Afghanistan and Pakistan

Afghanistan and Pakistan

Conflict, Extremism, and Resistance to Modernity

Riaz Mohammad Khan

Woodrow Wilson Center Press
Washington, D.C.

The Johns Hopkins University Press
Baltimore

EDITORIAL OFFICES

Woodrow Wilson Center Press
One Woodrow Wilson Plaza
1300 Pennsylvania Avenue, N.W.
Washington, D.C. 20004-3027
Telephone: 202-691-4029
www.wilsoncenter.org/press

ORDER FROM

The Johns Hopkins University Press
Hampden Station
P.O. Box 50370
Baltimore, Maryland 21211
Telephone: 1-800-537-5487
www.press.jhu.edu/books/

Library of Congress Cataloging-in-Publication Data

Khan, Riaz M. (Riaz Mohammad)
    Afghanistan and Pakistan : conflict, extremism, and resistance to modernity /
Riaz Mohammad Khan.
        p.   cm.
    Includes bibliographical references and index.
    ISBN-13: 978-1-4214-0384-7
    ISBN-10: 1-4214-0384-6
    1. Pakistan—Foreign relations—Afghanistan.   2. Afghanistan—Foreign
relations—Pakistan.   3. Pakistan—Politics and government—1988–   4. Islam
and politics—Pakistan.   5. Islamic fundamentalism—Pakistan.   6. Islamic
fundamentalism—Afghanistan.   7. Afghanistan—History—1989–2001.
8. Afghanistan—History—2001–.   9. Taliban.   I. Title.
DS383.5.A3K53 2011
327.58105491—dc22
                                                                                2011012027

 **Woodrow Wilson
International
Center
for Scholars**

The Woodrow Wilson International Center for Scholars is the national, living US memorial honoring President Woodrow Wilson. In providing an essential link between the worlds of ideas and public policy, the Center addresses current and emerging challenges confronting the United States and the world. The Center promotes policy-relevant research and dialogue to increase understanding and enhance the capabilities and knowledge of leaders, citizens, and institutions worldwide. Created by an act of Congress in 1968, the Center is a nonpartisan institution headquartered in Washington, D.C., and supported by both public and private funds.

Conclusions or opinions expressed in Center publications and programs are those of the authors and speakers and do not necessarily reflect the views of the Center staff, fellows, trustees, advisory groups, or any individuals or organizations that provide financial support to the Center.

The Center is the publisher of *The Wilson Quarterly* and home of Woodrow Wilson Center Press, dialogue television and radio. For more information about the Center's activities and publications, including the monthly newsletter "Centerpoint," please visit us on the Web at www.wilsoncenter.org.

Contents

Maps

Preface

This study was essentially completed by the end of 2009, and much of the narrative and analysis is based on events and experiences preceding that date. I have updated the study in the light of the relevant developments of 2010, during which the publishing process was under way. The study refers to the North-West Frontier Province (NWFP) of Pakistan by its old name, which was changed to Khyber Pakhtunkhwa (KPK) in April 2010.

I am indebted to the Woodrow Wilson Center for International Scholars for accepting me as a Pakistan Scholar from January to August 2009, which helped me to work on this book. I also deeply appreciate the contribution of Pakistani entrepreneurs in sponsoring the position of Pakistan Scholar at the Center, and I am thankful to my friend Dr. Ishrat Hussain, who thought of contacting me in late 2008 to inquire about my interest in the position. I am grateful to the members of the Asia Program at the Center, who made my stay both comfortable and memorable. My special thanks are due to Robert Hathaway, director of the Center's Asia Program, for his invaluable advice and suggestions as I put together the first draft of the book. I thank Joe Brinley, director of the Woodrow Wilson Center Press, and Yamile Kahn, managing editor, for helping me with the publication process. Brandon Lapsley and Daniel Greenberg assisted me with research, which I gratefully acknowledge. I am most grateful to Margery Boichel Thompson for her meticulous and excellent editing that has improved the language and presentation of the book. I am also highly obliged to many friends and colleagues who generously shared their experiences and views with me, some of whom I have mentioned in the text and the footnotes.

Riaz Mohammad Khan
December 2010

Map 1. Afghanistan and Pakistan

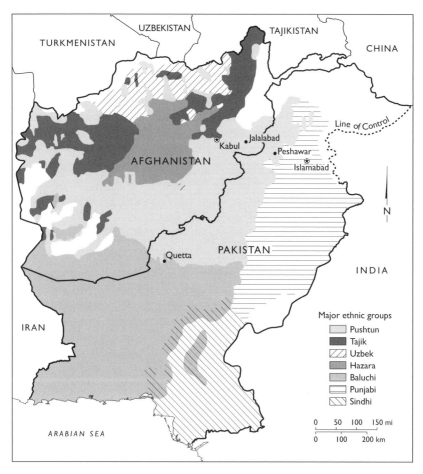

Map 2. Ethnic Groups in Afghanistan and Pakistan

Afghanistan and Pakistan

Introduction

The present study begins with developments in Afghanistan since the withdrawal of Soviet troops in February 1989, including the internecine conflicts that ravaged Afghanistan, and the interests and concerns of external powers. The conflicts involved first the Mujahedin groups, later the Taliban, and finally the U.S. and NATO military intervention.

The second part of the study focuses on the rise of extremism and religious militancy in Pakistan and the region, its antecedents, and its linkages with the Afghan Jihad. Surveying the past three decades' events and developments reveals the confusion that has clouded national discourse and perceptions in Pakistan concerning contemporary challenges that confront the society. These challenges must be addressed for Pakistan to survive, develop, and progress. More fundamentally, an intellectual crisis impedes Pakistan's progression to modernity.

The study is not based on rigorous or extensive research and in that sense cannot claim to be a work of scholarship. In fact, I was daunted by the vast material available on subjects related to Afghanistan and concede that it was difficult to throw a fresh light on the flow of events without being overstretched. Accordingly, the study presents a broad-brush treatment of events and attempts to weave personal experiences, perspectives, and evaluation into the larger narrative of events and developments relating to Afghanistan and Pakistan. For that purpose and for chronological specificity, I have benefited from published sources, which I have duly acknowledged. However, many of the events and developments described in chapters 1, 2, and 3 are based on personal impressions gathered while dealing with Afghanistan-

1

related issues during my various assignments at the Pakistan Foreign Office in Islamabad.[1]

The study discusses a number of issues that relate to the post-Soviet dynamics of the Afghan conflict, the fragmentation of Afghanistan under warlords, the accentuation of ethnic divisions, and the rise of the Taliban as the country suffered international indifference and isolation. In chapter 2, I have dwelt on some details about the genesis and early development of Taliban operations, drawing upon published sources and recollections of my colleagues. I refer to these details, most of which are known, for two reasons. First, they provide the background for important developments that intensified Taliban isolation and pushed Pakistani policy to fall between the ethnic divide in Afghanistan that I discuss and analyze. Secondly, and perhaps more interestingly, these operations, with their mobility, sudden moves, changing alliances, setbacks, and successes, were a close rerun of the old military campaigns by aspirants and pretenders to power in bygone centuries in Afghanistan and Central Asia, before the region became constricted by the advancing modern European empires. Such campaigns were possible because during the 1990s, Afghanistan was caught in a time warp, virtually isolated from the international community, a prospect unlikely to be repeated in the future.

The 1980s' Afghanistan episode had been a catalyst for two disparate but signal developments of the final decade of the twentieth century: the surge of freedom in Eastern Europe coupled with the disintegration of the Soviet Union, and the shaping of the militant radical Islamic impulse signified by Al Qaeda jihadist ideology. The events of September 11, 2001, the U.S. military intervention in Afghanistan, and the subsequent U.S. invasion of Iraq are among the defining developments of the beginning of the twenty-first century, with far-reaching consequences for the regional and global balance of power.

The U.S. intervention led to the collapse of Taliban rule and the successful Bonn process that shaped the new dispensation in Kabul under President Karzai. Yet, after the passage of nine years, the United States remains mired in Afghanistan in what has become the longest war in its history. The shift of U.S. focus to Iraq and failures in ensuring economic recovery and

---

1. My three assignments during the period covered in this study included responsibilities as director general in charge of Afghanistan and Soviet affairs 1986–92; additional secretary in charge of international organizations, disarmament and arms control 1998–2002; and foreign secretary from 2005 to 2008.

effective governance allowed the Afghan conflict to simmer, providing space for the Taliban to regroup and reassert themselves in the Pushtun-dominated southern and eastern parts of the country. The United States is still groping for options to improve the prospects of stabilization in Afghanistan. The present study analyzes these developments from a Pakistani perspective and discusses the role of Pakistan and other regional actors.

* * *

Here, it would be useful to provide a brief overview of events prior to the Soviet withdrawal from Afghanistan in 1989 that marks the point of departure for the present study.

Since the gathering of the chiefs of the Ghilzai and Abdali tribes near Qandahar and acceptance of Ahmed Shah Durrani as the king in 1747, the Kingdom of Afghanistan has survived as an independent state with a loose confederacy of Afghan tribes, often troubled by internal strife and under pressure from outside powers. The first external pressure came when Maharaja Ranjit Singh, the Sikh ruler of the Punjab, annexed Peshawar and adjacent districts west of the Indus River in 1823. Soon a far more formidable adversary in the shape of the British Indian Empire replaced the Sikh kingdom. British concerns over the expanding Czarist Empire in Central Asia led to a forward British policy. Britain's army invaded Afghanistan in 1838–42, a campaign that proved disastrous, and again in 1878, when the British briefly occupied Qandahar and Kabul. The second Anglo-Afghan war led to the 1879 treaty of Gandomak, which ceded the Khyber Pass and the districts of Kurram, Pishin, and Sibi to the British.

Earlier, in 1873, the British had reached an agreement with Russia (the Clarendon-Gorchakov agreement) in which Russia accepted Afghanistan as being outside its zone of influence and agreed to the Amu Darya as the limit of its future expansion in Central Asia. In this "Great Game," the British needed to establish the southern borders of Afghanistan, which had now evolved into a buffer state between the two suspicious and incrementally advancing European empires. Under pressure and with an assurance from the British of support against possible Russian ingression from across the Amu Darya, Amir Abdul Rahman Khan signed the Durand Agreement establishing the boundary that the successor state, Pakistan, inherited in 1947. The losses of the nineteenth century subsist in the psyche of the Afghans, but such are the burdens of history that many nations carry in their memory.

The next fateful development came in December 1979 with the Soviet invasion of Afghanistan and has ever since thrown Afghanistan in turmoil.

The Soviet intervention was intended to be brief. Moscow considered it necessary to save the shaky twenty-month-old Saur Revolution led by the Marxist People's Democratic Party of Afghanistan (PDPA). The 1979 Soviet invasion appeared at the time to be one of a succession of Soviet advances and U.S. setbacks in the same year, from Indochina to Iran to the Horn of Africa, Angola, and Nicaragua, in the backyard of the United States. For a decade the Soviets remained mired in Afghanistan, which became the last front of the Cold War.

Pakistan was sucked into the conflict primarily because of its geography and also because of the opportunity that the invasion offered to President Zia ul Haq to break out of international isolation following his military coup and the execution of his predecessor, Zulfikar Ali Bhutto. There was also the strategic consideration that even if the Soviets were not striving to reach for the warm waters of the Indian Ocean,[2] consolidation of their position in Afghanistan would make Pakistan, at least in theory, their next target. A fledgling tribal and Islamist resistance had already been forming in Afghanistan against the Marxist government in Kabul since 1978. The Soviet invasion legitimized it. Pakistani, U.S., and other international assistance, along with willing Afghan fighters from within Afghanistan and millions of refugees who had found shelter in Pakistan, turned the resistance into the high-profile Afghan Jihad.

Ten years later, in February 1989, as the last Soviet soldier crossed the Amu Darya, returning home as part of an arrangement concluded at Geneva under United Nations auspices, he was entering a transformed world, with the curtain closing on the Cold War and his own country on the verge of historic changes. The impact of the 1979 Soviet decision to invade had the most tragic consequences for Afghanistan. The rise of extremism and religious militancy and the coalescing of Al Qaeda are all linked to the Soviet military intervention and many of its unintended consequences. International indifference to Afghanistan and the region following the Soviet withdrawal compounded the problems. Chapters 1 and 2 discuss these developments and the forces that continue to ravage Afghanistan and torment Pakistan and the region.

The protracted UN-sponsored and other negotiations seeking Soviet withdrawal had also tentatively explored the possibility of a government of

---

2. The Russian push to the warm waters was generally attributed to an unauthenticated "will of Peter the Great." For further details see Peter Hopkirk, *The Great Game: The Struggle for Empire in Central Asia* (New York: Kodansha International Publishers, 1992), 20.

national reconciliation to facilitate withdrawal. Nonetheless, at the early stages, the only feasible demand could be for a timetable for withdrawal. Moscow had first insisted that even withdrawal of Soviet troops was no business of the United Nations and something that, if and when necessary, could only be discussed bilaterally with Kabul once interference from outside (Pakistan) stopped. In Pakistan, the early debates also focused on the profile of the Afghan resistance, in particular the question of a government in exile. There were influential promonarchy elements, mostly based in Europe and in Quetta, where Qandahar-connected families favored a government in exile built around King Zahir Shah's supporters.[3] The Pakistan government finally settled for the option of the seven Mujahedin Tanzeemat led by Peshawar-based Afghan leaders.

In part, the choice developed by default, but there was also wariness about having a government in exile based on Pakistani territory that could easily become a permanent headache, since no one could foresee a Soviet withdrawal. Also, the hard-line Peshawar-based Islamist leaders, who had fled Afghanistan in 1973 following a clampdown by Sardar Daoud, did not agree to any arrangement with a role for Zahir Shah. Importantly, Pakistan's Inter-Services Intelligence (ISI), which was given the lead role for liaison with Afghan resistance elements, felt comfortable dealing with the seven separate groups instead of one entity with a possible international profile.

Pakistan had agreed to drop the idea of pursuing a government of national reconciliation under UN-sponsored negotiations, because the United Nations, where the Kabul (PDPA) regime continued to occupy Afghanistan's seat, could not accommodate such a provision on the agenda. However, Pakistani negotiators and President Zia believed that if and when Moscow decided to withdraw, it would want to leave a stable, broad-based political dispensation in Kabul. As the years passed, this expectation receded into the background and the negotiations became ever more sharply focused on a time frame for withdrawal. But the expectation proved to be valid. Before indicating a time frame at Geneva, the Soviets hinted in December 1986 at seeking Pakistan's cooperation for a dialogue between the Kabul government and the Mujahedin Tanzeemat.

Ironically, Pakistan was unprepared. Politically, there was tension between President Zia and Prime Minister Muhammad Khan Junejo. The

3. Initially Pakistan was open to Zahir Shah's visiting Quetta, but Zahir Shah expected Pakistan to first prepare the ground to ensure support for his role before he would come to Pakistan. Zahir Shah was not known to be a proactive personality.

hard-line Afghan Mujahedin leaders were well entrenched and suspicious of any diplomatic moves. The ISI shared their doubts and distrusted the Soviet signals, driven by the Afghan Jihad's recent successes, scored with the help of the newly introduced Stinger missiles in mid-1986. Zia saw the opening and started calling for a government of reconciliation in Kabul only in late 1987, when Mikhail Gorbachev announced Moscow's offer of less than one year's time frame and called for the signing of the Geneva agreements that were almost ready. But the opportunity was already lost; the hard-line Mujahedin leaders rejected Zia's proposals for reconciliation or the possibility of dialogue. Gorbachev was in a hurry and not agreeable to an open-ended effort to achieve a government of national reconciliation. Zia could not deny Moscow the fig leaf of the Geneva Accords that Moscow needed for its withdrawal. The accords were signed after tortuous negotiations on an indirect understanding that both the Mujahedin groups and the Kabul government would continue to receive arms,[4] fueling the fires of the conflict in Afghanistan well after the Soviets left the scene.

For close to a decade, the ISI remained involved with the Mujahedin groups, which generated a good deal of suspicion and speculation about its preference for hard-line leaders, in particular Gulbadin Hekmatyar of Hisb e Islami. The moderate leaders, pro–King Zahir Shah elements, and intellectuals from among the Afghan Diaspora were critical of Pakistan's role. Within Pakistan, the ISI gained for the first time a major role in influencing external policy on an issue of importance for the country. Zia had rightly decided that all arms and funds to the Mujahedin leadership would be funneled through Pakistani channels; and no outside agencies, including the CIA, were to supply weapons directly to these groups. Accordingly, the position, resources, and influence of the ISI were vastly strengthened, and the organization became the mainstay of Pakistan's support to the Afghan Jihad. In the 1990s, the insurgency in Indian-controlled Jammu and Kashmir added to the role of the organization in helping yet another Jihad, which was legitimate from Pakistan's point of view.

---

4. Since a government of national reconciliation was not feasible, and backtracking by Pakistan on Geneva involved significant diplomatic costs, President Zia insisted on "positive symmetry" on the part of the guarantors, the United States and the Soviet Union, to keep open the supply lines to the Afghan Mujahedin. This was achieved through an exchange of letters the guarantors addressed to the UN secretary-general that are part of the Geneva agreements. Neither Zia nor Moscow favored the obligation of "negative symmetry," thus ending the supply of arms to both the Kabul regime and the Afghan Mujahedin.

The Afghan conflict and then the insurgency in Kashmir secured for the ISI and the army a prominent role in shaping Pakistan's foreign policy, in particular towards Afghanistan and India. This prominence led to an exaggerated perception internationally, echoed by many Pakistanis, about the ISI's overweening influence in state affairs and about the agency's behaving independently of the government or as a government within the government. There had been aberrations during the 1990s, when the ISI was used by the army high command to manipulate domestic politics, and civilian leaders often deferred to the army's point of view on foreign policy issues. At the same time, on many critical issues, the ISI and the army by and large acted in step with the overall policy of the government, which for long periods was headed by military rulers. For example, despite its opposition, the ISI could not block Pakistan's signing the Geneva Accords once Zia made up his mind to do so. At that time, the ISI wanted Pakistani diplomacy to somehow keep the Soviets tied down in Afghanistan and negotiate a change of government in Kabul.

Pakistan did not recognize the ISI-sponsored interim Afghan government in the early 1990s, and in the case of the Taliban did so only in 1998, four years after their emergence and two years after their firm control of Kabul. Similarly, like the Pakistan government, the ISI had to adjust to the new realities of the post–9/11 circumstances. This does not mean that the ISI (or for that matter the army) is monolithic; some of its personnel would suffer from attachment to the previous policies. Also, it cannot be denied that the Afghan Jihad enabled the ISI to grow into a powerful security agency with influence over internal as well as foreign policy matters, far beyond what is warranted by its grasp, capacity, and status as the premier intelligence agency of the country.

The present study picks up the Afghanistan story from 1989, when the Soviets left Afghanistan. In this sense, it is a sequel to my earlier book *Untying the Afghan Knot: Negotiating Soviet Withdrawal* (Duke University Press, 1991), which covered the period from the 1979 Soviet intervention until February 1989. Chapter 1 of the present study recounts major developments in Afghanistan relating to the final years of the Najibullah government and the Mujahedin rule over a fragmented Afghanistan. Chapter 2 focuses on the rise of the Taliban and their campaigns to extend their control over large parts of Afghanistan. The continuing conflict engaged the United Nations and Afghanistan's neighbors in efforts to bring about peace among the contending Afghan factions and help them reach political accommodation with each other. These efforts, which often lacked drive and convergence of interests, were blighted by mutual suspicions and the unwillingness of the Mujahedin leaders or later the Taliban leadership to share power with their adversaries within an agreed political framework. However, in describing events or offering analysis, it is not the study's intention to portray villains and heroes, but to throw light as far as possible on events and developments from the perspective of the various protagonists.

The first two chapters are not just a narrative of intra-Afghan strife involving successively the Afghan Mujahedin leaders and the Taliban. These chapters also bring out the failure of radical Islamist movements to provide political governance. This is an important development. The 1980s and 1990s had seen the rise of radical Islam and fundamentalism throughout the Islamic world along with a corresponding eclipse of secular thinking. This was in part because of generally secular-minded governments' inability to deliver on promised socioeconomic transformation and the failure of such governments in the Middle East to achieve a resolution of the Palestinian issue. The trend was propelled by the apparent success of the Jihad in Afghanistan, the Iranian revolution, the collapse of the Soviet Union, and the emergence of Islamist movements from the Balkans to the Caucasus to Central Asia.[5] The experience of Afghanistan with the Mujahedin and the Taliban during the 1990s represented the first setback for the radical Islamist doctrinaire thinking and approach by revealing its weakness, even bankruptcy, in governing a nation state in today's complex world. In the narrow and specific context of Pakistan, the same limitation was exposed by the local Taliban diktat in the tribal areas and to some extent by the bland and feckless rule by religious coalitions from 2002 to 2007 in the two Pakistani provinces bordering Afghanistan. This failing of fundamentalist and radical Islam, however, does not imply diminution of the relevance of Islam as a potent religious, political, and cultural force in Muslim societies.

Chapter 3 focuses on post–9/11 developments and the U.S. military intervention in Afghanistan to decimate Al Qaeda and dislodge the Taliban. The U.S. action spread the conflict to the bordering tribal areas of Pakistan, which obliged the Pakistani army to get engaged in military operations in these bordering regions. The nine long years since the United States and the NATO allies undertook Operation Enduring Freedom in Afghanistan have

---

5. An insightful discussion on the Islamist resurgence can be found in Ali A. Allawi, *The Crisis of Islamic Civilization* (New Haven: Yale University Press, 2009), 77–84.

produced unanticipated twists and turns without attenuating the challenge that the intervention had intended to address. In Washington, the Afghan war has become the major foreign policy preoccupation for the Obama administration. An added concern is the inflamed situation in Pakistan. This chapter discusses the course of the U.S. intervention, the consequences of the U.S. diversion to Iraq while the objectives in Afghanistan were far from achieved, and the friction and mistrust that characterized the post–9/11 cooperation between Pakistan and the United States.

Chapter 4 examines the interests and concerns of Afghanistan's neighbors and other external powers in the region, with specific relevance to Afghanistan and to prospects for the country's stability and peace. Chapters 5 and 6 concentrate on analyzing the situation in Pakistan, while the conclusions in chapter 7 focus on the present U.S. strategy for enhanced troop deployment before the expected winding down of its military involvement in Afghanistan. Chapter 7 also addresses the larger issue of combating the extremism and violence in the region that deeply engages Pakistan in a seminal struggle that would define its future orientation and ability to develop.

The Afghanistan conflict has had a deep impact on Pakistan. The Pakistani Taliban and other disparate militant groups wreaking violence in the country have drawn succor from the Afghan Taliban. At the same time, the rise of religious militancy and extremism has indigenous roots. In this context, this study looks at Pakistan's policies and their evolution; the much-debated role of Pakistan's military and intelligence establishment and the country's ability to contain extremism and militancy and neutralize Al Qaeda; and the nature of the Afghan and Pakistani Taliban and local militant groups. The discussion of these issues brings out the gravity and scale of the challenge faced by both Pakistan and Afghanistan and the stake that the international community has in helping the two countries to overcome this "existential" danger.

The situation in Pakistan and that in Afghanistan are, however, not quite parallel. Pakistan is a far more complex country, with a population seven times larger than Afghanistan's. Its institutions of governance are weak but not destroyed, unlike Afghanistan's; and it has a strong army. Pakistan is capable and will have to address by itself the challenge of extremism and religious militancy, whose history and roots are quite dissimilar to the background of the Afghan Taliban. Pakistan has a long tradition of religious parties and movements. The study attempts to explain the incremental growth of their influence in politics and public life in Pakistan and their contributions to a conducive environment; but they are not the precursor of the present-day extremism in the country.

Chapter 5 discusses the circumstances that have spawned religious militancy and the violent extremism practiced by the Pakistani Taliban. These relate to a number of factors, including the unique traditions of the autonomous tribal areas, the transmutation of militant groups meant to support the Afghan and Kashmiri jihads, the influence of the severe Saudi Salafi and Deobandi thinking, the proliferation of madrassas with narrow religious education, the depressed socioeconomic conditions, and the increasingly malfunctioning administrative and judicial systems, including the absence of speedy justice.

Chapter 6 discusses a major theme of the study by tracing the roots and growth of the pervasive intellectual confusion that characterizes public discourse in Pakistan on issues and challenges vital to national life and relating to the country's orientation, outlook, and identity. In the genesis of Pakistan, religion and politics got intertwined in a matrix distinct from the older traditions of Muslim governance or the contemporary precedents of countries like Turkey and Egypt or prerevolution Iran, where ruling elites introduced a secular agenda. Over the years, beyond the alliances of expediency and convenience between the political elite and religious elements, Pakistani society gradually ceded intellectual ground to activist religious conservatism and orthodoxy. The Iranian revolution of 1979 and the spread of Saudi Salafi dogma, facilitated by Saudi oil fortunes, the separation of East Pakistan, Zia ul Haq's policy of Islamization, and the Afghan Jihad all exerted powerful influences on the thinking and outlook of the expanding Pakistani urban and middle classes. In parallel, the country suffered dysfunction in governance caused by failure of political leadership and by changes in the constitution and in administrative and law enforcement institutions that successive civilian and military governments attempted. The consequent intellectual crisis distorts public discourse in Pakistan on the nature of the extremist violence and the threat it poses to the society. In a broader sense, this crisis is at the heart of the society's resistance to adjusting to contemporary modernizing trends, thereby impeding the country's socioeconomic progress.

The extremist militancy in Pakistan's northwestern tribal regions and the presence of Al Qaeda elements in the region help sustain the Afghan Taliban insurgency and continued instability in Afghanistan. Warlords, criminal and drug mafias, and corruption compound the problem. In this sense, success of efforts to bring stability in Afghanistan would depend on Pakistan's ability to reestablish its control over the tribal areas. The U.S. and Pakistani objectives converge in seeking disruption and defeat of Al Qaeda, which must be denied safe haven in ungoverned troubled spaces in Afghanistan and Pakistan. Beyond this convergence, the United States would have to pursue two separate trajectories for its respective strategies to stabilize Afghanistan and to help Pakistan with its counterterrorism effort. Accordingly, notwithstanding the nomenclature of Af-Pak policy, the U.S. administration will find little common ground in its dealings with the two countries. It cannot apply to Pakistan what it applies to Afghanistan.

Pakistan will deal with the situation and the challenge it faces in accordance with its own priorities and judgment. It distinguishes between the Afghan Taliban and the Pakistani Taliban that have challenged the writ of the government inside Pakistan. It cannot overlook the traditional source of threat to its security from India on its eastern border. The apparent disconnect in Pakistani and U.S. perceptions on these and other counts calls for regular and close consultations between U.S. and Pakistani civilian and military leaders, with the confidence that both sides are interested in stabilization of Afghanistan and promotion of a peaceful environment in the region. Nonetheless, notwithstanding any divergences in tactics or even perceptions, Pakistan must not allow its territory to be used by the Afghan Taliban or their allies in the tribal areas to carry their fight inside Afghanistan. The United States should also avoid actions and statements that could impinge on Pakistani sensitivities. Statements or demands that lend credibility to detractors who ascribe the turmoil in the region to the U.S. military intervention in Afghanistan, and to Pervez Musharraf's decision to become part of the American "war on terror," would distort public support for the efforts of the government and the army against extremists and Taliban militants.

Looking at Afghanistan, there is no well-defined center of gravity that if targeted would unravel the problems and set it moving towards stabilization. The Pakistani predicament is even more complicated. Accordingly, there is no quick fix for addressing the complex, sometimes overlapping challenges confronted by the two countries. The emphasis placed by analysts and policy makers on the need for a comprehensive approach is an admission of the complexity of the thirty-year-old problems that bedevil the region. Return to normalcy in the region will be a long haul even if the professedly well-intentioned efforts of all major players in the region succeed. Much will depend on the ability of the Afghan leaders to promote reconciliation and improve governance. The United States has indicated at de-escalating its military presence starting from 2011, but at the same time has reaffirmed its long-term commitment to remain engaged and help stabilization and economic reconstruction in Afghanistan. Other donor countries have made similar commitments to offer help, which Afghanistan needs and must continue to receive. Recent history demonstrates that turning away from Afghanistan in exasperation and indifference toward the region can be costly and does not offer an advisable option.

At the outset, I need to explain the book's style because of an observation that "the author's voice" is absent from the narrative and eschews first-person references. The impersonal narration is simply a matter of personal preference. Most of the events and developments described in the study are based on direct personal insights and experiences, or on participation in meetings and dealing with issues. The same holds true about the observations that relate particularly to concerns, policies, dilemmas, and workings of the Pakistan government, which I served in various capacities as part of the Foreign Office for almost four decades. There are a number of anecdotal accounts that I thought relevant to weave into the main text. Many other personal experiences have been recorded in the notes. I have done so in the interest of maintaining the flow of argument and because these stories in the notes, which I commend to the readers' attention, are supportive but not meant to serve as validation of a viewpoint. The analysis of developments interspersed throughout the study, including the survey of external interests in chapter 4, articulation of the intellectual crisis in chapter 6, and the conclusions in chapter 7, reflect and are based entirely on my personal perspectives.

Part I

The Afghanistan Context:
The Continuing Conflict

1

The Post–Soviet Withdrawal Phase of the Afghanistan Conflict (1989–1995)

As the last Soviet tanks rolled across the Hairatan Bridge over the Amu Darya on February 14, 1989, the withdrawal of Soviet troops from Afghanistan was completed according to the schedule laid down in the Geneva Accords signed in April 1988. There were no surprises. The world was by now convinced that the Soviet Union and the familiar political landscape of the Cold War were undergoing a momentous transformation. Kabul watched the events with some trepidation. Islamabad watched with a subdued excitement. The major world capitals had an interest in the development, but they approached it as if reaching an anticipated milestone. Washington and the West European capitals were already shifting their gaze away from Afghanistan to the East European arena. In South Asia, attention had turned to the issue of nuclear proliferation and the political change wrought by the election victory of Benazir Bhutto's Pakistan People's Party. The old dispute in Kashmir had started drawing fresh blood, as widespread agitation built in the Indian-controlled valley, caused by the controversial 1987 elections and mishandling of the subsequent protests.

In early February 1988, on the eve of the last round of the Geneva negotiations, President Zia ul Haq had received in Islamabad Soviet President Mikhail Gorbachev's special envoy, Yuri Vorontsov, an affable diplomat.[1] Vorontsov's mission was to ask Pakistan to accept Moscow's offer of a ten months' time frame for withdrawal and to sign the almost-ready agreement in Geneva. Zia ul Haq argued with Vorontsov that before leaving Afghani-

---

1. See Riaz M. Khan, *Untying the Afghan Knot: Negotiating Soviet Withdrawal* (Durham, N.C. and London: Duke University Press, 1991), 254–55, for details.

15

stan, the Soviets must work with Pakistan for a government of national reconciliation. Otherwise, he feared, there would be bloodshed in the country.
Zia went to the extent of suggesting that he would publicly endorse continued Soviet presence in Afghanistan for the purpose of promoting such a
government in Kabul. The argument stalled when Zia equivocated on
Vorontsov's insistence that Pakistan promise to deliver the Mujahedin leaders for a dialogue with Muhammad Najibullah, the Soviet-backed president
of Afghanistan, and to accept a deadline for reconciliation efforts. If the reconciliation efforts were to fail, Pakistan would sign the agreement.

In late 1986, almost one year before Moscow announced a realistic time
frame for withdrawal, Moscow had taken a strategic decision to withdraw
from Afghanistan and had discreetly sounded out Pakistan for its help in
pursuing a government of national reconciliation through dialogue between
the Mujahedin leaders and Najibullah.[2] Pakistan failed to make a serious
response, partly because of suspicions within the Pakistani military establishment that the Soviet overture might be tactical, to weaken the Afghan
resistance, and partly because of a lack of policy focus within the Pakistan government, which had fallen prey to tensions between President Zia
and Prime Minister Junejo. On the eve of the December 1987 U.S.-Soviet
summit in Washington, Gorbachev announced a one-year time frame. The
announcement caused Zia ul Haq to recognize the change in the Soviet position and to begin calling for an Afghan government of national reconciliation, an idea the hard-line Mujahedin leaders virtually rejected by refusing
to have any dialogue with Najibullah. The February 1988 meeting with Zia
came to an abrupt end when Vorontsov declared that Moscow did not wish
further blame for the troubles in Afghanistan and was withdrawing "with or
without Geneva." He warned of "incalculable consequences" for Moscow's
relations with Pakistan if there was no Geneva agreement. The Soviets
wanted to withdraw under the cover of a UN-negotiated agreement, which
Pakistan signed at Geneva in April 1988. Four months later, Zia ul Haq, the
principal architect of the seven Afghan Mujahedin parties (the Tanzeemat),
died in a mysterious plane crash. As the Soviet withdrawal proceeded, the
Afghanistan conflict entered its second decade and a new phase, now under
transformed regional and global circumstances.

2. Khan, *Untying the Afghan Knot,* 181.

Najibullah Defies Collapse

Moscow had assured its continuing support to the government of President Najibullah in Kabul during the postwithdrawal period. Statements by the two guarantors of the Geneva Accords, the United States and the Soviet Union, invoked symmetrical obligations to qualify the accords and created room for the two powers to provide military supplies to the contending Afghan parties. To further allay Najibullah's fears that the Soviets would abandon him, Moscow appointed a high-profile heavyweight ambassador to Kabul, Yuri Vorontsov, who was considered close to Gorbachev.

Defying some projections, the Afghan army did not disintegrate, nor were there any signs of an imminent collapse of the Najibullah government. There were no defections to the Mujahedin groups from within the Afghan government or the army, nor did Mujahedin activity increase. The opinion inside Pakistan about the survivability of the Kabul regime was divided; even Pakistan's premier intelligence agency, the Inter-Services Intelligence (ISI), was unsure of a quick Mujahedin victory. Pakistani chargé d'affaires in Kabul, Fida Yunus, had predicted soon after the Geneva Accords that the Najibullah government would be resilient, arguing that the groups within the Mujahedin Tanzeemat were deeply divided, lacking cohesion and without a common political platform.

During the period of withdrawal, under pressure from the ISI, the Tanzeemat had agreed to appoint a spokesman to serve on a six-monthly basis, but there was no consensus on forming a representative body. As the Soviet withdrawal progressed, the Tanzeemat came under some pressure from the Pakistan government to have a provisional coalition arrangement or an Afghan Interim Government (AIG). The Pakistan government thought it necessary that the Tanzeemat present a united front in response to the UN-initiated efforts to promote a government of national reconciliation, consistent with the UN commitment made at the time of the signing of the Geneva Accords. On the eve of the completion of the withdrawal, Soviet Foreign Minister Eduard Shevardnadze visited Islamabad to elicit Pakistan's cooperation in restraining a Mujahedin assault on Kabul and encouraging transition to a government of reconciliation in Afghanistan. The Soviets were nervous that Pakistan might take advantage of the Soviet withdrawal to orchestrate an attack on Kabul that could be deeply embarrassing to Moscow.

Shevardnadze's visit pushed the Pakistan government to further activate its efforts with the Tanzeemat to form a representative body. The ISI managed to convene a Tanzeemat *shura,* or consultative council, at Madinatul

Hujjaj near Rawalpindi with the participation of over four hundred Mujahedin delegates, Afghan notables, and Ulema (religious scholars). The shura was described as the gathering of Ahl al Hal wa Aqd, an Islamic concept of those with authority "to loosen or bind" and select a leader for the Muslim community. By late February 1989, the shura decided to nominate an Afghan Interim Government (AIG) and appointed Muhammad Nabi Muhammadi, a moderate leader, as its president and Engineer Ahmed Shah of the hard-line Yunas Khalis group as its prime minister.[3]

The AIG remained largely a façade on paper and dysfunctional as a representative entity, lacking the ability to devise a common policy or strategy to overturn and replace the Najibullah government in Kabul. In Afghanistan, the resistance remained a disparate guerrilla force of largely autonomous Mujahedin commanders affiliated with various Tanzeemat for the purpose of receiving financial and military assistance, for which each of the Tanzeemat had served as a channel. Major commanders who were part of the Tanzeemat leadership exercised influence and control in their respective areas but rarely coordinated operations with each other. As time passed without any sign of Najibullah losing his grip over Kabul, the enthusiasm of the supporters of the AIG further dampened.

Notwithstanding the differing views within the Pakistani establishment on Mujahedin ability to overthrow Najibullah, it was broadly agreed that there could be no recognition of the Afghan Interim Government or any government in exile based inside Pakistan's territory. Such a proposition was not acceptable even under President Zia ul Haq, and there was less justification to do so once the Soviets had left the country. Some officials within the Pakistani ISI, who recognized the divisions within the AIG and the difficulty in uniting the Tanzeemat on a common political platform, felt that Pakistan should recognize the AIG even if it was based on Pakistani soil. In their view, such recognition could become an incentive for cohesion within the Afghan Tanzeemat. The Foreign Office, however, remained firm that the AIG must be recognized only after it was able to establish itself in-

---

3. The Madinatul Hujjaj shura had cast the highest number of votes in favor of Sibghatullah Mojaddedi, a moderate activist personality, and Abdur Rab Rasool Sayyaf, a hard-line leader who enjoyed strong Saudi support and was the spokesman for the Tanzeemat in February 1989. The bitterness between the hard-line and moderate groups was so strong that it prevented approval of either of the two personalities to the top position, which eventually went to the mild-mannered and traditional religious leader of Harkat e Enqilab e Islami, Nabi Muhammadi.

side Afghanistan. This led to the Pakistan-sponsored attempt by the Tanzeemat to capture Jalalabad, the most important Afghan town between Kabul and Peshawar, nearly 75 kilometers from the Pakistan-Afghan border at the historic Khyber Pass.

Prime Minister Benazir Bhutto gave the green light for the operation when, in a meeting to discuss the question of recognizing the AIG, the ISI chief, Lt Gen. Hameed Gul, responded in the affirmative to a direct question on whether the Tanzeemat were militarily in a position to take Jalalabad. The ISI chief was perhaps entrapped by the rhetoric and publicity built assiduously around the Afghan resistance, crediting it for defeating the Soviet Union, the other superpower of the day.[4] Later, after the Mujahedin's failure to capture Jalalabad, and just before he relinquished his position as ISI chief, General Gul said that he had been under political pressure to launch an assault on Jalalabad despite his skepticism. He knew that the Mujahedin were a guerrilla force adept in ambush but without the experience of a siege or of a disciplined army's regular military operation.[5] This was a post-facto justification, as no politician could overrule military advice if it was firmly given and related to military strategy or operations.

In fact, Jalalabad was a botched-up operation, carried out in haste and without adequate preparations. Undoubtedly, the Mujahedin forces were unprepared for a long siege of the city, which was defended by a regular army using heavy equipment and supported by an air force. The fate of the operation was sealed early on, however, when seventy defectors from the Afghan army garrison at Samarkhel, surrounded by the Mujahedin, were massacred by elements of the Yunas Khalis group and their hacked bodies returned to the town in crates.[6] The Afghan government exploited the incident with the slogan "coffin or the country," meaning defend the country because surrender was no choice. The Afghan troops dug in, and the irregular Mujahedin forces dispersed after a couple of weeks' stalemate. A senior Kabul official who left Afghanistan after the exit of Najibullah later recalled that to start with, the Afghan army had considered the defense of Jalalabad a hopeless task and had plans to defend Kabul at the Sarobi

4. Steve Coll, *Ghost Wars* (New York: Penguin Books, 2004), 192–94, describes the meeting called by Benazir and General Gul's promise that Jalalabad would fall.

5. *New York Times* (hereafter *NYT*), April 23, 1989.

6. *Wall Street Journal,* March 27, 1989. There were also reports that the killing was done by the Arab Salafi jihadists linked to Yunas Khalis. See Marc Sageman, *Understanding Terror Networks* (Philadelphia: University of Pennsylvania Press, 2004), 58.

pass, but the scenario changed with the massacre of the Samarkhel garrison defectors.[7]

Obviously, the Tanzeemat leaders and the Mujahedin commanders were not prepared to handle defections, which should have been encouraged if the operation were to have any chance of success. This shortcoming in tactics was rectified three years later in the siege of Khost. Apart from this tactical blunder, the main Mujahedin contenders for power already had their sights on Kabul. They appeared less than enthusiastic about Jalalabad and hesitated to spend their resources on capturing a city that was only meant to serve as the short-term seat of the AIG. The Jalalabad campaign did not suit their individual ambitions.

The Jalalabad operation soon bogged down in a costly siege, with high civilian casualties and an exodus of refugees from the city.[8] The Mujahedin forces showed an inability to coordinate action. By late April the Jalalabad operation had petered out. Abandoning the siege, Mujahedin guerrilla forces started launching uncoordinated sporadic rocket attacks against Kabul and Qandahar in a futile attempt to put pressure on Najibullah's forces.

The Jalalabad debacle was a major setback with long-term consequences for the Mujahedin groups and for Afghanistan. Its success could have established an AIG of sorts in Jalalabad, with the possibility of significant international recognition and an impact on the political dynamics of Afghanistan, perhaps preventing the subsequent fratricidal conflict and destruction of Kabul. In the aftermath of Jalalabad, Najibullah gained in confidence and gave up his apparent quest for sharing power with the Mujahedin groups, earlier signaled by his appointment of a noncommunist prime minister, Muhammad Hassan Sharq, in 1988. Instead, Najibullah started portraying himself as an Afghan nationalist and the Tanzeemat as agents of Pakistan. On the other hand, while Pakistan supported the idea of a broadbased government in Afghanistan, the hard-line Tanzeemat leaders and the ISI insisted on the exclusion of Najibullah from any process aimed at reconciliation.

A power game among the main Mujahedin contenders had already ensued, with their sights fixed on Kabul. Sensing the declining fortunes of Najibullah, they started reaching out to elements within the power structure

---

7. This was narrated to the author by a former vice foreign minister under Najibullah, who was passing through Alma Ata in late 1992.

8. *NYT,* May 11 and May 12, 1989, put the casualty figure at 500 and the refugee figure at 50,000.

of the Kabul government. For these Mujahedin leaders, the Jalalabad setback was inconsequential; nor were they keen about a political process or any transitional arrangement that did not serve to clear the way for their individual ambitions to seize power. By late 1989, the intra-Mujahedin rivalry also started taking a violent turn when the Hizb e Islami of Gulbadin Hekmatyar, the most inflexible of the hard-line Mujahedin leaders and a known favorite of the ISI, was accused of killing several dozen fighters under the command of Ahmed Shah Massoud in Farkhar Valley in July 1989.[9]

International interest in Afghanistan had quickly waned, as gauged by the reduced presence of donor-supported NGO activity. Hundreds of foreign NGOs had operated in the heyday of the Afghan Jihad in the mid-1980s, but within one year of the Soviet withdrawal the numbers had dropped sharply. Remaining NGOs could be counted on one's fingers and were mostly linked to the UN refugee relief. The U.S. administration's interest in pursuing a broad-based government in Afghanistan diminished with the failure of the Jalalabad operation and the tenacity of the Najibullah regime, which continued to receive large supplies of arms from Moscow. Nevertheless, in 1990, the United States also explored with the Soviets the idea of a transitional arrangement to oversee elections in which Najibullah could participate, but the idea did not gain any traction.[10] The United States became preoccupied with another residual but urgent matter related to the Afghan war, namely the recovery of an estimated three hundred shoulder-carried Stinger missiles still in the hands of the Mujahedin forces.

Meanwhile, Pakistani politics regressed into a phase of chronic instability evident in the rapid changes of governments, alternating between Benazir Bhutto and Nawaz Sharif, with little policy focus on Afghanistan. Pakistan's Afghan policy was largely in the hands of the army and the ISI and depended on input from midlevel officials. These officials often scoffed at a diplomatic or political approach and were enamored of a romantic view of the Afghan Jihad, holding the hard-line Afghan Mujahedin leadership in veneration and remaining blind to its shortcomings. In May 1989, following the Jalalabad failure, Prime Minister Benazir Bhutto replaced General Hameed Gul with a retired general, Shamsur Rahman Kallu, who had little clout within the ISI or with the Afghan Tanzeemat. Benazir was in no position to bring about any significant shift in policy. Army chief General Mirza Aslam Beg had made it clear that he could not allow the (civilian) govern-

9. *NYT,* July 20, 1989.
10. *NYT,* May 3, 1990.

ment to control Pakistan's Afghan and Kashmir policy. Despite the Jalal-abad experience, the top brass in the Pakistani army and intelligence con-tinued to believe that only the most uncompromising and determined Mu-jahedin leaders would emerge ascendant in the Afghan domestic struggle. The army saw a strategic opportunity in this possibility, since many of these Mujahedin leaders appeared to be aligned to Pakistan and close to its pre-mier intelligence agency.

In the circumstances, any political or diplomatic initiative was bound to fail. Yet three efforts are worthy of mention. Diego Cordovez—the UN secretary-general's special representative on Afghanistan and interlocutor for the Geneva Accords—attempted the first post–Geneva Accords en-gagement, in pursuance of implementing the accords. His successor, Benon Sevan, continued the effort. The second initiative arose from Iran's in-creased interest in Afghanistan and desire to work with Pakistan, now that Iran's conflict with Iraq had cooled down and the Soviets had left Afghani-stan. While the Iranians grudgingly conceded that Pakistan had been the principal player in helping the Tanzeemat and other Afghan Mujahedin groups, they had maintained linkages with some of the Tanzeemat, in par-ticular the Jamiat e Islami of Burhanuddin Rabbani. They had also sup-ported eight Shia parties based in Tehran, comprising mostly ethnic Hazara elements, including Karim Khalili's Hizb e Wahdat. Iran did not want to be left out of a possible new international initiative on Afghanistan, especially with regard to the question of the return of Afghan refugees, which appeared to have become feasible following the Soviet withdrawal. During the course of 1991 the ISI launched the third effort—to put together a Mujahedin com-manders' shura in view of the apparent failure of the Tanzeemat leadership to forge unity and form a credible interim government. The Americans sup-ported this initiative.

UN Effort for a Political Solution

UN envoy Diego Cordovez visited Pakistan in June 1988 to initiate an ef-fort at reconciliation and promote a broad-based Afghan government. The UN secretary-general, Javier Pérez de Cuéllar, formally committed to the effort in a statement issued on his behalf at the time the completion of the Geneva Accords was announced a few days prior to their signing. Cordovez had no illusions about the success of such an effort, yet he spent nearly two weeks in the area, visiting Kabul a couple of times and mostly waiting in Islamabad for the Pakistanis to persuade the Tanzeemat leadership to receive him. Since reconciliation assumed dialogue, a broad-based government, and power sharing with Najibullah, the hard-line Tanzeemat rejected the UN effort outright. Objecting most strongly were Hizb e Islami factions of Gulbadin and Yunas Khalis and the Eittehad e Islami Mujahedin e Afghanistan of Abdur Rab Rasool Sayyaf,

With Zia ul Haq's intercession, the ISI finally arranged a meeting between Cordovez and the Tanzeemat's ad hoc spokesman, Yunas Khalis. The meeting was pro forma, and Diego Cordovez felt slighted, gave up, and never returned to the area. He continued to believe that Zia ul Haq and the ISI opposed dialogue, as they were in a position to put sufficient pressure on the recalcitrant Tanzeemat to fall into line. In fact, both Zia and the ISI were short on enthusiasm and ability to push the Tanzeemat to accept a dialogue with Najibullah. The Ojeri camp accident on the eve of the Geneva Accords that destroyed an ammunition dump meant for supplying the Mujahedin and that killed over a hundred people in the twin cities of Rawalpindi and Islamabad had darkened the mood within the ISI and sapped support for a Geneva-linked diplomatic effort.

In late 1988, Benon Sevan, an Armenian Cypriot with a congenial demeanor ready to reach out with a warm handshake and backslap, succeeded Cordovez as the United Nations special representative for Afghanistan.[11] He wore two hats on behalf of the UN secretary-general: first, as special representative to promote a possible political compromise that would reverse the intensifying struggle for political power within Afghanistan, a mandate derived from the Geneva Accords; and second, as a point person to facilitate the return of refugees and reconstruction of Afghanistan. Both objectives eluded his efforts, which remained in large part limited to coordination among the Afghanistan-related UN agencies. Like his predecessor, Benon believed that Pakistan held the key for promoting the political process, as it alone exercised influence with the Tanzeemat and could persuade their leadership to adopt a political course. His first meeting with the new prime minister, Mian Nawaz Sharif, in late 1990,[12] for which he had

11. Benon Sevan served as head of the UN Good Offices Mission in Afghanistan and Pakistan (UNGOMAP), then of its successor body, the Office of the UN Secretary-General in Afghanistan and Pakistan (OSGAP), from 1990 to 1992.
12. President Ghulam Ishaq Khan dismissed the Benazir government in July 1990, and the subsequent elections brought about a new coalition led by Mian Nawaz Sharif.

prepared enthusiastically and had waited for three months, turned out to be a nonevent.

Benon Sevan explained to Nawaz Sharif in some detail his ideas for a possible conference under UN auspices at which all Afghans, including some members of the Kabul regime, would be represented. The proposed conference would work for a government of national reconciliation, which, Benon emphasized, Zia ul Haq had vigorously advocated prior to the Geneva Accords. Nawaz, a man who learned a good deal on the job in subsequent years, made a few vacuous remarks about Pakistan's interest in political reconciliation and enquired about Benon's antecedents before winding up the meeting.

As UN envoy Benon departed, the prime minister wondered why "the gentleman" was talking so much about Afghanistan. Obviously, Nawaz had neither read the brief nor cared to find out whom he was meeting. But more important, the episode reflected the extent to which his government, at least in the initial phase of his first term, had left Afghan affairs in the hands of the ISI and the army. He was also deeply influenced by the thinking of Jamat e Islami, one of Pakistan's most influential religious political parties on the Afghan jihad, and one that favored the position of the hard-line Tanzeemat, who, regardless of their internal power struggle, rejected any accommodation with the Najibullah government.

Benon Sevan's ideas focused on starting a direct or indirect dialogue between the Najibullah regime and the Tanzeemat for a broad-based, if necessarily interim, government in a power-sharing arrangement. A start could be made with a congregation of Afghan representatives at an agreed venue under the auspices of the UN or jointly under the UN and the Organization of the Islamic Conference (OIC). The hard-line leaders, Gulbadin Hekmatyar, Yunas Khalis, and Rasool Sayyaf, rejected any role for the United Nations. Rabbani's Jamiat e Islami was ambivalent towards the UN, while the three moderate groups—the Afghan National Liberation Front of Sibghatullah Mojaddedi, National Islamic Front of Afghanistan of Sayed Ahmed Gailani, and Harkat e Enqilab e Islami Afghanistan of Maulvi Muhammad Nabi Muhammadi—were supportive of the idea. The opponents of the UN effort made the representation of the Kabul government into an issue, knowing that Kabul could not be bypassed under any UN-sponsored initiative. Discussions involving the ISI and the Pakistan Foreign Office dwelt on a suitable nomenclature to neutralize the hard-line objections and degenerated into considering formulations such as representatives of "Muslims" or "good Muslims" from Kabul. These were tactical posturings. The hard-line

Tanzeemat believed that the collapse of the Najibullah regime was simply a matter of time, and they needed to maneuver for that eventuality instead of offering the regime a lease on life through dialogue.

The first signs of the struggle within the Najibullah government and of the contacts between his associates and the Mujahedin leadership surfaced in early 1990. There were rumors of an abortive coup and later, in March, the defection of Najibullah's defense minister, Shahnawaz Tanai, who turned up in Pakistan to join Gulbadin Hekmatyar.[13] The incident followed an internal reshuffle in the Kabul government and the ouster of several Khalqi top leaders suspected of having contacts with the Mujahedin leaders. Khalq was the Pushtun-dominated segment of the Afghan left movement; Najibullah had belonged to Parcham. In 1978 the Khalq had engineered the overthrow of Sardar Muhammad Daoud, the Afghan president and cousin of former king Zahir Shah. Shahnawaz Tanai's defection came as a shock and revealed fissures within the Kabul regime that had withstood the exit of the Soviet forces.

By late 1990, the United States had begun pressing Moscow to agree to the cutting off of arms supply to all Afghan sides to bring about cessation of hostilities and promote the idea of a transitional arrangement.[14] These developments and Najibullah's apparent softening towards political accommodation encouraged UN Secretary-General Pérez de Cuéllar in May 1991to propose a plan that envisaged a cease-fire between the Mujahedin and the Kabul regime forces, a cessation of arms supplies by all countries involved in the conflict, and consultations for elections that would allow the Afghans to choose their own government. Najibullah showed willingness to accept the proposal and cease-fire offer. Abdur Rab Rasool Sayyaf, speaking on behalf of the AIG, and Gulbadin rejected the plan. Later on, AIG president Sibghatullah Mojaddedi, though known to personally favor a political approach, declared that there could be no cease-fire with Najibullah.

The new ISI chief, Lt. Gen. Asad Durrani, appointed following the dismissal of the Benazir government in July 1990, took charge of Afghan matters at a time when a certain degree of disillusion had set in towards the Mujahedin leadership. He had less reservation about trying various possibilities to break the logjam, including diplomatic efforts through the UN secretary-general's special representative. In mid-1991, Najibullah's de-

13. *NYT,* March 9, 1990.
14. *NYT,* May 3, 1990.

fense attaché in Islamabad hinted that Najibullah might abdicate. The ISI shared with the Foreign Office the view that if Najibullah were suddenly removed from the scene, Kabul would descend into chaos and turmoil. This convinced Asad Durrani to explore possibilities for a transition arrangement to cover the exit of Najibullah. Asad Durrani even met his Afghan counterpart Ghulam Faruq Yaqubi in Geneva to sound out Najibullah's thinking on dialogue and power sharing. Yaqubi suggested that if Pakistan could get the Mujahedin leaders to agree on some format for dialogue, a workable modality could be developed.[15]

Durrani also reached out to the former king, Zahir Shah, the other nemesis of the hard-line Mujahedin leaders, hinting that the king could come to Quetta to help organize an interim political arrangement. The king's spokesman and son-in-law, Abdul Wali, stuck to the familiar position that Pakistan needed to prepare the ground for acceptance of the king by the various parties, which he saw as the creation of Pakistan. These contacts were a long shot, but they revealed Pakistan's increasing anxiety to break the political impasse. The Mujahedin-Najibullah standoff denied Pakistan the expectation of a new, friendly Afghanistan emerging from the abortive Soviet venture in that country. Pakistan also increasingly felt the burden of nearly three and half million Afghan refugees, with vastly diminished international humanitarian support.

In mid-1991, the Pakistan Foreign Office prepared a paper, in consultation with the ISI, for approval by Prime Minister Nawaz Sharif. It basically supported a UN-sponsored indirect dialogue for a possible arrangement based on the principle of power sharing with elements from the Kabul regime, without Najibullah, who could be eased out as part of the transition process in Kabul. The prime minister agreed to convene a meeting of the Afghanistan cell, which included the top army, intelligence, and Foreign Office representation. Nawaz appeared a bit surprised that both the army chief and the ISI chief seemed to endorse the recommendation in the paper that the Foreign Office had formally submitted. He agreed that the ISI should work on the Tanzeemat leaders to cooperate with the UN secretary-general's representative and enter into an indirect dialogue with Kabul. Later, however, when the ISI chief pushed the proposal with the Tanzeemat leaders, Burhanuddin Rabbani claimed that he had received a message to

---

15. Asad Durrani's meeting encouraged Pir Sayed Ahmed Gailani, the pro-monarchy moderate leader of one of the Tanzeemat, the National Islamic Front of Afghanistan, to meet Najibullah in Geneva.

the contrary from the prime minister through the Jamat e Islami channels. Regardless of the veracity of the claim, at the time the prime minister showed no enthusiasm for dialogue and diplomacy and shared the populist faith in the jihadi struggle, which was seen as the primary factor in compelling the Soviets to leave Afghanistan.

On the other hand, Pakistan's president, Ghulam Ishaq Khan, saw benefit in the UN involvement and dialogue and was reportedly unhappy when he learned about Nawaz Sharif's disinterest in pushing the Tanzeemat to cooperate with the UN. However, intercession by the president could hardly have mattered in that complicated situation. The hard-line Mujahedin leaders would have stalled on any effort, as they had become quite autonomous in pursuit of their individual interests. The familiar tensions between the president and the prime minister in Pakistani politics had once again started taking shape. The Pakistani decision-making and policy-implementation processes had always suffered from the lack of rigor typical of the amorphous political environment of the country. Pakistan could not produce a sustained powerful push that would oblige the hard-line Tanzeemat leaders to change course and accept dialogue.

Pakistan Tries for a Political Solution as the International Focus Shifts Away from Afghanistan

During 1991, President Ghulam Ishaq Khan initiated a serious effort to bring about unity among the divided Afghan parties. A Pushtun with dignified bearing who commanded respect as an elder, Ghulam Ishaq Khan had risen from the ranks of the bureaucracy to the highest office of the land. He was a quintessential organization man who respected institutional practices and opinion. He thought that the Tanzeemat should agree on a plan of elections to constitute an interim government with a broad base and support among the masses. He would diligently prepare election plans and invite all Tanzeemat leaders for their comments and endorsement, explaining his meticulously worked-out representational bodies and structures based on elections in each *wuluswali* (district) and nominations from distinguished segments of society, including the Ulema, commanders, and tribal elders.

For an outsider, these discussions, conducted in Pushtu, were quite a tutorial in the Afghan and Pushtun tribal culture of courtesy and deception. For their own separate reasons, none of the participant Tanzeemat leaders were ready for an agreed plan, yet the way they kept putting monkey wrenches in the works was always a treat to watch. The first hour would be spent in praising the president for his concern and affection for the Afghan *Millat* (nation), his kindness and generosity, and his hard work in producing a most thoughtful plan. Then somebody (usually Gulbadin or Yunas Khalis or at times Rabbani) would start referring to the sacrifices made in the Jihad, the status that the commanders had earned in the eyes of the Afghan people, or the local leadership role assumed by the Ulema, and thus the need for substantial if not predominant representation for these segments of the society. Further questions would be raised about modalities and numbers, and within an hour or so the plan would be effectively scuttled and the meeting would disperse, with another round of effusive praise for Ghulam Ishaq Khan and a show of eagerness to benefit from his wisdom at the next meeting. After three such meetings, having twice reworked his election plans, Ghulam Ishaq Khan gave up the effort.

The president's efforts revealed the Pakistani approach in dealing with the Afghan Mujahedin leadership as inherently soft, tentative, and at times almost suppliant. In their meetings, Pakistani leaders, including the military chiefs, would begin by lauding the Mujahedin's achievements in defeating the Soviet Union before broaching the subject of the meeting, namely, proposals for their agreement. In this ambience, it was naïve to think that these hard-nosed Afghans would feel under pressure to make compromises or accept difficult decisions, when they could politely thwart the purpose of the meeting. They had come a long way since the early 1980s, when the Pakistani leadership under Zia ul Haq was in the driver's seat, making the important decisions concerning the Afghan resistance.

An early assertion of independence was the hard-line Tanzeemat's rejection of a formula offered by Zia ul Haq for a government of reconciliation in the wake of the Soviet offer in late 1987 of a one-year time frame for withdrawal. Furthermore, beyond their personal ambitions and the historical absence of a tradition of elections and democracy, the hard-line leaders were schooled in a version of orthodox Islam that scoffed at the idea of governance through popular vote that gave equal weight to every individual regardless of his character, status, and accomplishment.

The hard-line Tanzeemat made no bones about their intentions. In early 1991, at the request of the Foreign Office, the ISI arranged a meeting of about twenty-five second-rank Tanzeemat leaders for a briefing in Peshawar. The author, who was director general responsible for Afghanistan at the time, spoke to the gathering, emphasizing the need to end the bloodshed and to use the UN or the OIC intercession to force a transition in Kabul. The first objection followed the familiar theological harangue about the impropriety of shaking hands with godless communists and the betrayal of the Jihad. But the next observation was more to the point. A representative of the Hizb (Yunas Khalis group) got up and questioned the wisdom of sharing power. He reminded the gathering, "We have shed blood, not to share power at the end of the day; we have done so to wrest power for ourselves."

This remark was shorn of any pretension about their objective and reflected the motivation and implacable ambition of some of the Tanzeemat leaders. In this power game, elements within the army and the ISI were inclined to favor those who showed capacity to be ruthless rather than those wanting to be part of a future dispensation through maneuver and compromise. At the time, this seemed a realistic choice, but it proved to be fatal. The military mind is often attracted by strong personalities. It was understandable that ISI officials often applauded Gulbadin and Yunas Khalis for their effectiveness in the Jihad,[16] even though these men were the least amenable to political compromise and building bridges with others.

The Pakistan Foreign Office could not forcefully pursue the ideas for UN involvement to bring about a transitional arrangement or a broad-based government, because Benon Sevan, for his part, had failed to elicit a definitive response from Kabul in support of his ideas, especially the nature of a transitional process or representation in a broad-based government. The Kabul regime was reticent even to acknowledge the Tanzeemat as an equal interlocutor. Throughout 1990 and most of 1991, on the question of representation in a dialogue, Kabul would invariably use a euphemism—"the refugee elements" in Pakistan and Iran—to refer to the Tanzeemat.

In part to boost diplomatic efforts for a dialogue but mainly to rehabilitate Afghanistan so that the refugees could start returning following the Soviet withdrawal, Pakistan suggested that donor countries put together a package of $2 billion to $3 billion to serve as an incentive for the Afghans to abandon conflict and work for a stable new government of reconciliation. Donors were not prepared to consider any assistance, apart from minimal humanitarian help, until the Afghanistan situation settled down. While the United States maintained an interest in promoting a political settlement, by late 1989 the U.S. assistance to the Mujahedin groups had dried up, in-

---

16. Many Afghans resented the prominence given to Gulbadin. They argued that commanders associated with Nabi Muhammadi and Yunas Khalis were the most active on the ground, while Gulbadin was saving his forces and equipment for the anticipated struggle following the departure of the Soviets.

cluding a $30 million food-cum-cash program managed through the ISI.[17] France even decided to reopen its embassy in Kabul, as if to distance itself from the Mujahedin and signal its recognition that Afghanistan was on the mend and did not require any special effort on the part of the international community. In any event, by 1989 with the fall of the Berlin Wall, Afghanistan was no longer an area of primary interest to the West; its attention was now focused elsewhere—on developments in Eastern Europe and the Soviet Union itself.

This abandonment of Afghanistan, allowing it to drift on its own, was a historical letdown. The world needed to engage, to help ensure economic revival and stabilization in a country that had been devastated as the last front of the Cold War. The Afghan struggle, true to its traditions of fighting the outsider, had helped freedom movements in Eastern Europe and accelerated the unraveling of the Soviet Union. Afghanistan was the first substantive issue that raised doubts in the minds of the Soviet public about the propaganda claims of its closed Marxist regime. According to the official Moscow version, the Soviet soldiers were being sent to Afghanistan to fight the Americans, Pakistanis, and Chinese. These claims started losing credibility as young soldiers returned in body bags or brought back stories of the real conditions in Afghanistan. By conservative estimates, over one million Soviet soldiers were exposed to the war and more than fourteen thousand lost their lives.

In April 1999 at a Wilton Park seminar, former Soviet ambassador Oleg Grinevsky succinctly described the constraint the Afghan war placed on Moscow's ability to act in Eastern Europe. Grinevsky spoke to a group of Pakistanis and Indians about dangerous times during the Cold War. In the early 1980s, he had headed the Soviet side in the Helsinki Talks for promoting East-West détente in pursuance of the Helsinki Accords of 1975. At Wilton Park he stated that in 1982, upon returning from a Politburo meeting, Soviet President Yuri Andropov had remarked to him: "Today the Poles should go to Muslim churches and thank Allah; but for these problems in Afghanistan, I would have sent troops to Poland to take care of this [Solidarity] nuisance." Because of Afghanistan, the Soviets could not reenact in 1982 what they had done in 1956 and 1968.[18] It was an irony that once the

17. *NYT,* February 5 and February 16, 1990.

18. Pervez Musharraf, in his autobiography *In the Line of Fire* (New York: Free Press, 2006), 277–78, mentions that the chief of German intelligence presented to the

Soviets were out, the European and U.S. focus completely shifted to Eastern Europe and the former Soviet republics, now designated the Commonwealth of Independent States (CIS),[19] leaving Afghanistan in a state of ruin and civil war. Pakistan fared even worse. In 1990, it was subjected to sanctions on the nuclear issue and was left largely on its own to deal with over three million Afghan refugees and the deteriorating situation next door.

Pakistan's own relations with the West, especially the United States, had also become tense, specifically on the issue of nuclear proliferation. The Pressler Amendment, passed in the early eighties, became activated when President George H. W. Bush would not certify that Pakistan did not posses a nuclear device. The U.S. president had issued the certification until 1989, the year the Soviets left Afghanistan. Pakistan thereafter came under sanctions. As a consequence, the delivery of F-16 fighter aircraft, for which Pakistan had already paid close to $700 million, was canceled, and the United States refused to return the funds. In addition, the United States confiscated a good part of the U.S.-manufactured military equipment that was purchased earlier and sent for retrofitting and repairs. Ten years later, President Clinton admitted that this was unfair to Pakistan and agreed to negotiate the return of the funds Pakistan had paid.

These sanctions rankled the Pakistan establishment and contributed to rising popular sentiment against the United States. In the eyes of the Pakistani public, their erstwhile ally had not only left Pakistan holding the bag on war-torn Afghanistan after U.S. interests had been served but had also resorted to the pre-1979 pressures against Pakistan on the nuclear issue. Clearly, the special U.S. interest in Pakistan and Afghanistan had been linked to the Soviet military intervention. After the 1989 Soviet withdrawal from Afghanistan and the momentous changes set in motion in Eastern Europe, the United States and other donors had much bigger fish to fry elsewhere than in a continuing nettlesome engagement in Afghanistan.

---

visiting chief of Pakistani intelligence as a memento a piece of the Berlin Wall with the inscription, "To the one who struck the first blow." Later, the former German Foreign Minister, Joschka Fischer, remarked, "The security of Germany depended on what happened in the Hindu Kush."

19. During the first five years after the breakup of the Soviet Union, 1992–97, Russia alone received assistance from donor countries ranging between $50 billion and $100 billion, depending on calculations of balance-of-payments support, concessional loans, and rescheduling of loans.

Tentative Pakistan-Iran Joint Effort

Emerging from the shadows of the eight-year-long Iran-Iraq conflict (1980–88), Iran took an increasing interest in the evolving Afghanistan situation. During the 1980s, its main Afghanistan-related interest concerned the Afghan refugees. Unlike Pakistan, Iran largely kept the refugees in a restricted camp environment. It also sought to keep linkages with leaders of the Shia communities inside Afghanistan. In Islamabad, the Iranian embassy was known to have contacts with the moderate Tanzeemat leaders and with Burhanuddin Rabbani, the Tajik leader of the Jamiat e Islami. Iran had always felt empathy for the Persian-speaking Tajiks.

Iran had been careful to avoid a clear denunciation of the Soviet intervention, although it disapproved. It considered the intervention to have been instigated by the United States. In February 1989, Sibghatullah Mojaddedi visited Tehran at Iran's invitation. He promised the leadership of the eight Iranian-based Shia groups one hundred seats at the shura the ISI wanted to organize in Rawalpindi to decide an interim arrangement in anticipation of Soviet withdrawal. Back in Islamabad, Mojaddedi could not deliver on his promise, which was dismissed by the hard-line Tanzeemat leaders backed by the ISI and the Saudis.

In early 1991, Iran proposed to cooperate with Pakistan to build a Mujahedin united front and suggested a joint meeting of Pakistan, Iran, and all major Tanzeemat. The first trilateral meeting involving the three sides was organized in Islamabad in July 1991. The head of the Asian Affairs Division in the Iranian Foreign Office, Jafar Musavi, led the Iranian delegation; one day later, however, Foreign Minister Ali Akbar Vallayati came to Islamabad. In deference to the Iranian participation, leaders of the seven Peshawar-based Tanzeemat were joined in Islamabad by two additional Shia parties, Hizb e Wahdat, led by Karim Khalili and Haji Muhammad Mohaqeq, and Harkat e Islami, headed by Sheikh Asef Mohsini. The Iranians had two interests, one of substance, one of form. They wanted an assured Shia representation in a future Mujahedin government or in any representative conference intended to be a stepping-stone for a government of national reconciliation. Seeking formal recognition of the eight Tehran-based groups, Iran proposed a Shia representation of 25 percent.

The demanded share was far beyond the Pakistani estimation of the Shia population in Afghanistan and disproportionate to the perceived Shia contribution to the Jihad. Hazaras, Qizilbash, and Farsiwan, numbering barely three million, comprised the bulk of the Shia population in Afghanistan. In behind-the-scenes exchanges, Gulbadin Hekmatyar rejected the idea out of hand, saying that he could not endorse sectarian considerations for an Afghan government. He resisted an even much lower assured Shia representation. He made it into a point of principle and asserted, somewhat facetiously, that he would have no qualms if through an agreed nonsectarian procedure an all-Shia government emerged. He also argued that at no point in Afghan history had such a sectarian distinction been permitted for the purpose of governance.

The less important issue was the Iranian aversion to including the "voluntary" return of Afghan refugees in the formal communiqué, which in Iranian thinking clashed with the sovereign prerogative of a state to ask the refugees to return to their home country. The issue was resolved through a technical adjustment in drafting that went unnoticed by the Tanzeemat representatives. The communiqué produced at the end of the meeting failed to address Iran's principal demands but sounded upbeat, with a commitment to carry forward cooperation at the next meeting in Tehran.

Vallayati met Nawaz Sharif and wanted to discuss the results of the meeting. But he soon found that the prime minister was instead eager to show him the new prime ministerial residence to which he had shifted that very day. There were expressions of satisfaction, the expected pleasantries, and reaffirmation of goodwill and resolve for future cooperation. Nawaz knew that on the substantive concern of the Iranians, he had little to say or commit.

The follow-up meeting in Tehran in September 1991 started on a discordant note and came to its logical end in a stalemate. The Tanzeemat leaders who came with the Pakistani delegation included Sheikh Mohsini, a Hazara Shia leader who had attended the Islamabad meeting but whom the Iranians no longer supported. They now backed the rival Hazara leader Abdul Ali Mazari, in addition to the Hizb e Wahdat leadership. First, Iranian Vice Minister Alaeddin Broujerdi raised objections, and the meeting could not start until Iranian Intelligence Chief Mohsin Razai intervened to let Mohsini participate. The Iranians had also escalated their expectations beyond the 25 percent representation for the Shia. They now wanted Pakistan's endorsement to create a new militia along the lines of the Basij volunteer vigilante force that serves as the coercive arm of the clergy in Iran. The Pakistan side could not oblige.

Yunas Khalis reflected the mood of the hard-line Tanzeemat, plainly questioning the right of Iran to make any demand when it had been "impotent" in support of the Jihad. Putting together a communiqué that could show progress since the Islamabad meeting was excruciating; the trilateral dialogue had come to a dead end. Subsequently, Pakistan-Iran cooperation continued on a different trajectory, namely, helping negotiate cease-fires between the major Mujahedin groups engaged in the deadly struggle for control of Kabul. Later still, in the late 1990s, there was a parting of the ways between the two countries, as Pakistan supported the Taliban, who espoused an extremist Sunni and anti-Shia creed.

The trilateral meetings earned the Iranians the trust of the Shia elements in Afghanistan and also demonstrated that Iran was a player with a constituency and an agenda. Shia parties were relatively new entrants in the Jihad and had only marginal dealings with Pakistani intelligence, whereas the Iranians had started focusing on the Shia leaders, particularly in Hazarajat, as part of their effort to build influence in Afghanistan. By late 1991, Tehran had also developed considerable influence with Burhanuddin Rabbani and Ahmed Shah Massoud. As a result of the Iranian initiative and Soviet contacts with Ahmed Shah Massoud, in November 1991 Moscow invited Rabbani to join the Tehran-based Shia parties for the first-ever Mujahedin dialogue with the Soviet side.

For its part, Pakistan had no fresh proposal and simply wanted Iran to join hands to put pressure on the Tanzeemat to come up with a formula for future government and for hastening the demise of the Najibullah regime. What basically killed the trilateral initiative was the absence of any clear parameters for cooperation sufficiently attractive to the Pakistani side. Yunas Khalis's and Gulbadin's objections became a convenient excuse for abandoning the process. This did not imply that Pakistan's intelligence agency had used the two or exercised any decisive influence over the Tanzeemat leaders, including those who benefited most from its largesse. These leaders had no qualms about embarrassing Pakistan if it became necessary to protect their individual interests. They demonstrated this ability in December 1991, when Soviet vice president Alexander Rutskoy visited Pakistan, which came as a rude shock to the ISI and army top officials.

The Myth of Pakistan's Control over the Afghan Tanzeemat

Vice President Alexander Rutskoy arrived in Lahore on December 21, 1991, a rare visit to Pakistan from a Soviet leader at a time when the world watched in disbelief the breakup of the Soviet Union. Rutskoy had an association with Pakistan, as only four years earlier the Afghan Mujahedin had shot down his fighter plane in the border area. To his good fortune his parachute landed on the Pakistan side, where he was captured by personnel of the Pakistan Frontier Corps (FC) and handed over to the Soviet embassy in Islamabad. Remembering that he had been well treated by the Pakistani army, he traveled to Pakistan in December 1991 in the hope of getting some Russian POWs released from the custody of the Mujahedin groups and winning political kudos for himself. In Lahore, he was driven straight to the old colonial Governor's House, where Nawaz Sharif received him. Rutskoy explained the purpose of his visit: "You get a few Russian prisoners released by the Mujahedin to accompany me to Moscow, and I assure you that there will be a standing ovation for Pakistan in the Duma; we will turn a new page in our relations with Pakistan."

Nawaz was impressed by the opportunity. During the meeting, he received affirmation that Pakistan could also purchase advanced Russian defense equipment, including fighter planes. As a side issue, the prime minister wanted to verify whether following the establishment of the CIS, announced the previous evening in Alma Ata, it was appropriate to extend recognition to Russia and other former Soviet republics, in particular the Central Asian states. Rutskoy's affirmative response allowed Nawaz to immediately declare Pakistan's recognition of the newly emerged CIS states, making Pakistan the second country to have done so. Rutskoy, who was welcomed with the old Soviet hammer-and-sickle flag, was seen off at the Lahore airport as he departed for Islamabad the same evening with the new Russian tricolor flying atop the building.[20]

Nawaz Sharif contacted President Ghulam Ishaq Khan, army chief General Asif Nawaz, and ISI chief Lt. Gen. Asad Durrani to convey details of his meeting with Rutskoy. He emphasized that every effort be made to prevail upon the Tanzeemat leaders to oblige the Russian vice president. As it transpired, only the Gulbadin and Rabbani groups held some Russian prisoners inside Afghanistan.

Asad Durrani and Ashraf Jehangir Qazi, Pakistan's ambassador in Moscow who had come especially for the visit, along with other senior ISI officials, spent hours well past midnight trying to plead and convince these

---

20. The old Soviet flag was used at the welcome ceremony after advice had delicately been sought from Soviet embassy officials. Soviet ambassador Yakunin arrived at the airport flying the Soviet flag on his official car. He got his car flag changed at the airport and left after the welcome ceremony flying the Russian flag, a rare symbolic moment that captured a historic transformation.

leaders to hand over even a couple of prisoners, if not more, for the sake of Pakistan, where they had enjoyed shelter and hospitality for such long years. The responses were eloquent praise for Pakistan yet obfuscation on the main issue, with claims of inability for one reason or another, from denial to lack of knowledge of locations to absence of communications with field commanders. By morning, the ISI could get only a half-insane prisoner of Central Asian origin from Gulbadin and a promise from Rabbani to deliver two at a later stage. It was generally believed that the two groups held over a dozen ethnic Russian prisoners.

It was a deep disappointment for ISI chief Asad Durrani and army chief Asif Nawaz. Sitting in the side hall on the ground floor in the Pakistani Foreign Office with a swirl of Afghans and Pakistani officials milling around, Asif Nawaz confessed to Rutskoy that he was "ashamed" of not being able to deliver on the Russian vice president's request. To this, Rutskoy, unable to hide his dismay, responded, "Generals know how to get things done!"

There was speculation that the chief of Jamat e Islami, Qazi Hussain Ahmed, who had traveled from Peshawar to present Rutskoy with a translation in Russian of the holy Quran, had in fact come to restrain Gulbadin and Rabbani from making any gesture to the Pakistani government. What appears to be closer to the truth is Gulbadin's own desire to use the prisoners as pawns for direct negotiations with the Russians. Once again, the myth that Pakistan could prevail on the forces it had sponsored and nurtured for the Afghan Jihad lay embarrassingly exposed. Pakistani culture, despite its violence, remains soft at the core and tolerant of defiance and indiscipline. The Tanzeemat were in a sense a creation of Pakistan; yet at every critical juncture each leader acted autonomously, often guided by his own perceived narrow self-interest. The malaise continues to haunt Afghanistan on a broader canvas.

Initiative for a Commanders' Shura

On the military front, the siege of Khost and efforts to establish a commanders' shura, with reconciliation between Gulbadin and Ahmed Shah Massoud as its centerpiece, were worthy of note. Massoud was the legendary commander from the Panjshir valley north of Kabul, at the mouth of the Salang Pass, where he had repulsed several Soviet attacks and on occasion agreed to a cease-fire.

The Gulbadin-Massoud rivalry had a long history. In 1973 they had fled from Kabul following a crackdown on Islamist students by President Muhammad Daoud. Massoud was known to move in and out of Pakistan when, in 1977, he left for Panjshir following an assault by Gulbadin's men in Peshawar. He suspected that Gulbadin was targeting him with the blessings of the Pakistani intelligence operatives. In early October 1990, Ahmed Shah Massoud came to Gram Chashma in Chitral to attend an Afghan Mujahedin commanders' gathering encouraged by the Pakistani ISI. Massoud came to Islamabad at the invitation of the ISI chief, issued at Gram Chashma. In Islamabad, Massoud had meetings at the ISI and in the Foreign Office and was received by the top political and military leaders, including President Ghulam Ishaq Khan and Foreign Minister Sahabzada Yaqub Khan.

The Pakistanis sought to forge an alliance of all major Mujahedin commanders through a shura for coordinated military action inside Afghanistan. The idea was supported by U.S. special envoy Peter Tomsen, who believed in reaching out directly to the commanders to settle the Afghanistan conundrum. The ISI succeeded in bringing Ahmed Shah Massoud and Gulbadin together in Peshawar, where they agreed to coordinate action and also participate in the commanders' shura.

The first meeting of the shura was put together in Peshawar and was attended by Ismael Khan from Herat and Abdul Haq, who had been active in the Nangarhar area. The two rivals, Gulbadin and Massoud, and the assembled commanders readily agreed to expressions of unity and affirmed willingness for cooperation. Massoud announced in Peshawar a consensus on plans to topple the Kabul government and to hold elections in the northern provinces of Afghanistan by the following spring, with the participation of both Hizb e Islami and Jamiat e Islami.

Nonetheless, as the ISI would soon discover, none of these understandings led to practical implementation. In fact nothing could be agreed to as a common strategy on the ground. Ahmed Shah Massoud would procrastinate when asked to close the Salang tunnel. Gulbadin could not be trusted by any of the other commanders. One practical result of the shura was the expression of reservations by the participants to a suggestion by Gulbadin for a joint military operation against Kabul using rocket fire, which could cause heavy civilian casualties.[21]

21. *Keesing's Record of World Events,* October 1990, 37775.

The fall of Khost, a significant military development in April 1991, did not result from coordination among the commanders but from ISI pressure on Jallaluddin Haqqani, an influential commander nominally linked to the Yunas Khalis group who operated in the Paktika and Paktia regions. Khost was highly vulnerable, as the territory is surrounded by Pakistani tribal area from three sides. Anxious to show some success, the ISI was pushing Jallaluddin to move against the town. He was, however, in no hurry, as he suspected success could end Pakistan's interest in providing him with military supplies and that he might also be obliged to accommodate the moribund Afghan Interim Government. He agreed to launch an operation when faced with the threat of a supply cutoff.

Unlike in the Jalalabad operation, this time the ISI planned for encouraging defections and coordinated the operation closely with Haqqani. Kabul's paramilitary defenders, the Afghan Militia, were targeted first and encouraged to surrender, which they did on the fourth day of the siege upon receiving assurances of amnesty. According to some reports, General Shahnawaz Tanai, who had defected to Gulbadin, played a role in persuading the militia and subsequently the besieged Afghan army to surrender.[22] The militia personnel were treated well; they were allowed to keep their arms and leave for their villages and homes. On April 15, 1991, the third day after the militia had surrendered, the Afghan army, numbering close to six thousand, laid down its arms.

If Khost had fallen two years earlier around the time of the abortive Jalalabad operation, there was a good chance that the AIG might have been located in the town and secured some international recognition. By mid-1991, interest in the AIG had waned, and it was almost a forgotten entity. The Khost victory was celebrated by contingents of Pakistani Islamist political parties visiting the city, including the leader of Pakistan's Jamat e Islami, Qazi Hussain Ahmed. The euphoria was short-lived and without any political consequences. Nonetheless, Khost marked the first Mujahedin military victory against the Kabul government, which by now had started unraveling from within.

The main reason Pakistan's multidirectional efforts in late 1990 and 1991 remained fruitless was that by this time the Mujahedin leaders and commanders had become aware of the weakness of the Najibullah regime. It was the start of the end game for the seizure of Kabul. The influential commanders would not cooperate with each other or engage in major joint op-

22. _Keesing's Record of World Events,_ April 1991, 38153.

erations, fearing that such action could allow advantage to someone else. They all understood from history and tradition that in Afghanistan what mattered was control of Kabul. Therefore, it made no sense for Ahmed Shah Massoud to block Salang only to let his adversaries gain the upper hand against Najibullah.

Throughout 1989 to 1991, Gulbadin showed little interest in the Jalalabad or Khost campaign; his eyes were fixed on Kabul, as were those of his principal adversary, Ahmed Shah Massoud. Gulbadin made several plans to attack Kabul, especially following the defection of Shahnawaz Tanai, a development that gave rise to the expectation of the Najibullah's imminent collapse and provided a boost to Gulbadin. Nonetheless, the ISI did not encourage Gulbadin and did not consider his plans feasible. According to the ISI's assessment, neither Gulbadin nor, for that matter, any other Mujahedin commander could capture Kabul on his own.[23]

Najibullah's Exit and the Peshawar Accord

The collapse of the Soviet Union in December 1991 had a profoundly demoralizing impact on the Najibullah regime, which had survived the withdrawal of the Soviet forces with remarkable resilience and withstood the defection of its defense minister, Shahnawaz Tanai. As long as Najibullah appeared to enjoy the support of a superpower, most of his generals and allies held together. None of them was used to the idea of making a move without a hint or blessing of the big brother. The Soviet collapse came as a shock, and the Kabul government started pulling apart.

Early 1992 presented a different scenario. The struggle for power among the Mujahedin groups, in particular between the two strongmen of the Jihad, Gulbadin Hekmatyar and Ahmed Shah Massoud, had begun in earnest. Each was for some time trying to inveigle and win over Najibullah's military generals to his side. Despite the façade of public rejection by Muja-

---

23. In a different account, Steve Coll in *Ghost Wars,* 218–19, reports that after the Tanai episode, in October 1990, Gulbadin was ready to attack Kabul, with active support from the ISI, and the attack was aborted only after a stern warning from U.S. ambassador Robert Oakley. Coll comments that this intervention signaled the Pakistani army's deepening break with American priorities. The author, however, recalls that ISI chief Asad Durrani was quite clear in his mind that Kabul could not fall without a coordinated action by commanders belonging to all major Tanzeemat, and he was trying to organize a commanders' shura in the fall of 1990.

hedin leaders of any talks with the Kabul regime, the Tanai incident in 1990 had already brought out in the open the Mujahedin's contacts with Najibullah's men.

Gulbadin was known to be favored by the ISI, but he was intensely disliked by the other Tanzeemat and had completely alienated the outside world, including Saudi Arabia, Iran, and supporters of the Afghan Jihad in the West. His antipathy towards the United States was well known since his refusal to visit Washington when he was in New York in September 1985 leading a Tanzeemat delegation. Hours of persuasion by Pakistan Permanent Representative Sardar Shahnawaz and, by telephone, by the ISI chief Lt. Gen. Akhtar Abdur Rahman failed to convince him to change his mind. Gulbadin was in the forefront of those rejecting Iranian initiatives, regardless of their merit. He had annoyed his Saudi benefactors over his opposition to the presence of the U.S. forces in Saudi Arabia, echoing the objections of the then unknown Saudi Osama bin Laden.

In the diplomatic arena, Ahmed Shah Massoud acted with prudence and enjoyed international support that he had built by cultivating the European media, especially the French, with his early schooling in the French language. He established linkages with Iran benefiting from his Persian-speaking Tajik background. Massoud was affiliated with the Jamiat e Islami of Burhanuddin Rabbani, a mild-mannered leader. Massoud had remained largely aloof, confined to his base in Panjshir; he and Rabbani did not engender the ill will that many of the other Tanzeemat leaders had developed towards Gulbadin Hekmatyar for his arrogant demeanor towards other parties and allegedly ruthless targeting of opponents. At one Tanzeemat meeting to discuss possible leadership questions, Gulbadin lost his temper and taunted Mojaddedi, who had opposed his view, saying that Mojaddedi's party could fit into his pocket. Gulbadin was believed to be behind the murder of Professor Syed Bahauddin Majrooh, a well-respected intellectual among Afghan expatriates, who supported the Zahir Shah option for return of normalcy to Afghanistan. Moderate Tanzeemat hated Gulbadin. His only kindred soul, Yunas Khalis, at heart a simple cleric, had become inactive for reasons of age and a new marriage, as well as his disillusionment with his peers who were reaching out to elements within the Kabul regime.[24] As the Najibullah regime began to falter, Gulbadin and Massoud were the two principal actors on the stage in Afghanistan for the unfolding of a sinister new phase of the internecine conflict.

24. *Keesing's Record of World Events,* May 1991, 38194.

Najibullah made a few conciliatory moves that only betrayed his weakness. In September 1991, he welcomed the U.S.-Soviet agreement for ending all military support to the Afghan combatants and offered a cease-fire, only to be rejected by the Mujahedin commanders.[25] There was a hint of desperation when, in the wake of the dissolution of the Soviet Union, Najibullah appealed to the United States in March 1992 to help his country become a "bulwark against the spread of fundamentalism" in Central Asia. He also supported the U.S. proposal for a UN-sponsored transitional government.[26] For Najibullah, the writing on the wall was clear, and within a few days, he announced his intention to step down in favor of an interim government to be put together by the United Nations.

In the third week of March 1992, Benon Sevan wanted to meet Prime Minister Nawaz Sharif urgently. Sensing the changing scenario, the meeting was arranged for March 20 in Lahore, where Nawaz was joined by the newly appointed ISI chief, Lt. Gen. Javed Nasir, a born-again Islamist preoccupied with new opportunities in Central Asia and more obsessed with India than with the affairs of the squabbling Tanzeemat leaders. Benon Sevan issued a dramatic salvo, suggesting that Pakistan ask the Tanzeemat leaders to come up with an agreed panel of neutral personalities, and he would arrange a transfer of power to the panel in Kabul. He underscored the urgency in the situation, which without such a transfer of power could lapse into bloodshed. This was music to the ears of Nawaz Sharif, who, like many in the ISI, believed that a Mujahedin government must eventually replace Najibullah and that the talk of dialogue and sharing of power was not an option worthy of pursuit. The transfer of power to a panel nominated by the Tanzeemat could be a definitive, short prelude to a Mujahedin government, with the obvious advantage of heading off a conflict. Nawaz immediately instructed the equally excited ISI chief to press the Tanzeemat to agree on a panel and coordinate the transfer of power with Benon Sevan, whose stock had suddenly risen in the eyes of the prime minister.

More than two weeks later, there was still no agreement on a panel of names, despite all the pressure that the ISI could bring to bear on the Tanzeemat leaders, who held endless meetings at the Tanzeemat office in Peshawar. Gulbadin, however, remained in Parachinar close to the border and designated his second in command, Qutubuddin Hillal, to attend the meetings. Javed Nasir had camped in Peshawar, constantly pleading with the

25. *NYT,* September 14 and 17, 1991.
26. *NYT,* March 10, 1992.

Tanzeemat leaders to reach an agreement, invoking scripture and the teachings of Islam and stressing the need to avoid bloodshed in Kabul.

Javed Nasir had just been appointed to head the ISI. He played no favorites and desperately wanted the leaders to reach some agreement to show success to the prime minister. In the second week of April, he reported signs of an agreement on a list of neutral personalities who could affect transfer of power. The prime minister convened a meeting on April 15 in Islamabad, inviting all Tanzeemat leaders and Benon Sevan to formalize the agreement. The meeting, scheduled for late afternoon, could not get under way when it transpired that Rabbani had reneged on the agreement. Meanwhile, in Kabul, matters were taking a turn for the worse for Najibullah. It was rumored that his military generals were defecting to Ahmed Shah Massoud and Gulbadin along ethnic lines and that Najibullah faced a threat to his life.

The meeting convened by the prime minister did take place briefly late in the evening. Rabbani took the position that the situation in and around Kabul was grim and an effective team rather than a group of weak neutrals was needed to keep calm and avoid bloodshed. He proposed that each party nominate two strong persons other than the leaders, who could immediately take over in Kabul. From his party, he offered the names of Ahmed Shah Massoud and Engineer Syed Muhammad Ayub. Benon Sevan had by now indicated that he would arrange transfer of power to any panel nominated by the Tanzeemat and had dropped the earlier condition of neutral personalities.

Although Rabbani was the leader of the Jamiat, Ahmed Shah Massoud called the shots, and by now Massoud's strategy was quite evident. He had militarily upstaged his archrival Gulbadin and wanted to enter Kabul, preferably under an arrangement with UN blessings. He had built alliances with the Hizb e Wahdat of Karim Khalili, who put pressure on Kabul from the north, and with Abdul Rashid Dostum, an Uzbek from Mazar e Sharif, who commanded Uzbek militia and was aligned to Najibullah. Dostum's defection proved critical, as this influenced non-Pushtun (Parchami) commanders, along with their heavy military equipment, to side with Massoud. Dostum moved over two thousand of his militia to Kabul. Meanwhile, Massoud's forces had moved out of Panjshir towards Charikar, a mere forty miles from the capital. Massoud had thus militarily outflanked Gulbadin in the race for Kabul. In Islamabad, Gulbadin's representative rejected Rabbani's proposal and insisted on maintaining the agreement on the list of neutral personalities that was reportedly reached earlier in the morning. Others were prepared to show flexibility in varying degrees, and it became clear that an agreement depended on the Hizb and the Jamiat and that there was no possibility of reaching it that evening.

In a separate room in the prime minister's house, Benon Sevan waited impatiently for a breakthrough. He was constantly in touch with Kabul, where the situation was deteriorating by the hour. By midnight, he met Nawaz Sharif and informed him of his intention to fly to Kabul right away. Nawaz tried to dissuade him, suggesting that he should leave in the morning, but Benon was adamant and revealed that Najibullah had sought refuge in the UN compound in Kabul. He had to keep his word to be helpful and left for Kabul within the hour. The meeting ended inconclusively and a deeply disappointed Javed Nasir wistfully remarked: "The only person who proved worthy of his word this evening was a non-Muslim." The prime minister desired to meet the Tanzeemat leaders the next day and asked Javed Nasir to ensure the presence of Gulbadin, who was reportedly in Parachinar preparing to move inside Afghanistan to his base near Sarobi.

On April 16, 1992, a clearer picture emerged. Najibullah had moved to the UN compound, where he remained for the remaining days of his life.[27] Benon later requested that Pakistan help with his exit. Nawaz agreed on condition that Najibullah would not step out of the plane in Pakistan and his first destination should be any place other than India, where his family had already moved. Kabul was under the effective control of General Dostum, with his cousin General Majid in charge of the airport. Ahmed Shah Massoud had positioned himself in Charikar, within striking distance of Kabul. Abdur Rahim Hatef assumed the position of acting president, declaring that he would step aside in favor of a government agreed to by the Mujahedin leaders.

In Islamabad, in late afternoon, Gulbadin was brought to an ISI safe house by helicopter. There the other Tanzeemat leaders had gathered to meet the prime minister. Before the meeting and before the prime minister's arrival, Javed Nasir along with secretary-general of the Foreign Office, Akram Zaki, and a few other senior Foreign Office and ISI officials met separately with Gulbadin to brief him about the previous evening's meeting and the ground situation. Gulbadin was glum. He showed little interest in the previous evening's proceedings, kept eerily quiet, and spoke only once, with grim foreboding, when informed that Ahmed Shah Massoud had moved to Charikar. "Now there will be bloodshed."

27. *NYT,* April 17, 1992.

During the meeting with the prime minister, Gulbadin remained calm but tense, firmly maintaining the Hizb position on adopting the neutral-panel formula, and once accused Jamiat of perfidy for turning away from an agreed position. Appeals and platitudes once again proved fruitless, and the prime minister left it to the ISI to keep pressure on the Tanzeemat to come up with an agreed formula. Nonetheless, the meeting helped to bury the idea of a neutral panel. The majority of the Tanzeemat leaders, especially the moderate leaders, saw a chance to be represented in a possible dispensation, and they drifted towards the idea of representatives of each of the parties forming the interim arrangement. This raised the issues of the modality of the arrangement and its leader.

The venue of the Tanzeemat then shifted to Peshawar, where the prime minister came, once again to weigh in for an early agreement. Meanwhile, Benon Sevan kept sending urgent messages for a Tanzeemat agreement to avoid bloodshed. Gulbadin moved to his base in Sarobi and positioned his forces on the pass overlooking Kabul, which was now effectively in the hands of generals aligned with Ahmed Shah Massoud.

On April 20, Nawaz Sharif traveled to Peshawar, this time also inviting Qazi Hussain Ahmed, leader of Jamat e Islami, Maulana Sami ul Haq, leader of his faction of Jamiat Ulema e Islam, and Maulana Abdus Sattar Khan Niazi, another political religious luminary. This was an effort by Nawaz to bring in the political religious heavyweights, who he believed could have helped in forging a consensus among the divided Tanzeemat.

A few days prior to this meeting, Akram Zaki had also approached Qazi Hussain Ahmed, who had been making critical statements against the Foreign Office for misunderstanding and mishandling the Tanzeemat leadership. Akram Zaki requested that the Jamat leader help with the Tanzeemat at a crucial juncture. Knowing the complications, Qazi at first demurred but then agreed to speak to Rabbani and to Qutubuddin Hillal, who was representing Gulbadin.

It was arranged for Qazi Hussain Ahmed to meet the two leaders on the afternoon of April 20 in Peshawar, where he was to join the prime minister after the late evening prayers to meet the Tanzeemat leadership. After meeting for several hours with Rabbani and Qutubuddin Hilal, Qazi Hussain Ahmed came to the governor's house for the prime minister's meeting frothing at the mouth, exceedingly upset with the Jamiat and Hizb leaders. When asked about his discussions, he remarked, showing his exasperation, "There was a time when these people had turned up at my doorstep in tatters. Today they refuse to listen to me." Throughout the evening's meeting, which lasted for nearly five hours until well past midnight, Qazi Hussain Ahmed sat stone-faced without making a single intervention.

In most aspects the meeting proved to be a rerun of the earlier inconclusive discussions. Everyone listened with courtesy and silence to the appeal for unity from Maulana Sami ul Haq and Maulana Abdus Sattar Niazi, who cited the holy book and parables from Islamic history. Even the indiscreet remark by Maulana Niazi that an opportunity had arisen to build a "Sunni state" in Afghanistan on the ashes of communism did not cause a stir, except for a gentle whispered reminder from the prime minister that the participants included leaders of the two Afghan Shia parties. The issue of who should lead the interim arrangement, comprising nominees of each of the Tanzeemat, kept surfacing. Late in the night when this issue once again became a subject of contention, Nawaz mentioned the practice in his party of resorting to secret voting. In a show of efficiency, an aide present in the room immediately distributed blank slips of paper to the Tanzeemat leaders, who politely kept these in their pockets and continued expressing their different points of view. Next day, Nawaz felt upset when Qazi Hussain Ahmed, who had kept quiet throughout the meeting, responded to a press question by dismissing the meeting as a vain attempt to decide the destiny of Afghanistan on slips of paper.

The breakthrough came on April 24, when an excited Javed Nasir, singing praises to the glory of the Almighty, conveyed to the prime minister that an accord had been reached and was to be signed in Peshawar that evening. Witnessed by the prime minister and the Iranian foreign minister, who had flown to Peshawar from Tehran for the purpose, the leaders of the eight Afghan parties and the second in command from the Hizb placed their signatures on what came to be known as the Peshawar Accord, forged together under the pressure of circumstances.

The lack of ISI input or interference was evident from the substance of the accord. It defined two phases of two months and six months for an interim government to be headed respectively by Sibghatullah Mojaddedi and Burhanuddin Rabbani. All other cabinet positions were divided among the parties with the understanding that the top leaders would not be eligible for the positions. Thus the prime ministership went to Hizb, but Gulbadin could not designate himself for the post. In the event, he nominated commander Abdus Sabur Fareed, who was unable to move to Kabul. Deputy prime ministerships were given to three parties, those of Yunas Khalis, Sayed Gailani, and one in which the Shia groups joined as the Ittihad e Islami party. Most important, the Ministry of Defense was given to the Jamiat e Islami of Burhanuddin Rabbani, who wasted no time in nominating Ahmed Shah Massoud as its head.

The way was thus cleared for Ahmed Shah Massoud to enter Kabul with reportedly close to ten thousand troops under his command.[28] Massoud's control over the security forces was decisive; within days of Mojaddedi's appointment of former general Muhammad Yahya Nauroze as a nonparty minister for national security (the intelligence apparatus), Nauroze was pushed out unceremoniously, allegedly under pressure from Massoud. Other persons of note felt ineffective and insecure and were obliged to leave Kabul soon after the takeover by the Mujahedin government under Mojaddedi. These included the well-reputed commander Abdul Haq, who was briefly associated with Hizb e Islami of Yunas Khalis, and General Abdul Rahim Wardak, who belonged to the party of Pir Gailani. Ahmed Shah Massoud alone exercised effective control of Kabul, which reflected the reality on the ground and rendered the Peshawar Accord ineffective as an instrument of peace.

The Iranians were suspicious of Pakistani manipulation and initially had reservations because of insufficient Shia representation. But they could also see that Gulbadin, the reputed ISI favorite, was the big loser. The Peshawar Accord had placed political control of Kabul in the hands of Ahmed Shah Massoud, a close ally of Iran. The accord was a political defeat for Gulbadin, who had alienated the other Afghan parties. It was a failure of those ISI elements who preferred Gulbadin but did not provide sound political counsel to their protégé. Apart from the military advantage on the ground, Ahmed Shah Massoud was helped by the polite and deceptively modest temperament of the Jamiat leader, Burhanuddin Rabbani, who succeeded in winning the support of the moderate parties.

The Peshawar Accord was a cleverly crafted document that designated by name only two persons for the symbolic position of president of the interim government, effectively excluding other top leaders by leaving cabinet positions to their nominees. The accord further envisaged the establishment of a body to prepare a constitution, which was eventually set up under Nabi Muhammadi in 1993. The signing of the Peshawar Accord had engendered a certain optimism that the stalemate persisting since the Soviet withdrawal

28. *NYT,* May 1, 1992.

had ended and that Afghanistan might finally be able to turn a new page for the better. But in strife-riven Afghanistan, peace remained elusive.

On 24 April 1992, already anointed by the accord as the defense minister, Ahmed Shah Massoud moved into Kabul. In Peshawar, Mojaddedi made preparations to proceed to Kabul in a big caravan to take over as president, which he did on 28 April 1992. Nawaz Sharif desired to visit Kabul on the day after the arrival of Mojaddedi in the capital to congratulate the new Afghan president. This presented a nightmarish scenario for the Pakistani Foreign Office and intelligence agencies. In Kabul, Pakistani Chargé D'affaires Fida Yunus remained constantly in touch with the local commanders, especially General Majid, who controlled the airport and gave clearance on 29 April around noon. In Peshawar, two C-130s were ready. A large throng of press had already been invited to the Peshawar governor's house, ostensibly for a press conference by the prime minister, and at the last moment were driven to the airport, where the prime minister and his close associates and the army top brass soon joined them for the flight to Kabul.

Kabul airport presented a crowded, chaotic scene, with hundreds of ragtag Kalashnikov-toting Afghan Mujahedin, scores of them armed with shoulder-carried bazookas and rocket launchers. Mojaddedi and Tanzeemat leaders received the Pakistani prime minister and his party and accompanied them to Arg Palace. There everyone was led to a small chamber with two chairs, for Nawaz and Mojaddedi (a third was later added to seat Asif Nawaz, the Pakistani army chief). The room was filled with the Pakistani party and the Afghans, many standing on a couple of tables lying on one side. After the usual felicitations and eloquent encomiums by Mojaddedi for Pakistan and its prime minister, Nawaz presented Mojaddedi a check for US $10 million. This largely symbolic visit to Kabul partly reflected Nawaz's personal desire to savor the drama of the moment. A vivid reminder of the chaos that had now gripped Afghanistan occurred while the Pakistani party waited at the airport for a weather system to pass before taking off. Booms from rockets fired by Gulbadin's forces targeting the nearby hills foreshadowed an ominous future of violence.

The battle for Kabul between Gulbadin and Ahmed Shah Massoud intensified in the ensuing months and turned into a disastrous conflict, with shifting alliances and attempts to bring about cease-fires that always proved short-lived. Other forces jostling for the control of parts of the city included the Hazaras under Abdul Ali Mazari, at times supported by Dostum, leading to tension and intermittent clashes with Ahmed Shah Massoud and transient understanding with his rival Gulbadin. In the couple of years after the takeover by the Mujahedin leadership, much of Kabul, especially the suburbs, was destroyed. Years later, visitors could see the ruins of the Aman Palace just outside the city, the destroyed residential areas, and twisted metal electric poles with scores of bullet marks as reminders of the brutal struggle and villainy of the Afghan leadership who perpetrated destruction on the city with medieval abandon. None of the leaders vying for control of Kabul showed sensitivity to the need for peace and rehabilitation of a devastated country and its suffering population.

Mujahedin Interregnum and the Fragmentation of Afghanistan

After the passage of close to two months following the April ceremonies inaugurating the new government, signs appeared of Mojaddedi's intention to extend his tenure.[29] Barely two weeks before his designated term was to expire, he visited several cities and made speeches claiming that he was the only leader with broad enough support to unite the nation. He needed time, he said, to address the ongoing strife among the Mujahedin, something that could not be accomplished in his two-month tenure. These reports prompted Nawaz Sharif to send a delegation to Kabul in late June 1992, led by Secretary-General Akram Zaki, to dissuade Mojaddedi from acting in violation of the Peshawar Accord. Even though there was nothing in writing, Nawaz was presumed to have assumed the role of a guarantor of the accord. He did not accept the argument that Pakistan should no longer intercede and let the Afghans settle their affairs as they pleased, regardless of the Peshawar Accord.

By the time Akram Zaki left for Kabul, an incident had already disabused Mojaddedi of entertaining any idea of continuing in office. On his return to Kabul from Mazar e Sharif, two missiles attacked his plane as it flew low and prepared to touch down at Kabul airport. One missile struck, knocking off the nose of the plane, but Mojaddedi landed safely. It was the narrowest of escapes, and a deadly disaster was averted literally by a hair's breadth.

29. *NYT,* June 1 and 22, 1992.

When the Pakistani delegation met him in the Arg Palace, he looked scared and isolated. He was visibly bitter and blamed Ahmed Shah Massoud for the attack. He showed no intention of continuing. He had been chosen by the other parties to serve a period of two months as president because he led the weakest of the Afghan parties and could facilitate an early transition. Gulbadin or Ahmed Shah Massoud could not have tolerated a stronger personality. Mojaddedi passed on the presidency, as stipulated by the Peshawar Accord, to Burhanuddin Rabbani.

A significant aspect of the transition from Najibullah to the Mujahedin government had been the dispersal of the former communist regime without a witch hunt or violence targeted against them. With the exception of Najibullah and his brother, who sought refuge in the UN office in Kabul, most of the other regime members became part of the new political landscape. A few of them left the country. There was no mayhem, no retributions. The ease with which one Mujahedin group or another absorbed them showed strong tribal and ethnic linkages that made the ideological partisanship no longer relevant. Many of them were military elite whose alliances were critical in the new power struggle. In fact, those siding with Ahmed Shah Massoud had decided the fate of Kabul in his favor. Most of the remnants of the former regime, especially the non-Pushtuns, aligned themselves with Ahmed Shah Massoud and other groups supported by Iran.

As the relentless strife between the forces of Gulbadin and Ahmed Shah Massoud continued around Kabul, the rest of Afghanistan was divided up among powerful warlords, each with his own militia, generating revenue through taxes and road tolls. Jallaluddin Haqqani controlled Khost, Paktika and Paktia regions; Ismael Khan was entrenched in Herat; Abdur Rashid Dostum in Mazar e Sharif; Karim Khalili, Abdul Ali Mazari, and Sheikh Mohsini in the Hazarajat; and Haji Qadeer, Abdul Haq, and Deen Muhammad had influence in the Jalalabad area. North of Jalalabad was Gulbadin's territory. The only region of significance not under a powerful warlord was Qandahar. Traditionally a Durrani territory, Qandahar did not fall to any influential commander, as most of the notable Durrani families had left Afghanistan following the Saur Revolution in 1978 and the assassination of Sardar Daoud and several members of his family. In and around Qandahar, small-time Mujahedin commanders asserted their control and lived on extortion, especially by exacting tolls on goods passing through their respective areas to and from Pakistan. Much of the commerce through the area consisted of the smuggling of commodities into Pakistan, where high duties made them expensive. Afghanistan was thus effectively fragmented, without a central control or authority.

Pakistan, Iran, and Saudi Arabia made efforts to bring about the cessation of hostilities among the Afghan factions. Nawaz invited Gulbadin and Burhanuddin Rabbani to Islamabad in March 1993, which led to a new accord.[30] This attempt at reconciliation was based on what appeared to have become the key defect in the Peshawar Accord: Gulbadin, an important figure, had been effectively kept out of any office. The new accord rectified the apparent error by designating Gulbadin as prime minister. Rabbani's tenure as president was extended by eighteen months. The Saudi monarch invited all Tanzeemat leaders to gather at Mecca for a solemn oath at the holy sanctuary of the Ka'aba. There, on the holy Quran, they committed themselves to peace, reconciliation, and the welfare of the Afghan nation.

But peace remained elusive. Gulbadin, now prime minister, was unwilling to enter Kabul without his forces or the exit of Panjshiris and other pro–Ahmed Shah Massoud forces. According to the Islamabad Accord, the prime minister and the president were to decide the cabinet in consultation with each other and other Mujahedin leaders. Gulbadin's objection to Ahmed Shah Massoud's keeping the portfolio of defense minister became a point of contention and resulted in an early breakdown of the Islamabad Accord. The fighting continued.[31]

Afghanistan's misfortune thus persisted, as none of the Mujahedin leaders was capable of inspiring confidence among his peers and building viable alliances that could steer the country towards calm and normalcy. Of the two major military leaders, Ahmed Shah Massoud and Gulbadin, the former was better disposed to reaching out to others, yet he remained essentially insular, suspicious, and parochial. Dostum, Ismael Khan, Jallaluddin Haqqani, and other prominent commanders remained on the periphery, preoccupied with their regional holds. High-profile political leaders inclined to build and work within coalitions, in particular Rabbani, Mojaddedi, and Sayed Ahmed Gailani, lacked military muscle or the backing of strong commanders. Afghanistan remained divided, mired in conflict and ungoverned. Conflicting interests of the region's countries and disinterest on the part of the major powers did not help.

30. *NYT,* March 4, 1993.
31. Kamal Matinuddin, *The Taliban Phenomenon: Afghanistan 1994–1997* (Oxford: Oxford University Press, 1999), Appendix III, text of the Islamabad Accord, 246–51.

Islamabad's Concerns as Afghan Factions Fight for Kabul

Towards late 1993, Pakistan experienced yet another political change. Benazir Bhutto became prime minister for the second time, following President Ghulam Ishaq Khan's dismissal of the Nawaz government. Besides her preoccupation with the chronic internal political wrangling, Benazir showed only peripheral interest in the affairs of Afghanistan. In terms of policy, Benazir's attention was focused on Kashmir, where an indigenous agitation had virtually coincided with the beginning of her first term as prime minister. The Kashmiri movement had turned violent in reaction to early mishandling of the situation by the Indian authorities. By the mid-1990s, the violence reached a high point, actively abetted by militant elements from the Pakistani side. Kashmir has been a deeply emotive issue for Pakistan. For Benazir, with a politician's point of view, it carried far greater relevance than the seemingly intractable internecine strife in Afghanistan.

Pakistan's Afghan policy stagnated, with midlevel intelligence officials continuing their liaison with the various warlords and factions. During Benazir's second term there was no significant move by the Pakistani political leadership to push for reconciliation inside Afghanistan or to bring about a cease-fire or an end to hostilities. The ISI, now headed by Lt. Gen. Javed Ashraf Qazi, was focused on Kashmir and resigned to the simmering conflict inside Afghanistan, with little interest in shaping a new Afghan policy or engagement.

One exception was Interior Minister Naseerullah Khan Babar, who paid attention but for a different reason. He was an old Pakistan People's Party hand who had served with Zulfikar Ali Bhutto and been responsible for offering protection to young Afghan dissidents, including Gulbadin and Massoud, in the early 1970s. Babar was possessed by the idea of opening a caravan, or trade, route to the newly independent states of Central Asia. In 1994, he made two trips by road from Quetta in Pakistan to Turkmenistan, Uzbekistan, Kazakhstan, and Kyrgyzstan, entering China through the Turgut Pass and Pakistan through the Khunjerab Pass, to observe the route personally.

There was a sense of disappointment that, because of the conflict in Afghanistan, Pakistan was unable to reap dividends from the transformed regional situation produced by the emergence of the independent Central Asian states, which had generated a great deal of enthusiasm and expectation in the country. Pakistan's policy establishment was unhappy that the turmoil in Afghanistan was blocking the country's access to the Central Asian republics. Pakistan thus had an unquestionable interest in the stability of Afghanistan, reinforced by the burden of over three million Afghan refugees, large numbers of whom mixed with the urban population, giving rise to problems of crime and security. External support for the Afghans and the refugees had dried up, and there was a pervasive feeling that Pakistan had been left alone to deal with the problems of a collapsed state next door. The West, in particular the United States, appeared to have turned its back on Pakistan and abandoned Afghanistan, which had served the interests of the West at a critical juncture in the Cold War. In addition to sanctions under the Pressler Amendment, Pakistan faced pressure on account of the rising militancy in Kashmir. The American and European governments and the Western media had started linking the violence in Kashmir to sponsorship by Pakistan's military, specifically the ISI, and accusing Pakistan of supporting terrorism in Kashmir. In this scenario, Afghanistan took a back seat in Pakistan's foreign policy concerns and focus.

Notwithstanding the conflict and instability, developments in Afghanistan still appeared broadly favorable to Pakistan's interests. There was the consolation that Afghanistan was now governed by elements that, despite their individual grievances, had been beholden to Pakistan and had strong personal connection to the country. Almost every Afghan leader had family members and property in Pakistan. In the absence of a settled government in Kabul, Pakistan began developing direct relations with the powerful warlords that governed Afghanistan's various regions. Where such linkages had not existed previously, the Pakistani ISI developed them. Dostum in Mazar e Sharif and Ismael Khan in Herat visited Pakistan several times and received ISI support.

Ahmed Shah Massoud, however, stood out as an exception. His relations with Pakistan betrayed mutual unease. During the fight against the Soviets, Pakistan had supported him with the direct supply of arms on a few occasions, apart from what he received by virtue of his association with Rabbani's Jamiat, which as a party was among the top recipients of funds and military equipment. Many in the ISI were suspicious about his commitment to fighting the Soviets. Some argued that since his stronghold of Panjshir was located at the mouth of the Salang tunnel, Ahmed Shah Massoud could have choked the Soviets' main supply line. This was not a reasonable expectation. The Mujahedin commanders could only engage in guerrilla tactics, never holding fixed positions that may have been necessary for a prolonged blockade of the Salang tunnel. While mostly holed up in the narrow Panjshir valley, Massoud could not afford to provoke the Soviets to the point of drawing strong retribution. He did put up stiff resistance whenever the Kabul regime's forces tried to overrun the valley.

The ISI's view was apparently colored by the known rivalries between the various Mujahedin groups and leaders, including the antipathy between Massoud and Gulbadin. Since the 1970s, Massoud had visited Pakistan only once—in late 1990, when the ISI tried to mend relations with him and encourage reconciliation between him and Gulbadin. But he and Gulbadin were destined to be on a collision course for control of Kabul.

Pakistani intelligence had anxiety about yet another development in 1991 —the emergence of a non-Pushtun coalition of parties known as Shura e Nazar, which included mainly Panjshiris and Tajik commanders and rallied around Ahmed Shah Massoud. Pakistan saw the coalition as a product of Iranian encouragement and as a potential counter to the Pakistan-supported groups of Gulbadin and Yunas Khalis. Even without outside prompting, Shura e Nazar was part of the early positioning by the various groups, in this case the Tajiks and Panjshiris, for an incipient power struggle as the curtain closed on the Najibullah regime. Later, following Najibullah's ouster, Shura e Nazar became part of the larger non-Pushtun coalition, the Northern Alliance, which included Uzbek and Hazara elements as well. Pakistani intelligence had contacts with some of the individual Northern Alliance leaders but viewed the coalition as an ominous new factor on the Afghan scene that could potentially challenge Pakistani interests. This was an unfortunate prejudice that vitiated Islamabad's future relations with Kabul and contributed to ethnic rivalry in the country.

The Gulbadin-Massoud confrontation presaged the ethnic divide between Pushtuns and non-Pushtuns, even though it remained a bit obscure because of the shifting alliances among Afghan factions during the course of 1992–93. Within days of Najibullah's collapse and Ahmed Shah Massoud's move to position himself closer to Kabul, slogans started appearing in Peshawar—how could Tajiks rule Kabul?—comparing Massoud to Bacha Saqao, a Tajik rebel who briefly usurped the throne in Kabul in 1929. The ethnic fault line and the tension dividing the Pushtuns and the non-Pushtuns had been barely visible during the days of Zahir Shah, They had surfaced, after the Saur Revolution in April 1978, in the infighting between the two Afghan Marxist factions of Khlaq and Parcham, and once again threatened the country with fresh and more fatal tremors.[32] The ethnic tension and antipathy between Pushtuns and non-Pushtuns has a long history. Its roots lie

32. Barnett R. Rubin, "Fragmentation of Afghanistan," *Foreign Affairs,* Winter 1989/ 90; and "A Tribe Apart," *Boston Review,* January/February 2009. In these two articles, published with a gap of nearly two decades, Rubin provides a graphic account of the ethnic divisions.

in the memory of the excesses that Pushtun rulers committed to control their non-Pushtun subjects since the establishment of the Durrani Dynasty.

The promise of the much-romanticized Afghan Jihad died in the internecine strife in Afghanistan that followed the collapse of the Najibullah regime. The abysmal failure of the Mujahedin leaders to bring peace and stability to war-torn Afghanistan and comfort to its suffering population was not just a disappointment to the Afghan people and a tragic loss of opportunity to rebuild Afghanistan. These leaders represented a new face of fundamentalist Islam, which had led a widely acclaimed struggle against the outrageous military intervention in their country by one of the superpowers of the day. The main contenders for power during the Mujahedin interregnum were the product of Islamic revivalist movements of the late 1960s and early 1970s. Their failure to accommodate each other and work together within an agreed political framework revealed fundamentalist and radical Islam's inability to provide functional national governance. Their Islamist background appeared to have hardened rather than softened their individual intransigence and their intolerance of political opponents. In stubbornness, these leaders were exceeded only by their successors, the Taliban, whose austere background and narrow interpretation of Islam made them unable to recognize flexibility and accommodation as part of their religious/political lexicon.

Political analysts often point out that two considerations preoccupied the Pakistani army's strategic thinking regarding its support of various Afghan Mujahedin groups: first, its view of Afghanistan as providing strategic depth to Pakistan; and second, its interest in having a friendly government in Afghanistan. While the concept of a friendly government was flawed, the aspiration of strategic depth in Afghanistan defied reason from the point of view of the traditional interpretation of the concept. "Friendly government" is a highly subjective concept that encourages patronage and interference and spawns suspicion and provocation. Loose talk asserting that Pakistan's sacrifices had earned it the right to have a friendly government in Afghanistan was resented by Afghan intellectuals and elite, who saw it as a Pakistani justification to impose its diktat on Afghanistan.

The idea of Pakistan seeking strategic depth on its western border made little sense by any measure, when its threat perception was almost entirely linked to India. Pakistan's major cities and communication corridors remain close to India, and a friendly Afghanistan could not put distance between these two hostile neighbors. At times, the concept was defended in terms of shifting strategic assets to safety, which at best reflected naïveté. Assets in times of tension or conflict are meant for use, not for safekeeping. Parking assets anywhere also requires sophisticated infrastructure, and Pakistan has locations at greater distances from its eastern border than Kabul. Later a more benign and plausible interpretation was constructed to suggest that the concept only meant that Pakistan should feel secure along its western border[33] in times of tension with India. Even this apology for a fallacious concept does not hold, since Pakistan never faced a conventional military threat from Afghanistan, as had been evident during the 1965 and 1971 conflicts with India. Furthermore, if the purpose is simply a legitimate interest in a friendly border, instead of talking about "seeking strategic depth," Pakistan should refer to its desire to pursue normal friendly relations with Afghanistan.

Stability in Afghanistan and normal relations with Kabul would strengthen security on Pakistan's northwestern borders. Pursuit of dubious and impractical doctrines and ideas would only give rise to misgivings and distrust. The danger arose from an unstable Afghanistan and extremist religious elements that in part were the product of circumstances in Pakistan. Ideas such as strategic depth only reflected confused and warped thinking that sometimes clouded Pakistan's policy and approach to Afghanistan. Nonetheless, the seduction of these fanciful ideas and the dynamics of the Pushtun population of the two countries' bordering regions sucked Pakistan deeper into the Afghanistan quagmire, especially when its intelligence establishment saw an opportunity in the gathering of a new unexpected force, the Taliban, in southwestern Afghanistan.

33. Gen. Ashfaq Parvez Kayani was quoted by the *Daily Times* of Lahore, February 2, 2010, as saying, "If Afghanistan is peaceful, stable and friendly, we have our strategic depth, because our western border is secure. You (the Pakistani army) are not looking both ways."

2

The Advent of the Taliban (1995–2001)

Political observers have often suggested that the Taliban in Afghanistan are a creation of Pakistan's ISI. This credits the agency for an accomplishment beyond its prowess or imagination. The Taliban were a phenomenon waiting to happen in a situation devastated by ten years of Soviet intervention and five years of internecine conflict. The Taliban (plural of Talib, a student, a seeker of knowledge) were the product of madrassas that had mushroomed in the tribal areas and refugee camps in Pakistan and Afghanistan, especially after the exit of Soviet troops. The Afghan Jihad had provided the environment for the growth of madrassas in Pakistan's tribal areas adjoining Afghanistan. In Pakistan especially, Afghan youth among the three million–plus refugees grew up receiving madrassa education supported by Muslim charities worldwide. Most of the funds came from the Gulf countries and from collections by religious political parties in Pakistan. Education of thousands of Afghan refugee children was completely left to these private seminaries. Neither the United Nations nor the Pakistan government did anything to establish proper schools in the refugee camps. The Islamist organizations, especially those with Wahabi and Deobandi leanings supported by Saudi charities, filled the need to educate Afghan children, while the official-level assistance effort remained focused on feeding the Afghans and arming them to fight the Soviets.

During the 1980s, in the environment created by the Afghan Jihad and President Zia ul Haq's policy of Islamization, thousands of new madrassas were added to the large numbers already operating in the country. They welcomed Afghan students. Since most Afghans identified with Sunni Islam, they gravitated to the Deobandi and Wahabi (Saudi Salafi) madrassas that actively advocated jihad and received the bulk of the charity. Three principal centers attracted the largest number of Afghan students and later served as a source of inspiration for the Taliban—Darul Uloom Haqqania in Akora Khattak, managed by Maulana Sami ul Haq; Darul Uloom in Dera Ismail Khan, managed by Maulana Fazal ur Rahman; and Jamiatul Uloom e Islamiyah attached to Binori Mosque in Karachi, managed by Mufti Nizamuddin Shamzai. With the exception of Mufti Shamzai, a well-respected cleric, the other two personalities headed separate factions of the religious political party Jamiat Ulema e Islam. Following the Soviet withdrawal, madrassas proliferated adding to the existing numbers inside Afghanistan, particularly in the Pushtun belt and the countryside. Thus a generation of Afghan youth who had grown up under the most austere circumstances received their education in madrassas based on a narrow, rigid, orthodox interpretation of Islam.

A large number of Afghan madrassa students had shifted to Afghanistan and participated in fighting the Soviets alongside the Mujahedin commanders. They were as disappointed and angry as the rest of the Afghan population with the infighting among the major Mujahedin leaders, who had failed miserably to bring peace and economic health to Afghanistan. The excesses and corruption among small bands of Mujahedin led by unruly commanders roaming the country aggravated these feelings of anger and disappointment.

By the mid-1990s, discontent was on the rise throughout the country, but Qandahar and Helmand regions were suffering the most, as these areas were not under the control of a major warlord who could maintain any semblance of order. Over a dozen low-ranking local commanders affiliated with various parties operated in the region. Despite encouragement from the ISI, they never moved against Qandahar, which remained in the hands of a small contingent loyal to Najibullah following the Soviet withdrawal. The same motley bands continued to jostle for territorial control after the fall of Najibullah. From Chaman on the Pakistani side of the border to Qandahar, a distance of barely 120 kilometers, local commanders erected more than twenty toll-collection barriers[1] to extort money to allow passage of trading goods.

---

1. As mentioned by Aziz Ahmed Khan, Pakistan's ambassador in Kabul during the Taliban period.

Emergence of the Taliban in Qandahar

It was no coincidence that Qandahar and Helmand became the venue for the growth of the Taliban movement. Versions vary. According to a widespread story that some dismiss as a deliberately promoted myth, in August 1994, a local commander picked up some members of a Herati family from the Helmand area on their way to Qandahar, molested and killed them, and burned their bodies. The ensuing outrage led a local notable, Mullah Muhammad Ghaus, who had been a fighter with the Yunas Khalis group during the Afghan Jihad of the 1980s, to rally men and madrassa students, some with experience as Mujahedin fighters. They took action against the culprit and hung him from the barrel of a tank and disarmed his men.[2] This was a newfound power.

Soon many from the ranks of the Mujahedin fighters and students (Taliban) from madrassas in and around Qandahar gathered to rein in the corrupt and rapacious commanders and bring peace to the city. The local population supported the Taliban action and welcomed the new rulers, who appeared to bring safety and order to the city. Even if the reported incidents had been a fabrication, it was the tyranny of the warring factions and notorious commanders like Nadir Jan, Saleh, and Daro Khan in the Qandahar area that had sparked the Taliban action. With their altruistic zeal and ready recruits from madrassas in the region, the Taliban ranks swelled and over one thousand joined their colleagues in Qandahar.[3] As their influence started spreading, they were soon to emerge as a new force in the southern provinces.

Meanwhile, another incident linked the phenomenon to Pakistani intelligence. Around October 1994, Naseerullah Khan Babar, the interior minister under Prime Minister Benazir Bhutto, had planned to send a caravan of goods to Central Asia in forty trucks belonging to National Logistics Cell (NLC), a transport company run by the military as part of its enterprises.

2. For other versions, see Ahmed Rashid, *Taliban: Militant Islam, Oil and Fundamentalism in Central Asia* (London: I. B. Tauris (2000), 25; Matiuddin, *The Taliban Phenomenon,* 23–26; and S. Iftikhar Murshed, *Afghanistan: The Taliban Years* (London: Bennet and Bloom, 2006), 43.

3. S. Fida Yunus, *Afghanistan: Political Parties, Groups, Movements and Mujahedeen Alliances and Governments 1879–1997,* Vol II (collected documents compiled in collaboration with Area Study Center, Central Asia), Peshawar, Pakistan: Peshawar University (1997) 868–69.

Arrangements for their passage through the territories of the major warlords were made, and in Qandahar, the first destination across the border, understandings were reached with various commanders who operated in the area. In the event, however, the caravan was hijacked near Qandahar. The Pakistani security agencies, in particular the ISI, were desperately trying to salvage whatever remained of the trucks, as the goods, mostly food items and textiles, had already been confiscated by errant commanders.

This episode coincided with the emergence of the Taliban in the area. The ISI approached the new group to rescue the NLC trucks. The Taliban, who had by November assumed control of Qandahar and its surroundings, obliged and earned the gratitude and recognition of the powerful Pakistani intelligence agency. Since the Taliban were soon on the march in Afghanistan, the ISI also began supporting the new ascendant force. When asked at a press conference if the Taliban had been created by Pakistan, Naseerullah Babar reportedly nodded with a certain satisfaction. According to another version, he even suggested that the Taliban were "our boys," which became the basis for the speculation that the Taliban were Pakistan's creation.[4]

In the beginning there was considerable suspicion against the Taliban in Pakistan, especially among the religious-political elements who sided with Bulbadin Hekmatyar or other Mujahedin parties. Outlandish speculation included the conjecture by the Jamat e Islami–backed *Weekly Takbeer* that the British and the CIA had conjured up the Taliban after their failure to prop up pro–King Zahir Shah elements in Qandahar.[5] Some Afghans suggested that the UN secretary-general's special representative, Mehmoud Mestiri, had come up with the idea of a third force to balance and bring together the warlords. However, it was widely believed that ISI support accounted for the Taliban's rise, in particular its help in the Taliban's defeat of a local commander, Mansur, who had been instrumental in the plunder of the NLC caravan, and in the Taliban's subsequent capture of an ammunition depot near Spin Buldak controlled by Gulbadin's men. But much of the equipment the Taliban later possessed, including tanks and warplanes, fell into their hands as a result of their expanding control and the swelling of their ranks by local Mujahedin groups. This phenomenon was not unique. It is consistent

---

4. Musharraf, *In the Line of Fire,* 211, argues that the Taliban had emerged independently of Pakistan; he also suggested that the United States had welcomed the Taliban as the "third force," hoping for a return of normalcy in Afghanistan.

5. Rafiq Afghan, *Weekly Takbeer,* March 2, 1995, Lahore, 17–20.

with the traditions of changing alliances typical of domestic Afghan warfare, such as occurred when the Najibullah regime collapsed and his military commanders joined the ranks of rival Mujahedin groups.

There is no clear account of how early associates came to choose Mullah Muhammad Omar as their leader. A tall ascetic individual belonging to the influential Hotak subtribe of Ghilzai Pushtuns, Mullah Omar was a veteran of the Jihad with his own madrassa in Maiwand, Qandahar. He and his associates were all part of the madrassa network and had forged connections when they were Mujahedin fighters, mostly under the Yunas Khalis group. According to Mullah Wakil Ahmed Mutawakil, who later served as Taliban Foreign Minister, Mullah Omar was proposed because of his piety and his services to the Afghan Jihad, during which he had lost an eye and suffered a leg injury. Another factor may have been that, among his peers, Mullah Omar belonged to the largest subtribe.

He demonstrated an uncanny instinct for leadership when he convened an assembly of more than one thousand Ulema and notables in Qandahar in March 1996, primarily to gain legitimacy and backing for the Taliban and to have a discourse on the objectives and character of their rule. He proclaimed the gathering the shura of "Ahl al Hal wa Aqd." One day during the course of the assembly, the sacred *Kharqa* (cloak), reputedly belonging to the Holy Prophet, was brought out for display from a shrine located near the tomb of Ahmed Shah Durrani. During this rare event, in a dramatic gesture, Mullah Omar wrapped himself in the cloak, which won him instantaneous endorsement as Amir ul Momineen (leader of the faithful).[6] Mojaddedi and other Mujahedin leaders criticized the act, but with this medieval flourish, Mullah Omar established himself as the undisputed leader of the Taliban. Thus began a rule in Afghanistan that, in every facet, was an anachronism for a nation state on the eve of the twentieth-first century.

Expansion of the Taliban Control

By early 1996, the Taliban leadership had seen considerable fluctuation in their fortunes. Soon after their emergence in Qandahar in October 1994, the Taliban scored a series of remarkable successes and swept through Uruz-

---

6. Rashid, *Taliban,* 42. According to Ambassador Aziz Ahmed Khan, the proposal for declaring Mullah Omar "Amir ul Momineen" was mooted in a meeting during the Ulema gathering by Mullah Ehsanullah, who later served as the Taliban finance minister.

gan, Zabul, Paktia, and Paktika, where they met little resistance. Mullah Jallaluddin Haqqani, the strongman of Paktia and a well-respected Mujahedin commander, joined them. Indeed, many of the Taliban leaders had been part of his or Yunas Khalis' forces fighting the Soviets. Burhanuddin Rabbani, the nominal president of the Kabul government, had also reached out to the Taliban leadership in a bid to enlist their cooperation against Gulbadin Hekmatyar. By early 1995, the Taliban had captured Wardak and by mid-February, Charasyab, the headquarters of Gulbadin, who retreated to Sarobi.

The Taliban had received support from Pakistan as well as from traders and transporters who found relief as the Taliban cleared roads of barriers and extortionist practices. Thousands of Afghan madrassa students from within the Pashtun regions of Afghanistan and Pakistan filled the Taliban ranks. The Taliban commanders were proving to be skillful fighters, drawing upon their experience of warfare as part of the Mujahedin groups during the Jihad of the 1980s. But this alone could not explain the scale of the Taliban successes. These were largely attributable to the frustration and disappointment of the Afghan populace, who had grown tired of the excesses and anarchy perpetrated by the unruly Mujahedin commanders, while the Taliban appeared to offer hope and security.

The Taliban were soon knocking at the gates of Kabul, where their seemingly unstoppable roll came to a temporary halt. Kabul had been under the tenuous control of Ahmed Shah Massoud and was the scene of a vicious strife engaging forces of Gulbadin, Dostum, Hazaras under Mazari and Ahmed Shah Massoud. Parts of the city were in the hands of Hazaras' and Gulbadin's forces when the Taliban ousted Gulbadin. Faced with a new threat, Ahmed Shah Massoud first tried to evict Hazaras from the city, forcing Mazari to reach out to the Taliban. In the confusion, Mazari fell into the hands of the Taliban and was killed while in their custody. The Hazaras and, more important, Iran blamed the Taliban for Mazari's death and never forgave them.[7]

Ahmed Shah Massoud then turned on the Taliban and inflicted heavy damage, obliging them to retreat from the vicinity of the capital. In the following months the fighting shifted to the west. Massoud wanted Ismael Khan, the warlord controlling Herat and longtime ally of Burhanuddin Rabbani, to engage the Taliban in order to relieve pressure on Kabul. By late February 1995, after having moved into Helmand, Nimroze, and Farah, the Taliban were close to Shindand, the important airbase developed by the So-

---

7. Ibid., 35.

viets. With reinforcements from Kabul, Ismael Khan pushed the Taliban out and regained control of Farah and Nimroze. The Taliban withdrew, facing a setback and the loss of four of the twelve provinces they had controlled at the beginning of February. However, they began regrouping, a capacity they were to demonstrate again in the future.

Meanwhile, suspecting that the Taliban had been mortally weakened after their successive defeats on both the eastern and western fronts, Ismael Khan made a tactical error. In August 1995, he ventured beyond his territory into Helmand toward the Taliban stronghold in Qandahar. His forces were routed near Girishk in Helmand. The Taliban kept up the pursuit and within one week captured Shindand.[8] In panic, on September 5, Ismael Khan abandoned Herat and fled to Iran. The fall of Herat shocked Massoud and Rabbani, who suspected a Pakistani hand in the rejuvenation of the Taliban and their military victory against Ismael Khan. The next day, in obvious anger and retaliation, the Kabul government connived at, if not instigated, the ransacking of the Pakistani embassy by a mob in which the Pakistani ambassador, Qazi Humayun, barely escaped with his life. One staff member was killed and many, including the ambassador, were injured, while the grand colonial structure, with elegant wood paneling, which had once served as the embassy of the British Empire in the city, was reduced to ashes and rubble. The incident irreparably damaged relations between Pakistan and Ahmed Shah Massoud.

By spring 1996, Mullah Omar had consolidated his grip on the Taliban leadership, having gained the endorsement of a shura largely attended by Ulema. The Taliban now controlled the entire southwest of Afghanistan including Herat. They once again turned their attention to the east and advanced closer to Kabul. The increasing Taliban pressure with rocket attacks on Kabul brought together for the first time the two sworn adversaries of the Afghan conflict, Ahmed Shah Massoud and Gulbadin Hekmatyar. Burhanuddin Rabbani signed a peace accord that enabled Gulbadin for the first time to enter the city[9] as its nominal prime minister, the post to which he had been appointed three years earlier under the Islamabad Accord. Gulbadin also sent his troops to defend the city. President Rabbani then reached out to Dostum, Hizb e Wahdat, and the Jalalabad shura built around Haji Qadeer and his brothers. He tried to reach out to erstwhile adversaries to forge a grand alliance, but the effort was obviously prompted by the threat

8. Ibid., 39–40.
9. *NYT*, June 27, 1996.

of the Taliban. Rabbani also sought support in Iran and the Central Asian Republics.

Pakistan, stung by the attack on its embassy, now backed the Taliban as the new promising force on the Afghan scene that controlled more territory than any other Afghan faction. The ISI tried to encourage a Taliban alliance with Dostum's Junbish e Milli and the Jalalabad shura, but the Taliban showed disinterest, as they had other military designs for expanding their control.[10] At the behest of the ISI, Taliban commander Mullah Rabbani did meet Dostum in a bid to isolate Massoud; Dostum, however, reckoned the Taliban a greater threat and instead joined an alliance worked out by Burhanuddin Rabbani that brought together Massoud, Dostum, and Hazara leader Karim Khalili to form the Shura e Aali e Difa e Afghanistan (the Supreme Council for the Defense of Afghanistan), commonly known as the Northern Alliance. This proved to be a more stable arrangement than the numerous other alliances and understandings that a plethora of factions had reached, which kept breaking up in the fluid Afghan political landscape. The Northern Alliance also represented the non-Pushtun side of the ethnic divide that has been one of the dominant features in the Afghan conflict.

In mid-1996, Taliban forces intensified military pressure against Kabul, which came under incessant Taliban rocket attacks. Then, in a surprise move and with large reinforcements of madrassa youth, including some from across the border in Pakistan, the Taliban commanders Mullah Rabbani and Mullah Borjan turned away from Kabul and advanced on Jalalabad, which fell to them on August 25. Within a couple of weeks, the Taliban forces swept through the eastern provinces of Nangarhar, Laghman, and Kunar and launched an offensive against Sarobi, forcing Gulbadin to leave his stronghold and flee to Pakistan. Later in 1997, the Taliban complained that he was organizing attacks in the Kunar area. When the Pakistanis tried to restrain him, Gulbadin sought protection in Iran. With the capture of Sarobi, the Taliban forces converged on Kabul from three sides with lightning speed. The Taliban commanders had demonstrated unusual mobility and tactical acumen. A dispirited Ahmed Shah Massoud saw the futility of defending Kabul. He vacated the city on September 26 and withdrew to his base in Panjshir. In the flush of victory, the Taliban continued their advance in pursuit of Ahmed Shah Massoud, but soon lost steam and stalled close to Salang.[11]

10. Rashid, *Taliban,* 44.
11. *NYT,* October 16, 1996.

The Taliban now controlled the capital and nearly 70 percent of Afghanistan. They set up a new government in Kabul, led by Mullah Rabbani as president and as head of a six-member interim shura, which also included Haji Muhammad Hassan Rehmani, governor of Qandahar, Mullah Abdul Razzaq, Mullah Fazil Muhammad, Maulvi Ghyasuddin, an Uzbek from Faryab, and Mullah Muhammad Ghaus, in charge of foreign affairs. The shura enforced a harsh version of Sharia law that was already enforced in the Taliban-controlled territories and sought international recognition, which would continue to elude the Taliban.

With the passage of time and especially after the convening of the Ulema shura and subsequent capture of Kabul, the Taliban completely shed the early pretensions that they had entered the scene only to bring order and peace and were disinterested in governance. Their declared objectives now included the establishment of a "pure Islamic state," implementation of the Sharia laws, establishment of a religious Amr bil Maroof wa Nahi al Munkir (promote virtue, forbid vice) police (vigilantes), appointment of pious Muslim people to government jobs, enforcement of the hijab (veil) for women making them cover themselves from head to foot, changing the school system to ensure that students not come under alien cultural influences and that they be imbued with teachings of the Quran and Sunnah and become Mujahid in the path of Allah.[12] On the surface, they claimed to eradicate linguistic, racial, and regional discriminations, and although the Taliban cab-

---

12. Detailed aims and objectives proclaimed by the Taliban are enumerated in the documents collected by Fida Yunus and published in *Afghanistan: Political Parties, Groups, Movements and Mujahidin Alliances and Governments (1879–1997)*, Vol II, 872–74. These aims and objectives included, inter alia: establishing a "pure Islamic state"; implementing Shariat; appointing pious Muslim people to government jobs; eradicating linguistic, racial, and regional discrimination and preparing the ground for Islamic brotherhood; ensuring the protection and security of non-Muslim people in Afghanistan; ensuring Hijab dress style; establishing a religious police; establishing an Islamic army for defense; preparing programs for schools so that students do not come under alien cultural influence and are imbued with love for the Quran and Sunnah and become Mujahid in the path of Allah; dealing with international problems in the light of the Quran and Sunnah; transforming the state economy with the assistance of other Islamic countries; and collecting Islamic revenues such as Zakat and Jazya. In an interview in the Jeddah daily *Al-Hayat,* published on December 4, 1995, two members of the High Council of the Taliban stated that once in Kabul, the Taliban would form a council of religious scholars to choose a Khalifa and that there would be no elections in Afghanistan, because elections were an un-Islamic practice. The above tabulation reflected the mind-set of Ulema schooled in orthodox Islamic institutions and, broadly speaking, their prescription for Islamic governance.

inet in Kabul and their provincial governors included other ethnic groups, they remained largely a Pushtun dispensation always reluctant to accommodate or build alliances with other ethnic groups. However, what caused them to be ostracized internationally was their treatment of women. The closure of all girls' schools and banning women from work as well as the ouster of international NGOs from Kabul earned them bitter hostility from human rights activists and organizations worldwide.[13]

The capture of Kabul exposed the Taliban to interaction with the outside world, especially the United Nations, and dealings with the country's other ethnic groups and political forces. In both arenas, the Taliban were found wanting and stubborn. They showed no skill in winning political allies, nor could they reform or display flexibility to build international support. Isolated, they obsessively pursued the expansion of their control, which they were convinced owed to a providential design. The Taliban did not pause to consolidate their position or improve conditions in the large parts of Afghanistan that fell under their control or reach accommodation with their rivals. They were constantly on the move to expand their hold, and the conflict never ceased. They dogmatically believed in a military approach. The Taliban leadership continued to describe it as jihad, perhaps the only vocation they had ever known.

As in Kabul, the Taliban victories in the north came slowly and at great cost in human life, suffering, and bloodshed. In the confusion of alternating successes and setbacks, shifting loyalties and massacres, the mainstay of the Taliban strength remained the fresh recruits from the madrassas of Afghanistan's southern and eastern Pushtun belt and Pakistan's madrassas. They enjoyed the backing of Pakistan and Saudi Arabia. For Pakistan, the Taliban appeared to offer the best hope for Afghan stabilization and they drew strength from the ethnic Pushtuns who straddle the Pakistan-Afghanistan border. Saudi Arabia had its own reasons to support the conservative brand of Islam practiced by the Taliban. The speculation that the Taliban military successes were indebted to ISI guidance is, however, incompatible with the character of the Taliban. Like their predecessors, the

---

13. Ahmed Rashid in *Taliban,* 105–16, analyzed the Taliban's misogynist mind-set and behavior. In April 1999, the author visited Kabul, where Pakistani ambassador Aziz Ahmed Khan organized a lunch to which he invited Mullah Hassan Akhundzade, the Taliban Foreign Minister. Akhundzade refused to listen to a suggestion by the author that the Taliban government appeal to expatriate Afghans living in the Gulf region to create a fund to help widows. The Taliban indifference to the plight of women was disturbing.

Afghan Mujahedin leaders, the Taliban were independent minded and not amenable to direction and control by outsiders. The Taliban operations, with their drama and fluidity, reflected a peculiar Afghan genius and were reminiscent of warfare often enacted in the vast stretches of Afghanistan and Central Asia before these regions experienced the pressures of the expanding Tsarist and British empires.

Meanwhile, the United Nations, in consultation with Pakistan and Iran, launched successive efforts, with limited success, to bring about cease-fires between the Taliban and various contending forces, to negotiate exchange of prisoners, and to address humanitarian crises. The United Nations was only peripherally engaged, with no means of influencing the course of the fighting. On the other hand, Iran and Pakistan, who distrusted each other,[14] supported contending parties. Russia and the Central Asians were wary of the Taliban and sympathized with the non-Pushtun ethnic groups of northern Afghanistan. Ahmed Shah Massoud appealed for U.S. intercession and "backing for moderate Muslims to avert a new era of fundamentalism" in Afghanistan.[15] The United States, however, while supportive of the UN efforts, remained largely disengaged from the country, which appeared to remain mired in an endemic strife.

Conflict Shifts to the North

Beyond Herat, Dostum had effectively kept the Taliban advance in check. Mazar e Sharif, Dostum's headquarters and the largest city in northern Afghanistan, had all along been relatively peaceful and undisturbed by the Soviet intervention and the subsequent civil war. But this was soon to change because of dissension, intrigue, and shifting loyalties within the ranks of Dostum's army.

The troubles in the north started with a rebellion against Dostum by his second in command, General Malik Pahlawan, who suspected that Dostum had had his brother assassinated in June 1996 and ordered the same fate for Malik. The Pakistani officials from the consulate they maintained in Mazar

---

14. Murshed, *Afghanistan: the Taliban Years,* 196, lists Iranian grievances against Pakistan and their view of the Taliban. The Iranians regarded the Taliban as a brainchild of the Americans, financed by the Saudis and trained by the Pakistanis.

15. *NYT,* March 7, 1995.

e Sharif knew that Malik was nursing this bitterness.[16] But there is little evidence of Pakistani complicity in brokering any understanding between the Taliban and Malik for Dostum's ouster, notwithstanding Pakistani unhappiness at their own failure to bring about a deal between Dostum and the Taliban and Dostum's choosing to join the Northern Alliance. The Taliban promised Malik a share of power, and he conspired with other Uzbek generals, who had their own grievances against Dostum's well-known ruthless and high-handed behavior. On May 21, 1997, from his base in Faryab, Malik revolted against Dostum and soon captured Badghis and Sare Pul. In a coordinated action, the Taliban forces converged on Jowsjan, Dostum's home province. Dostum was forced to escape into Uzbekistan and then sought refuge in Turkey. On May 24, Malik and Taliban forces moved into Mazar e Sharif.[17]

Pakistan had long resisted the Taliban pressure for diplomatic recognition, but in these new circumstances, with Mazar falling under Taliban control, Pakistan changed its position.[18] Pakistan could be faulted for condoning the Taliban's narrow and oppressive creed and practices, but not for extending recognition to a political force that now controlled the capital and most of the country. Saudi Arabia and the UAE followed suit, but others opted for a wait-and-see policy. Soon, the Taliban were to court a disaster in Mazar e Sharif.

Once in Mazar e Sharif, the Taliban commanders, in particular Mullah Razzaq, were dismissive of Malik, who had expected to enjoy autonomy to rule in Mazar, as an ally of the Taliban, more or less as Dostum had done as part of the Northern Alliance. The Taliban, on the other hand, offered Malik only a post as deputy foreign minister, which infuriated him. The Taliban also began behaving as they did elsewhere, trying to disarm the local population, imposing restrictions, and thus heightening tension in a city already waiting to explode. The Taliban ignored Pakistani officials in Mazar when, at the behest of Malik, they tried to remind Mullah Razzaq to honor the Taliban agreement with Malik.[19] In their hubris, the Taliban commanders did not realize that they were no longer operating in the Pushtun areas but in an ethnically alien territory, where their ostensible ally did not fully

16. Murshed, *Afghanistan: The Taliban Years,* 75–77.
17. *NYT,* May 25, 1997.
18. For details, see Murshed, *Afghanistan: The Taliban Years,* 82–83.
19. Ibid., 89–92. Also see Matinuddin, *The Taliban Phenomenon,* 100.

exercise control over armed groups. Uzbek loyalties were divided, and Hazaras listened to Hizb e Wahdat. The local population was also seething against Pakistan, seeing it as complicit in inflicting the Taliban upon them.

Taliban attempts to disarm the local population led to an inevitable scuffle between the Hazara and Taliban soldiers, which ignited the fuse for a massacre of the Taliban, who, being unfamiliar with the city, found themselves trapped. Thousands were killed including Mullah Borjan, who had launched the successful offensive against Jalalabad. Mullah Ghaus, Mullah Razzaq, and Mullah Ehsanullah were captured along with several thousand Taliban.[20] Taliban fleeing from the northern provinces mostly perished.[21]

Suddenly the fortunes were reversed. Malik still could not fully assert his control in Mazar because of the Hazara presence. He joined a new alliance with Massoud and Hizb e Wahdat, but mutual distrust prevented any significant cooperation between them.[22] Dostum returned to Mazar in September when fighting between his supporters and Malik's forced Malik to withdraw to his base in Faryab. Before long, Dostum moved to Shibergan, as the tension between the Hazara and Uzbek troops escalated in Mazar e Sharif. Hazaras took credit for ousting the Taliban from the city. Within one year of the Taliban defeat and retreat from the north, Taliban forces regained enough strength to go on the offensive again, blockading the Hazarajat partly to avenge the Hazara excesses in Mazar. Twice, the Pakistan government, along with the United Nations, interceded to airlift food supplies and provide relief to the population facing acute shortages in the region.[23]

The Taliban retribution against Mazar e Sharif came in August 1998 when they had reinforced their ranks and gathered resources. They first advanced to Jowsjan, effecting desertions by Dostum's commanders and forcing Dostum to once again seek exile in Turkey. The Taliban moved with speed, capturing Maimana and Shibergan. On August 8 they reached Mazar, taking the Hazara defenders by surprise. What followed was another wave of massacre, this time targeted at the city's Hazaras.[24] Repeating an earlier

---

20. Rashid, *Taliban,* 58–59, put the figure of captured Taliban at 3600 including prisoners held by the Hazara Hizb e Wahdat and Ahmed Shah Massoud.

21. According to a UN report published one year later, as many as 2000 Taliban fighters were killed and buried in mass graves after being taken as prisoners. *NYT,* November 18, 1997.

22. Rashid, *Taliban,* 61.

23. *NYT,* November 28, 1997, and May 4, 1998.

24. Rashid, *Taliban,* 72–73, estimates that between 5000 and 6000 people were killed.

pattern of swift military maneuvers, after taking over Mazar the Taliban turned to the Hazarajat and captured Bamiyan in September 1998. This time the Taliban leadership issued instructions to prevent the excesses against the local population and thus tempered Taliban violence, avoiding repetition of the Mazar massacres.

As the Taliban attack against Mazar proceeded, eleven Iranian "diplomats" who were mostly intelligence personnel stationed in the Iranian Consulate were murdered, reportedly at the hands of elements of a Pakistani militant group, the virulently anti-Shia Sipah e Sahaba. The incident drew a sharp reaction from Iran against both the Taliban and Pakistan. The Taliban had also captured more than forty Iranian truck drivers who used to carry Iranian military supplies to the Hizb e Wahdat (Hazara) forces. The truck drivers and the bodies of the slain Iranians were handed over to Iran through Pakistani and UN intercession. The episode brought to full view Pakistani extremist groups' involvement and support of the Taliban. The Talibanized Afghanistan had become an incubator for the growth and training of Pakistani extremist and militant groups, who, in time, would threaten to destabilize Pakistan and the region.

The strife in the north had also sharpened international divisions over Afghanistan. Iran, Russia, and the Central Asian Republics, disturbed by the Taliban successes, sided with elements of the Northern Alliance, while Pakistan and Saudi Arabia had cast their lot with the Taliban leadership. This was an intractable situation. In Pakistani thinking, which was itself a casualty of political vicissitude and drift, once the Taliban were helped to gain control of the entire country, the world would acquiesce in the reality on the ground and accept them. The Pakistanis saw them as a friendly dispensation in neighboring Afghanistan. The Pakistani military and intelligence had developed a deep antipathy towards the Northern Alliance, in particular Ahmed Shah Massoud. They accused him of double-dealing during the days of the Afghan Jihad against the Soviets and later playing the game of Iran and India in Afghanistan at the expense of Pakistan's interests. Former president Pervez Musharraf reflected this thinking in his memoir, citing among the reasons for Pakistan's support for the Taliban that the Taliban's success would spell the defeat of the "anti-Pakistan Northern Alliance."[25] Quite often these views were formed on the basis of reports from midlevel operatives in the field who empathized with the Taliban. Their reports put a simplistic Manichean construct on a complex situation; but, trag-

25. Musharraf, *In the Line of Fire,* 209, 211.

ically, these inputs colored perceptions at the senior-most levels of decision making in Pakistan.

Meanwhile, the recapture of Mazar and massacres in the north delivered a fatal blow to the weak, but at one point promising, diplomatic initiatives aimed at bringing about peace, in particular those involving the United Nations. Ever since they gained control of Kabul, the Taliban had become increasingly desperate for international recognition. For this reason, their leadership in Kabul had remained engaged with the United Nations, though Mullah Omar had remained aloof. The massacre at Mazar, however, extinguished prospects for such recognition.

UN Engagement with the Taliban

After the advent of the Taliban, the UN secretary-general appointed three successive special representatives for Afghanistan: Mehmoud Mestiri from January 1995 to June 1996, Norbert Holl from July 1996 to November 1997, and James N'gobi from December 1997 to December 1998, all serving as head of the UN Special Mission in Afghanistan (UNSMA). Lakhdar Brahimi, appointed by Secretary-General Kofi Annan, served as special envoy from September 1997 to December 2004. Brahimi, who had based himself in New York, was the only UN official who had ever met Mullah Omar. The UN's Sisyphean efforts mostly revolved around encouraging ceasefires, preventing attacks against cities, forming commissions for reconciliation, and the more ambitious goals of promoting a broad-based government and prohibiting the supply of arms to the warring factions.

The same themes ran across bilateral efforts by Pakistan or in combination with Iran and at times with Saudi Arabia. The results were invariably disappointing. No Afghan party would ever show willingness to let go of the slightest military advantage that it appeared to enjoy at a given point of time. For example, suggestions for a broad-based government or a government of neutral personalities in Kabul could never find favor with the faction in control of Kabul. The same applied to suggestions for deweaponization or demilitarization of Kabul that were, off and on, floated to initiate a peace process and create an environment conducive for a reconciliation process.

The issue of legitimacy always posed a stumbling block. As long as Burhanuddin Rabbani was treated as the president or his representative occupied the UN seat for Afghanistan, he could only agree to add to the existing government but not to replace it with any agreed broad-based arrangement. The issue constricted the UN's ability to play a mediator's role or to institute intra-Afghan dialogue, even before the Taliban had captured Kabul. The Rabbani government insisted on being treated as the sole legitimate government, whereas others saw it as a representative of one faction with limited control in Afghanistan. The dilemma was reminiscent of the situation in the 1980s when the UN failed to initiate a dialogue between the Kabul regime and the Mujahedin Tanzeemat. Once in Kabul, the Taliban expected nothing short of recognition in exchange for co-opting a few members of the opposition. In fact, the Taliban in their rhetoric went a step beyond; they often mixed the idea of broadening the base of the government with accommodating "good Muslims" from other ethnic groups. They claimed that the Taliban had no ethnic prejudices and had included members of other ethnic groups in the Council of Ministers and as governors of provinces. In most instances, Afghan factions indulged in posturing rather than searching for a serious basis for reconciliation and mutual understanding. Instead of concerns for peace and economic rehabilitation, it was primarily individual interests and military successes or setbacks that determined the positions of the Afghan protagonists.

In dealing with the Taliban, particularly after they gained control of Kabul and most of the Afghanistan territory, the United Nations and UNSMA were handicapped by nonrecognition of the Taliban. In the autumn of 1997, after the fall of Mazar e Sharif and Pakistani recognition, the Taliban sent a delegation to New York headed by Mullah Abdul Hakim Mujahid. But their delegation failed to elicit support in the world body, where most membership saw the Taliban as a repressive regime with little regard for human rights. The views of the educated Afghan diaspora strengthened this impression. With their narrow and insular mind-set, the Taliban had never tried to reach out to the prominent Afghans living outside the country to elicit their support. Moreover, the Taliban had lost control of Mazar after holding the city for less than one week, thus weakening their claim that they controlled most of Afghanistan.

The Rabbani representative continued to occupy the Afghan seat at the United Nations. There had been UN precedents for such anomalies, as when the representative of the exiled Sihanouk regime remained in the Kampuchea seat instead of the Khmer Rouge, who controlled the country. For their part, the minimum the Taliban expected was a vacant-seat formula such as the Organization of the Islamic Conference (OIC) had adopted. Thus ostracized, the Taliban considered the United Nations inherently biased and had no incentive to cooperate with it.

The Taliban's treatment of women proved an additional obstacle in dealing with them or in raising funds for programs in Taliban-controlled areas. Nonetheless, UN humanitarian operations played a significant humanitarian role in the supply of food items. The World Food Program in particular remained an important lifeline for many starving Afghans, especially in the central parts of Afghanistan. In addition, the UN intercession in October 1998 was effective in putting pressure on the Taliban to release the Iranian captives following the fall of Mazar e Sharif, although it can be argued that it was the threat of Iranian military intervention that forced Mullah Omar to yield, inducing him to take advantage of the UN and Pakistani mediation.[26]

This was not the only occasion when the UN had some success in bringing the opposing parties together. In February 1997, UN Special Representative Norbert Holl was able to organize working-level talks between the Taliban, Hizb e Wahdat, and Dostum's Junbish e Milli to focus on the question of exchange of prisoners in the hope that the process could then lead to political-level talks for peace.[27] In April–May 1998, before the Taliban's Mazar offensive in July 1998, the UN and the Organization of the Islamic Conference launched a significant effort. They developed a proposal for the formation of a commission of Ulema to be nominated by the Taliban and the Northern Alliance that would decide measures for restoration of peace and stability in Afghanistan. The proposal, which had Mullah Omar's blessings, had evolved as a result of Pakistan's initiative and discussions with Mullah Rabbani and Burhanuddin Rabbani, who were separately invited by Nawaz Sharif to Islamabad. The two sides agreed to have a steering committee comprising nominees of the Taliban and the Northern Alliance to meet under the auspices of the United Nations and the OIC. The Taliban acceptance of the UN appeared to be a concession, as they had accused the organization of denying them recognition as the legitimate government with control over Kabul.

There was fuzziness over the agenda for the steering committee. Mullah Omar wanted it to be restricted to preparations for the Ulema commission, while Northern Alliance leaders wanted it to include related issues of ceasefire, exchange of prisoners, and removal of the Taliban blockade of Hazarajat. Mullah Omar insisted that these matters should be left to the commis-

---

26. *NYT,* September 5, 1998, reported Iran amassing 70,000 troops near the Afghan border. *NYT,* September 10, 1998, reported a warning by Iranian President Muhammad Khatami.

27. Murshed, *Afghanistan: The Taliban Years,* 252.

sion. The proposal was actively pursued not only by senior Pakistani officials, but also by Lakhdar Brahimi and OIC envoy Ibrahim Saleh Bakr. In mid-Aprii 1998, the U.S. permanent representative to the UN Bill Richardson met Mullah Rabbani in Kabul and the Northern Alliance leadership in Shibergan. He raised the matter with both sides and confirmed their convergence on convening a steering committee for face-to-face talks.[28]

The steering committee met on April 26, leading to some optimism for a breakthrough. The Taliban had sent a team led by Foreign Minister Mullah Wakil Ahmed Mutawakil. There was progress on the issue of the Ulema commission, with both sides agreeing to nominate twenty members each; but the committee soon faced a deadlock when the Hizb e Wahdat representative demanded a decision for immediate lifting of the blockade of Hazarajat. Wakil left for Qandahar to persuade Mullah Omar to agree and did not return, extinguishing the faint hope raised by several months of active diplomacy.[29]

Failing to bring together the warring factions for reconciliation, UN special envoys also tried to work with outside players in an effort to promote peace in Afghanistan. The most significant of these initiatives was Lakhdar Brahimi's "Six-plus-Two" format to get Afghanistan's six neighbors and Russia and the United States. Since its inception in early 1998, the arrangement became a forum for the eight participants, mostly at the ambassadorial level, to discuss the situation in Afghanistan. The resulting communiqués included reaffirming commitment to Afghanistan's independence, sovereignty, and territorial integrity; noninterference in the country's internal affairs; establishment of a broad-based multiethnic government in Kabul; and asking the Taliban to improve human rights and control narcotic trafficking. The first important document from the forum, the "Points of Common Understanding," was adopted in September 1998, against the backdrop of the fall of Mazar and the killing and capture of the Iranian personnel.

Thus, it carried a strong demand for the detainees' release and the return of the remains of the Iranian personnel and asked the Taliban to cooperate with an international investigation into the matter. UN Secretary-General Kofi Annan's subsequent report accused the Taliban of "massive human rights violations."[30] The September "Six-plus-Two" meeting generated more

28. *NYT,* April 13, 1998.
29. Details are based on conversations with Ambassador Aziz Ahmed Khan. Also see Murshed, *Afghanistan: the Taliban Years,* 133–47, and *NYT,* May 20, 1998.
30. UN Document A/53/455, S/1998/913, October 2, 1998.

interest in the possibility of a face-to-face encounter between Iranian Foreign Minister Kamal Kharazi and U.S. Secretary of State Madeleine Albright than in the prospect of promoting reconciliation in Afghanistan.

Later, in October, under the threat of an imminent Iranian action against the Taliban, Mullah Omar decided to receive Brahimi and promised the release of the Iranian personnel and the return of bodies of those killed. He also agreed to establish an inquiry commission to investigate the killings and asked Brahimi to look into the massacre of the Taliban in Mazar more than a year earlier. The Taliban leaders accused the Iranians of providing massive supplies of arms to the Northern Alliance. Fortuitously for them, only a few days later, a train carrying such supplies to Tajikistan was interdicted in Osh, Kyrgyzstan, and the incident was publicized in the press.[31] Mullah Omar showed willingness to talk to the Iranians directly or through the auspices of the United Nations. However, once the crisis was diffused, the Brahimi initiative lost momentum.

The other highlights of the "Six-plus-Two" initiative were the meetings held in Ashgabat and Tashkent in March and July 1999, which resulted from the enthusiasm of Turkmenistan and Uzbekistan, two of Afghanistan's Central Asian neighbors, to play a prominent role. The Ashgabat meeting showed some signs of progress. After the fall of Mazar and Bamiyan, the Northern Alliance and Massoud were under pressure and, virtually confined to Badakhshan and a small area of eastern Afghanistan, wanted to negotiate a ceasefire. However, the subsequent Tashkent meeting proved sterile, despite representation by both the Taliban and Ahmed Shah Massoud. The meeting ended in adopting a declaration, pushed by both Iran and the United States, that was highly critical of the Taliban.

The "Six-plus-Two" group had started on the wrong foot, failing to focus on pressuring the contending Afghan factions for peace and reconciliation; instead, the group remained hostage to the interests of individual members and their rivalries and differing interests. Following the murder of Iranian personnel in Mazar e Sharif, the group turned its focus on the Iranian reaction and concerns. After the attacks on the U.S. embassies in Kenya and Tanzania in August 1998, the U.S. priority shifted to putting pressure on the Taliban to hand over Osama bin Laden, the leader of Al Qaeda, who was believed to be behind the attacks. The proposals for a comprehensive arms embargo, being considered by the "Six-plus-Two" and supported by Pakistan, turned into a demand for cutting off supplies of fuel to the Tali-

---

31. *NYT,* October 30, 1998.

ban. Pakistan balked, because Taliban-controlled Afghanistan almost entirely depended on Pakistan for fuel for domestic consumption. At the behest of the United States, the United Nations now started to consider imposing sanctions against the Taliban for providing safe haven to Al Qaeda. The U.S. view of the Taliban had by now turned from ambivalence to hostility.

Initial U.S. Ambivalence

American policy was largely circumscribed by the hostility of American civil society towards the Taliban human rights record, especially their treatment of women, and, following the Kenya and Tanzania attacks, by the presence of Al Qaeda in Afghanistan. Initially, however, U.S. officials listened to Pakistan's arguments that the Taliban brought hope for stability and peace in Afghanistan. The relative ease of the Taliban success at the early stages and their ability to disarm populations in areas under their control had not gone unnoticed by the United States. Indeed, within Pakistan many supporters of Gulbadin and Rabbani blamed the rise of the Taliban on U.S. encouragement. Soon this view changed. Yet this early impression was of U.S. neutrality, if not positive acquiescence in the rise of the Taliban. The U.S. view was also influenced by two factors: first, the Iranian antipathy towards the Taliban, and second, a growing interest in pipelines from Central Asia to the Baluchistan coast in Pakistan, which depended on stable political conditions in Afghanistan.

Union Oil Company of California, Unocal, was one of the first in the area as soon as the prospects of access to the energy resources of the Caspian Basin materialized with the breakup of the Soviet Union. Unocal had its eyes on a possible project for a gas pipeline over 1500 kilometers long from Turkmenistan to Pakistan through Afghanistan, initially estimated at $2.5 billion. The company set up its office in Qandahar in 1996. Its rivalry with an Argentinean oil company, Bridas, for the same project raised considerable speculation about a new "great game" in the region and about funding of the Taliban by the two interested parties.[32] The facts were far less sensational, and the prospective pipeline never became feasible, yet the possibility remained tantalizing as long as it was alive.

The visit to Kabul in April 1998 by U.S. permanent representative to the

---

32. Rashid, *Taliban,* 157–69. Ahmed Shah Massoud had accused Unocal of funding the Taliban for the capture of Kabul.

UN Bill Richardson, accompanied by Ambassador Thomas Simons and Assistant Secretary of State Karl "Rick" Inderfurth, was an unexpected culmination of informal contacts that the United States had continued to maintain with the Taliban. It was an exploratory mission during which the visitors had meetings with Mullah Rabbani, the Afghan president, and other Taliban officials. They also visited Shibergan to meet the Northern Alliance leadership, although Ahmed Shah Massoud was unable to attend that meeting. A visit by Mullah Rabbani to Islamabad one month earlier, in March 1998, may have encouraged the Americans to establish such a high-profile contact. In Islamabad, Mullah Rabbani had demonstrated a moderate political stance and publicly suggested that the Taliban were not opposed to girls' education, an issue that greatly rankled the West. Politically, Rabbani was agreeable to the formation of a commission of Ulema under the auspices of the OIC and the United Nations and endorsed the Pakistani idea of a comprehensive arms embargo. There were thus enough issues on which Bill Richardson could directly elicit Taliban views, including those germane to "Six-plus-Two" discussions that he himself had joined in New York. He also wanted to sound out the Taliban on cooperation against Osama bin Laden, who was allegedly involved in anti-U.S. activities. But at this stage Osama was still a "secondary issue" for the Americans.[33]

For their part, the Taliban, especially the Kabul-based leadership, were looking for recognition and financial assistance to revive an economy in a state of total collapse. Following the meeting, Bill Richardson gave an upbeat account.[34] Mullah Rabbani had promised to open girls' schools, provided funds were made available, and to relax the ban on NGO operations. He further suggested that the United States and Saudi Arabia could bring a case in an Afghan court against Osama on the basis of evidence, and that the Taliban government would respect the verdict if it were in favor of deportation.

Later, the Taliban kept reminding Pakistani ambassador Aziz Ahmed Khan about Bill Richardson's promise for help that never materialized. In Europe and the United States the human rights lobbies were so riled up against the Taliban that no government in the West could contemplate dealings with the Taliban. International assistance to the Taliban government was restricted to food, largely through the World Food Program, in the

---

33. Steve Coll, *Ghost Wars* (New York: Penguin Books, 2004), 384.
34. *NYT,* April 18, 1998.

range of 200,000 tons of wheat.[35] There was little appreciation that the Taliban had ensured security, confiscating large quantities of personal arms. Travel in the Taliban-controlled territories was safe, and there were no toll barriers. The author witnessed this when he traveled to Kabul by road in April 2000.[36] The Taliban had reduced poppy cultivation and declared its eradication in 1999, which many international observers cynically dismissed as a measure to control production to keep a high street value for the commodity. The U.S. attitude's shift to one of hostility, following the attacks on the U.S. embassies in Kenya and Tanzania, intensified Taliban isolation.

Mullah Rabbani's offers may have been sincere in view of the pressures on Kabul at the time, but the Taliban obduracy on NGO and gender issues was ingrained in their psyche and left little room for convincing either the Europeans or the United States of a change of position. Another fleeting opportunity to show goodwill and to put up an acceptable face had arisen in September 1997, when Emma Bonino, the EU commissioner for humanitarian affairs, visited Kabul on a familiarization mission. Instead of taking advantage of the occasion, the Taliban's Amr Bil Maroof police detained her entourage at a hospital she was visiting for nearly four hours objecting to the presence of television cameras. She later described the Taliban as a "repressive, grotesquely misogynistic regime."[37] This may appear to be a harsh comment, but because of their environment and antiquated education, most of the Taliban rank and file and the hard-line Qandahar leadership were narrow-minded and xenophobic, especially on gender issues and in their conduct with non-Muslims.

Bill Richardson's visit had taken place against the backdrop of a less publicized rivalry that was shaping up between two distinct centers of the Tali-

35. The total bilateral and World Food Program allocation for the supply of wheat was around $200 million. Taliban officials used to point out that they could buy more than one million tons of wheat with this amount from the open market.

36. The author also witnessed the shockingly abject poverty in Afghanistan under the Taliban rule. In his travel from Torkham to Kabul, every four to five kilometers along the entire stretch of the dusty road destroyed by fifteen years of conflict, clusters of old people and children could be found standing and begging passersby to throw them some money.

37. In 2000, speaking to Afghan refugee women in the Nasir Bagh refugee camp near Peshawar, Secretary of State Madeleine Albright had similarly harsh words, calling the Taliban treatment of women "despicable."

ban power in Kabul and in Qandahar. The Taliban leadership in Kabul was slightly more exposed to the outside world and felt the pressure of isolation and the need for international financial assistance to run the government. In contrast, the group based in Qandahar, led by Mullah Omar, had little sensitivity to such pressures and felt secure in its hard-line behavior and isolation. The potential of the incipient division was never tested. The United States remained disinterested, and Pakistan had no stake in looking for, much less exploiting, any divisions among the Taliban. Meanwhile, Qandahar found another financier, Al Qaeda and its chief, Osama bin Laden, who was well versed in tribal codes and customs and had gradually gained influence with Mullah Omar and his band of Taliban in Qandahar. Kabul's authority and influence were further eclipsed as Mullah Rabbani suffered from cancer and died in April 2001.

Al Qaeda Gains as Taliban Isolation Deepens

Al Qaeda (Arabic for the "base") had coalesced around the remnants of the thousands of Arab youth who had come to fight the Soviets in Afghanistan. They were prompted by a range of motivations, from inspiration to fight a jihad to alienation from their own societies, and included those the CIA had encouraged to come to Afghanistan. A large number had stayed behind after the Soviets withdrew, as their own countries were unprepared to take back these radicalized young men, tempered by the Afghan conflict.[38] Many of those who did return home were incarcerated, and there were even reports of executions in Egypt and Algeria.

Osama bin Laden, a member of the Saudi billionaire bin Laden family, first came to Peshawar to provide financial help to Maktab al Khadmat (Services Office) established there in 1980 by an eminent Palestinian scholar activist, Sheikh Abdullah Yusuf Azzam, to support the Afghan Jihad. Abdullah Azzam had shifted to Peshawar after he was expelled from the King Abdul Aziz University in Jeddah following the Saudi crackdown on radical Islamists triggered by the seizure of the Haram Sharif in Mecca in Novem-

---

38. *NYT,* March 28, 1993, reported that thousands of "Islamic militants" from Algeria, Egypt, Tunisia, Jordan, and Turkey had found a base in Afghanistan to work against governments in their home countries and that they had been recipients of large funds from the United States and Saudi Arabia during the Afghan resistance against the Soviets. See also *NYT,* April 18, 1993.

ber 1979. Having been educated at Al Azhar University in Cairo, Azzam had contacts with Ikhwanis (members of the Egyptian fundamentalist Muslim Brotherhood Movement) whom he attracted to Peshawar, including Ayman Al Zawahiri.[39] The Maktab recruited Arabs, known as "Afghan-Arabs" for the Jihad, most of whom had the Wahabi orientation.[40] In the late 1980s, Osama started organizing his own Afghan-Arab jihadi group for operations against the Soviets inside Afghanistan. At that time, he was known to have contacts with the American embassy in Islamabad. Following the assassination of Abdullah Azzam in late 1989, Osama emerged as the leader of the Afghan-Arabs. His turnabout came with the first Gulf War in late 1990 and his strong opposition to the deployment of U.S. troops in Saudi Arabia. The Saudi government reportedly ignored his offer to bring Afghan Mujahedin to oust Saddam Hussein's forces from Kuwait.

Osama set up Al Qaeda with two professed objectives: pushing the U.S. forces from his home country, the land of the two holy mosques; and the liberation of Palestine, an issue that gnaws at the psyche of every Arab and has caused a deep sense of indignation and humiliation. As he later described publicly, he regarded the presence of "the American crusader armed forces" in the Gulf countries as "the greatest danger and the biggest harm." He insisted that "the infidels must be thrown out of the Arabian peninsula."[41] Osama had moved to Sudan in 1992, where he was hounded by U.S. intelligence, forcing him to return to Afghanistan in May 1996. Conflict-riven Afghanistan proved a safe base in which to work out his agenda, which now included an ideological commitment to target American and Western interests worldwide. In Afghanistan, he sought refuge with Deen Muhammad and his brother Haji Qadeer in Jalalabad. Once the Taliban moved in, Osama approached Mullah Rabbani, who had led the Taliban assault against the city. Mullah Rabbani assured Osama the same protection, in appreciation for Osama's services for the cause of the Afghan Jihad.[42] Thus by providing refuge to the leader of Al Qaeda, an alien body with an obsession to confront the West globally, the insular Taliban, steeped in medieval tribal traditions, had unwittingly created the circumstances to turn Afghanistan

39. There is a view that some Arab governments were happy to push dissidents and radicalized youth towards the Afghan Jihad.

40. The Salafi influence was evident in the *Takfiri* (apostasy) dogma embraced by Al Qaeda and other religious extremists. Azzam was opposed to applying *Takfir* to other Muslims.

41. *NYT,* August 31, 1996.

42. Conversation with Ambassador Aziz Ahmed Khan.

into a new twenty-first-century storm center. That country would soon draw the wrath of the sole superpower of the day.

Osama moved to Qandahar in late 1996 and started building relations with the Taliban leadership. Later, he constructed residential quarters for Mullah Omar and started providing financial help to the cash-starved Taliban. At an early stage, the Saudi government had an opportunity to get him extradited to Saudi Arabia but found it expedient to let him remain in Afghanistan. No link had yet been established between Osama and Saudi extremist elements in the terrorist attack on Khobar Towers in June 1996. Meanwhile, the support for the Taliban by Arab and Pakistani elements was proving critical to Taliban successes. Osama was gaining time to build influence with the Taliban and strengthen himself through recruitment and training. Al Qaeda also began developing linkages with other extremist militant groups. In particular, these included the Chechens escaping from Russian military campaigns and persecution; Uzbeks fleeing President Islam Karimov's clampdown on the Islamic Movement of Uzbekistan in Ferghana and elsewhere; Sunni militant groups of Pakistan; and the Kashmiri jihadi groups. Afghanistan had become an ungoverned space conducive for jihadist militancy and extremists. In the early years of Osama's stay, his anti-U.S. rhetoric did not attract particular attention, as such sentiment was commonplace in the region.

The isolation of the Taliban and their grievances against the international community over nonrecognition, apathy towards the massacre of the Taliban in Mazar e Sharif in 1997, and the routinely harsh international criticism of the Taliban hardened Mullah Omar's view that only a military approach could bring success to the Taliban. He grew more dependent on the foreign militant elements, in particular the Arabs, who were also a source of funds. Furthermore, the Taliban leaders were receptive to the austere and harsh Wahabi (Salafi) ideology of the Saudis, given their madrassa background and Deobandi persuasion. The Saudi Salafi and Al Qaeda influence on Omar became visible when, two years after the capture of the Hazarajat and one year after his decree to preserve the eighteen-hundred-year-old colossal Buddhas carved into the sandstone hills facing the city of Bamiyan, the statues were allowed to be defiled.

Later, in March 2001, it became known that the Taliban intended to completely destroy this world heritage. The international community, in particular the Buddhist nations, raised an outcry and appealed to save the statues. President Musharraf sent his interior minister, retired Lt. Gen. Moinuddin Haider, to plead with Mullah Omar, who remained unmoved. That the Taliban leader decided to rebuff the Pakistanis and the rest of the international community suggested, other than the Al Qaeda and Salafi influences, the arrogance and rigidity the Taliban had developed as a result of their successes. This was reflected in Mullah Omar's comments to Moinuddin that he was answerable to God alone. Later, reacting to the worldwide condemnation of the destruction of the Bamiyan Buddhas, the Taliban Foreign Minister Mullah Wakil Ahmed Mutawakil sarcastically remarked that the world could hear the Buddha statues exploding but "failed to listen to the cries of our hungry children." The Taliban leadership should not have been so apathetic to the squalor of their people, in the first place, while not giving a second thought to their unceasing military effort to control all of Afghanistan. The Taliban rule had become increasingly repressive in its zealotry; they had even told Hindus, the only non-Muslims left in the country, to wear distinctive marks on their dress,[43] and their policies against women and foreign aid workers had further stiffened.

By 2001, despite their control of almost 90 percent of the territory of Afghanistan, the Taliban had become further isolated, with Pakistan the only country maintaining diplomatic relations. Saudi Arabia and the United Arab Emirates had severed relations mainly as a consequence of the Osama issue, which increasingly preoccupied the Americans after the bombing of their embassies in Kenya and Tanzania in early August 1998 and the suicide attack against the USS *Cole* in October 2000. Following the embassy attacks, the immediate U.S. reaction was to blame Osama. Within days, on August 20, President Clinton ordered the United States to hit Osama's base in Zawar Kili, Khost, with a batch of seventy-five Cruise missiles. But Osama escaped, as he did not turn up in Khost, contrary to the information of the U.S. intelligence sources.[44] Over thirty persons died in the attack, including a number of Afghans, several Pakistanis reportedly belonging to the Kashmir-related jihadi group Harkat ul Ansar, and some Arab nationals. The mix pointed to the close linkages that had developed between Al Qaeda and other militant jihadi groups in the region. It also lent credibility to the charge that the ISI was training militants for Kashmir in camps inside

43. *NYT,* May 23, 2001.

44. The Americans were highly cautious prior to the launching of the attack. General Anthony Zinni, chief of the U.S. Central Command (CENTCOM), was in Islamabad on the day of the attack and had meetings at the military headquarters during the day. Only when he was proceeding to the airport, nearly an hour after the attack, did he break the news to his Pakistani counterpart. He had supposedly come to Islamabad to alert the Pakistani side that the missiles were not being fired by India.

Afghanistan. A few of the missiles even fell within Pakistani territory, giving the country valuable technology for reverse engineering.

Simultaneously, the American missiles struck a pharmaceutical factory in Khartoum reportedly owned by Osama. The Americans alleged that the factory was being used for manufacturing precursors for chemical weapons. The charge could not be proved. These attacks brought Osama into the limelight and built up his popular appeal throughout the Islamic world. In Pakistan, Islamist parties held demonstrations in his support. The Americans were now vigorously pursuing Osama and had declared a bounty for his capture; they linked Al Qaeda with almost every recent attack on U.S. targets, including the 1993 bombing of the World Trade Center and the Americans killed in Mogadishu the same year. Osama's rhetoric had also shifted from a criticism of Arab regimes and denunciation of Israel to declaring a "global jihad" attacking U.S. and Western interests everywhere as being a duty of all Muslims.

Following Osama's return to Afghanistan from Sudan, the Americans asked the Saudis and the Pakistanis to approach Mullah Omar to hand over Osama. The Taliban, however, took the position that they could not hand over a guest to the United States but would be ready to consider a trial by an Ulema court. That court could include Ulema from Saudi Arabia and proceed on the basis of evidence to be provided by the Americans. The last joint effort for this purpose was made when Prince Turki al Faisal, the Saudi intelligence chief, accompanied by his Pakistani counterpart, Lt. Gen. Nasim Rana, and Pakistan's special envoy on Afghanistan, Syed Iftikhar Murshed, traveled to Qandahar in September 1998 to meet the Taliban leader. Prince Turki's demarche and threat ended in an angry exchange with Mullah Omar. According to an eyewitness account by Iftikhar, the outburst was triggered by Prince Turki's accusation that Mullah Omar was "lying" in denying that he had ever promised to hand over Osama to the Saudis. Prince Turki left the meeting in anger and Saudi Arabia immediately severed diplomatic relations with the Taliban, an act that was to be followed by the UAE.[45]

45. Murshed, *Afghanistan: the Taliban Years,* 300–302. Also see a corroborative account in Musharraf, *In the Line of Fire,* 213–14. According to Musharraf, Omar did propose the formation of a council of Ulema from Afghanistan and Saudi Arabia to decide Osama's fate. At the same time he "bitterly objected" to the presence of U.S. troops in Saudi Arabia, asserting that the "older generation" of self-respecting Saudi rulers would never have allowed such presence. This annoyed Prince Turki, and he left the meeting. The sudden departure of Turki surprised Mullah Omar who, according to Musharraf, appeared to have been "playing to the gallery" and "did not comprehend that he had made

After the failure of the Turki mission, U.S. officials sought Pakistani co-operation to arrest Osama. In mid-1999, the U.S. side suggested raising a special force to operate inside Afghanistan to capture Osama. When Nawaz Sharif went to Washington to bring the Kargil skirmish with India to a close, President Clinton spoke with him about the suggestion.[46] Later in September, the new ISI chief, Lt. Gen. Ziauddin Khwaja, visited Washington and gave his consent, partly because President Clinton had played a positive role in diffusing the Kargil crisis. After the dismissal of the Nawaz Sharif government in October 1999 and imposition of military rule by Pervez Musharraf, the United States did not pursue the plan.

The Dilemma of Pakistan's Taliban Policy

The months following the Musharraf takeover in Pakistan were relatively uneventful. Pakistani-U.S. relations had again hit a nadir; the military takeover had compounded the sanctions already placed on Pakistan because of the May 1998 nuclear tests. At India's behest, the United States kept up its pressure on Pakistan to disband militant organizations committed to jihad in Kashmir. At times, there were implied threats of declaring Pakistan a terrorist state, although these never took a tangible shape. The issue of un-delivered F-16s continued to add bitterness to the relations. In April 2000, President Clinton had reluctantly agreed to touch down in Islamabad for a four-hour stopover after a five-day visit to India, but he refused to make a public appearance with President Musharraf.[47] In this environment of mis-trust, there was hardly room for substantive cooperation. Moreover, it was pointless to approach the Taliban without convincing evidence of Osama's culpability. So far, the evidence collected by the Americans was largely cir-cumstantial, and it clearly appeared to be insufficient for conviction in any court of law, not to speak of a politically biased Taliban Ulema court.

---

an enemy out of one of the few people who could have truly helped extricate [the] Taliban from the mess created by Osama's presence in Afghanistan."

46. The 9/11 Commission, *The Final Report of the National Commission on Terrorist Attacks on the United States,* issued on July 22, 2004, 125.

47. In September 2000, on the occasion of the UN General Assembly, Musharraf had met Yasir Arafat and spoken to him about the difficulties faced by Pakistan in its relations with the United States. Yasir Arafat volunteered to intercede with Bill Clinton on Pakistan's behalf. This was the extent of the downturn.

In May 2000, U.S. Under Secretary of State Thomas Pickering visited Islamabad where, in addition to Pakistani leaders, he met Taliban Deputy Foreign Minister Mullah Abdul Jalil to discuss extradition of Osama as required by the relevant UN Security Council resolutions.[48] Pickering handed over evidence of Al Qaeda involvement in the Tanzania and Kenya U.S. embassy bombings and Osama's invocation of jihad against the Americans.[49] Mullah Jalil did not agree with Pickering's arguments, asserting that the Taliban would nonetheless not allow Afghan territory to be used against the United States. The Taliban leadership was unlikely to oblige, especially when the United States and the rest of the world were ostracizing the regime.

Still under the shadows of the Kargil episode, Pakistan was far too preoccupied with Kashmir to anticipate the danger brewing on its western borders or to view Al Qaeda, much less the Taliban, as a threat. Musharraf's agenda, announced in his first address to the nation, was socioeconomic development. On the foreign relations front, his priority was to internationalize Kashmir, the stated justification for the ill-fated Kargil venture. The ISI was deeply involved with the Kashmiri Mujahedin groups under the new ISI chief, an architect of Kargil, Lt. Gen. Mahmud Ahmed, who had begun developing the traits of a born-again religious enthusiast. A glaring example of this was the patronage enjoyed by Maulana Masood Azhar immediately after his release from Indian custody in exchange for an end to the hijacking of an Indian Airlines plane from Delhi to Qandahar in December 1999. There was no evidence that the ISI had engineered the hijacking, as alleged by India; but once released, Masood Azhar headed straight to Pakistan, where he immediately set up a militant outfit, Jaish e Muhammad, with the declared objective of carrying out jihad in Kashmir. Masood Azhar could not have acted without the connivance, if not the support, of Pakistan's premier intelligence agency. Later, Musharraf had to ban the organization. It still exists as a fanatical militant group, but this time with guns turned against the host country.

General Mahmud was an admirer of the Taliban, like many within the Pakistani military whose perception of the Taliban was grounded in religious naïveté. In early 2001, at a conference of Pakistani envoys in Islamabad to discuss the Afghanistan situation, several participants criticized Pakistan's policy of support for the Taliban, as it rebounded internationally

48. In particular, Security Council Resolution 1267 of October 1999.
49. Murshed, *Afghanistan: the Taliban Years,* 298. Also see *The 9/11 Commission Report,* 126.

to sully the image of Pakistan. They suggested that Pakistan should put pressure on the Taliban to change their attitude on girls' education, treatment of UN humanitarian agencies, and reconciliation with the opposition. Mahmud reacted almost disdainfully, dismissing the arguments by saying that in the two-hour briefing he did not once hear a reference to Providence. It was an irony that on September 11, 2001, he was in Washington and the next day faced U.S. demands from Deputy Secretary of State Richard Armitage.

The religious elements in Pakistan vociferously eulogized the Taliban for their simplicity, honesty, piety, and commitment to Islam and as harbingers of peace in Afghanistan. In their zeal, they would even describe Taliban rule as reminiscent of the pristine times of the pious first four caliphs of Islam. At times, these exaggerations were deliberate and calculated to bolster public acceptance of the Taliban in Pakistan. A combination of the political ambitions of religious forces and the prevailing military view that Afghanistan under the Taliban could best serve the interests of Pakistan in the area was the underlying impulse of this campaign, a heady blend of a revivalist Islam and simplistic Realpolitik. At the intellectual level, the protagonists on the religious right have been assertive and adept in propagating their views, especially in the local Urdu press. They have often indulged in self-righteous rhetoric and patriotic blandishments, projecting themselves as a force that stands for truth and against the West's machinations to dominate Islam. They have demonstrated ability to influence populist opinion, especially when it resonates with the military establishment.

The more realistic view within Pakistan's military establishment, also generally supportive of the Taliban, argued that once they settled down and established control over the entirety of Afghanistan, they would be ripe to undergo an internal metamorphosis towards moderation. This was an illusion, if not a pretext, to defend a regime that seemed friendly and completely dependent on Pakistan. No doubt, the Taliban enjoyed certain grass-roots support and legitimacy and were able to bring peace and successfully reintegrate much of Afghanistan. But most of the world saw them as an abomination. The prevalent Pakistani public opinion remained oblivious to the international opprobrium against the Taliban and to the Afghan émigré community's almost universal dislike of Pakistan's pro-Taliban policy. Pakistan lost much of the goodwill it had earned over a decade among most Afghans, including a great many in the Afghan émigré community, in addition to the Afghan Mujahedin leadership and significant elements within the Afghan elite.

Iran, in contrast, despite its ideological proclivities and international diplomatic isolation, acted with pragmatism and recovered from the handicap of its earlier 1980s aloofness from the Afghan Jihad. Following the emergence of the Taliban, Iran provided refuge to Gulbadin, Ismael Khan, and the Shia leaders from Hazarajat. More important, Iran strengthened its links with the Northern Alliance, while Pakistan gratuitously and publicly justified the Taliban push to extend their control over all of Afghanistan. The Northern Alliance saw this as Pakistani complicity with the Taliban in an attempt to decimate it militarily.

International Pressure on the Taliban Intensifies

The United States turned up pressure on the Taliban through the United Nations Security Council, which had first addressed the Afghanistan internal strife in a fairly mild resolution in October 1996 following the Taliban takeover of Kabul. The resolutions adopted in August and December 1998, after the fall of Mazar e Sharif and the accompanying violence, were the first to be critical of the Taliban and were mainly sponsored by Iran, Russia, and the Central Asian Republics. Iran, in particular, was indignant at the murder of its personnel at the Iranian Consulate General in Mazar. The December resolution had for the first time demanded that the Taliban not provide sanctuary to terrorist elements.

The sentiment changed sharply in Resolution 1267, adopted in October 1999, which specifically referred to the Taliban as continuing to provide "safe haven" to Osama bin Laden and cooperating with other terrorist networks. The resolution demanded that the Taliban "turn over" Osama to a country where he had been indicted or where he could be effectively brought to justice. The resolution went a step further. Under chapter VII of the UN Charter, it barred air flights from Taliban-controlled areas and froze financial resources belonging to the Taliban, except those approved, on a case-by-case basis, by a committee the resolution established to monitor implementation of its provisions.

Resolution 1333, adopted one year later, in December 2000, further toughened the sanctions, imposed a comprehensive arms embargo against the Taliban, and adopted additional specific provisions for freezing assets belonging to Osama and Al Qaeda members. The Security Council resolutions represented an escalating pressure to stifle the friendless Taliban. Pakistan, the only country that sided with them, no longer carried any clout in UN corridors, especially on Afghanistan-related matters. Within the Pakistani establishment, the Foreign Office recognized the potential mischief of these mandatory resolutions under chapter VII. The ISI and the military saw it as just a failure on the diplomatic front and maintained a smug attitude. In the past, they believed, Pakistan had been able to put up with many such setbacks, the recent most being on Kargil. The Taliban were even less sensitive to the UN demands and dismissed them as unjustified and biased against an Islamic regime. They declared a complete boycott of any United Nations–sponsored peace talks[50] and became ever more intransigent, as evidenced in their defiance of the worldwide appeals not to blow up the Bamiyan Buddhas.

Internationally, Pakistani officials continued to advocate for the Taliban on the grounds that the unacceptable aspects of their rule were temporary and likely to change as they settled into governing. They argued that international engagement could even hasten the process. This was the line taken by Pakistan Foreign Minister Abdul Sattar as late as June 2001 when he visited Washington and met National Security Advisor Condoleezza Rice. She bluntly told him that the United States could not ignore that Pakistan was "in bed with our (U.S.) enemies" and that Pakistan "must drop the Taliban." A luncheon meeting with his counterpart, Colin Powell, was more congenial. The same evening, Sattar was embarrassed at the National Press Club in Washington, when he faced a volley of abuse from two Afghan journalists, who were then forcibly removed from the conference room. Despite such obloquy, Pakistan maintained its support for the Taliban, hoping that eventually, like many regimes, the Taliban would survive sanctions and change just enough to gain some international recognition. No one in Pakistan or among the Taliban had expected the fateful events that followed in September and drastically changed the global political environment.

Just two days before 9/11, Afghanistan was rocked by the reports of Ahmed Shah Massoud's assassination in a suicide attack carried out by Al Qaeda members, disguised as TV cameramen; the assassins had been pursuing a request for an interview with the Afghan commander for some time.[51] Massoud's removal was Al Qaeda's gift to the Taliban. Its far-reaching implications extended beyond the ouster of the Taliban in the next couple of months. Massoud was absent when the U.S. intervention cleared the field for the Northern Alliance. His was the first murder of a leading Mujahedin leader, other than that of the Shia leader Mazari, who was killed in a confusing situation, allegedly at the hands of the Taliban. This major develop-

50. *NYT,* December 11, 2000.
51. Coll, *Ghost Wars,* 574–76.

ment was, however, completely eclipsed by the events two days later when flights hijacked by nineteen young Arab youth slammed into the World Trade Center towers in New York and the Pentagon in Washington, the two outstanding symbols of the wealth and power of the United States.

9/11 Impacts Afghanistan and Pakistan

Within hours of the horrors of 9/11, President Bush had described the attack as "Pearl Harbor of the twenty first century,"[52] a "war not a crime," and his war rhetoric was given an ideological construct. On September 21, 2001, addressing a joint session of the U.S. Congress, President George W. Bush stated: "This is not just America's fight. . . . This is the world's fight. This is a civilization's fight . . . of all who believe in progress and pluralism, tolerance and freedom. . . . The course of the conflict is not known, yet its outcome is certain. Freedom and fear, justice and cruelty, have always been at war, and we know that God is not neutral between them." Importantly, Bush made it clear that the United States would look beyond Al Qaeda and also punish those who harbored Al Qaeda.

President Musharraf and the Pakistani Foreign Office had little doubt about the implications of the shocking attacks that were witnessed worldwide in real time. Musharraf read a strong statement condemning the attack. Pakistan again obliged when, the next day, appreciating the president's statement, a suggestion came from the U.S. embassy that Pakistan should explicitly state that it stood by the United States and would extend cooperation in bringing the perpetrators of the terrorist act to justice. On September 12, Deputy Secretary of State Richard Armitage summoned ISI chief Lt. Gen. Mahmud Ahmed and Pakistan's ambassador to Washington Maleeha Lodhi. Armitage was polite but firm and plainly put the choice before Pakistan in the now famous phrase, "Either you are with us or against us." There have been references, including in Musharraf's autobiography, to an alleged statement by Armitage that, in case of noncooperation, Pakistan would be bombed "back to [the] Stone Age." Armitage denied having made such a threat, and it certainly was not in the records.[53] Mahmud reassured Armitage that Pakistan would stand by the United States.

---

52. The *Washington Post,* January 27, 2002, reported that President Bush recorded the remark in his diary on September 11, 2001.

53. Following the publication of Musharraf's autobiography in 2006, which carried

On September 13, Colin Powell conveyed to Musharraf a list of seven demands. The key points asked Pakistan's consent for logistical support, such as "blanket overflight and landing rights"; "territorial access," including "use of ports, air bases, and strategic locations on the borders" to conduct military operations against "perpetrators of terrorism and those who harbor them"; intelligence sharing; agreement to cut off all fuel supplies to the Taliban and to interdict supplies and recruits that could help the Taliban's offensive capability; and the use of Pakistani airspace for possible military action inside Afghanistan.[54]

On September 14, Musharraf convened a corps commanders' meeting, the country's highest military body, to discuss the situation and the U.S. demands. There was no dissent, only the raising of some issues of tactics and what Pakistan must ask in return. The impact of 9/11 was so overwhelming and fresh that the question of denying support to the United States appeared foolhardy, regardless of the perceived importance of the Taliban regime to Pakistan's interests. September 11 had changed international sentiment. Pakistan hoped to convince the Taliban to extradite Osama and avert the oncoming disaster. The issue of what to ask seemed secondary, although in a note, the Foreign Office had made a case for committing support in principle and offering discussions for mutually agreed understandings.[55] The counterargument discussed within the military establishment, which Musharraf favored, had been that this was not the time to quibble, since the basic decision and policy line were clear. To bargain at a time of extraordinary gravity appeared to detract from the quality of a gesture that was considered both inevitable and in Pakistan's national interest. On September 19, in explaining his unequivocal and speedy response, Musharraf said that he had done everything for Afghanistan and the Taliban when the whole world

---

a reference to the threat, Richard Armitage denied it on the CBS program *Sixty Minutes* on September 22, 2006. The first such reference was carried by November 15, 2001, in an *LA Weekly* article by Ali Ahmed Rind, who cited Armitage as having said, "Help us and breathe in the 21st century along with the international community or be prepared to live in the Stone Age." This reference may have been a fabrication or mixed up with a comment appearing in the *New York Times* of September 13 that if the Americans were clamoring to bomb Afghanistan "back to the Stone Age," they ought to know that Afghanistan "does not have so far to go."

54. The seven demands made in a nonpaper presented by Wendy Chamberlin, U.S. ambassador in Islamabad, on behalf of Secretary of State Colin Powell have been detailed in Musharraf's autobiography, *In the Line of Fire,* 204–5.

55. Inam ul Haq, the foreign secretary at the time, recalled that the paper was handed over by Musharraf to Ambassador Wendy Chamberlain.

was against them; now he was trying to do his best to get Pakistan out of a "critical situation."

In practical terms, Pakistan was not in a position to block airspace.[56] The United States could overcome its logistical handicap by using its existing base in Diego Garcia or aircraft carriers; the Indian media had also hinted at extending facilities to the United States to fight terrorism in the region.[57] Of further importance, Musharraf saw an opportunity to bring Pakistan into international focus as a frontline state in the fight against terrorism, similar to the one the Soviet military intervention presented to Zia ul Haq in 1979. Soon after the corps commanders' meeting, Musharraf conveyed Pakistan's acceptance of the seven demands to Colin Powell, who was both pleased and surprised.[58] He had expected Pakistan to ask for discussions, instead of giving an expeditious and unconditional response. The response ended Musharraf's isolation, and he instantly became a key ally in the "war on terror."

Pakistan tried quite desperately to persuade the Taliban leader to relent on his refusal to hand over Osama. There was a sense of urgency, as the opportunity to avert a showdown on the issue was narrow. U.S military preparations, reminiscent of the Gulf War mobilization a decade earlier, were in hand. The key interlocutor was Lt. Gen. Mahmud Ahmed, who met Mullah Omar on September 16, accompanied only by a few ISI confidants. The effort by Foreign Secretary Inam ul Haq, who had Musharraf's approval for inclusion of Aziz Ahmed Khan in the delegation, was politely finessed. Aziz had been Pakistan's ambassador to the Taliban and had returned to Islamabad in the year 2000 after completing his tenure. When the helicopter carrying the delegation stopped in Kabul, it was suggested that Aziz should brief the Taliban leadership in the capital. Aziz insisted on going to Qandahar. Once in Qandahar, however, he was asked, ostensibly to save time, to separately brief Taliban Foreign Minister Mutawakil while Mahmud met Mullah Omar. Aziz got the hint.

The points for Mahmud's meeting had been discussed and approved by Musharraf. Mahmud was mandated to convey with utter candor to the Taliban leader that Afghanistan faced the gravest of dangers and that the Tali-

---

56. In the 1980s, Soviet military planes carrying military supplies to Ethiopia used to fly over Pakistani airspace, without official clearance or advance information.

57. In Pakistani official perception, such media comments, suggesting that India could take the place of Pakistan, were inspired by the Indian government.

58. Bob Woodward, *Bush at War* (New York: Simon and Schuster, 2002), 59.

ban were in no position to withstand the overwhelming U.S. military might. Mahmud was asked to impress upon Mullah Omar that as a sincere friend that had stood by the Taliban despite all pressures, Pakistan wanted him to act in the interest of saving the Taliban government. Mullah Omar had answers to what Mahmud had to convey, often invoking his faith in Allah to close any argument. Mullah Omar's answer to the warning of danger and the potential of U.S. military power was a rhetorical question whether the U.S. might was greater than that of Allah. As for Osama, he essentially reiterated the earlier position that an Afghan court could hold a trial and could even decide on extradition on the basis of the evidence to be provided by the U.S. side.

Whether Mahmud Ahmed read the riot act or behaved in an obsequious manner, as he allegedly had done in his earlier interaction with Mullah Omar, is a moot point.[59] Later, referring to the meeting, Mahmud admitted to the author of an authoritative work on the Pakistani military, Shuja Nawaz, how difficult it was to argue with a man of faith.[60] Even if Mahmud had been firm, the result would have been no different. Aziz Khan's separate meeting with Foreign Minister Mutawakil on these points was equally fruitless, which was understandable given that the same subject was being discussed at a higher level with the Taliban leader in the next building.

Repeatedly and at critical junctures since the 1980s, Pakistanis had failed to influence their Afghan interlocutors. Pakistanis are capable of taking tough positions and showing stubbornness and rigidity, but they do not practice hard diplomacy. In dealing with the Mujahedin and then the Taliban, the Pakistanis' empathy with their clients made them more willing to get converted to their clients' point of view than the other way round. Intellectually weak, the midlevel officials, especially those from the ISI, were often impressed and overawed by the certitude of conviction and faith the Taliban demonstrated.[61] Earlier, they had shown similar deference to the

59. Pakistanis are generally impressed by religious personalities from Central Asia and the Arab lands. This is almost ingrained in their psyche, partly because much of the Islamic inspiration and tradition in Pakistan derived from revered personalities from these regions.

60. Shuja Nawaz, *Cross Swords: Pakistan, Its Army and the War Within* (Karachi, Oxford University Press 2008), 542–43.

61. To illustrate the point, the author would recall his conversation in late 1988 with Brig. Muhammad Anwer of the ISI (*nom de guerre* Colonel Badshah), a key liaison person with the Tanzeemat and Mujahedin commanders. I had sought a meeting with him before I proceeded on a sabbatical to Georgetown University to write about the Geneva

Mujahedin leaders who often rejected calls for accommodation and pragmatism, not because of their convictions but because such suggestions did not suit their individual interests.

In a last-ditch effort towards the end of September 2001, the ISI put together a delegation of Ulema drawn from the madrassas where many Taliban leaders were known to have received their education, including Mufti Nizamuddin Shamzai of the Binori Mosque and Maulana Sami ul Haq of the Akora Khattak Darul Uloom Haqqania. The delegation spent a day with Mullah Omar. According to some perhaps cynical reports, the meetings ended up in expressions of solidarity with the Taliban leader's point of view. In the local tradition, the Taliban did make an attempt to get over the Osama issue. Afghan clerics issued an edict requesting Osama to leave the country. This was a nonstarter, first, because Osama had nowhere to go. Secondly, the United States demanded nothing short of the surrender of Osama. Given the rigidity of the Taliban mind-set, this was not possible; the Taliban ambassador in Islamabad rejected the notion that the clerics' decree could lead to the handing over of Osama.[62] The Taliban deputy prime minister Haji Abdul Kabir reportedly made an offer to hand over Osama to a third country after the U.S. military action had begun, provided the Americans stopped bombing and gave evidence.[63] The United States rejected the overture, saying the surrender of Osama was nonnegotiable.

Though pessimistic about the efficacy of further efforts, the Pakistani Foreign Office pressed the U.S. side to provide material evidence against Al Qaeda and Osama to help the Pakistan side at least meet the justifiable Taliban demand for evidence. Pakistani officials argued that the Security Council had demanded extradition of Osama to a country such as Saudi Arabia where he could be tried under a mandatory resolution, but this argument did not cut much ice, as the Taliban viewed the United Nations as a biased

---

negotiating process. In response to my observation that the Mujahedin leaders needed to be persuaded to participate in dialogue and a government of reconciliation, Anwer simply narrated a story that he said was told to him by an Afghan Mujahid fighter. The Afghan fighter was on a ridge overlooking a mountain road when a large Soviet convoy of military vehicles appeared. He had only one shoulder-carried rocket launcher and knew that he could only damage one vehicle and that he would in turn meet a sure death. He fired the shot and it hit one vehicle carrying some explosive material that destroyed the entire convoy. The Afghan Jihad, Anwer added, was not guided by human plans but by the power of faith.

62. *NYT,* September 21, 2001.
63. *Guardian* (London), October 14, 2001.

organization. The U.S. embassy in Islamabad finally handed over, on a confidential basis, a twenty-plus-page document that appeared to be part of the evidence submitted to secure an indictment by a New York court to pursue Osama. It did not contain any material directly relating to 9/11, but it detailed connections among alleged Al Qaeda operatives involved in the bombings of the U.S. embassies in Kenya and Tanzania and the attack on USS *Cole*. Receiving the document enabled the Foreign Office to make a statement that the material could justify an indictment in a court of law against Al Qaeda and its chief, Osama bin Laden. For the Taliban, the statement and the evidence provided carried little value, and they showed it the same indifference that they had maintained towards the UN Security Council resolutions.

Apart from the Pakistani efforts, there was no international diplomacy pressing the Taliban to hand over Osama that resembled diplomatic efforts prior to the first Gulf War to persuade Saddam Hussein to vacate Kuwait. The Taliban were set in their isolation and stoical absolutism and determined to face the might of the sole superpower. They once again drew upon their madrassa-trained youth, including thousands of young men from Pakistan, most of whom perished in Afghanistan as a result of the U.S. military action or the revenge of the local population especially in northern Afghanistan. A few thousand were led by an old cleric, Sufi Muhammad, from Swat in Pakistan, who had launched a movement, Tehrik Nifaz e Shariat e Muhammadi, that had been pushing since the early 1990s for enforcement of Sharia in the district. He escaped but did not return to Swat, reportedly out of fear for his life. He resurfaced five years later to lead a virtual revolt, which will be discussed later in the book.

Predictably, the U.S. military action, described as Operation Enduring Freedom, began on October 7, 2001, within four weeks of the 9/11 atrocities. The United States was riding a sympathy wave; in less than one month, it had put together an impressive coalition. The United States did not need to go to the Security Council, as chapter VII resolutions on the Taliban and Osama seemingly provided the international legal framework for military action against the Taliban. The U.S. military tactics were simple: pulverize the Taliban through aerial bombardment and encourage and build a coalition against them inside Afghanistan before U.S. forces set foot on the ground. The Taliban had thought they would take on the Americans in a land combat. Some pro-Taliban elements in Pakistan with military background had predicted that a disaster, similar to the one suffered by the Soviets at the hands of the Mujahedin, awaited the American forces in Afghanistan.

Within a few weeks, however, the Taliban forces began to crumble under the impact of heavy bombardment in the north. Meanwhile, Northern Alliance troops and Uzbek forces under the command of Rashid Dostum, who had returned to Mazar e Sharif, started regrouping in anticipation of the collapse of the Taliban.

In retreat, the Taliban faced disaster and atrocities worse than those they had suffered in 1997. This time the American forces had joined the ethnic opposition forces to pursue and target the Taliban. In late November 2001, at Qala e Jungi near Mazar, several hundred Taliban prisoners were mowed down with aerial bombardment when a few of the U.S. soldiers holding them were attacked. Similarly, when a large number of Taliban surrendered in Qundus, hundreds were stuffed in containers to be shifted to Shibergan, and scores if not hundreds died of suffocation and were buried in mass graves. These massacres deeply scarred Pushtun sentiments and generated sympathy for the Taliban in southern Afghanistan and the Pushtun belt of Pakistan.

It was generally expected by analysts in Pakistan that the Taliban would put up a fight in Kabul, where it would be impossible for the allied forces to bomb without causing massive collateral damage. However, as forces of the Northern Alliance (renamed United Front) closed in on Kabul under the command of General Muhammad Fahim, a Panjshiri Tajik and longtime lieutenant of his slain leader, Ahmed Shah Massoud, whom he had now replaced, the Taliban defensive lines north of the capital collapsed under severe B-52 bombardment. Overnight, the Taliban decided to withdraw without putting up any fight and without even informing the Pakistani and other elements fighting alongside them. In the morning, there was a power vacuum in the city, with these remaining elements trapped and massacred by the local population. It appeared that the Taliban had already gauged the local population's alienation as a result of their harsh rule. The Taliban retreat came as a great relief to the allied forces. On November 12, Kabul fell to the advancing forces of the United Front. Its foreign minister, Abdullah Abdullah, announced control of the city.

As the focus of the U.S. military effort shifted to the south, Osama and large numbers of Al Qaeda men moved towards the Tora Bora mountains east of the border at Parachinar, the closest point in Pakistan's tribal belt to Kabul and Jalalabad and often referred to as "the jutting parrot's beak." In late November and early December 2001, the cave and tunnel structures in the Tora Bora mountains, which were once effectively used by the Afghan Mujahedin in their fight against the Soviets, came under heavy U.S. shelling.

But Osama and his men had taken advantage of the absence of any U.S. strategy to interdict their movement toward the Tora Bora region, from where it was virtually impossible to seal mountain paths and routes leading into the ungoverned tribal areas of Pakistan. With no coordination with the Pakistani side, the indiscriminate U.S. bombing of the mountains and increase in the bounty on Osama to $25 million did not prevent his escape into the bordering regions of Pakistan and Afghanistan.[64]

The United States had enlisted support of a local commander, Hazrat Ali, who later became the head of the eastern Shura set up by the interim arrangement under Hamid Karzai. But such measures yielded no result. In late 2002, Senator John Kerry blamed President Bush for "outsourcing" the capture of Osama to Afghan warlords and "taking his eye off the ball."[65] Several thousand Al Qaeda and other foreign militants were able to escape into the tribal areas of Pakistan.[66] Assuming that Osama was the primary target of the U.S. military campaign, Senator Kerry's criticism was valid.

There is little evidence of coordination between the Pakistani military and the American action in southern Afghanistan, in particular the Tora Bora bombardment in late December 2001, intended to interdict Al Qaeda and the remnants of the Afghan Taliban fighters who started heading for the bordering regions of Pakistan. Pakistani army and paramilitary forces (mainly the Frontier Corps) had a thin presence in the area.

An unrelated incident also diverted the Pakistani army's attention to the country's eastern borders at a time when it should have heightened its watch on the northwestern border. A terrorist attack on the Indian Parliament on December 13, 2001, and Indian accusations of Pakistani complicity led to an escalation of tension between the two countries. India mobilized over one million troops against Pakistan in the course of 2002, with a similar response by the Pakistani military. U.S. and European diplomacy failed to act expeditiously and only moved at a much later stage when the threat of conflict appeared real. Clearly, the need for the Pakistani army to attend to the northwestern border was overlooked, allowing the Taliban and Al Qaeda relative

64. Osama is believed to be hiding in the bordering regions of Afghanistan and Pakistan inhabited by Pushtun tribes. The bounty did not produce information about his location. Bush, in a September 2005 meeting with Musharraf, wondered "whether these tribal people had any idea how much money $25 million was." (Publisher's note: Osama was killed in May 2011 by a U.S. military operation in Abbottabad where he had lived for five years.)

65. *NYT,* October 19, 2002.

66. *NYT,* December 17, 2001, reported that more than 2000 Al Qaeda fighters were trying to flee from Tora Bora.

ease in fleeing into the tribal areas of Pakistan. Most probably, the army deployment would not have thwarted the escape of the Taliban fighters, who easily mixed with the Afghan refugees; but the foreign elements such as Uzbeks and Chechens who had become Al Qaeda's coercive arm could have been checked and kept away from the tribal populations. Notwithstanding the outcome, the point regarding lack of coordination remains valid.

Qandahar, the Taliban's last stronghold, fell to the coalition on 11 December 2001 when Hamid Karzai, who had been appointed as head of the provisional arrangement signed at Bonn on December 5, brokered a deal with former Mujahedin commanders Mullah Naquib and Mullah Haji Bashar that forced the Taliban to abandon the city. The deals in Qandahar and Jalalabad that brought back the old commanders and leaders the Taliban had ousted and the return of the Northern Alliance commanders were ominous signs of the revival of the pre-Taliban warlords days. Within two months of the start of the U.S. offensive, the era of the Taliban, who had risen in Qandahar seven years prior and had come to control 90 percent of Afghanistan, had abruptly ended. But the ouster of the Taliban with relative ease and the dazzling military success of the U.S. forces did not bring peace and an end to violence or a democratic dispensation for Afghanistan. Instead, the country remained in turmoil, and the threat of the Taliban and Al Qaeda, which appeared to have dissipated, began to reemerge as the Bush administration set its eyes on Iraq.

Some analysts are of the view that if the international community had engaged the Taliban, Al Qaeda could not have had free rein in Afghanistan and 9/11 would have been avoided.[67] Related questions include: Was it possible to change the Taliban through engagement? Was there any possibility that the Taliban would have handed over Osama? And was there a chance to avert 9/11? These are now academic questions, and any examination would be influenced by the advantage of hindsight and would overlook the circumstances, attitudes, and preoccupation of the principal actors prior to September 2001.

Nonetheless, they deserve a serious look. Before proceeding with any analysis, it is worth repeating the point already made in this study, namely,

---

67. Musharraf, *In the Line of Fire,* 215, makes the point in the context of the Bamiyan Buddhas and the absence of any international leverage on the Taliban; Murshed argues in *Afghanistan: The Taliban years,* 304–5, that "the stabilization of Afghanistan could have been achieved much earlier had the international community engaged with and not isolated the Taliban . . . (and) the tragedy of 9/11 might not have happened."

that a bigger mistake was the abandonment of Afghanistan following the Soviet withdrawal. A focused and intensive international engagement in the post Soviet withdrawal phase might possibly have moved Afghanistan towards normalcy.

The Taliban, mostly the sons of illiterate farmers, had been raised and schooled in the most severe environment of a relentless war, stark refugee camps, and austere madrassas. In their outlook and orientation, they were more difficult to deal with and far more intransigent in their attitudes compared to their forerunners, the Mujahedin leaders.[68] Nonetheless, the Taliban leadership nursed a deep grievance over nonrecognition after they had assumed control of Kabul and large parts of Afghanistan, and recognition and interaction by the international community would have affected their behavior. Though the Taliban were unlikely to yield to U.S. demands on the issue of Osama bin Laden, an international presence and recognition might have made them more sensitive to international concerns and perhaps led them to constrict the activities of Al Qaeda.

The Saudis had the best chance of negotiating extradition of the Al Qaeda chief. The Saudis and the Taliban leaders shared tribal, religious affinities that the Saudis could have leveraged. Ironically, disregard for tribal traditions vitiated the Saudi effort in 1997 when Prince Turki, showing lack of sensitivity, accused Mullah Omar of lying. Subsequently, the Saudi government simply withdrew and shunned the Taliban, leaving the Americans and Pakistanis to deal with the problem. During the brief period between 9/11 and the American military action, they stayed away from Pakistani attempts to persuade the Taliban leadership to hand over Osama.

It is difficult to say whether Saudi custody of Osama before 9/11 would have averted the event. Osama never directly or unambiguously claimed responsibility for the 9/11 attacks. The closest he came to an admission was in a videotape released to Al Jazeera on October 29, 2004. Osama remarked that while watching the destruction inflicted by the Israeli invasion on Lebanon in 1982 he thought that, like the destruction of towers in Lebanon, "towers in America" should be destroyed. Subsequent inquiries revealed that Khalid Sheikh Muhammad was the mastermind of the 9/11 attacks. In any event, the nineteen hijackers involved with the attack lived and received

---

68. Matinuddin, *The Taliban Phenomenon*, 28, mentions that the madrassa training insisted on a strict religious code that did not permit any accommodation with those having a different religious persuasion. The same intransigence was reflected in the Taliban behavior in political matters.

training outside Afghanistan. It is thus doubtful that extradition of Osama to Saudi Arabia or the United States would necessarily have prevented 9/11. Also, such a development alone was unlikely to have neutralized Al Qaeda, which had other firebrand leaders, in particular Ayman Al Zawahiri and Khalid Sheikh Muhammad, and had built a following with ideological inspiration rather than structural discipline.

Over a decade of international isolation, internal fragmentation, and conflict had allowed Al Qaeda to grow and plan in Afghanistan. Modern technology and the use of cyberspace enabled Al Qaeda to develop its outward reach even while embedded in the war-ravaged and medieval environment of Afghanistan. Clearly, in today's globalized world, conflict situations can become infectious breeding grounds for new dangers; these can be remedied not through insulation but through anticipation, engagement, and constructive involvement by the international community.

3

Post–9/11 Afghanistan

On the day the Taliban withdrew from Kabul, efforts were set afoot to put together a political arrangement to fill the vacuum left by the Taliban. The moribund Six-plus-Two group at the United Nations revived to call for the establishment of a broad-based government and reiterated its commitment to the preservation of Afghan independence and territorial integrity. More important, the Security Council adopted a resolution on November 14, 2001, endorsing efforts of the "Afghan people" for a multiethnic, broad-based, and representative government committed to respecting human rights and to peace with Afghanistan's neighbors.[1] In reality, the United States was calling the shots both militarily and politically. The United States had an ally on the ground in the shape of the Northern Alliance, whose forces now controlled Kabul, but the Americans also understood that replacing the Taliban with the pre-Taliban arrangement that had existed in Kabul under Burhanuddin Rabbani would not help. A Pushtun front and adequate representation, with a modicum of credibility, were the minimum requirements.

The Americans tried to build up two personalities for leadership. First, they encouraged commander Abdul Haq, a flamboyant personality from an influential family in Jalalabad who had lost one foot in operations against the Soviets.[2] With U.S. encouragement, he went into Afghanistan in late October in what proved to be an ill-conceived move, with insufficient caution and without assurances from local elements, and while U.S. military

1. UN Security Council document S/RES/1378/2001.
2. Abdul Haq was the brother of Haji Abdul Qadeer, one of three vice presidents assassinated in July 2002, and Deen Muhammad, a former governor of Nangahar Province and former deputy prime minister appointed under the Peshawar Accord in April 1992.

operations were still focused in the north. Abdul Haq fell into a Taliban trap and his mentors, the U.S. military, could not rescue him from swift execution on October 26, 2001.

Hamid Karzai, a Popalzai Pushtun from a prominent Qandahar family, who had worked with Professor Mojaddedi while living in Quetta, was the other personality the Americans encouraged. Karzai had even supported the Taliban in their early years but had turned against them, suspecting their complicity in the murder of his father, Ahad Karzai, who was a strong supporter of the former king, Zahir Shah. In late October 2001, Hamid Karzai entered Afghanistan closer to Qandahar and reportedly became a target of accidental friendly fire in Uruzgan region; but he was rescued in time to play the most prominent role in the post-Taliban Afghanistan.

For Pakistan, the developments in the wake of the U.S. military action in Afghanistan had no silver lining. Its policy of support to the Taliban was in shambles; its nemesis, the Northern Alliance, was back in Kabul; and Al Qaeda and Taliban remnants were descending into the tribal areas where traditional governance had long collapsed, largely as a result of the Afghan Jihad. The Pakistan government had made an effort to convince the Americans to take Pushtun interests into account and prevent entry of Northern Alliance troops into Kabul. In early October, Pervez Musharraf called on the United States not to allow its intervention to give way to a "government unfriendly to Pakistan" and said that he supported a government under Zahir Shah. Later, he even threatened to withdraw permission for overflights and other promised facilities if the U.S. bombing enabled the Northern Alliance to take over Kabul, claiming that he had an understanding with the United States that the Northern Alliance would not be allowed to "draw mileage" from American action.[3] He suggested inclusion of some moderate Taliban leaders in a new political dispensation, only to have his suggestion dismissed the next day by the Northern Alliance leader Abdullah Abdullah.[4] In late October, Muttawakil traveled to Islamabad to suggest cessation of U.S. military action to enable the Taliban leaders to persuade

---

3. *NYT,* September 26, 2001, reported that Abdul Sattar had indicated that Pakistan would oppose any plan to link the American-led military thrust in Afghanistan with moves for a new government to replace the Taliban. *NYT,* October 9, 2001, reported that Musharraf had called upon the United States to make the air strikes brief and warned against pressing for change so fast that the Taliban could give way to a new government unfriendly to Pakistan. He indicated that Pakistan would accept Zahir Shah.

4. *NYT,* October 17, 2001.

Mullah Omar to hand over Osama. However, the die was cast. The Americans were in a hurry to remove the Taliban and effect a political change.

Pakistan had lost its voice on Afghan matters on the international stage. Pakistani Foreign Minister Abdul Sattar had accompanied President Musharraf to New York and was expected to attend the Six-plus-Two meeting at the UN building on November 12. Because of a bomb scare, he was unable to leave his hotel for several hours, and the meeting proceeded and adopted a communiqué without the Pakistani foreign minister. Lakhdar Brahimi later briefed him on the outcome, which primarily endorsed Brahimi's efforts for putting together an interim arrangement in Kabul. One day earlier, Musharraf had tried to make a case for associating acceptable Taliban elements with the new interim arrangement in Kabul and cautioned President Bush against the overweening military presence of the Northern Alliance in Kabul, which was bound to ruffle Pushtun sentiment. Briefing the press following the meeting, Musharraf stated that Pakistan and the United States had identical views on a post-Taliban setup in Kabul and that, while the Northern Alliance troops would be encouraged to move south, the United States would not want the Alliance troops to "enter" Kabul.[5] Days later, the Northern Alliance troops were pouring into Kabul. Foreign Minister Abdul Sattar later accused the Alliance of violating its understanding with the United States; but closer to truth was that Pakistan and the United States were not on the same wavelength.

Meanwhile, religious political parties in Pakistan staged large protest rallies against the American action in Afghanistan. But these were overtaken by the breathtaking pace of developments in Afghanistan and the Taliban's precipitous exit from Kabul. As the protests fizzled out, Pervez Musharraf consolidated his position by effecting changes within the army top brass, replacing the ISI chief, Lt. General Mahmud Ahmed, and the chief of general staff, Lt. Gen. Muhammad Aziz Khan. Both had been his allies in the 1999 military coup but were well known for their religious fervor and their sympathies with the Taliban.

One of the immediate U.S. worries in the aftermath of the fall of Kabul was the eight Americans from Christian Aid, an NGO, whom the Taliban had captured in early August 2001.[6] Once their release had been secured, the United States pushed Pakistan to close down the Taliban embassy and

5. *Dawn,* November 12, 2001.
6. *NYT,* August 7, 2001.

consulates in Pakistan, even though Pakistan was committed to doing so once a new arrangement was in place in Kabul. The regular briefings to the large media present in Islamabad by the Taliban ambassador, Mullah Abdus Salam Zaeef, who displayed a good sense of humor, irritated U.S. officials in Islamabad. At U.S. insistence, Zaeef was forced to leave Islamabad. He was later captured by the Americans and kept at the Americans' Guantánamo Bay facility until his release in 2007.

The Bonn Process

On December 5, 2001, the landmark Bonn Agreement was signed by a group of twenty-two notable Afghans, who represented supporters of the former king (the Rome Delegation), moderate Peshawar-based Mujahedin factions (the Peshawar Group), the Northern Alliance, and prominent Afghan émigrés, including those based in Iran (the Cyprus Group). They had been invited by Lakhdar Brahimi, who had finally found an opportunity to contribute meaningfully to the Afghan political process, thanks to the U.S. intervention. Among the prominent invited Afghans credited with drafting the Bonn Agreement, many were the same as those considered over the years for an interim setup on the sidelines of the Geneva negotiations and as late as early 1992, when the Najibullah regime collapsed. They included Abdul Sattar Sirat, Hedayat Amin Arsala, Houmayon Jareer, Dr. Azizullah Ludin, Professor Muhammad Ishaq Nadiri, Dr. Muhammad Jalil Shams, Dr. Zalmai Rassoul, and General Abdul Rahim Wardak. Conspicuously absent were the Taliban and representatives of the hard-line Mujahedin groups.

The top-ranking Afghan Mujahedin leaders like Mojaddedi and Burhanuddin Rabbani also remained behind the scenes to keep the Bonn group less controversial. Having been the nominal president since mid-1992, Rabbani was particularly unhappy about his exclusion.[7] For its part, Pakistan had no option but to acquiesce in the Bonn decisions; Musharraf formally extended congratulations to Hamid Karzai when he was appointed head of the interim arrangement envisaged under the Bonn agreement. Musharraf welcomed the agreement and the Bonn process, although Islamabad was deeply concerned over Pushtun underrepresentation and Northern Alliance dominance in the new political setup in Kabul.

7. *NYT,* December 6, 2001.

The Bonn Agreement, a blueprint for the political evolution of Afghanistan, established an interim administration, a special independent commission for the convening of a Loya Jirga in six months, to be opened by the former king, in keeping with Afghan tradition. The Loya Jirga was to appoint a Transitional Authority and a constitutional jirga to prepare the constitution and hold elections within two years. Hamid Karzai was nominated as chairman of the twenty-nine-member interim administration, which would be in charge of various ministerial portfolios. The Interior Ministry and the important Defense Ministry remained with General Muhammad Qasim Fahim, whose mainly Panjshiri and Tajik forces controlled Kabul as well as the defense and intelligence apparatus. The Afghan army chief of staff, Bismillah Khan Muhammadi, and intelligence chief Amarullah Saleh were Tajiks and Panjshiris. Fahim was also one of five vice chairmen of the interim administration. Later, Karzai expressed dissatisfaction with the choice of the transitional cabinet, saying that it was product of a "backroom" deal.[8]

The Bonn Agreement gave sweeping authority to the United Nations to guide the interim administration. It also called for the setting up of the UN-mandated International Security Assistance Force (ISAF) to help the interim authority carry the process forward. On December 7, 2001, the Security Council endorsed the Agreement. ISAF consisted mainly of U.S. and NATO troops, with some Australians.[9] This was the first NATO mission outside the European theater, a fact that generated some debate as to how the organization would reinvent itself for similar interventions outside Europe.

The Bonn Agreement set a new direction for a political resolution of the Afghan conflict. Notwithstanding Brahimi's consummate and experienced handling of the talks at Bonn, the Agreement was not the fruit of diplomacy but more a recognition of the changed realities on the ground brought about by the U.S. military intervention. In March 1997, in an interview with Rahimullah Yusufzai, a well-respected correspondent based in Peshawar, Mullah Omar averred that a military solution had better prospects of bringing about a settlement than diplomatic efforts.[10] He was prescient, but his error was the assumption that the Taliban could alter the military situation

8. *NYT,* June 24, 2002.

9. UN Security Council document S/RES/1386/2001.

10. Rashid, *Taliban,* 54, quotes Rahimullah Yusufzai writing in the (Islamabad) *News* of March 30, 1997.

in their favor. He had discounted the correlation of forces outside Afghanistan. Change in Afghanistan, as in the past, did result from the use of military might, but this time by the sole superpower of the day in response to the tragedy of 9/11. However, once again, the passage of a few years would demonstrate that outside military intervention alone cannot suffice to bring peace. That requires a broader engagement.

The Bonn process unfolded according to the prescribed timelines. In June 2002, the former king convened and inaugurated the Loya Jirga. Hamid Karzai was nominated to head the transition arrangement, with changes in the ministries bringing a few more Pushtun faces and the positions of vice president going to two prominent political personalities, Ahmed Zia Massoud, brother of Ahmed Shah Massoud, and Karim Khalili, leader of the Shia Hizb e Wahdat. On January 4, 2004, a new constitution was adopted; and in October, elections for the president were held as scheduled, with Karzai sweeping 21 of the 34 provinces. The constitution provided for a lower house, Wolesi Jirga, and an upper house, Meshrano Jirga. The election of 249 members of the Wolesi Jirga, distributed among the provinces on the basis of population, were held in September 2005, thus broadly completing the Bonn process for reconstructing a new governmental structure for Afghanistan. Yunus Qanooni was elected as the speaker of the lower house, while Mojaddedi headed the Meshrano Jirga. The new cabinet, though with a large infusion of technocrats, was ethnically more balanced than its precursors. The important Defense Ministry portfolio was given to Abdul Rahim Wardak,[11] an ethnic Pushtun and former commander from the moderate pro-monarchy party of Sayed Ahmed Gailani.

The 2004 elections, by any measure, had been successful; despite the Taliban threats, the turnout was respectable. There were a number of candidates, including Qanooni and Rashid Dostum, who carried majorities in their areas, as should have been expected. Karzai displayed a democratic temperament while he headed the interim arrangement and did not resort to the familiar manipulation in the region to stay in power. And the elections were held on schedule. The heavy presence of the international force and UN over-

---

11. The Afghan army remained under the charge of Bismillah Khan, a Tajik from Panjshir, who is known to be dismissive of Abdul Rahim Wardak, a respected Pushtun but with weak credentials regarding his contribution in fighting the Soviets during the 1980s. He belonged to the party of Pir Sayed Ahmed Gailani, whose associates were often derided by other Tanzeemat as "Gucci Mujahids."

sight ensured the process. Still, some credit must go to Karzai for providing a leadership of moderation and sensitivity, more so than any of his peers among the Mujahedin leaders. This fact needs to be acknowledged, even if, cynically, one were to concede that Karzai lacked the option of manipulation, since in 2004 he did not command the wherewithal to do so.

The UN oversight had imparted a degree of efficiency to the Bonn process; and the presence of the ISAF forces gave an assurance that in most parts the voting was held peacefully and in difficult areas problems remained contained. Pakistan closed the main crossing points as a check against any Afghan refugee activity disrupting the elections. But although the architecture of the government envisaged by the Bonn agreement was in place in Kabul, the country appeared to suffer from absence of governance. On the ground, Afghanistan remained fragmented and under the control of warlords, many of whom governed their respective provinces and exercised arbitrary local autonomy antithetical to political stabilization. Central control was tenuous. In south and southeast Afghanistan, large areas were troubled with gradual revival of the Taliban and their insurgent activity. The Taliban also operated from across the border in the tribal areas of Pakistan, where they enjoyed sympathy and support. The much-bruited economic support was slow and seemed to dissipate before making a difference on the ground because of corruption, the absence of governance, and UN and donor failure to devise an effective strategy.

Following the Bonn Agreement, had Afghanistan received sustained and focused world attention and an intensive economic and political engagement on the part of the agreement's sponsors, the country could have been on the path of political stabilization and economic recovery, which go hand in hand. But the United States was distracted by another fatal temptation that had preoccupied President George W. Bush even before he was confronted by the Al Qaeda assault. The Bush administration had its eyes set on Iraq and dislodging Saddam Hussein.[12]

12. In a discussion about the early days of the U.S. military action in Afghanistan, William B. Milam, former ambassador to Pakistan and senior scholar at the Woodrow Wilson International Center for Scholars, mentioned to the author that by early 2002 he had detected a certain disinterest in the Bush administration's attitude towards Afghanistan. This upset him to the extent that he sought an assignment abroad, even though he had been especially asked to join the South Asia Bureau in the U.S. State Department as an advisor soon after 9/11. Also see William Safire's op-ed in the *New York Times,* October 8, 2001, emphasizing that Baghdad was "the center of world terror" run by Sad-

Instability Persists as the United States Shifts Focus

Once the Bonn process was put on course and the first donors' conference, in Tokyo in January 2002, had committed over $3 billion for the reconstruction and rehabilitation of Afghanistan, the Western coalition, in particular the United States, became complacent. The violence in Afghanistan appeared to have been contained, Pakistan had cooperated in capturing and eliminating a large number of Al Qaeda members, and the threat appeared to be receding. By late 2002 and early 2003, it was not Afghanistan but Iraq that became the focus of the Bush administration's attention.[13] Unlike the Afghanistan intervention, which had broad international acceptance, the Iraqi intervention proved controversial. It provoked adverse reaction and spawned resentment in the Islamic world. Almost every neighbor of Iraq opposed the military intervention. The charge that Iraq possessed or was acquiring weapons of mass destruction (WMDs) lacked credibility. While the International Atomic Energy Agency (IAEA) was able to verify in March 2003 that it had found "no evidence or plausible indication of the revival of a nuclear weapons program in Iraq," Hans Blix, the head of the UN Monitoring and Verification Commission (UNMOVIC), had not finished the mandated investigation and needed more time to reach a conclusive determination. The war was widely seen as a U.S. attempt to control Iraqi oil and neutralize a country that could threaten the security of Israel.[14]

---

dam Hussein. *NYT,* December 1, 2001, reported that President Bush "intended to use the momentum (achieved in Afghanistan) to force Iraq to open its borders to United Nations inspectors looking for weapons of mass destruction."

13. An anecdote worth recalling is a discussion in May 2002 among Pakistan's former Foreign Minister Agha Shahi, prominent Indian political analyst A.G. Noorani, and Foreign Office colleagues of the author. Except for Agha Shahi, no one saw the inevitability of the U.S. attack on Iraq. Shahi cited the new administration's psychological impulses and Israeli obsession with security as the motivating factors. Bush had shown an evangelical streak, reflected in his January 2002 State of the Union address when he labeled Iraq, Iran, and North Korea "the axis of evil." There were reports of strong division within his cabinet and of his own initial reluctance; yet, quite apart from the pressure of neoconservatives, the mind-set of conviction prevailed over prudence.

14. In the author's view, which he stated at a UN conference on WMDs convened at Jeju Island in the Republic of Korea in late 2002, chemical and biological weapons cannot be compared to nuclear weapons in lethal or strategic impact or characteristics. Chemical weapons (or for that matter biological weapons) do not have a decisive impact on wars, as shown by the Iran-Iraq War of the 1980s. Furthermore, nuclear weapons programs are detectable, and it is possible to verify if a country is or is not pursuing a

Political stabilization of Afghanistan required an effective government and more than commitments to reconstruction. The promised assistance was far short of meeting the challenge of rebuilding Afghanistan's economy, shattered by more than two decades of warfare. The Bonn process, while important in itself, had merely introduced a gloss of stability. The Taliban, the main adversary, were still licking their wounds; they had received a devastating blow, but they were not destroyed. Their top leadership, in particular Mullah Omar, Mullah Dadullah, Mullah Mansur, Jallaluddin Haqqani, and his son Sirajuddin Haqqani, was largely intact and only needed time to revive and become active again. Al Qaeda had suffered more severely, with a large number of its top leaders captured or killed. However, the fountainhead of inspiration, Osama bin Laden, and his deputy and chief strategist, Ayman Al Zawahiri, had survived. Following the invasion of Iraq, Al Qaeda had found a new cause and a powerful argument with which to gain new recruits to its ranks. Indeed, the Iraqi invasion spawned widespread popular anger in the Muslim world, which infused a second life into Al Qaeda.

The political process envisaged under the Bonn Agreement required the government to be transitional until 2004. This limited its ability to consolidate control. Meanwhile, the old warlords who accepted the Karzai government, in particular Rashid Dostum, Ismael Khan, Fahim, and Abdur Rab Rassool Sayyaf, were more interested in consolidating their position in their respective areas than in strengthening the central government and democratic institutions as the Bonn process intended. Powerful governors in various regions and the Wahdat leaders in central Afghanistan reasserted their control and literally pushed the country into the pre-Taliban fragmented anarchy. This time, however, the leaders of the north were more discreet and less capricious in their rule, though they did keep the center's authority at bay.

Clearly, the political dispensation brought about by the Bonn process failed to pacify the south and southeast of the country or to overcome the simmering Taliban insurgency. The fault did not lie entirely with the Karzai government, as the seeds of failure preceded its inception. The United Nations Security Council committee established to implement UN Security

---

nuclear option. In contrast, short of physical occupation, such deniability is almost impossible to verify if a country is accused of possessing or developing chemical or biological weapons. Hans Blix was, therefore, assigned an impossible task. It was only the occupation of Iraq and months of thorough scouring by the allied forces that finally determined that Iraq did not possess chemical or biological weapons.

Council resolutions 1267 and 1333, which imposed sanctions against the Taliban, lumped the Taliban leaders together with Al Qaeda on its list of terrorists, which in addition to freezing assets proscribed any contacts with those on the list. This was a serious mistake. Al Qaeda, which was alien to Afghanistan, flourished in the hospitable and conducive environment of the Taliban rule, while its agenda focused on issues beyond Afghanistan.

The Taliban, in contrast, were an integral part of the Afghan society and had ruled large parts of Afghanistan with a certain grassroots legitimacy and support. Their rule may have offended the sensibilities of the urbanized Afghans and ethnic non-Pushtuns; but it did not appear repressive to a considerable segment of the rural, economically depressed, and illiterate Pushtun population of the south and southeast, which had found relief from the insecurity and ravages wrought by the fighting warlords. By designating the Taliban as terrorists, the United Nations had barred the Karzai government from reaching out to them. The government was thus inherently handicapped in pursuing a meaningful reconciliation within the country, because the Taliban were beyond the pale and could not be involved in the effort. An opportunity was lost to isolate the hard-line Taliban leadership and break Taliban cohesion by reaching out to leaders like Wakil Ahmed Muttawakil, who was jailed and released in 2003, and Abdus Salam Zaeef, who had sought asylum in Pakistan but ended up languishing for years in Guantánamo Bay.[15]

Pakistani officials felt that Jallaluddin Haqqani, the strongman of Khost, could be persuaded to be supportive of the new administration in Kabul if the United States were to make him an overture. Nonetheless, any accommodation with the Taliban or pro-Taliban leaders was ruled out by the occupation authorities, as was clear from the treatment meted out to Muttawakil and Zaeef. Unfortunately, U.S. and UN officials' lack of political savvy was exacerbated by the hostility of the Northern Alliance leaders towards their erstwhile nemesis. By definition, efforts for reconciliation

---

15. Fotini Christia and Michael Semple, "Flipping the Taliban," *Foreign Affairs* (July/August 2009), make a strong argument for reaching out to those Taliban leaders who may be reconcilable and point to the mistake of proscribing all Taliban, made in the wake of the U.S. intervention in 2001. They add the names of Abdul Haq Wasiq, the Taliban deputy minister of intelligence, Rahmatullah Sangaryar, a commander from Uruzgan, and Sahib Rohullah Wakil, leader of the Salafi movement in eastern Afghanistan, as persons inclined to join the new political dispensation. *NYT,* January 27, 2002, reported that Hekmatullah Hekmati, the Taliban intelligence chief in Herat, joined Ismael Khan in denouncing the Taliban leaders as "power-hungry opportunists."

should have been targeted at the Taliban. The taboo against contact was first broken, in 2007, by British units who struck a cease-fire deal with the Taliban in Helmand Province. That was six years after the Taliban had been designated as terrorists. Much time had been lost. The possibility of a Taliban response to a reconciliation gesture would have been far more viable immediately after the American intervention, when they were militarily in dire straits, than later when they were seen to be resurgent.

Slowly, the Taliban and other insurgent elements opposed to Kabul started regrouping and launching military activity. The armed opposition to the Kabul government and the coalition was identified as three distinct segments. The Taliban affiliated with Mullah Omar and his associates became active in southwestern Afghanistan, in particular Qandahar, Helmand, and Uruzgan provinces. The Haqqani group operated in the Paktika and Paktia region, the traditional stronghold of Jallaluddin Haqqani. Gulbadin and his militants resumed armed attacks in the Kunar area. Insurgent activity in these three areas developed quite independently of each other.

Kabul under the new dispensation appeared only nominally in the hands of President Karzai. While the United Nations and the coalition, in particular the United States, played a dominant role, calling the shots to ensure that the Bonn process remained on course, the Afghan National Army (ANA) and the security apparatus were visibly Tajik and non-Pushtun, thus provoking old prejudices. Until 2004, the funds allocated to build the ANA went to General Fahim or some of the warlords. The most prominent face in Kabul was that of Ahmed Shah Massoud, the fallen hero of the Northern Alliance and the lion of Panjshir. His ubiquitous presence was close to a personality cult that could not have sat well with the Pushtuns, most of whom treated Massoud like one among many prominent Mujahedin commanders, and one who had even made compromises with the Soviets.

The brutal Afghan conflict had seen massacres along ethnic lines, and the mutual bitterness had not subsided. Following the American intervention, the Pushtun population in the north, in particular in Qundus and Takhar, suffered attacks aimed at ethnic cleansing.[16] Many had trekked south, even over to Pakistan, with stories of excesses that circulated in Peshawar and evoked local sympathy with these uprooted people and anger over the turn of events in Afghanistan. The Pushtun intellectuals in Peshawar would often speak passionately about the predicament of the Pushtuns in Afghanistan and were dismissive of Karzai as an American puppet. The United Na-

16. *NYT,* March 7, 2002.

tions officials actively promoting reconciliation were mostly technocrats and lacked the political sensitivity needed to address the problem; along with representatives of the foreign NGOs, they also nursed a deep antipathy toward the Taliban.

Lakhdar Brahimi, the author of the Bonn process and the UN secretary-general's special representative, had virtually withdrawn, having resigned in 2002 after setting the Bonn process in motion. The UN was now represented by the United Nations Assistance Mission in Afghanistan (UNAMA), established in late March 2002 by a UN Security Council resolution with a mandate to support the Bonn process, to provide political and strategic advice for the implementation of the process, to help formulate a development strategy and a drug-control strategy, and to promote human rights and recovery and reconstruction efforts. Since its inception, UNAMA has been successively headed by four special representatives of the UN secretary-general: Lakhdar Brahimi, who remained in the post in New York until the appointment of his successor, Jean Arnault in January 2004, followed by Tom Koenigs from March 2006 to December 2007, who was succeeded by Kai Eide. UNAMA's deputy also headed the UN Development Program (UNDP) in the country.

The new administration installed in Kabul by the Bonn process did not produce effective governance, nor did it serve as a catalyst for reconciliation. The Karzai government, especially in its transitional phase, included a heavy contingent of prominent Afghan émigrés who were competent, reform-minded individuals. However, their influence and linkages were limited within the country, which had radically changed because of the protracted conflict. The government's outreach to the provinces remained correspondingly tentative; security concerns constrained the ministers in their travel outside Kabul, curtailing the effectiveness of programs, especially in the country's troubled regions. Some high-profile ministers remained mostly preoccupied with their regional concerns, narrow interests, and political maneuvering—for example, Interior Minister Muhammad Yunus Qanooni, Muhammad Mohaqeq and then Karim Khalili, who successively took charge of planning, Ismael Khan, who became minister for water and energy, and other Afghan leaders restored by the ouster of the Taliban. In March–April 2004, heightened tensions reminiscent of the Mujahedin interregnum reportedly stemmed from infighting in Herat over the murder of Ismael Khan's son[17] and then in Faryab, where Dostum resisted Karzai's

17. *NYT,* March 23, 2004.

appointment of a governor.[18] These situations remained contained largely because of the presence of coalition forces in the country.

Absence of a security apparatus to convey the central government's authority remained the most debilitating aspect of governmental functioning. The first priority had been the reconstitution of the Afghan National Army. During the transitional period the task of rebuilding the ANA and the police was in the hands of General Fahim, who favored recruitment from among the Tajiks and other elements from the north. Nearly 70,000 troops raised in the first four years were mostly non-Pushtuns. The resultant ethnic imbalance in the security apparatus hurt the new government. Furthermore, Tajik and other non-Pushtun troops could hardly be expected to operate or ensure government authority in the Pushtun-dominated south and southeast of the country. There were rumors that parts of the ANA and police were raised only nominally, on paper, to collect funds.

The Karzai government started taking corrective measures after the elections, but by then the increasingly active Taliban had succeeded in promoting the view that they stood for the protection of Pushtun rights, a nationalist twist to their insurgency. In the Pushtun regions, the Taliban also adopted the terror tactics of Al Qaeda, resorting to suicide bombings and brutal killings to terrorize the population and thereby prevent it from cooperating with the government or the foreign military forces. Local recruitment centers for the police and the army were special targets, thus impeding the rebuilding of the local police force to bring about stability. The ANA also suffered both from the lack of recruits in the Pushtun areas, especially southern and southeastern Afghanistan, and from the endemic desertions caused by fear of Taliban retaliation.

Moreover, the private militias maintained by warlords compounded the challenges the Taliban insurgency posed. Karzai admitted government inability to rein in private militias, which he described in 2004 as a greater danger than that posed by the Taliban.[19] An important program identified under the Bonn process was that of demilitarization, demobilization, and reintegration of private militias to transform their members into normal citizens. By early 2005, the government released figures claiming success in reintegrating over thirty thousand militia into the society, with similar numbers having surrendered their light and heavy arms. However, the veracity of such assertions, in the fluid situation prevailing in Afghanistan, remained

18. *NYT,* April 9, 2004.
19. *NYT,* July 12, 2004.

questionable. The issue presented a chicken-and-egg problem: if there was no police or security apparatus to protect people, they would be hard-pressed to disarm and would drift towards seeking safety in their clan or tribe or in the local strongman, who may have been an erstwhile Mujahedin commander or a local Taliban leader.

Traditionally, much of the Afghan population had rarely experienced regular central authority. The country therefore easily regressed into the pre-Taliban mode, and the government's control beyond the capital remained tenuous. The sporadic UN presence could not supplant a government functionary representing central authority. Administrative dysfunction became contagious and manifested itself in crime, corruption, drug trafficking, and absence of the rule of law. This did not imply that the Karzai government had been totally hapless against warlords and crime syndicates. It enjoyed the important support of the coalition forces, which arguably enabled Karzai to dislodge Ismael Khan prior to the elections in 2004 and, similarly, to successfully sideline Fahim when he tried to challenge Karzai in the elections. Karzai could make his weight felt in Kabul politics, but away from the capital, it was a different story.

The failures of the Karzai government and of UNAMA and thus the international community in redressing the conflict situation and the collapsed Afghan economy should not make us lose sight of some of the remarkable achievements of the Bonn process. After a lapse of three decades, there was now a government in Kabul that enjoyed international credibility and recognition. It had a structure, however weak, with a functioning parliament and administration. These institutions of governance are likely to survive the exit of the coalition forces. The country is increasingly resistant to a relapse into the pre-9/11 conditions prevailing under the Taliban rule and the preceding Afghan Mujahedin factionalism. No doubt the goal of national reconciliation remains elusive, but that is a difficult process and can hardly be imposed from outside when domestic impulses are absent or weak. The process has been difficult even in Bosnia, where the international intervention and the framework provided by the Dayton Accords have been robust in comparison to Afghanistan, a country with a largely illiterate population and without a history of strong institutions of governance.

Considerable progress has been made in the health and education sectors, in particular the education of girls; women have been pulled out from under the pall of the Taliban's oppressive practices. Large parts of northern Afghanistan have achieved relative stability and calm. Consolidation of peace in these areas can become an ingredient for a new national consensus, once the challenge in the Pushtun areas has been met. If troubles persist in the Pushtun areas of the south and southeast, the Kabul government alone cannot be held responsible for the situation. The history of the Afghan conflict imposes an obligation on the international community to help Afghanistan towards stabilization, especially now that it has intervened militarily in the country.

The Afghanistan Compact: A Comprehensive Approach to Reconciliation and Reconstruction

September 2005 saw the formal end of the Bonn process with the completion of the parliamentary and provincial elections, but Afghanistan was far from being stable. Taliban activity was on the rise, and the security situation had started to deteriorate. The promise of Afghan economic revival had not materialized as envisaged in early 2002 at the Tokyo donors' conference. This apparent failure had provoked a comment from former U.S. envoy to Afghanistan James Dobbins in October 2005, four years after the U.S. intervention and one year since Karzai's election as president. Dobbins asserted that the "largest sector" of the Afghan economy was the "opium business."[20] The realization grew that greater cohesion was needed between the efforts of the Afghan government and the international community. Badly lacking was a comprehensive strategy that could rectify the earlier ad hoc approach and encompass all areas of governance, security, and development, with benchmarks and mutual obligations identified.

Such a new strategy was delineated in the Afghanistan Compact, a high-sounding document produced essentially by UN experts, adopted at a conference in London held January 31–February 1, 2006. The conference was co-chaired by Afghanistan and the United Nations, with the participation of fifty-one countries and a number of political and financial organizations, including the World Bank, International Monetary Fund, Asian Development Bank, Islamic Development Bank along with the European Union, NATO, and the Organization of the Islamic Conference. The Security Council expanded the mandate of UNAMA to include help to the Afghan government in implementing the new compact.

The compact identified critical areas of activity for the ensuing five years —security, governance, rule of law and human rights, economic and social

---

20. Report by Philip Kurata, http://www.America.gov, U.S. Department of State, October 6, 2005.

development, and elimination of narcotics—and outlined elaborate principles of cooperation between the participating international community and Afghanistan. The ambitious benchmarks to be achieved included the raising by 2010 of a 70,000-strong "professional and ethnically balanced" Afghan National Army and 62,000 "functional and ethnically balanced" national and border police, and the disbanding by 2007 of all illegal armed groups. Notwithstanding the concern over private militias, the target of disbanding them in one year, when the ANA and police were to be built over four years, revealed a certain unrealistic optimism that sometimes characterizes UN declarations. The benchmarks set out in the economic and social sector reflected the Millennium Development Goals prescribed by the United Nations.

UNAMA established an elaborate structure with over a dozen regional offices in selected provincial headquarters. Under the UN secretary-general's special representative, there were two deputies, each responsible for one of the two main areas of UNAMA responsibility: political affairs and development matters, which included relief, recovery, and reconstruction programs. The assistance programs coordinated by the UN or the international NGOs had a particular emphasis on the gender issues that had been the focus of international concern for a long time because of the Taliban's denial of education and work opportunities for women. On the political side, UNAMA had initially been mandated to provide advice to the interim authority and oversee the Bonn process, and the completion of the process had been a creditable achievement. However, the intrusive UN involvement, especially after the main institutions of the state had been established and begun functioning, had a downside.

The continued role of the United Nations in political matters detracted from the authority of the government and limited room for it to grow and operate in accordance with the Afghan realities on the ground, rather than as an academic blueprint evolved through UN conferences and subject to UN scrutiny. The presence of the powerful U.S. ambassador in Kabul, Zalmay Khalilzad, also eclipsed the government's authority.[21] Iraq is a case in point. The early departure of the U.S.-appointed head of the Coalition Provisional Authority as Prime Minister Nuri al Maliki took charge in 2006 after a transitional period helped the Iraqi government to strengthen itself and directly cope with the country's political problems. Meanwhile, the U.S.-

21. *NYT,* April 17, 2004.

led multinational force in Iraq remained engaged with security and rebuilding the national army.

In Afghanistan, the overweening UN and U.S. advice and oversight appeared to overwhelm Karzai and his government and to cramp his domestic stature, especially his ability to lead the reconciliation effort. Afghanistan is a complex situation with low literacy and a subsistence economy, a mix of tribal and medieval circumstances, and the present-day bane of warlords, drug trafficking, crime, and corruption. In these conditions, apart from the role that an outside coercive force can play to ensure a certain degree of security, improvement will largely depend on the initiative and credibility of the government and its leaders as independent actors.

Efforts for Reconstruction Falter

Despite the upbeat expectations at the adoption of the Afghanistan Compact, progress in economic reconstruction and recovery remained dismal. A good deal of blame was placed on domestic corruption, conditions of insecurity, and lack of governance; but much of this predicament owed to the insufficiency of development funds, combined with the gap between commitments and disbursement. Further complicating matters were the modalities of channeling the assistance, as well as priorities and programs not necessarily designed for a comprehensive strategy to address the country's economic, political, and military problems. Afghanistan deserved and needed a Marshall plan–type of engagement;[22] what it received was perhaps enough to run a fledgling administration but far short of making a difference on the ground. Compared to the U.S. Department of Defense's $173 billion funding for Operation Enduring Freedom between 2001 and 2009,[23] the total amount of pledges for reconstruction in Afghanistan made at the

22. Some observers make the valid point that Afghanistan could not be compared to post–World War II Europe. The success of the Marshall Plan owed, in large measure, to the effective use of the assistance by literate and organized communities in the recipient countries. However, in the case of Afghanistan, reference to the Marshall Plan is made rhetorically to suggest that to make a difference in the lives of the people requires a large quantity of economic assistance and its appropriate use.

23. Congressional Research Service (CRS) Report for Congress, "The Cost of Iraq, Afghanistan, and other Global War on Terror Operations since 9/11," updated October 15, 2008, CRS-6.

donors' conferences of Tokyo (2002), Berlin (2004), London (2006), and Rome (2007), for the period 2002–2011 have been $23.5 billion.[24] The Paris Conference in June 2008 announced commitments of nearly $20 billion, some of which were carried over from the past, making the total assistance committed over the next several years around $25 billion.

According to the review published by the Aid Coordination Unit of the Afghan Ministry of Finance in June 2008, $19.6 billion had been fully committed by the donors from the estimated pledges of $44.5 billion, which included U.S. pledges amounting to over $26 billion.[25] However, the figures published in a June 2009 *Washington Post* article citing the special inspector general for Afghanistan reconstruction present a different and perhaps more realistic picture. According to this source, the United States spent around $4 billion on reconstruction from 2001 to 2008, with $1.8 billion on roads, $861 million on power, $560 million on health, $448 million on education and schools, and $331 million on agriculture.[26] The discrepancies arise from the confusion over parallel commitments,[27] but the real issue had been the actual disbursements and their effectiveness.

If the *Washington Post* figures are an indicator, it is understandable why the reconstruction effort did not make a difference on the ground. The same article cited examples of wastage. It was widely alleged that as much as half of the committed assistance was siphoned back to the donor countries in the form of consultancies, expensive training programs, and inflated contracts.[28] There have been visible changes in the rehabilitation of infrastructure and construction in the cities, in particular Kabul, but these were not commensurate with the scale of the commitments. In the rural areas, especially in the south and southeast, the centers of resistance, the impact was almost absent.

24. International commitments made at the Tokyo Conference (January 2002) to help Afghanistan were $4.5 billion, with $1.8 billion for the first year. The subsequent Berlin Conference in March 2004 elicited commitments of $8.2 billion, with $4.4 billion for the first year. The London Conference in January 2006 received multiyear commitments of $10.5 billion.

25. Ministry of Finance, Budget Department, Kabul, June 2008, 3.

26. *Washington Post,* June 19, 2009.

27. For example, Pakistan had committed $300 million at the Tokyo Conference and reiterated it on subsequent occasions. Moreover, it had only disbursed half of the amount for construction of the Torkham-Jalalabad road, completed in 2007.

28. *NYT,* November 7, 2005, details how many Afghans saw U.S.-led reconstruction projects as "wasteful, slow-moving efforts" that benefited the foreigners more than the Afghans; and contracts worth hundreds of millions of dollars for construction of schools, clinics, and power systems did not have much to show for them on the ground.

Allocations announced at the 2002 Tokyo conference were weighted in favor of capacity building, schools and education, and health care. Of the $1.7 billion allocated for reconstruction and recovery in the first year, not counting relief assistance, only $70 million was set aside for agriculture and $170 million for rebuilding infrastructure, the two main areas for generating economic activity. Almost one year later, media reports lamented that this assistance had made little difference in the lives of the people.[29] Even six years later, on the eve of the Paris Conference, the Kabul government and the media were criticizing the international community for its light footprint in the reconstruction of Afghanistan.[30] Foreign donors were accused of failing to deliver on what had been promised or attaching conditions to aid disbursement.

Besides funds, a focused strategy was necessary, with high priority on economic revival, job creation, and poverty alleviation. This would have required large-scale investment in agriculture, infrastructure projects throughout the country, and capital infusion at the grassroots levels. In November 2003, Barnett Rubin of the Center for International Cooperation in New York estimated that, to that point, projects worth only $100 million were completed, as against an aid disbursement of $2.9 billion. In 2009, writing for *Boston Review,* Rubin pointed to the complaints of the Afghans that the international community had neither a plan nor adequate funding for recovery, adding his own lament that international projects in Afghanistan were out of touch with "local realities," sometimes with "disastrous" consequences. In December 2007, Oxfam policy advisor Matt Waldman observed that millions of Afghans faced severe hardship, comparable to sub-Saharan Africa, and that "peace could not be achieved in Afghanistan without more determined efforts to reduce poverty." He advocated that priority be accorded to rural development through strengthening local governmental institutions and directing more resources to local communities.[31] At the same time, the government at the local level remained either absent or without active involvement, as the preferred method was to channel assistance through NGOs. This approach was dysfunctional in conflict zones, while in other areas it led to waste, lack of accountability, corrupt practices, and sidelining of the local administration.

29. *NYT,* December 8, 2002.
30. Press statement by the Afghan embassy spokesman in Washington, Ashraf Haidri, June 12, 2008.
31. Statement by Matt Waldman on the sixth anniversary of the signing of the Bonn Agreement, Oxfam International Web site, http://www.oxfam.org/en/news/2007/pr071205-six-years-after-bonn (accessed December 5, 2007).

Agriculture, where traditionally half of the population was employed, also received less attention, because rehabilitation of this sector required strong involvement of the local administration, especially in dealing with land and water disputes. UN agencies had considerable experience in providing relief assistance but had little to show for agricultural development in any developing country. With slow progress in the initial years of relative calm, the task became more complicated as the Taliban insurgency gained momentum and warlords grew increasingly entrenched in their areas. Thus the international community lost a critical window of opportunity, which had been available in the early years following the Tokyo Conference, to generate economic activity and make a difference on the ground.

The Taliban claim to have eradicated poppy cultivation was never contested, but it was often dismissed as an attempt to boost the value of their ample existing stocks to fetch better returns. Regardless of the motive, the Taliban did control poppy cultivation and contain drug trafficking. Since their ouster, poppy cultivation and drug production has been jumping up every year.[32] Scores of thousands of hectares of land are under poppy cultivation, and the Western media have even accused Wali Karzai, the brother of Hamid Karzai, of drug trafficking.[33] The problem has been serious not just in provinces such as Helmand, where the Taliban have become active, but also in Badakhshan, a traditional Tajik stronghold. It is widely believed that drugs are one of the main financial sources for insurgents and warlords. Drug traffickers have a stake in keeping the situation destabilized. The former finance minister of Afghanistan, Ashraf Ghani, spoke in late 2004 of the direct link between drug production and "terrorism," emphasizing that success in the war on drugs depended on economic growth and political stability.[34] The efforts to stamp out this evil have fallen into the conventional grooves. The UN Organization for Drug Control (UNDOC), in coordination with ISAF, launched well-publicized campaigns to destroy the poppy crop, which achieved only partial success and provoked local resentment.

Besides eradication, other antinarcotics plans and efforts are based on the familiar approaches of interdiction, law enforcement, information campaigns, rehabilitation programs, and alternative livelihoods. The entire effort, however, has suffered from a paucity of funds. If the problem was

---

32. Opium production has doubled since 2003 and accounts for 93 percent of the total world production, *NYT*, June 18, 2009.

33. AFP report, October 4, 2008.

34. *NYT*, December 11, 2004.

deemed serious enough and undermined the strategic objective of counterinsurgency, on which tens of billions of dollars a year were being spent
for the military effort, then the less than ten million dollars currently spent
annually on the antinarcotics effort neither made sense nor would it help.
The effort would require a manifold increase in funds allocated to induce
farmers to pursue crop substitution. It may be worthwhile to consider other
innovative approaches to the problem.

At an informal meeting in Islamabad, when it was suggested to President
Karzai that Afghanistan should be designated as the sole, or one, legal exporter
of opium for pharmaceutical purposes, he appeared quite interested. After all,
more than the existing legal exporters, which are all reasonably prosperous
countries, Afghanistan deserved revenues from such exports, monitored under a well-defined regime. The country deserved this privilege if only to contain the huge problems that opium production and drug trafficking posed to
Afghanistan, to the region, and to Europe, which was part of the coalition striving to help Afghanistan attain normalcy. Current efforts have, however, been
completely out of sync with the scale and gravity of the problem.

The elevation of Hamid Karzai from a transitional head to the president
of the country, through largely acceptable democratic elections in October
2004, brought no change in the authority and influence of his government.
The ground realities remained the same, with Afghanistan fragmented
among warlords and Taliban activities slowly on the rise. Militarily, U.S.-
led ISAF forces called the shots, while developmental activity in the hands
of the UN or foreign donor agencies remained minimal. The Bonn process
had been completed with an elected political structure in place, but its promise of peace, reconciliation, and development remained elusive.

Iraqi Distraction at the Heart of Failures in Afghanistan

The disappointment expressed at the end of the Bush administration over
the deteriorating conditions in Afghanistan and questions about the results
of the billions spent and hundreds of allied soldiers' lost lives missed the essential point about the enormity of the challenge in Afghanistan and the loss
of focus that relegated the country to a lower priority as compared to the
U.S. engagement and interest in Iraq.[35] The heady mix of neoconservative

35. Estimated war funding for FY 2001—2009 data published in CRS Report to
Congress on October 15, 2008, shows $657.3 billion for Iraq operations and $172.9 bil-

ambition to reshape the Middle East and corporate interests in the Gulf propelled the intervention in Iraq. No such motivation or grand design underpinned the Afghanistan engagement.

The resources and oversight needed to transform Afghanistan and restore
it to normalcy required resolute endeavors in multiple economic, political,
and military dimensions. U.S. attention was divided from the start, and complacency set in with the easy exit of the Taliban. The professed U.S. objective was to build democracy in Afghanistan, but after the intervention, as
Paul Krugman noted, the Bush administration had "no taste for nation building."[36] In an editorial on July 16, 2004, the *New York Times* rightly criticized President Bush's decision to fight the war against the Taliban "on the
cheap" and then "leave the job of nation building undone," while he diverted American forces to Iraq.[37]

The U.S. and ISAF military presence in 2003 was limited to 14,000
troops, barely sufficient to protect Kabul and vicinity. After 2005, the numbers increased significantly in response to heightened Taliban military activity. Nevertheless, the level of 62,000 troops reached by 2008, including
29,820 U.S. troops,[38] remained insufficient to provide security in population centers while combating and defeating the Taliban, whose numbers did
not exceed 30,000, according to various estimates. The coalition efforts to
reconstitute the Afghan National Army and police had been a failure, as the
responsibility to counter the Taliban fell almost entirely on the shoulders of
the NATO/ISAF forces.

In June 2009, President Barack Obama appointed General Stanley A.
McChrystal U.S. commander in Afghanistan and asked him to design a new
strategy. McChrystal pointed out that even to achieve the limited goal of
defeating Al Qaeda and the Taliban, it was necessary to protect the population rather than simply target the offenders waging a "silent war" through

---

lion for Operation Enduring Freedom in Afghanistan. The U.S. troop commitment for
Afghanistan was as low as 9,000 in 2003, whereas it launched the Iraqi operation with
150,000 troops; by May 2009, the United States deployed 43,000 troops in Afghanistan,
compared to 134,000 in Iraq. *NYT,* June 18, 2009.

36. *NYT,* February 24, 2003.

37. Also see the op-ed article by J. Alexander, former legal advisor to Afghanistan,
complaining that the U.S. effort in Afghanistan was "underfinanced and undermanned,"
NYT, September 23, 2004; and op-ed article by Nicholas D. Kristof, *NYT,* October 2,
2004.

38. ISAF deployment; http://www.nato.int/isaf/docu/epub/pdf/isaf_placemat.pdf
updated as of March 13, 2009.

intimidation and persuasion to control the population. This required, he emphasized, "proper resourcing, rigorous implementation and sustained political will." These ingredients were absent from the international, primarily U.S., engagement in Afghanistan, especially after the opening of the Iraq front. Even the sole superpower was unable to handle two active military theaters requiring far more than a military approach to achieve the minimum desired normalcy and containment of the turmoil the military action caused. Furthermore, the coalition suffered from lack of cohesion and coordination in its internal functioning, with responsibilities compartmentalized. The coalition troops were assigned sectoral responsibilities and operated virtually independent of each other. The McChrystal analysis of August 2009 highlighted the need for an integrated approach to address the multidimensional challenges in Afghanistan.

Lacking was a coherent strategy for political reconciliation sensitive to the ethnic realities of the country. Reconstituting the army was left to General Fahim, who recruited mostly non-Pushtuns, who could not be deployed in the Pushtun areas. The effort for reconstruction and economic recovery appeared to have little coordination with promoting the political objective of reconciliation. A vast gap remained in the resources promised and those actually deployed. More important, the realization that the situation in many parts of the country, especially the rural areas, had not improved came late, after almost four critical years had elapsed.

The Afghanistan Compact reached in London in 2006 was a renewal of commitment based on this realization, but it did not lead to a correspondingly rigorous implementation. The United States, which had all along provided the leadership, was embroiled in Iraq and planned a new surge strategy that committed more resources and troops to that front. The relative lack of focus on Afghanistan and the gathering threat there emerged as an issue in the 2008 U.S. presidential campaign.

The Situation Deteriorates in the Afghanistan-Pakistan Border Regions

The other important contributing factor to Afghanistan's problems lay across the border in Pakistan, in particular in the ungoverned border regions of the Federally Administered Tribal Areas (FATA). U.S. military action in Afghanistan pushed the Taliban and Al Qaeda elements into these areas, destabilizing them and creating a new source of friction and exchange of accusations between Pakistan and Afghanistan. Kabul argued that the conflict's center of gravity lay in the Taliban sanctuaries inside Pakistan. The Taliban and Al Qaeda flow into the FATA upset in its infancy a policy the Musharraf government introduced in 2000 to deploy the army in the area to open roads and undertake projects to improve conditions and earn the army the goodwill of local tribes. The events of September 2001 changed the entire political and military landscape. For Lt. Gen. Jan Orakzai, corps commander stationed in Peshawar and a tribal Pushtun, the U.S. military action across the border now dictated a new priority. With the post-9/11 change in government policy, the Pakistani army was required to interdict the fleeing Taliban and Al Qaeda, who enjoyed local sympathies in the tribal belt.

The thin Pakistani military presence was reinforced and redeployed in the tribal agencies that lay across areas affected by the U.S. military action, particularly the North and South Waziristan tribal agencies, among the main springboards for the Jihad against the Soviet Union. The Waziri and Mahsud tribes there had a particularly long history of rebellion and fierce independence.[39] During the 1980s, the Soviet forces regularly bombarded Angoorada, a border town in North Waziristan, to stop infiltration of the Afghan Mujahedin from the area. Throughout the 1990s, the tribal belt allowed free passage for the Afghan Mujahedin, the Taliban, and their supporters. Generally, there was calm except for sectarian violence in the Kurram agency, where Shia-Sunni tensions had escalated since the Afghan Jihad. This changed with the U.S. military action in Afghanistan and the expulsion of Al Qaeda and many Taliban fighters and part of their leadership.

The wild terrain of the FATA, especially South and North Waziristan, now became host to Al Qaeda and the Taliban, obliging the Pakistani military to pursue them, as an ally of the United States in the "war on terror." Slowly, Pakistan got sucked more deeply into the conflict, provoking its domestic militant groups, who found common cause with Al Qaeda and the fugitive Taliban. It was as if a dormant virus had become newly activated. At the same time, opinion ranging from the extreme Islamists to the mainstream political analysts criticized the government for involving the country in America's war. They asserted that the misguided government policy of siding with the Americans had brought the conflict to the tribal areas.

---

39. Waziristan first gained a reputation for its fiercely independent tribes because of the jihad against the British in the late 1930s and 1940s launched by Mirza Ali Khan, who belonged to North Waziristan and was known as "Faqir of Ipi." At one time, the British government had reportedly engaged nearly 40,000 troops to suppress the rebellion.

Even the liberal elements, especially those aligned with the Pakistan People's Party (PPP), who blamed Musharraf for the military takeover and for undermining the country's democracy, criticized government policy and argued that an effective fight against terrorism and militancy demanded a democratic polity. These critical views had characterized the public discourse on the "war on terror" since 2001; but they gained resonance as the conflict intensified in the tribal areas, especially after March 2007, when Musharraf began losing his grip on the government as a result of the popular movement against his fateful dismissal of the country's chief justice.

On the Afghan side, Hamid Karzai placed the blame for the country's woes and for his government's failure to effect improvements squarely on the continuing Taliban insurgency, which in his view was sustained solely because of support from elements in Pakistan. He believed that the Taliban leadership operated from inside Pakistan, where it had found refuge. UN and ISAF midlevel officials aired the same accusations, often through calculated leaks to the media to explain the failure to stabilize the country and contain the escalating insurgency. By mid-2005, it was alleged that Mullah Omar was hiding in Quetta and that Pakistani intelligence was protecting him and his associates, now dubbed the Quetta shura, who were guiding the Taliban insurgency in southern Afghanistan. Similar claims were made about the top Al Qaeda leaders, in particular Osama bin Laden. The Kabul-based international media carried stories suggesting that after conducting their raids, the Taliban groups withdrew to the safety of the border areas of Pakistan, in particular to the sprawling camps around Quetta.

Pakistani officials countered that much of the Taliban activity during most of 2005 and 2006 had been away from the Pakistani border—in Uruzgan and northern districts of Helmand in the Sangin, Nawzad, Musa Qala, and Lashkar Gah areas—and could not be carried out from hideouts in Quetta or elsewhere in Pakistan. These areas were far removed from the Pakistani border and had been the former Taliban stronghold. They also pointed to the failure of the reconciliation process in Afghanistan and claimed that it was Pakistan that was the victim of the unsettled situation in Afghanistan.

The frequent bitter exchanges and mutual recrimination persisted and vitiated relations between the two countries, especially at the diplomatic level. The resulting tension preoccupied most of the bilateral interaction during the remaining Musharraf years. The same years also saw heightened militant activity by Pakistan-based extremists, the Pakistani Taliban, Al Qaeda, and local tribal insurgents, who had been challenging the writ of the government since early 2004, targeting the military and progovernment leaders in the FATA area.

The Afghan accusations were disingenuous in the sense that the Afghan leadership, more than anyone else, were aware of the border's porous nature and that it could not be sealed. Expecting Pakistan to do so was asking the impossible. They themselves had taken advantage of the terrain in carrying out forays against the Soviet army from the soil of Pakistan. Whenever the conflict had flared in any Afghan region, especially the south and southeast, a part of the affected population would simply walk into the Pakistani side of the tribal belt. The Taliban leaders also moved across this border and did not maintain any permanent headquarters such as was alleged by the location of the so-called Quetta shura. They used the sprawling refugee camps as their temporary hideouts, where it was difficult to find them. If the ISAF presence was thinly spread, so were the Pakistani forces deployed in these historically ungovernable regions.

Pakistan never claimed that there could be no Taliban crossing into Afghanistan to aid the insurgency. Instead, they argued, equally untenably, that the Afghan National Army and ISAF stationed on the Afghan side of the Durand Line bore the responsibility for interdicting this cross-border movement. Pakistan's initial assertions that none of the top Taliban or Al Qaeda leaders could be in Pakistan owed in part to the psychology of denial it had developed in its diplomacy during the 1980s. Then, most of the international community accepted the denial of interference from the Pakistani side of the border, which was a ruse to avoid diplomatic inconvenience, especially at the United Nations. In the current circumstances, resort to such denials as a defensive posture came at the cost of Pakistan's credibility. In its public statements, Pakistan should have limited itself to insisting on evidence and reiterating its commitment to follow leads, as was its obligation under the mandatory UN Security Council resolutions.

Friction Increases between Pakistan and Afghanistan

At various levels, however, Pakistan did ask for evidence. Only once, in early 2006, President Karzai provided addresses and telephone numbers used by the Taliban and records of calls they had made, which were found to be either several months old or nonexistent and useless as leads. The ISI pursued the matter, claiming that it had associated the Pakistan-based CIA representatives with the effort to look into the information shared by the

Afghan side. The follow-up on the information proved futile. On an earlier occasion, when the Pakistan side had pressed for concrete information in response to Kabul's repeated accusations that the Taliban network was operating from inside Pakistan, the Afghan side had passed on information that made little operational sense. They provided a list of four names including Mullah Omar, Gulbadin Hekmatyar, and two high-profile political personalities from Pakistan known for their views against the U.S. intervention in Afghanistan. Musharraf publicly dismissed it as the "nonsense list."[40] The repetition of the accusations deepened the distrust that already existed between the two sides.

Another widely held view among foreigners based in Kabul and Islamabad was that Pakistan always seemed able to eliminate a high-value target close to some high-profile visit to substantiate the impression of cooperation. In fact, Pakistan could be blamed for half-hearted cooperation but not for such a sinister, calculated game. Pakistan hardly eliminated any high-profile Afghan Taliban personalities, except in May 2007, when Mullah Daddullah was tracked by human intelligence on the Pakistan side and picked up by aerial surveillance as soon as he crossed into Afghanistan. Most other high-value militants the Pakistanis targeted were either Al Qaeda or Pakistani extremists. Their capture or elimination at times coincided with dates close to high-level U.S. officials' visits because these visits occurred quite frequently, rarely missing a month in any calendar year. In the case of Al Qaeda, Pakistan could not be accused of "running with the hare and hunting with the hounds." Pakistani officials viewed these allegations as inspired by hostility from within the Afghan government and by the pervasive suspicion and prejudice developed over many years against Pakistan and its intelligence agencies.

The tension between Islamabad and Kabul was also attributable to the lack of chemistry between Musharraf and Karzai. Both leaders carried a certain baggage. Pakistan had actively opposed the Northern Alliance and advocated Pushtun representation, albeit discreetly, which irritated the Afghan side. For his part, Musharraf listened sympathetically to the military assessment that suspected the Northern Alliance of close liaison with India and Iran at the expense of what Pakistan perceived as its interests in Afghanistan. Karzai, on the other hand, had to be responsive to advisors from his intelligence agency, Riyasat e Amniyat e Milli (RAM), headed by Amarullah Saleh, a young Panjshiri close to Ahmed Shah Massoud. Foreign visitors to Islamabad would at times remark about Amrullah's harsh words

40. *NYT,* March 7, 2006.

about Pakistan. As a result, the prospects that the two sides might show understanding and act with restraint in public statements remained narrow. There could be psychological factors in the two leaders' being ill at ease with each other. Some of Musharraf's close confidants had a low opinion of Karzai. And although Musharraf could not be accused of condescending behavior towards Karzai, at times he could be faulted as undiplomatic, failing to suppress his feelings and becoming irate, especially if he thought his interlocutor deliberately disingenuous.

The numerous visits the two presidents paid to each other's capitals, as well as visits by Pakistani Prime Minister Shaukat Aziz, would temporarily help ease tensions, though they would invariably revive. In July 2005, Shaukat Aziz visited Kabul for a day and thought he had had a good meeting with Karzai, until the two leaders held a joint press conference. Shaukat Aziz received a shock when Karzai, in his opening remarks, spoke for several minutes about how infiltrators from Pakistan came to Afghanistan to torch and destroy schools and deprive Afghan children of education. The point could have been made in simple inoffensive terms if the intention had not been to embarrass the visitor by virtually designating Pakistan an accomplice of the "terrorist Taliban." Musharraf did not face such a situation in public, but during his visit to Kabul in August 2006, a meeting organized for him with Afghan elders was attended by Vice President Karim Khalili and the chairmen of the Meshrano Jirga (the upper house) and the Wolesi Jirga, Sibghatullah Mojaddedi and Yunus Qanooni, among over two dozen notables. Many in attendance took the floor to argue that there were no ethnic differences in Afghanistan and that all the trouble owed to a handful of militant leaders with an obscurantist ideology who must be defeated. This was clearly staged to politely reject the Pakistani argument that the Taliban were trying, with some success, to give their struggle a nationalist twist by playing on the ruffled sentiments of the Pushtuns. This Pakistani view was meant less for the Kabul leaders than for the outside visitors to Islamabad, especially the Americans, who had begun showing exasperation over the Taliban's resurgence and wondering about the reasons for it.

By late 2005 and early 2006, Pakistan faced persistent criticism in the Western media, which claimed that it was not fighting the terrorists and even had an interest in the survival of the Taliban leadership.[41] This would sup-

---

41. Editorial comment in the *New York Times,* August 5, 2005, accused Pakistan of being "passive" in countering Taliban; *NYT,* September 22, 2005, an editorial called upon the world to put "pressure" on Pakistan to end Taliban activity.

posedly keep their options open to help their erstwhile clients, the Taliban, in case the Americans decided to leave the area. Pakistani officials believed that the Kabul government was planting these stories to malign Pakistan and to instigate coalition pressure on Pakistan or worse, take action inside Pakistani territories.

Pakistan had direct contacts with the U.S. and ISAF high command. General John P. Abizaid, who had succeeded General Tommy Franks as U.S. CENTCOM commander in 2003, visited the area regularly. Such apprehensions had not been raised by Abizaid nor in the biennial meetings of the Tripartite Military Commission convened at the highest military level. In public statements, Pakistani officials would note that rather than trading accusations in the media, any complaints should be brought to the Tripartite Military Commission or, alternatively, discussed through the CENTCOM chief.

On several occasions, Musharraf enunciated Pakistan's stand, which was summarized in the three-point overview he presented at a press conference with British prime minister Tony Blair in Lahore in late November 2006. Musharraf stated that the real problem lay inside Afghanistan and that the heart of the issue was reconciliation. Such cross-border activity as occurred was a consequence of the conflict inside Afghanistan rather than the cause of the conflict's continuation. He once again invited better coordination through existing mechanisms rather than the exchange of accusations. He also made a strong appeal to the world community to help Afghanistan on a Marshall Plan–like scale and to pursue a comprehensive strategy that would combine political and economic elements with military action.

Apart from media stories citing midlevel officials, a clear and formal U.S. request to Pakistan to clamp down on the Afghan Taliban, which underscored U.S. skepticism of Pakistani efforts, did not come before the beginning of 2007. Until then, Pakistani officials saw the complaints primarily as an attempt by the Kabul government to divert international attention from its fecklessness in addressing the issues it faced. By arguing that the real problem was located in Pakistan rather than Afghanistan, Kabul appeared to want to shift the burden of the conflict onto Pakistan and convince ISAF to broaden the war to include Pakistan's border regions. Pakistan had already deployed close to 80,000 troops in the FATA, where the Pakistani army's headaches were local militants and insurgents rather than the Afghan Taliban. Nonetheless, in late 2006, to counter the persistent charges, the Pakistani government initiated new steps for better control of the border.

Pakistan's Stillborn Proposals and Countercomplaints

The new measures included increasing the number of border posts to nearly 1000, as compared to nearly 100 ISAF/ANA posts along the border on the Afghan side; selective fencing and mining of the border; and creating a three-kilometer no-go zone near particularly notorious pathways that criss-crossed the difficult terrain. According to the military's assessment, of the long border of over 1000 kilometers that the North-West Frontier Province (NWFP) shares with Afghanistan, no more than 60 to 70 kilometers of mining and fencing would be required in short stretches to block the most sensitive parts of the border, while another 100-plus kilometers of mining and fencing would be required along Baluchistan's similarly long border. In view of the easement rights for the tribes living in the border regions, recognized since the British colonial period, Pakistan proposed the establishment of designated crossing points and an identification system possibly to include biometric cards. An additional measure that would require the cooperation of the Afghan government and international agencies was to relocate the Afghan refugees inside Afghanistan, since refugee camps close to the border inside Pakistan provided safe haven to Afghan Taliban and militants.

All three suggestions drew a negative reaction from Kabul. President Karzai strongly opposed the ideas, asserting that the proposed measures were neither "helpful nor practical" and would only hurt the people living in the region and not stem "cross-border terrorism." He reiterated that Pakistan must eliminate Taliban sanctuaries on its territory, which were the "source of terrorism."[42] The Pakistani proposals, moreover, provoked Afghan sensitivities regarding the Durand Line as the international border. The issue dates to the partition of British India, though Kabul had never been able to define the issue with any precision. For Pakistan, the Durand Line was the border it had inherited as the successor state to British India and was, therefore, nonnegotiable. At the Geneva negotiations in 1988, the reference to international borders had arisen as the last hurdle and required the intercession of Soviet Foreign Minister Eduard Shevardnadze before acceptable language was injected to finalize the texts.

Kabul objected to fencing and mining any portion of the border, arguing that these measures would cause inconvenience and hardship to the tribesmen inhabiting the area. Pakistan attempted to introduce biometric cards to

---

42. *NYT,* December 27 and 29, 2006.

regulate movement of people across the Chaman border post north of Quetta, which is the main artery for commerce on Afghanistan's southwestern border. Afghan officials on the other side of the border actively thwarted the attempt by shredding the cards.

Coalition representatives were visibly on the defensive, as they could neither oppose nor clearly support the suggestions. The UN and European officials objected to the proposed selective mining. Pakistan argued that extraordinary measures were justified to respond to Kabul's constant complaints. The Canadian Foreign Minister, Peter Mackay, visiting Pakistan in early January 2007, was visibly uncomfortable trying to dissuade the Pakistani side from taking steps that caused difficulties for Kabul. Finally, he agreed to consider Pakistan's request for capacity building, to include supplying helicopters and other equipment, so that Pakistani troops could act with speed in the area. This could obviate the need to mine or fence the border. Later on, Canada opted for an easier recourse, namely, to organize technical-level meetings of Afghan and Pakistani officials to discuss ways and means for an improved functional border arrangement relating to customs, transit commerce, and movement under easement rights.

Notwithstanding the negative responses, the Pakistani proposals served temporarily to lessen criticism against Pakistan. On the ground, the army took measures short of selective mining. It identified about 75 kilometers of border in bits and pieces in Waziristan and a similar length for the Baluchistan-Afghan border for fencing, and created a no-man's zone, within three kilometers of the fence, to be monitored. The fence was partly completed when the idea was abandoned for lack of interest by the Afghans and the international community. The setting up of designated crossing points and biometrics never took off, as it required the cooperation of the Afghan side. Nonetheless, the idea has since been kept alive.[43]

In 2007, a Turkish mediation effort underscored the desirability of some Pakistan-Afghanistan understanding and a code of conduct to reduce tension along the border. The Turks, however, discovered the sensitivities involved both in Pakistan's unwillingness to open the border issue and in the Afghan reservations on accepting any reference that could be regarded as their recognition of the Durand Line. Some officials from the coalition and from UNAMA naively thought there was an opportunity for the international community to intercede to reach a settlement of the border issue

43. *Jang,* July 26, 2009. The Pakistani interior minister discussed with his counterpart enforcement of a biometric system at Chaman and two other crossing points.

between the two countries. They should have consulted Diego Cordovez, the architect of the 1980s Geneva talks, to understand the futility of a wild goose chase. For Pakistan it was a folly to open an issue for discussion that it considered settled. For Afghanistan, it was an ill-defined idea that was a throwback to the nineteenth century, when the Afghan state encountered the expanding British Empire in South Asia. Notwithstanding the border co-nundrum, there was need for an international role to keep tensions contained and optimize cooperation in fighting against the militants.

On refugees, after receiving Musharraf's approval, the Pakistani Foreign Office began pressing the United Nations High Commissioner for Refugees (UNHCR) to shift the refugee camps from Pakistan to relatively safe areas inside Afghanistan, where refugee families could be provided relief assis-tance. Apart from the Afghan accusation that the camps served as hideouts for Afghan militants, the Pakistani Foreign Office believed that the ex-tended presence in camps of hundreds of thousands of refugees in condi-tions of squalor was already creating problems for Pakistan. In Baluchistan, two large camps, at Girdi Jungle and Bramchah, housed more than 150,000 refugees, awash with weapons and literally off-limits to the Pakistani po-lice and security personnel. Bramchah straddled both sides of the border and was a well-known conduit for drug smugglers. The camps had become breeding grounds for crime and religious militancy and provided shelter to the Taliban. They also served as convenient meeting points for the Taliban and elements from Pakistani extremist militant groups.

Surprisingly, the Afghan government, UNHCR officials, and Pakistani vested bureaucratic and local political interests resisted the Foreign Office suggestions. The UNHCR held that these refugees should return voluntar-ily and should not be shifted only to become displaced persons inside Afghanistan, and the Afghan government pleaded its inability to cope with such repatriation. UNHCR was also afraid that it would lose funding once the refugees lost their status and became internally displaced persons (IDPs). Thus technical arguments prevailed over strategic considerations because of vested interest. With some difficulty, refugees from Kacha Garhi near Peshawar were shifted to Afghanistan. This became possible in part because of the pressure exerted by land speculators who wanted to acquire the camp's urban site for a housing development.

Another factor that embittered meetings between Musharraf and Karzai was Pakistan's complaint that RAM, the Afghan intelligence agency, was cooperating with its Indian counterpart, the Research and Analysis Wing

(RAW), to undermine Pakistani interests both in Afghanistan and in its frontier provinces of NWFP and Baluchistan. India and Pakistan used to maintain four consulates in addition to their respective embassies in Kabul, namely in Jalalabad, Qandahar, Herat, and Mazar e Sharif, a diplomatic arrangement inherited from the days of the British. The Pakistanis always suspected the activities of the Indian consulates in Qandahar and Jalalabad so close to their border, where consular staff was more than a token presence and which did not appear to serve any ostensible trade or consular interests. Following the ouster of Najibullah, the Indians closed down their consulates; but they reopened them after ten years' absence when the transitional government was set up under Karzai. The Pakistani press would often publish unsubstantiated reports of over a dozen Indian offices or consulates in Afghan provinces bordering Pakistan, to suggest growing Indian influence and interference to the detriment of Pakistani interests. Having suffered a setback with the exit of the Taliban, Islamabad viewed the reopening of the Indian consulates as a provocation with no apparent purpose but to create mischief for Pakistan, especially in the insurgency-prone province of Baluchistan.

The Pakistan government long suspected the Indian intelligence agency of providing funds and weapons to Baluch nationalist elements. The ISI managed to produce documentary evidence of RAW activity, such as visits by RAW agents close to the border, or RAM and RAW cooperation in regard to Bramdagh Bugti, a leader of the Baluch Liberation Front, a nationalist group that seeks secession of the province. Bramdagh Bugti and another dissident Baluch nationalist leader, Balach Marri, sought refuge in Afghanistan following the killing of Bramdagh's grandfather, Akbar Bugti, a Baluch tribal chief, in a botched military operation in August 2006. Bramdagh later proceeded to Delhi, indicating obvious collaboration between RAM and RAW. The ISI had collected incontrovertible evidence of the presence of Bramdagh and his family in Kabul and then in Delhi. Balach was killed inside Afghanistan in November 2007, apparently caught in cross fire between the Taliban and ANA forces. Musharraf presented documentary evidence of RAM and RAW cooperation and tried to put Karzai on the defensive in some of their one-on-one bilateral summits, and once in Ankara in 2006, when the Turkish leadership tried to mediate between the two sides. Musharraf always took pride in the professionalism demonstrated by the ISI in gathering evidence for the Pakistani case and dismissed Afghan charges as being mostly based on hearsay.

Mediatory Efforts and the Idea of a Joint Grand Jirga

President Bush tried to reduce tensions by inviting the two presidents for a dinner on September 30, 2006. The media expected rough exchanges between Karzai and Musharraf.[44] The tone of the two leaders had been harsh. Karzai blamed Pakistan for providing sanctuary to the Taliban and asked the international community to act, while Musharraf targeted the Afghan government for failing to improve security within Afghanistan and trying to throw the blame onto Pakistan. When asked about his expectations for the meeting, given the strained relations between the two leaders, Bush admitted the bitterness between the two allies and cited it as the very reason for the dinner meeting. The event led to an unexpected development.

At the dinner, Karzai proposed and Musharraf agreed that there ought to be a joint grand jirga, with the participation of representatives of the two countries, to address issues that had been causing tension. It was further agreed that the first session of the joint grand jirga would be held in Kabul and the second in Islamabad, and that both were to be attended by the two presidents. Pakistan was thus pushed into a situation that, at the diplomatic level, it had been trying to avoid, namely transforming the Afghan problem into a bilateral problem between the two countries. Musharraf had misunderstood a position explained by Lieutenant General Orakzai, now the governor of NWFP, at a luncheon meeting that President Bush held for Musharraf and his delegation a few days prior. At Musharraf's instance, Orakzai explained to Bush how he was involving local jirgas in pacifying militants active in Waziristan. These steps eventually led to a controversial peace deal between the government and the militants earlier in the month. The Americans were uncomfortable about this initiative and doubted the wisdom of a deal that could further embolden the militants on both sides. During his explanation, Orakzai remarked that a local jirga initiative, with participation of notable Pushtuns from the Pakistan side, could help reduce resistance and violence on the Afghanistan side as well. This was a far cry from the concept of the bilateral joint grand jirga proposed by Karzai. The modality of the Karzai proposal, which Musharraf had already accepted, be-

---

44. *NYT,* September 28, 2006. An editorial comment appearing in the next day's *New York Times* blamed all three participants at the dinner for the deteriorating situation: Musharraf for his "remarkable ineffectiveness" at stopping the Taliban from crossing into Afghanistan, Karzai for being indulgent of corruption, and Bush for not committing enough troops.

came the subject of considerable discussion within the relevant Pakistani ministries and agencies, including the military.

The plan for the joint grand jirga started taking shape in early 2007. The initial Pakistani reservations on the format of the joint grand jirga gave way to acquiescence in participation limited to leaders from Pakistan's two provinces bordering Afghanistan. These participants could consider ways and means to improve friendly bilateral cooperation and to fight terrorism that affected both countries. Pakistan rejected any references that could allow discussion on border-related issues or Afghan intercession with tribes on the Pakistani side. Furthermore, Pakistan could not accept any role for the international community or the UN, except for their presence as guests during the inaugural and closing events. On the Afghan side, the jirga included representatives from each province, as the non-Pushtuns became nervous about the unprecedented gathering of Pushtuns from both sides of the border. Pakistan and Afghanistan set up their respective jirga commissions, headed by Aftab Ahmed Khan Sherpao, the Pakistani interior minister, and Pir Sayed Ahmed Gailani, head of the National Islamic Front of Afghanistan and a moderate leader from the days of the Afghan Jihad.

The jirga was convened on August 9–12, 2007, with over 500 representatives from each side gathered for the occasion. From Pakistan the representation was mostly from NWFP. Instead of Musharraf, Prime Minister Shaukat Aziz cochaired the inauguration session with Karzai. Musharraf was prevented from attending by a meeting convened to consider the growing internal political crisis triggered by his dismissal of the country's chief justice; but he did join the closing session. The speeches at the jirga were platitudes, with the Pakistani leaders emphasizing that the conflict was fundamentally an Afghan issue, as the Taliban were Afghans and the solution depended on the success of reconciliation. They reiterated their commitment join with Afghanistan to fight the forces of terrorism and extremism.

A potentially important outcome of the otherwise symbolic joint grand jirga was a decision to constitute a "permanent" smaller jirga of fifty members, twenty-five from each side, to "pursue a process of dialogue for peace and reconciliation with the opponents (*mukhalifeen*),[45] "opponents" being a euphemism for the militants and the Taliban. The proposed process, however, could not be established anytime soon. Pakistani politics had become turbulent, with Musharraf increasingly embroiled in the domestic crisis and

45. Source: Regional Institute of Policy Research and Training, Peshawar.

the election process. Musharraf's presence to co-chair the concluding session of the joint grand jirga had assuaged Karzai's pride, and he visited Pakistan on December 26–27, 2007. He suggested that Musharraf activate the jirga process, as Pakistan had yet to nominate its twenty-five members. Before leaving for Kabul, Karzai met Benazir Bhutto hours before her assassination in the evening that transformed Pakistan's political landscape. Once again, the idea of the jirga was thrown into limbo, especially because most of the prominent Pakistani members of the jirga commission and the ruling party lost the February 2008 elections, which were followed by Musharraf's resignation later in August.

During 2007, the public bickering between the leaders of Pakistan and Afghanistan had prompted a few outside attempts at intercession and mediation. Turkey, UAE, and the G-8 offered to play a mediatory role. UNAMA also sensed an opportunity to expand its mandate from an exclusive focus on Afghanistan to include facilitation between Pakistan and Afghanistan and to adopt a formal role in the convening of the joint grand jirga. In fact, the first-draft format for the proposed jirga was delivered to the Pakistan Foreign Office, purportedly on behalf of Karzai, by the deputy chief of UNAMA, Alexander Christopher. Pakistan was wary of such attempts and saw no justification for an intermediary when the two countries had direct contacts and were already engaged in discussions on all the issues at various levels. The UAE initiative did not go beyond a couple of meetings at the foreign ministers' level, held on the sidelines of the Shanghai Cooperation Organization (SCO) summit in Shanghai in June 2006 and later at the UN General Assembly.

The Turks were more serious and persistent. During an Arab League Summit in Riyadh in late March 2007, which Musharraf and Turkish Prime Minister Recep Tayyip Erdoğan attended as guests, Erdoğan suggested a trilateral summit in Ankara with the participation of the presidents of Afghanistan and Pakistan. Musharraf agreed to the idea and suggested that he could stop over in Ankara on his return from a planned European visit in late July 2007. The Ankara trilateral summit demonstrated to the Turkish leaders, then locked in their own domestic wrangles challenging the legitimacy of the ruling party, the futility of a third-party intercession, even though they wished to continue with their initiative. In a closed meeting between Karzai and Musharraf in the presence of the Turkish president and prime minister, Musharraf began by saying he did not wish to be either diplomatic or hypocritical. He poured out the evidence that had been pieced together about RAW and RAM cooperation to undermine Pakistan's interests. Drafting of the communiqué proved to be equally testy, but finally a format was agreed in which the commitments on principles and actionable points between the two countries were placed in an essentially bilateral framework.

The G-8 effort was launched on the sidelines of the May 2007 foreign ministers' meeting in Potsdam by inviting the foreign ministers of the two countries. It did not take off and ended with the adoption of a text in the G-8 declaration that reaffirmed cooperation in the fight against terrorism and support to the Afghan government.

A Flawed Waziristan Agreement and the Predicament of the Pakistani Army

Pakistani moves to forge a peace accord with militants in Waziristan, through a series of jirgas in the autumn of 2006, came under considerable criticism and marked the start of a debate on whether the Pakistani army was unwilling or unable to take on the militants. The September 2006 Waziristan Accord, to be discussed in some detail in chapter 5, was mainly an initiative of retired Lt. Gen. Jan Orakzai, governor of NWFP, who felt that military action alone was not yielding results in the area and the situation needed to be handled politically. Musharraf supported Orakzai and deferred to his knowledge of the region because of his tribal background.

The Kabul government expressed objection to the Waziristan Accord, alleging that it would only provide respite to the Taliban and other terrorist elements and encourage militancy inside Afghanistan. The Americans had similar reservations. However, when Musharraf visited Kabul on September 7, 2006, the Afghan side acknowledged, in a joint statement, some positive elements and underscored the importance of their implementation.[46] The Americans remained skeptical, but their criticism toned down somewhat following reports that British troops fighting in the north of Helmand Province were reaching out to the local Taliban in the Musa Qala area for cease-fire or peace deals in the late autumn of 2006.[47]

The Waziristan Accord was negotiated at a time when the army action in the area had come to a stalemate. In substance, it underestimated the in-

---

46. According to the Joint Statement of September 7, 2006, "President Karzai appreciated the recent agreement between the government of Pakistan and the Pakistani Taliban in North Waziristan, which forbids, among other things, the cross-border infiltration of Taliban into Afghanistan."

47. *NYT,* December 2, 2006.

tractable character of the militancy, which was not primarily tribal but had a strong mix of Al Qaeda and Pakistani extremist elements. In terms of timing, the negotiations had coincided with serious military setbacks, notably, the capture of nearly two hundred soldiers trapped by a ruse laid by the local Taliban under the command of Baitullah Mahsud, a new militant leader from the Mahsud tribe in South Waziristan. Baitullah later launched the Tehrik Taliban Pakistan (TTP) and declared an open rebellion against the government, establishing a Taliban-type Islamic emirate in his area with the support of Al Qaeda. The year 2006 also saw suicide bombings in Pakistan, a bane that bore the stamp of Al Qaeda, whose remnants had embedded themselves in the tribal areas and were becoming part of the core of insurgency and militancy in the area. In these circumstances, the Waziristan agreement appeared a product of weakness on the part of the Pakistan government. Within months, the agreement fell apart. The rebellious tribesmen blamed drone attacks and bad faith on the part of the Pakistani military in maintaining its presence in the area; at the same time there was nothing to show in the way of reduction in militancy or restraint on the activities of foreign elements or the Afghan Taliban in the area.

The question arises why the Pakistani army was finding counterinsurgency so difficult. First, the army's deployment had been incremental and somewhat ad hoc, based on an initial misjudgment of the gravity of the problem. The realization of its seriousness developed gradually with the insurgency's increasing intensity. The army was thus mostly in a reactive mode, putting out fires where they seemed to erupt. Second, the army's orientation was to engage in regular warfare, specifically to address India's military threat. Fighting a thinly dispersed, elusive enemy that sought refuge in a terrorized population or in inaccessible mountainous terrain was a new experience, entailing several handicaps. Any bombardment of suspected compounds to take out hiding militants often resulted in collateral damage to local inhabitants. This caused resentment and created hostility among affected families steeped in the local tribal code and custom of Pushtunwali, which emphasized *badal,* code for revenge.[48]

---

48. Pushtunwali is the Pushtun tribal code, which combined with a sprinkling of Sharia elements is the law for the Pushtun tribes in the bordering regions of Pakistan and Afghanistan. The main elements of Pushtunwali include: *nang* (honor), *badal* (revenge), *malmastai* (hospitality), and *nanawatai* (sanctuary or refuge). The code is normally applied through the institution of the local jirga of elders, *spingeeri,* which literally means "white beards."

Third, the collapse of administrative structures in the tribal areas because of the 1980s' Jihad and the general decline in governance over the years resulted in weak ground intelligence and no force other than the army to protect those who may side with the government and the armed forces. The army could not perform the police or paramilitary functions required to secure the area once the army had cleared it of militants. Consequently, as soon as the army would withdraw, militants could again become active and target those who may have cooperated with the army. According to official figures, between 2005 and 2007 the militants brutally slaughtered more than 600 people, including 150 tribal elders. In addition to tribal insurgent elements and the Pakistani Taliban, these forces included disparate Arab, Chechen, Uzbek, and other central Asian elements, which loosely formed a part of Al Qaeda. Estimates ranged from 3,000 to 6,000 foreigners, who were known to be tough, ruthless fighters, constantly on the move in small bands and mixed with local sympathizers.

Fourth, the Pakistani forces were ill equipped to carry out rapid actions or to move with speed in largely unfamiliar terrain where the adversary held a decisive advantage. Pakistan had requested in late 2005 that the United States provide helicopter gunships and sophisticated equipment, such as night goggles, to build its capacity for effective counterinsurgency. The U.S. response was slow to materialize. The United States had reservations, concerned lest Pakistan deploy the helicopters on their eastern front with India or let the night goggles fall into the hands of the Taliban fighters. Six helicopters were delivered in 2006, but five of these remained grounded for lack of spare parts, finally provided in mid-2007. Another ten MI-17 helicopters were delivered in 2009. Night goggles were finally supplied in late 2007, subject to scrutiny and periodic counting.

President Bush was personally well disposed to President Musharraf, but the U.S. administration tended to drag its feet and often treated Pakistan as part of the region's problem. There was an obvious deficit of trust on both sides. The administration did not respond to Pakistan's requests for the much-needed funds for expanding the Frontier Corps (FC) and developing the FATA. In 2004, Pakistan requested the United States to provide $150 million annually for five years for FATA development projects and $300 million for expanding the Frontier Corps. Funds for the FC were not made available until 2008. The U.S. advisors were unsure of FC loyalties, because the corps was drawn from local tribesmen mixed with regular troops and kept under the command of regular army officers. The FC expansion was not meant simply to strengthen this paramilitary force, but also to provide employment in the tribal areas and create the possibility of weaning local youth and their families away from the militants. As for development assistance, the first tranche of $71 million was released in late 2007 to be used by the U.S. Agency for International Development (USAID) through local NGOs. At that time, Pakistan was spending from its own resources around Rupees 8 billion (approximately $125 million) on FATA development. The proposal for Reconstruction Opportunity Zones (ROZs), initiated in early 2006 and meant to generate economic activity in the FATA and the border regions, is still under consideration.[49]

The Pakistani military and Musharraf faced a dilemma: their counterinsurgency operations had been unsuccessful, yet they could not admit failure. By 2007, pressure on Musharraf was mounting, with contradictory pulls from the United States and the coalition on one hand and from within Pakistan on the other. The United States wanted more active cooperation on controlling the Afghan Taliban and cross-border activity.

American Resort to Drone Attacks

The Pakistan-U.S. military relationship has hardly ever been based on mutual trust, with lurking suspicions about each other's objectives even in the best of times. As early as 2005, U.S. army personnel complained that Pakistanis could not be trusted with intelligence, as in many cases the target would escape once information was passed to the Pakistan side. On the Pakistan side, inadequate capacity meant that as troops were mobilized, their ground movements were exposed and the target, normally a small band of militants or even an individual, would be alerted and shift locale. When the U.S. and Pakistani militaries agreed to intelligence sharing and Pakistan allowed surveillance through unmanned drone flights over tribal airspace, the drones took off from bases agreed to by Pakistan as part of the logistical support the United States requested after 9/11, as later reports revealed.

---

49. *Washington Post,* March 21, 2009, in an editorial comment, applauded the proposal, nearly four years after it was initiated. Among U.S. reservations were worries about the possibility of labor from other areas of Pakistan seizing jobs in ROZs from local labor in the FATA, losing sight of the nature of the area and the strategic requirement of job creation in the tribal areas. The proposal has been emasculated by excluding textile items and by the related misplaced fear of causing disruption to the U.S. textile industry. *Daily Times* (Lahore), July 20, 2009, reported opposition by the U.S. textile industry to inclusion of textiles in the ROZ plan.

Pakistan's inability to act against targets identified by electronic means gave the Americans the opportunity to stretch the original understanding. They unilaterally decided to take matters into their own hands, with an apparent go-ahead from President Bush, and equipped Predator drones with Hellfire missiles to strike high-value Al Qaeda and Taliban targets inside Pakistani tribal territory.

The Americans first used the weapon on January 13, 2006, against a gathering in Damadola in the Bajaur Agency, where, according to American information, Al Qaeda's second in command, Ayman Al Zawahiri, was present. Pakistan's military spokesman obfuscated the cause of the incident, attributing it to shelling from across the border. While the Pakistani army knew that the United States operated drones for intelligence gathering from facilities inside Pakistan, there was no understanding on the use of drones as weapons. The Americans apparently interpreted Pakistan's reaction as acquiescence in the use of drones for striking at targets. After a couple of minor drone attacks, barely noticed by the media, a high-visibility incident on October 30, 2006, embarrassed the Pakistan government. On that day, a drone strike targeted a madrassa in Damadola, where again the presence of Zawahiri was suspected. It led to the killing of more than eighty persons. Zawahiri, if at all there, had managed to escape.

Pakistan's official reaction, issued by the army spokesman, was to claim responsibility for the incident, explaining that the army had targeted the madrassa because of a gathering of foreign militants.[50] This claim was ill advised, because the lie was exposed by the electronic media, which reached the site the very next day and showed the debris of the American missiles on television, vindicating the opposition religious parties, who had blamed the United States for the attack. The Pakistani government, already facing growing media criticism for having dragged the country into an American war and for fighting against its own people in the process, now was attacked for failing to defend the country's sovereignty. Since the October 30 incident there have been sporadic drone attacks, each time drawing diplomatic protests from the Pakistan Foreign Office. The frequency of the attacks increased exponentially after the new Pakistani government took over following the February 2008 elections.

The issue of intelligence sharing and targeting of Al Qaeda and Taliban militants was long the focus of meetings between the U.S. and Pakistani military leadership. Pakistan had made several suggestions, from transfer-

50. *NYT,* October 31, 2006.

ring drone technology to Pakistan to placing drones under joint control. The U.S. officials feared that drone technology, if shared, could be replicated by the Pakistanis. In 2007, the United States finally agreed to establish centers near the border for joint monitoring of drone images to ensure joint responsibility and elimination of error as far as possible. By mid-2008, the U.S. CENTCOM set up a facility near Khyber, which faced considerable teething problems.

The collateral damage caused by U.S. drone strikes in Pakistan and U.S. aerial and ground action in Afghanistan raises hackles in both countries. On a number of occasions, for the sake of his political credibility, President Karzai has sharply criticized U.S. attacks, especially aerial bombings that sometimes hit wedding parties and other gatherings, resulting in large civilian casualties. The Pakistani government faced strong pressure from public and political opposition demanding cessation of the drone attacks. The government could not appear to be insensitive to civilian deaths or to overlook the issue of sovereignty. The government continued to make routine demarches, despite the awkward evidence that the U.S. drone flights originated from Pakistani facilities.[51] Hamid Karzai publicly embarrassed Pakistani Prime Minister Yousaf Raza Gilani in a joint press conference in Islamabad on March 11, 2010, by stating that drones did not fly from Afghan territory, implying that the United States was using Pakistani bases.[52] The successful targeting of a few high-profile Pakistani Taliban leaders in 2009, however, somewhat attenuated the public pressure and pointed to improved cooperation in intelligence sharing between Pakistan and the coalition forces.

The effectiveness of drone attacks in weakening Al Qaeda and the Taliban is much debated. Pakistani political analysts argue that the attacks fuel militancy. According to press reports through early 2009, more than seven hundred civilians had died in drone attacks as compared to a dozen or so Al Qaeda

51. *The Times* (London), February 19, 2009, identified "Shamsie base" in Baluchistan as being used for drone flights; *Los Angles Times,* February 13, 2009, attributed to U.S. Senator Dianne Feinstein a remark revealing that drones flew from bases inside Pakistan.

52. President Hamid Karzai stated: "We are not responsible for these attacks. They are being carried out by a powerful sovereign country, namely the United States, which is also a close ally of Pakistan. They [the drones] do not fly from our territory, but in our airspace; it is beyond our capacity to stop them." This quote is from an article by Robert Fisk, published in *The Independent* (London), April 6, 2010. A similar version was cited by the *News* (Islamabad), March 12, 2010.

members killed.[53] In tribal areas, extremists exploited the deaths resulting from attacks to recruit suicide bombers, invoking tribal traditions of revenge. At the same time, these attacks have been effective against some of the Pakistani Taliban leaders, pointing to a certain acquiescence in these operations on the part of the Pakistani government. Since 2008, drone attacks increased severalfold in frequency and, especially during 2010, showed improved precision in ground intelligence and targeting militants. Drone attacks overall thus underscored the sensitivities and complications of operations in the border regions and the need for better coordination with the Pakistani army, which has a definite interest in targeting the Pakistani Taliban leadership. The Pakistan government's ambivalence and its diplomatic protests are prompted by its desire to minimize unavoidable public embarrassment.

Pakistan has drawn two red lines. First, it has resisted repeated U.S. suggestions to expand drone operations to areas outside the tribal belt, in particular Baluchistan, where refugee camps, especially near Quetta, are suspected of sheltering Afghan Taliban leaders. Second, and particularly important, Pakistan firmly opposes any ingress by U.S. or ISAF troops across the Durand Line into Pakistani territory. The Americans wanted Pakistan to allow joint ground action, at least against high-value targets, but Pakistan declined for political reasons.[54] The attack by two U.S. military helicopters with troops, which entered the Pakistani border village of Jala Khel on September 3, 2008, to target a house allegedly occupied by militants, became a test case. The Pakistani army threatened that a repetition of such ground attacks would have consequences for mutual cooperation, including transit of NATO supplies through Pakistan. Pakistani authorities made good on the threat with a temporary suspension of the supply line two years later when NATO/U.S. helicopters attacked a Pakistani border post in the Kurram Agency on September 30, 2010. Both Admiral Mike Mullen, chairman of the U.S. Joint Chiefs of Staff, and Anders Fogh Rasmussen, NATO secretary-general, formally expressed regret for the incident. The Western mind takes seriously a firm and calm response backed by a clear willingness to act; noisy protests are often dismissed as ignorable paroxysms.

53. David Kilcullen and Andrew McDonald Exum, "Death from Above," *NYT,* May 17, 2009.

54. In *NYT,* December 1, 2010, documents released by WikiLeaks stated that in late 2009 Pakistan allowed "12 U.S. Special Operations soldiers" to deploy with Pakistani troops operating in the tribal area but not to conduct combat missions. The U.S. embassy cable described this as a "sea change in thinking." But the author does not draw the same conclusion from this revelation.

The Disconnect and Distrust

On the Afghan Taliban, the U.S. and Pakistani perceptions and approaches, especially at the operational levels, suffered from disconnect, if not divergence. The U.S. and ISAF forces were interested in targeting Al Qaeda and the Afghan Taliban and their supporters, while the Pakistani government, including the army and the ISI, were still adjusting their thinking to the new realities created by 9/11. The U-turn over the Afghan Taliban had become stated policy in late 2001, but on the ground the change could not be made that precipitously. Pakistan did focus on capturing and eliminating Al Qaeda, but the same rigor was not evident regarding the Taliban.

Those who criticize the Pakistan government and army for being soft on the Afghan Taliban fail to appreciate that Pakistan could not have acted to destroy and decimate them as the coalition forces did. Though it did target Al Qaeda members on the run, it did not target the Afghan Taliban fleeing from U.S. action in 2001 and 2002. This was not because Pakistan necessarily viewed them as assets for a future political dispensation in Afghanistan. Nor did the distinction that Pakistan made between the Afghan Taliban and Al Qaeda imply that the Pakistani military was scheming to develop active cooperation with the Afghan Taliban to keep the Afghanistan situation destabilized or willfully protect them for manipulation at a later stage.

Under Pakistan's reversed policy and U.S. pressure not to allow cross-border activity by the Afghan Taliban, the Pakistan government did take measures to restrain Taliban movement into Afghanistan, adding checkpoints, fencing, and troop deployment and increasing border monitoring. Intelligence sharing increased, resulting most notably in the targeting of Mullah Dadullah. Nevertheless, on top of Pakistani empathy with the Taliban, Pakistan had different priorities and limited capacity to interdict and control the Afghan Taliban movement. The Afghan Taliban did not take on Pakistani troops or carry out acts of violence inside Pakistan. The Pakistan government and army had as their primary concerns the Pakistani Taliban and other militants, including Al Qaeda, in the FATA. It was these elements rather than the Afghan Taliban who challenged Islamabad's writ and targeted government officials and army personnel in the area.

The divergence in coalition and Pakistani priorities came into sharp relief in Waziristan. From 2006 onward, U.S. and ISAF worries focused on the activities of Maulvi Nazir, a Waziri leader, and Sirajuddin Haqqani, the son of the well-known aging Mujahedin commander from Khost, Jallaluddin Haqqani. Maulvi Nazir protected Sirajuddin and his lieutenant, commander Hafiz Gul Bahadur, who shuttled between Afghanistan and North Waziristan organizing Taliban activities against the coalition forces in Paktia and Paktika, a stronghold of Jallaluddin since the 1980s. Pakistani military operations in Waziristan had been soft on Sirajuddin and his ally, Maulvi Nazir, in part because of the tribal rivalry between Nazir and Baitullah Mahsud, who had become the leader of the Tehrik Taliban Pakistan. In collusion with Al Qaeda, local militants, and extremist elements, Baitullah Mahsud had vowed to destabilize the government. Baitullah Mahsud and the TTP were the Pakistani army's priority target and nemesis, leading the insurgency in the tribal areas and causing mayhem in other parts of Pakistan, including major cities. They had been responsible for numerous suicide bombings and, according to the Musharraf government, the assassination of Benazir Bhutto in December 2007.

At the operational level, these differences caused considerable mistrust. Pakistan wanted information about Mahsud and his hideouts through U.S. electronic surveillance and wanted to use Mullah Nazir to squeeze Mahsud with the promise to weaken Nazir's alliance with Sirajuddin. U.S. and NATO officials believed that Pakistan was only interested in pursuing its own enemies and not those carrying out attacks inside Afghanistan against the U.S. and NATO forces. Even worse, they suspected that the Pakistani army was protecting Nazir and Sirajuddin as future assets. For their part, Pakistanis believed that U.S. drone attacks targeted Maulvi Nazir territory and spared the Mahsud area. The apparent U.S. reluctance to pursue Baitullah Mahsud gave rise to Pakistani misgivings and even somewhat outlandish speculation in the Urdu press that the United States and Kabul were helping Mahsud with arms and funds to undermine Pakistan. But Mahsud was no friend of the United States, as was evident from his bluster in late March 2009 threatening to attack Washington. He was eventually killed by an American drone attack in August 2009, which demonstrated better understanding and coordination at the armed forces and intelligence level under the new army chief, Gen. Ashfaq Parvez Kayani.

In a conflict situation, misgivings can easily be fed by the absence of coordination in the timing of various moves. The coalition decision in the autumn of 2009 to remove some border checkpoints was prompted by the new strategy, introduced by General McChrystal, to secure population centers rather than fight the Taliban in bordering regions. But the move came at a time when the Pakistani army was engaged against the Pakistani Taliban in Bajaur and Swat. The implication of the removal of ISAF posts, at least in the eyes of the Pakistani media, was connivance to let the Pakistani Taliban

escape into the adjoining Afghan territory. This gave rise to much speculation about the seriousness of the coalition in helping the Pakistani army's
operations to counter the TTP. Such misunderstanding and lack of coordination at the operational level are not exceptional and have even plagued
coordination among the coalition forces.

Beyond the question of differing perceptions and priorities, the Pakistani
army had limited capacity to interdict Afghan Taliban movement across the
border or to flush them out of their hideouts in Pakistan. Such an operation
would require huge resources and manpower. The Afghan Taliban have
taken advantage of the open border, free movement in the country, and the
natural hideout offered by the sprawling refugee camps and refugee populations in bordering towns in Pakistan. They blended in and lived among
the millions of Afghan refugees. It was also unrealistic to expect the Pakistani army to turn its focus to sealing the border and squeezing the Afghan
Taliban when it was preoccupied with the enormous problem of trying to
contain and neutralize the Pakistani Taliban and foreign militants in the
tribal areas. Taking on the Afghan Taliban while dealing with the local insurgency could have stirred up troubles that the Pakistani army would pre-
fer to avoid. The army was heavily engaged in countering insurgents and
militants in the border regions, with over 100,000 troops deployed by late
2007 and suffering large numbers of casualties.

Another disconnect is that between U.S. expectations and what the Pakistani military or civilian establishment could agree on counterterrorism cooperation. Since early 2007, as the Taliban insurgency grew alongside terrorist threats linked to militants in Pakistan and targeted against the West,
U.S. officials suggested that Pakistan provide access to data on all airline
passenger travel in and out of Pakistan to discern patterns that could help
preempt terrorist plots. Similarly, the United States sought access to all data
maintained by the ISI on terrorists beyond the information and investigations regarding specific cases of U.S. interest. Pakistan could not agree. No
responsible government could provide travel data on all its citizens, and
such an arrangement could invite an instant challenge in the courts. Later
in 2008, frictions developed over Pakistani refusal to allow a blanket provision of visas to U.S. security personnel, particularly in view of the notoriety already earned by the Blackwater (now Xe) security company in Iraq
and Afghanistan. These requests and suggestions for joint counterterrorism
operations and army action in North Waziristan continued to surface. Bob
Woodward in his book *Obama's Wars* identified them as the "four requests"
strongly taken up by National Security Adviser Gen. James L. Jones and

CIA chief Leon Panetta with Pakistani army chief General Kayani[55] in May 2010 following the abortive attempt by Faisal Shahzad, a U.S. citizen of Pakistani origin, to blow up an SUV in New York's Times Square on the first day of that month. Kayani was in no position to oblige in any significant measure beyond committing full cooperation on the Faisal Shahzad investigation.

FATA in the Crosshairs as the United States Increases Pressure on Pakistan

The years 2006 and 2007 saw a significant rise in suicide bombings inside Afghanistan that indicated increasing coordination between the Taliban and Al Qaeda and other extremist militant groups. In the eighteen months between January 2006 and June 2007, there were 193 suicide attacks targeting both NATO and Afghan government personnel and installations.[56] By late 2006, the increasing U.S. and NATO concern over the Taliban activity was reflected in officially expressed unhappiness with Pakistan. In February 2007, Secretary of Defense Robert M. Gates publicly called upon Pakistan to "do more."[57] Against a backdrop of heightened clamor about Pakistan's failing to do its share in combating the Taliban threat to Afghanistan, if not abetting the Taliban, and an increase in drone attacks, U.S. Vice President Dick Cheney visited Kabul and Islamabad in February 2007. His real intended destination was Islamabad, where he had a detailed one-on-one meeting with President Musharraf.

Cheney surprised and alarmed Musharraf when he consulted him about a plan predicated on extensive and simultaneous bombing of militant hideouts and compounds in Waziristan stretching over several days. Musharraf rejected the plan as untenable. Following Cheney's departure he contacted Bush, who reassured Musharraf that the United States would not pursue any such operation without consultations and Pakistan's consent. The episode was clear evidence that, like Kabul, Washington was now convinced that the FATA should be viewed along with Afghanistan as part of the theater of conflict. Pakistan could no longer effectively argue that the main problem

55. Bob Woodward, *Obama's Wars* (New York: Simon and Schuster, 2010), 364–66.
56. *NYT,* July 1, 2007.
57. *NYT,* February 13, 2007; and *NYT,* March 13, 2007, statement by Ronald E. Neumann, U.S. ambassador to Kabul.

ought to be addressed inside Afghanistan.[58] More important, in reaction to a serious incident, the United States could possibly resurrect the Cheney plan. One year later, the American assessment was baldly stated in a February 27, 2008, report to the Senate Armed Services Committee by Director of National Intelligence Michael McConnell. Al Qaeda, the report said, continued to maintain "active connections and relationships that radiate outwards from their leaders' hideout in Pakistan to affiliates throughout the Middle East, northern Africa, and Europe."

The year 2008 witnessed a sharp escalation in U.S. drone attacks in Pakistan, frequent expression of U.S. concern over Pakistan's inability to check Taliban and extremist militancy in the FATA, and increasing U.S. disappointment with the performance of the Karzai government. These were the dying days of the Bush administration, which had come under heavy attack in the election year for the misadventure in Iraq. Later in the year, as the economic crisis developed, it was partly linked to the hemorrhage caused by the war effort.[59] The administration wanted to show some dramatic successes and hoped to take out a few high-value Al Qaeda or Taliban targets. The drone attacks were justified to the U.S. public on the basis of lack of trust in the willingness or capability of the Pakistani army. An additional twist in media commentaries was that Musharraf, whose fortunes had by now collapsed, had engaged in double-dealing and was not sincere in fighting terrorism. American think tanks again resonated with the view that Pakistan was an unreliable ally and that it wanted to keep the Taliban option alive. The U.S. media charged that the United States had poured "billions" into Pakistan's economy but that Pakistan did little to defeat the Taliban and terrorism. This criticism obviously upset the Pakistani army and, coupled with the drone attacks, aggravated public opinion in the country.

Pakistan's perspective concentrated on the thousands of Pakistani citizens killed. By 2008, Pakistan had lost over fifteen hundred soldiers, with many times more civilians killed in the violence. Pakistan had suffered economic losses in the scores of billions of dollars in a war Pakistanis saw themselves as fighting largely at the behest of the United States. At the least,

58. *NYT,* February 27, 2007, reported that Cheney had gone to Pakistan to deliver a "stiff private message," expressing U.S. concerns about the ISI and the Waziristan peace agreement. *NYT,* February 28, 2007, carried an official denial that Dick Cheney's mission was to pressure Musharraf for failing to confront Al Qaeda and the Taliban.

59. In a November 17, 2010, *Washington Post* op-ed titled "In Memoir, Bush Spins Fiscal Fiction," Ruth Marcus, commenting on George W. Bush's memoir *Decision Points,* argued that Bush chose to go to war in Iraq with borrowed funds.

U.S. commentators were expected to appreciate the Pakistani military's efforts in capturing Al Qaeda members and dismantling the organization's structure. Moreover, Pakistan was facing a grim, complex situation domestically in the form of bomb blasts, suicide bombings, and rising militancy, especially in the FATA. If the efforts of the Pakistani army appeared less focused on pursuing the Afghan Taliban and more on fighting the homegrown insurgency, the local Taliban, Al Qaeda, and other extremists and militants, it was wrong to attribute this to any Machiavellian game or double-dealing on the part of Pakistan.

Notwithstanding these exacerbated antagonisms, here a clarification is in order. By 2008, the U.S. media and analysts often cited the figure of $11 billion in assistance (at times citing $15 billion for the period FY 2002–FY 2009) when criticizing Pakistan for not "delivering" on countering terrorism. The $11 billion figure wrongly characterized as assistance an amount of $6 billion, on top of the actual $5 billion assistance package. The $6 billion were "coalition support funds" reimbursed to Pakistan as payments for logistical support Pakistan provided and to supplement Pakistan's FATA deployments within the framework of Operation Enduring Freedom. These support funds accrued on the basis of a loosely negotiated understanding between the two defense establishments rather than on a formal negotiated accord. The practice that evolved on the basis of this understanding linked reimbursements mostly to Pakistani deployments in the counterterrorism effort rather than to the logistical support extended by Pakistan to the coalition forces. In addition to the use of Pakistani military bases, 70 percent of coalition (NATO/US) supplies passed through Pakistan. The reimbursements for deployments were ill conceived, as they undermined the position that Pakistan was fighting essentially its own war. They also entailed a cumbersome procedure that involved scrutiny on the part of the U.S. institutions, and differences began surfacing in early 2007.

Accusing the Pakistani army of double-dealing not only reflected a disregard for the difficulties of the situation inside Pakistan; it also denied the reality that the Afghan Taliban were both a byproduct and part and parcel of the circumstances in Afghanistan. The attitude of the coalition and the United States towards the Afghan Taliban started slowly changing by 2009, with cautious support to the Karzai government's reaching out to the Afghan Taliban for reconciliation. If, as the coalition expected, Pakistan had vigorously interdicted and eliminated the Afghan Taliban, how would it have looked in the face of this shift in U.S. policy? Besides being contrary to the position Pakistan had taken on the eve of the Bonn process and the difficulties it would have entailed, such an effort on the part of Pakistan would have been a source of deep bitterness and embarrassment.

Responsibility for the failure of the reconstruction effort and the sad economic conditions throughout Afghanistan, however, could not be laid at the doorstep of Pakistan or its tolerance of the Afghan Taliban. In 2008, a new emphasis emerged in Western public commentaries on the rampant corruption infesting the Karzai government. Part of this criticism was valid, but the timing raised questions about the underlying motivation. Blaming corruption and cronyism within the Karzai government for the dismal predicament of Afghanistan after spending $173 billion in the war effort did not help the image of the Bush administration, nor could it cover up the fact that the assistance disbursed fell far short of the challenge and the promises. The problem was compounded by the absence of an effective strategy for economic revival designed to suit the ground realities, which lent urgency to the need for a policy review by Bush's successor.

More than any other factor, however, it was the U.S. preoccupation with Iraq that distracted and weakened the U.S. engagement in Afghanistan. The United States simply could not commit sufficient troops or funds for reconstruction that might have made the critical difference in moving the country towards stabilization. The United States and its allies also could not focus on reconciliation and promoting democratic institutions in Afghanistan—the declared, albeit ambitious, objective of the U.S. military intervention. The coalition soon found it expedient to cooperate with many of the erstwhile warlords and ended up restoring their authority in their fiefdoms rather than strengthening governance under Kabul. In an article contributed jointly by former U.S. Secretary of State Madeleine Albright and former British Foreign Secretary Robin Cook in October 2004, the authors attributed the turmoil in Afghanistan to two realities: first, the world community had "never given Afghanistan the priority it deserved," and second, "tactics" used in Afghanistan had been inconsistent with "long-term objectives of stability and democracy."[60]

The apparent weakening of the coalition and the change of sentiment in the West, as exemplified by the controversies over Guantánamo Bay and Abu Ghraib, encouraged the Afghan Taliban and their supporters among religious elements in Pakistan. The European coalition started showing signs

60. "The World Needs to Step Up Its Help in Afghanistan," Center for American Progress, http://www.americanprogress.org/issues/2004/10/b213009html (accessed October 5, 2004).

of fragility in terms of commitment to the war effort, and President Bush lost two of his staunch European allies. Following the Madrid terrorist bombings, Prime Minister José María Aznar López lost the elections in April 2004. Three years later, British Prime Minister Tony Blair had to step down in June 2007, under the shadow of increasingly questionable policies relating to Iraq and Afghanistan. In Pakistan, Musharraf faced an ominous domestic political crisis. Within the international community, the United States remained the principal player and its attention was divided, with Afghanistan relegated to the position of a secondary theater of engagement. Even with a complete focus, the task of restoring peace and rebuilding the country was daunting. A diminished approach made it impossible.

The New U.S. Administration's Review and Shift in Strategy

During the election campaign Barack Obama had committed himself to continuing military engagement in Afghanistan, which he described as a war of necessity as distinct from the Iraqi war of choice. As expected, the new U.S. administration lost no time in instituting a policy review on a strategy for the next phase of the military engagement in Afghanistan. The public and academic discussion in the United States coinciding with the policy review revealed a range of opinion, generally reflecting fatigue with the military effort and little enthusiasm for restructuring domestic politics in Afghanistan. The minimalists asserted that Afghanistan had been as it was (anarchic) for a thousand years and was likely to remain so for another thousand years; the United States, they said, should simply focus on the Al Qaeda threat, eliminate it, and leave the country. It should, however, maintain its commitment to provide humanitarian and economic assistance. The broader view recognized the complexity of the problem while seeking a clear objective focused on security and stability rather than on promoting democracy. The debate leaned towards pragmatism and circumspection and awareness that not everything that might be desirable could be accomplished in Afghanistan.

The March 2009 review emphasized a comprehensive strategy, combining military action with political and economic elements. In this fundamental aspect, it was a continuation of the old policy outlined in the Afghanistan Compact adopted in London in 2006. The need to extend a hand to reconcilable opposition was no longer in question; it was the single most important conclusion of the joint grand jirga in the autumn of 2007. On the ground, both the Karzai government and, separately in the FATA context, the Pakistani government were making limited efforts to win "hearts and minds."

The U.S. objection to reaching out politically to Taliban leaders had led to certain confusion about good Taliban versus bad Taliban; yet, it had become clear by the end of the Bush administration that exclusive reliance on military action was no longer viable. The economic dimension was never in question; its success depended on resources and their effective application. The new approach under the Obama administration differed from the earlier U.S. position in its clear acceptance of the Afghan Taliban as part of the Afghan political landscape. The comprehensive strategy also demanded improved coordination among the allies, not only for military operations but also for reconstruction activity in Afghanistan. Thus far, the NATO allies had compartmentalized responsibility and divided the country into sectors for enforcing security and overseeing development.

The second distinctive feature of the review was the recognition of Pakistan as part of the theater of conflict, especially because the FATA was becoming the new sanctuary for Al Qaeda, Afghan and Pakistani Taliban, and their affiliated militant groups. In Pakistan, the new government accepted the hyphenated Af-Pak policy and did not object to this bracketing, which the official Pakistani position had resisted earlier. The new government had its sights fixed on a $7.5 billion five-year assistance package that Joe Biden, in his capacity as chairman of the Senate Foreign Relations Committee, had first promised during his visit to Islamabad in early 2008. However, it very soon became evident that the issues and problems facing the two countries were quite separate and could not be addressed by one policy. In practical terms, "Af-Pak" referred to two distinct policies.

The third significant difference between the old and the new policies lay in the vaguely defined desirability of regional cooperation, which, in theory, ought to involve India as well as Iran, Russia, and China in the efforts for stabilization and peace in the region. The role of the regional players, in particular improvement of relations and understanding between Pakistan and India, is important to peace and stability in Afghanistan and the region. However, because of India's strong resistance to discussion of its problems with Pakistan in any modality other than an essentially bilateral context, this element of the new approach, which was not clearly spelled out, was later quietly dropped. Nonetheless, the early contacts by Ambassador Richard Holbrooke, the U.S. special envoy for Afghanistan and Pakistan appointed by the Obama administration, included travel to New Delhi in his itinerary, and it was recognized that India-Pakistan tensions had an impact on problems and concerns involving Afghanistan and Pakistan and the conflict situation in the region.

Following the March 2009 review, the Obama administration decided to add another 21,000 troops to bring the U.S. military presence in Afghanistan close to 68,000 troops. This did not point to a major change in the military strategy, but it did reflect an enhanced focus on Afghanistan and the intention to facilitate robust deployments and tactics for the implementation of the existing military strategy. The March review did not foreshadow significantly intensified military activity, which would have required the dispatch of far greater numbers than the existing troop strength. The Iraq conflict engaged close to three times the number of troops for a country of smaller size and easier terrain than Afghanistan's. The American policy debates showed a clear reluctance to greatly increase the military commitment, as the United States remained watchful of a Vietnam-like incremental drift towards a wider commitment.

The change of U.S. command in Afghanistan, notably, the appointment of General McChrystal to replace Gen. David McKiernan in June 2009, led to a second review of the policy along the lines of the famous "troop surge" applied by General David Petraeus in Iraq's Anbar Province in 2007–8 to neutralize radical Sunni insurgents. Presenting his "candid" assessment to Secretary of Defense Robert Gates on August 31, 2009, General McChrystal requested an additional 40,000 troops for a new counterinsurgency strategy of protecting the population and building the Afghan army. He cautioned that the situation was "serious," and unless the United States gained the initiative and reversed the "momentum" of the militants in the next year, the "United States risks the outcome where defeating the insurgency is no longer possible." He concluded that "success was achievable" but depended on winning the people by protecting them. Briefly, McChrystal's strategy was based on several elements: protecting population centers instead of spreading troops over Afghanistan's mountains and valleys; halting the advance of the Taliban and breaking the momentum of violence; gradual transfer of responsibility to the Afghan security forces; improved coordination among the NATO/ISAF forces; improved governance and economic development; and efforts at weaning away mid- and lower-level Taliban and reintegrating them, and offering reconciliation to senior-level Taliban.[61]

61. Report to the Secretary of Defense dated August 30, 2009. Facsimile of the report can be found at http://media.washingtonpost.com/w.p-srv/politics/documents/assessment_Redated_092109.pdf.

The public controversy generated by the revelation to the press of this confidential report in September 2009 brought out the opposing view, attributed to Vice President Joe Biden, predicated on a limited counterterrorism strategy to be pursued with the existing troop strength. In November 2009, another confidential communication was leaked to the media, this time from U.S. ambassador in Kabul Karl Eikenberry expressing opposition to General McChrystal's proposal for additional troops unless the newly re-elected President Karzai agreed to clean up his administration. Finally, President Obama decided in favor of his appointed general, supported by Gates, Mike Mullen, and Petraeus, and agreed to an increase of another 30,000 troops by early 2010. At the same time, after reportedly consulting his top generals, Obama hinted at an eighteen-month timeline, identifying July 2011 as the time to start returning U.S. troops from Afghanistan.[62] The Republicans, led by Senator John McCain, severely criticized declaring a timeline for beginning troop withdrawals as an encouraging signal to the Taliban and others fighting Karzai and the coalition forces, forcing the administration to clarify that any reduction would be initiated only after a review. Nonetheless, indicating the timeline represents an acceptance of the reality that the U.S. military commitment to Afghanistan was not open-ended. It may also have been intended to serve as a message to the Karzai government to get its act together.

General McChrystal's candid analysis acknowledged the rising influence of the Afghan Taliban, especially in rural southern and eastern Afghanistan, and attributed the problem primarily to the failure of the U.S. and allied approach, which lacked focus and clarity of objectives. Meanwhile the Taliban had regrouped. More than half the provinces of Afghanistan, including a number of districts in northern and western provinces such as Faryab, Badghis, Herat, Baghlan, and Qundus, appeared to be under the influence of local Taliban commanders and shadow governors. The Taliban operated in these areas with ease and, by maintaining a coercive presence and appealing to tradition and nationalistic sentiment, ensured the cooperation of the local population, which knew little more than poverty and subsistence living. It was therefore argued that the new U.S. strategy was unlikely to

---

62. *NYT,* August 16, 2010. In an op-ed piece, "No 'Graceful Exit,'" Bob Herbert quoted Jonathan Alter's book on Obama's first year in the White House, *The Promise,* alleging a categorical affirmation by General David Petraeus and Admiral Mike Mullen that the United States could "train and hand over" to the Afghan National Army by July 2011 so that the drawdown could begin.

work. The Taliban could wait and choose their timing, whereas Americans were in a hurry and could not remain engaged indefinitely. U.S. and NATO forces could only bring temporary calm, but once they started moving out, the Taliban would return and reassert themselves.

This prognosis may not necessarily prove true. The population is tired of conflict and violence and may not stand by the Taliban. If the local economy of important population centers starts showing improvement and local and national elements begin to assume responsibility for security, the drawdown of U.S. and NATO troops would not favor the Taliban, as their rationale for fighting would weaken in the eyes of the ordinary Afghan.

Nonetheless, the intriguing leakage of the McChrystal review and the indication of a timeline, however equivocal, highlighted certain familiar aspects of the U.S. policymaking process that potentially run counter to the stated policy objective. The debate laid bare the weakness of the U.S. resolve in the face of limited public support for substantial escalation in troop numbers or a prolonged military engagement in Afghanistan. In spite of statements by the U.S. military leadership that the drawdown would depend on review of the ground situation, the reduction of the U.S. military presence would commence well before the next presidential elections in 2012. Equally obvious is that the exit strategy would not be precipitous. Its trajectory would be a shift from counterinsurgency towards counterterrorism, which has already two active elements in place for targeting insurgents: increased drone attacks and the CIA-organized Counterterrorism Pursuit Teams (CTPT) comprising Afghan and American components for covert operations. Meanwhile, the number of U.S. and NATO forces would gradually decrease, with the expectation that reconstituted ANA and police would take over responsibility for security, with residual NATO/ISAF forces receding in the background. The target for this transition has been set tentatively for 2014.

The first well-publicized operation in accordance with General McChrystal's blueprint came in February–March 2010 and concentrated in the Helmand region at Marja and Nad Ali, with a population barely above one hundred thousand. Along with Qandahar and its vicinity, Marja had long been regarded as the Taliban stronghold. Success in this area could become a turning point. On the other hand, this was an area where the Taliban had been operating against the British and been well adapted to a warfare of ambush, retreat, regrouping, and attack at the time of their choosing. The two months' battle petered out inconclusively, with the Taliban fighters melting away and merging with the surrounding population. Now the coalition and Afghan troops, estimated at around 15,000 for the operation, would need to stay long enough to oversee changes in local conditions that would deny the potential for an eventual Taliban return. Variants of the same strategy would have to apply to other population centers, in particular Qandahar, Paktia and Paktika, and Kunar to achieve the thus-far-elusive objective of reversing the momentum of insurgency. A weak link is the capacity of governmental administrative and security structures in an area and a population that have seen little central authority for decades.

The Pakistani establishment had initial concerns that the enhanced deployment of US/NATO troops and surge-like operations in southern and eastern Afghanistan might produce new refugee flows and an influx of Taliban into Pakistan. In the event, the surge and operations like the one in Marja did not presage a qualitatively different level of military engagement, which would have been the case had the United States sent a substantially larger number of troops into Afghanistan. Furthermore, such operations, involving troop concentrations, were meant to protect rather than dislocate the civilian population. A "surge" is supposed to be for a limited duration, just long enough to ensure that the Afghan government and army are sufficiently strengthened to be able to survive and help Afghanistan towards stabilization as the U.S. and coalition forces begin withdrawing. The fear of an influx of refugees or fleeing Taliban proved unfounded, but the possibility calls for continued monitoring and coordination between Pakistan and the US/coalition forces.

The minimal objective of dismantling and defeating Al Qaeda would require a protracted effort on the part of the United States. Efforts to stabilize Afghanistan and help Pakistan overcome its internal problems of militancy and extremism would require a long time and necessitate continuing U.S. engagement. Whether achieving these goals would be possible without a significant military presence is arguable. The U.S. military presence poses a paradoxical situation in that it has become as much a part of the problem as of the solution. The Afghan Taliban and militants claim legitimacy for the insurgency, describing it as a nationalist struggle against foreign occupation. Afghans are known to have resisted any foreign military presence historically, and such resistance is part of their folklore and sense of pride. But until a credible and effective national army is built in Afghanistan, a foreign military presence would be required to counter and pacify the militancy.

The Obama strategy faced another dilemma that came to light during the August 2009 Afghan elections. Part of the problem had been the expectation of the sponsors of the Bonn process, in particular U.S. and UN officials and activists, that Afghanistan needed transparent and fair elections to replace the Hamid Karzai's dysfunctional and corrupt government. The campaign by Western media and NGOs against Karzai became tantamount to interference in the election process. In tribal, ethnically divided, and conflict-ravaged Afghanistan it was difficult to envisage elections that would come close to withstanding international scrutiny. To start with, the environment was not conducive to elections in many troubled areas in the south and southeast. A candidate elected largely on the basis of a mandate from the north could have been ineffective in meeting the challenge of insurgency and helping the process of reconciliation. In the end, despite his reputation and the tainted process, Karzai emerged elected and enjoyed that modicum of credibility necessary to lead Afghanistan towards stabilization, provided he could assert himself politically.

General McChrystal's departure as a consequence of an article in the July issue of *Rolling Stone* magazine citing loose remarks by the general and his close associates, followed later in the month by WikiLeaks' release of thousands of operational-level communications and documents, were not just bizarre developments. They cast a shadow on the conduct of the war and ominously revealed U.S. weariness and frustration with the war. The lack of propriety and discipline underlying the reported remarks betrayed a psychology of unease. It was fortuitous for President Obama to have Gen. David Petraeus, the architect of the surge operation in Iraq, available to head the command and avert more serious consequences. With Petraeus stepping in, the Obama administration could credibly assert that the policy and strategy remained unaffected. Petraeus is politically savvier than McChrystal and better suited for managing a drawdown as soon as an upturn in the situation starts taking shape, though Petraeus has asserted that he was not mandated to preside over a "graceful exit."[63] He has already demonstrated his political skills by persuading President Karzai to agree to organizing and arming local vigilante groups to neutralize the Taliban. The challenge, however, continues to lie in enabling the Afghan government and security forces to contain and break the Taliban momentum in southern and eastern Afghanistan.

Credited with success in Iraq and as the author of counterinsurgency strategy, Petraeus would not be inhibited about escalating the heat on the Taliban through the use of force. It is argued that the Taliban must be militarily coerced and weakened before they would be willing to respond meaningfully to efforts for conciliation. However, the dilemma lies in the fact that "winning hearts and minds"—essential to counterinsurgency efforts—

---

63. *NYT,* August 16, 2010.

could easily be offset by intensive military efforts bound to displace and hurt ordinary Afghans.

The WikiLeaks episode is reminiscent of the Pentagon Papers disclosure in 1973. The first batch of documents released in July 2010 was primarily an embarrassment to the U.S. military over the compromising of their sources and contacts on the ground in Afghanistan. Broadly, these documents are field communications that reveal the mistakes and problems, especially civilian casualties, encountered during ground operations, reinforcing the already pervasive impression of a plagued war effort. Since the documents, mostly raw intelligence and updates, covered a period before the Obama administration, the White House and Pentagon could easily be dismissive of their significance.

Many of the leaked documents carried reports of linkages between the insurgent Taliban and Pakistani ISI operatives, attributed mostly to Afghan intelligence, which considered Pakistan an "enemy," as reported by the *New York Times* on July 26, 2010. There was nothing new in these revelations, which were the staple of Afghan complaints and media reports in 2006 and 2007. Whenever Karzai raised this issue in one-on-one meetings, Musharraf would ask for actionable information or evidence and accuse the Afghan intelligence of prejudice. On a couple of occasions he showed Karzai intercepted communications obtained from sources in Kabul saying that so many "ISI-trained terrorists" had entered Afghanistan. Musharraf would rhetorically ask how the Afghan intelligence had determined that these individuals were "ISI-trained." This in his view reflected the inherent hostility of the Afghan intelligence under Amarullah Saleh.[64] The specific references in the leaked documents to General Hameed Gul suggest that most of the Afghans' field intelligence was based on hearsay. General Gul, long retired from army service, had served as ISI chief in 1987–89 and was well known for his sympathies with the Taliban and as an implacable critic of the U.S. military intervention. However, his presence in Taliban strategy sessions to plan revenge for the killing of an Al Qaeda member[65] or similar activities at micromanaging Taliban tactics, as cited in press reports on WikiLeaks, made little sense.

The November 2010 batch of WikiLeaks documents comprises diplomatic communications. According to news accounts of the leaks, commu-

---

64. Following his removal, Amarullah Saleh publicly labeled Pakistan Afghanistan's "enemy number one."

65. *NYT,* July 26, 2010.

nications emanating from Islamabad reveal U.S. insistence that Pakistan act against the Afghan Taliban and U.S. frustration that Pakistan protected the Afghan Taliban as part of its strategic goals. U.S. officials remained skeptical of assurances from the Pakistani army chief that Pakistan and the United States were essentially on "the same page in Afghanistan."[66] They did not understand, as explained earlier in this chapter, that Pakistan (and for that matter many Afghans) could not treat the Afghan Taliban the same as the coalition did, and that this was not because Pakistan considered them future assets.

As expected, the WikiLeaks revived the familiar buzz in the U.S. press and electronic media about duplicitous games played by the Pakistani intelligence agency and Pakistan's unreliability as an ally. It fed into the distrust that grows with U.S. frustration in its military effort against the Taliban. An equally strong reaction to the perceived allegations appeared in the Pakistani media. Even those in Pakistan who value relations with the United States and U.S. support to Pakistan feel disappointed that U.S. opinion makers fail to appreciate the complexity of the problems Pakistan faces, the enormous loss in civilian and military casualties it has suffered, and the havoc wreaked inside Pakistan by the impact of the U.S. intervention next door, notwithstanding that the pathology of extremist violence has a lot to do with Pakistan itself.

Af-Pak Follow-up for Pakistan

While the Obama administration has formally linked Afghanistan and Pakistan in the overall strategy for the region, the Bush administration had also attached importance to Pakistan and its role for achieving U.S. objectives in Afghanistan. At the strategic level, the United States regarded Pakistan's cooperation as critical. This was evident in the expeditious moves by the United States to help Pakistan immediately after 9/11 and Pakistan's commitment of support. The United States removed all sanctions imposed following Pakistan's nuclear tests and the 1999 military coup and was helpful in the negotiations on rescheduling Pakistan's debts from international donors and the International Monetary Fund. The United States also offered an assistance package of $5 billion spread over six years (FY 2002–FY 2007), divided almost equally between military and economic assistance. At the

66. *NYT,* December 1, 2010.

same time, U.S.-Pakistan interaction, especially at the working levels in the context of Operation Enduring Freedom, reflected the distrust and misgivings discussed earlier in this chapter.

The essentials of the Obama administration's approach towards Pakistan are similar, with some differences in emphasis and changes in Pakistan's political circumstances and a more determined Pakistani effort to fight resurgent homegrown Taliban and extremist militancy.

The new assistance package, called the Enhanced Partnership with Pakistan Act of 2009, popularly known as the Kerry-Lugar Bill, and approved by the U.S. Congress in September 2009, is considerably larger than the assistance program under the Bush administration. The new package promised $1.5 billion annually for five years. But this offer has not been without controversy and the bickering that has become typical of the unsteady Pakistan-U.S. relationship. At the level of military cooperation, the Obama administration soon realized that with the exit of Musharraf, U.S. officials needed to have direct access to Pakistan's military leadership, somewhat in parallel with its dealings with the civilian government. Top U.S. military officials, including Admiral Mullen, General Petraeus, and General McChrystal, have been frequent visitors to Islamabad to maintain regular and direct contact with the Pakistani military leadership. Publicly, the understanding and consultations at this high level have a positive tone, and the U.S. generals have often lauded the efforts of the Pakistani military in Swat and then in South Waziristan and other parts of the FATA, to be discussed in some detail in chapter 5. The United States has also become more responsive to Pakistan's capacity-building needs. Yet this intensified and improved cooperative interaction has a subtext of frustration, evident in the repeated suggestion that the Pakistani army expand its theater of operations to North Waziristan.

The acrid debate in Pakistan as soon as the Kerry-Lugar Bill was adopted and became public pointed to the persistent unease and uncertainty in bilateral relations. The bill tied the release of military assistance to certification related to counterterrorism, nuclear nonproliferation, and an assurance of civilian control over the army. The somewhat gratuitous specificity impinged on the internal workings of Pakistani institutions and verged on indictment. For example, certification had to confirm Pakistan's cooperation in "closing terrorist camps in the FATA [and] dismantling terrorist bases in other parts of the country, including Quetta and Muridke," or that "the security forces of Pakistan are not materially and substantially subverting the political and judicial processes of Pakistan" or that "the Government of

Pakistan exercises effective civilian control of the military, including . . . approval of military budgets, the chain of command, [and] the process of promotion for senior military leaders."

Predictably, the media, the political parties, and, importantly, the military reacted sharply. The corps commanders' meeting on October 7, 2009, issued an unprecedented statement expressing its "serious concern" over the impact on "national security" of the clauses relating to the military, while deferring to the Parliament for a "national response." The controversy obliged Senator John Kerry, one of the authors of the bill, and Secretary of State Hillary Clinton to undertake visits to Pakistan in late October 2009 to clarify that the bill did not in any manner impinge on Pakistan's sovereignty and only referred to internal U.S. procedures required for monitoring. Stung by the criticism, the U.S. dignitaries visiting Pakistan to explain the bill even remarked publicly that Pakistan was not obliged to accept the package. The controversy thus eclipsed the significance of a measure that was meant to be the centerpiece of U.S. policy for helping Pakistan and enhancing cooperation and understanding between the two countries.

The conditions implied in the bill have only strengthened the voice of those who argue that the "war on terror" is not Pakistan's fight and that Pakistan is being used as hired help by the United States, which maintains an essentially transactional relationship with the country. The United States has the right to monitor how Pakistan uses its assistance, but the onerous Kerry-Lugar conditions and accusatory inferences were damaging to the common purpose. This was especially so after the Swat operation, when the Pakistani army was engaged in a massive and critical operation in South Waziristan, backed by strong and growing public opinion against Al Qaeda and Pakistani Taliban and militants. Ironically, these detailed conditions were unnecessary. The assistance is based on mutual interest and can be curtailed or turned off at any point of time for any reason the United States determines. But once built into the new assistance package, these conditions are seen by many in Pakistan as merely advancing the U.S. agenda. While to be helpful, the United States must be mindful of Pakistan's internal debate, the Pakistan government could not escape responsibility for its inexplicable failure to anticipate and forcefully engage the U.S. administration and Congress to remove the offensive language prior to the bill's passage.

In the military arena, in the autumn of 2009 following the difficult operations in Swat and South Waziristan, the coalition exerted considerable pressure on the Pakistani army, partly through the media, to launch similar actions against the Taliban and militant groups, in particular the Haqqani group in North Waziristan. The Pakistani army spokesman, however, made it clear that the army would act in accordance with its own strategy and priorities, as army chief General Kayani explained in detail when he visited NATO headquarters in Brussels in late January 2010. The general pointed to the four-phase strategy of "clear, hold, build, and transfer" and explained that the army would first consolidate gains and fully stabilize the areas already secured to prevent their falling back into militants' hands. He was frank about the army's overstretched deployment, noting "constraints on [its] capability to absorb and operate and [its] limited cutting-edge counter-intelligence/counter-terrorism capability, as well as limited budgetary space."[67] He dismissed aspersions on the army's motives by emphasizing that Pakistan was fighting its own war and that the army's credibility was at stake. By 2009, the army had lost 2,273 soldiers as compared to the 1,582 fatalities suffered by coalition forces. In its own "silent surge," Pakistan had deployed 147,000 troops in the FATA, as compared to the nearly 100,000 US/NATO troops in Afghanistan.[68] Despite the position taken by the Pakistani army chief, pressure on Pakistan to launch large-scale operations in North Waziristan will persist as long as it remains a base for Taliban activities inside Afghanistan and a suspected sanctuary for Al Qaeda operatives.

Another issue that has stirred misgivings from time to time has been the expectation that Pakistan could deploy more troops away from its eastern border to the FATA region. In early 2009, the Pakistani media had reacted sharply to expressions of concern in the U.S. media over Pakistan's move to shift some troops from the northwestern border to the east, in the aftermath of heightened tensions with India following the Mumbai terrorist attack of November 26, 2008.[69] The Pakistani media viewed it as an assault on Pakistan's sovereign right to make adjustments according to its own threat perception. Beyond this question of principle, the fact remains that the bulk of the Indian army, eight out of its thirteen corps, remains deployed against Pakistan.[70] There could be no assurance against a repetition of

67. *The News* (Islamabad), February 2, 2010.

68. Mariana Baber's interview with General Kayani, *The News* (Islamabad), February 13, 2010.

69. Pakistani officials later explained the move as a routine reshuffle involving two brigades. Even discounting this explanation, the scale of movement was not substantive enough to have stirred official and media concern in the West.

70. Ejaz Haider, "Debunking Arguments against Eastern Deployment," *Daily Times* (Lahore), May 27, 2009. Earlier, in 2002, Pakistan had shifted some of its troops from the FATA to the eastern border during heightened tension with India.

Mumbai-type incidents and an Indian threat of retaliation. India also has in the works a "Cold Start" strategy of close-range deployments for swift military strikes against targets inside Pakistan. Accordingly, the insurgency in the FATA region does not materially alter the Pakistani army's India-centric threat perception. In deference to Indian sensitivities, the United States remains shy about asking India to thin out its presence along the Pakistani border or to avoid issuing threatening statements.

While the Obama administration's new strategy on the Afghan war and U.S. engagement with Afghanistan and Pakistan are unfolding, American public sentiment has already pared the objectives in Afghanistan and set the direction towards gradual military disengagement. The U.S. military exit on the horizon will have far-reaching consequences just like those that flowed from its intervention more than nine years ago. Much will also depend on the circumstances and modality of U.S. disengagement. The United States will continue to have an important stake in Afghanistan and the region, where the interests of major regional powers also intersect. The next chapter will attempt an overview of these interests and an evaluation of future perspectives.

4

The External Powers:
Interests and Concerns

For three decades, the Afghan conflict in its various phases has been a source of turbulence in the region and a catalyst for developments far beyond its borders. During much of this time, the country has also been subject to the interplay of the competing interests of regional as well as major powers. In the 1980s, freedom movements in Eastern Europe were able to consolidate while the Soviet Union remained mired in Afghanistan. The Afghan conflict affected Soviet society in various ways and slowly raised public doubts about the official justification for the country's military intervention in Afghanistan, at the same time revealing the unassailable Soviet Union's vulnerability.

More than a decade after the Soviet Union's 1989 withdrawal and subsequent disintegration, Afghanistan became the epicenter of the 9/11 shockwaves and has ever since remained a major preoccupation of U.S. policy, figuring prominently in the 2008 U.S. elections. The U.S. area of concern has since broadened; the border regions of Pakistan that are contiguous to Afghanistan are seen as sanctuaries where Al Qaeda and Taliban militants can plan their next attacks against the United States or Europe.

Pakistan remains locked in the Afghan conflict, which has spread to its tribal areas (FATA) and parts of its two provinces bordering Afghanistan—North-West Frontier Province (NWFP) and Baluchistan. The Afghan Taliban struggle appeared to have conferred legitimacy on the Pakistani Taliban and extremist militants because of the growing perception of U.S. presence in Afghanistan as the source of the region's turmoil. The public debate emphasizing this perception complicates the task of the Pakistani government and military in countering domestic militancy and extremism.

Further complicating the situation is what can only be described as rivalry among the regional players, particularly Iran, India, and Pakistan, as they pursue their competing interests. This chapter examines the interests and concerns of the major external players in the region as they relate to the continuing conflict in Afghanistan, but it will not attempt to dwell on the history of Pakistan-India relations or the dynamics of U.S. relations with the two countries, except where relevant to the conflict situation.

Pakistan

In their overview of developments in Afghanistan since the Soviet troop withdrawal, the preceding chapters discussed a range of perceived Pakistani interests and motives. It is difficult to provide a definitive assessment of Pakistani interests, as several independent actors operate on both sides of the border in a peculiarly intertwined environment, combining both natural affinities and mutual unease, often described as two countries "joined at the hip."[1] The dynamics of Pakistan-Afghanistan relations and their mutual problems should not be viewed merely from the perspective of official policies and Kabul-Islamabad exchanges. There are massive informal interactions among a range of interest groups and people, including tribes and traders, operating in the border regions independently of the two countries' governments. Since the 1980s, religious-political elements on the two sides, especially the madrassa networks in the border regions, have assumed prominence. The phenomenon of these informal interactions is unique in terms of its scale, its roots in custom and tradition, and the high degree of public acceptance. It has been sustained and strengthened by the soft nature of the border, stretching over difficult mountainous terrain, and varying degrees of weak institutional governance on both sides of the border.

A policy of detachment between the two countries is inconceivable. Such an approach would be academic, if not outright impractical, in view of the virtually free interaction among tribes with ethnic kinship in a rough terrain across a border more than 2000 kilometers long. The interaction can be regulated but it cannot be stopped. The Afghans have contested this border, established as the Durand Line, without ever clearly stating the nature of their

---

1. President Karzai used this expression in his formal banquet speeches on several occasions during visits to Islamabad.

claim. Nonetheless, on the ground, the current conflict has reinforced an operational recognition of the border. The U.S. and ISAF forces respect the demarcation in terms of their ground operations. The coalition attack across the border into Pakistan at Jala Khel in September 2008 reconfirmed the position. The U.S. and ISAF forces acknowledged the border violation with a commitment to investigate and an assurance against its repetition. Pakistan has rejected offers by friendly interlocutors for diplomatic intercession to settle the Durand Line question, maintaining that it is a nonissue. Opening the issue could only add to confusion without in any manner helping to resolve the problems that have engaged the two countries and the international community.

The Pakistanis must understand that there cannot be a conventional firm border formally recognized by Afghanistan, because such a notion would defy the region's history, geography, and demographic realities. For their part, the Afghans must appreciate the necessity for a line marking the juridical and legal boundary between the two countries; and, as the colonial precedents dictate, that has to be the Durand Line. Improved operational and functional management of the border is in the interest of both countries. The two countries had a workable arrangement in the past, disrupted by the thirty years of conflict, with the refugee influx adding to the unregulated movement across the border. As the situation eventually settles down, regulatory measures will become necessary. To make these measures palatable and publicly salable, Kabul may expect Islamabad to improve facilitation of Afghanistan's trade with India.

The Pakistani debate on relations with Afghanistan has often focused on Islamabad's apparently legitimate interest in avoiding a two-front situation. Historically, in view of the chronic tension with India, Pakistan has been wary of close relations between Afghanistan and India, suspecting them of colluding to the detriment of Pakistani interests. In addition to Pakistan's belief that the Indian consulates close to its border in Jalalabad and Qandahar serve as centers of Indian intelligence activity, the visibly expanded influence of India in post–9/11 Afghanistan stirs anxiety within Pakistan's civil and military establishment. There have also been signs that the coalition is encouraging India to assume a larger role beyond participating in the reconstruction effort, including possible Indian involvement in rebuilding and training the Afghan National Army (ANA). This could open up the prospect of ANA dependence on India, especially when the U.S. and coalition forces start withdrawing from Afghanistan. Such an eventuality could raise hackles in Pakistan and become a new source of instability in the region. The Pakistani army chief's offer in late 2009 to train the ANA appeared to be essentially to preempt the coalition and Kabul from considering such a proposal from India.[2]

In mid-2010, however, Karzai accepted the Pakistani army chief's offer in principle, reflecting an upturn in Kabul-Islamabad relations. Karzai was asserting himself politically, as signaled by his domestic reshuffle and overture to the Taliban for reconciliation. In June 2010, Karzai removed Amarullah Saleh as head of intelligence and shifted the Tajik ANA chief Bismillah Khan to head the interior ministry. Amarullah Saleh was a particularly staunch opponent of any dealings with the Taliban and known for his strong views blaming Pakistan entirely for the conflict in Afghanistan. Since his removal, Amarullah Saleh has publicly turned his ire against Karzai. Nonetheless, it would not be helpful for Pakistani analysts to see these developments as diluting Kabul's interest in developing close ties with India.

Another source of rancor between Islamabad and Kabul had been the irredentist Pushtunistan claim, which, like the Durand Line issue, has had a fluid quality never clearly defined by successive Afghan governments. Pakistan was irate that Afghanistan was the only country to have opposed Pakistan's admission to the United Nations. Under King Zahir Shah, Sardar Muhammad Daoud, Afghan prime minister from 1953 to 1963, was a principal protagonist of the Pushtunistan idea. But Daoud did little to articulate or push it when he overthrew Zahir Shah and declared himself president of the country in 1973. During the five years of his presidency, his most provocative act came in his first presidential speech to the nation, when he mentioned Afghan interest in the separated Pushtuns living in Pakistan. Before his overthrow, and wary of Soviet pressure, he was eager to improve relations with Pakistan. But over the years, the naming of a "Pushtunistan Square" in Kabul and occasional gatherings of Pushtuns in Kabul, including invitees from the Pakistani tribal belt or opposition Pushtun political leaders, agitated many in the Pakistani government establishment. On its part, Pakistani intelligence agencies sheltered Afghan dissidents, including some latter-day Mujahedin leaders, who opposed the monarchy and the Daoud regime.

The issue has a psychological undertone on both sides. As noted in the introduction, the Afghans never reconciled to the Durand Line and claimed a historical and cultural interest in the affairs of the Pushtuns on the Paki-

2. Comment by Rahimullah Yusufzai, "Behind Kayani's Training Offer to Afghans," in *The News* (Islamabad), February 9, 2010.

stan side. At the time of the partition of British India in 1947, the most prominent Pushtun leader, Khan Abdul Ghaffar Khan, had opposed the accession of NWFP to Pakistan. Kabul's rhetoric about Pushtunistan encouraged dissidents in the province. In retrospect, however, neither the Afghan reservations to the Durand Line nor the Pushtunistan issue ever posed a real threat to Pakistan.

During the 1980s, in the several contacts that Pakistani officials had with King Zahir Shah, he invariably impressed upon his Pakistani interlocutors that in 1965 and 1971, when Pakistan was locked in conflicts with India, its border with Afghanistan had been secure and he had conveyed assurances in this regard to the Pakistani leadership. Indeed, Zulfikar Ali Bhutto had publicly acknowledged his appreciation that Afghanistan had assured security on Pakistan's northwestern border during 1965 and 1971. Sardar Daoud, suspicious of increasing Soviet influence and the activities of the left-leaning People's Democratic Party of Afghanistan (PDPA), reached out to Pakistan. Between June 1976 and March 1978, his talks with Zulfikar Ali Bhutto and then with Zia ul Haq laid the beginnings of an emerging understanding towards settling "the difference," that is, the Durand Line.[3] In April 1978, however, Daoud was overthrown in the leftist coup led by PDPA elements.

In the early 1980s, to assuage any Pakistani concerns, the Soviets and Afghan leader Babrak Karmal offered assurances against raking up the border or the Pushtunistan issue, provided Pakistan stopped supporting the Afghan Mujahedin. Apart from the perceived strategic threat to Pakistan implicit in the prospect of consolidation of the Soviet presence in Afghanistan, it was nonetheless Pakistan that, with international backing, stirred things up on its northwestern border by helping the Afghan Mujahedin. Today, the danger emanating from this direction is of an unconventional character that threatens both Afghanistan and Pakistan and has a global reach.

The kind of conventional security threat that Pakistan faces on its eastern border is inconceivable along its northwestern border with Afghanistan. The force imbalance between the two countries notwithstanding, the ethnic mix of the ungoverned and autonomous populations that inhabit both sides

---

3. Sardar Daoud had begun to feel pressure from Moscow and wanted to open up to Pakistan and Iran, which were then formally allied to the West. Details of his conversations with Zulfikar Ali Bhutto and later with Zia ul Haq are recorded by Abdus Samad Ghaus, former Afghan deputy foreign minister, in his book *The Fall of Afghanistan: An Insider's Account* (Washington: Pergamon-Brassey's International Defense Publishers, 1988), 127–46.

of the border turns it into a buffer that would deter any conventional maneuvering in a military offensive. Nonetheless, the apprehension of a two-front threat led Pakistan to seek a "friendly government" and "strategic depth" in Afghanistan. These dubious propositions, which gained currency —especially after the ouster of Najibullah and the advent of the Taliban— have only hurt Pakistan. They have deepened distrust and misgivings among the educated Afghan elite, who have a history of unease with Pakistan and have suspected that Pakistan wanted to treat Afghanistan as its backyard.

Furthermore, a "friendly government" and "strategic depth" were inherently problematic concepts. Pakistan's apparently legitimate interest in a friendly government led to the temptation of supporting favorites, an elusive pursuit that ignored the fundamental lessons of history and politics in Afghanistan, where meddling by neighbors and attempts to install favorites have only aggravated problems. The idea of seeking strategic depth in Afghanistan made little military sense. Even as a natural desire for a secure border in the northwest in the event of a military conflict on the eastern front,[4] it was at best awkward, if not devious and offensive to Afghan sensibilities.

The mirror image of these questionable concepts has been the widespread presumption in Kabul and among Western political analysts that Pakistan, in particular the ISI, continued to view the Afghan Taliban as assets for a time when the Americans, like the Soviets, would abandon Afghanistan out of fatigue and that country would experience another political convulsion. The disconnect in the approaches of the Pakistani army and the coalition forces towards the Afghan Taliban and the divergence in their priorities and tactics were examined in the previous chapter. Pakistan's position on the Afghan Taliban has been partly vindicated by the Obama administration's review and its acquiescence in the Karzai government's reaching out to the Afghan Taliban. Pakistan had argued that Pushtun interests and the Afghan Taliban could not be ignored in any political dispensation aimed at bringing peace and normalcy to the country. For Pakistan, this was a legitimate position to take, as intertwined as it is with Afghanistan in several dimensions of ethnicity, culture, and politics, in addition to history and geography. However, the contention that Pakistan views the Afghan Taliban as assets for the post-U.S. period in Afghanistan requires a closer examination.

4. When subjected to scrutiny, Pakistani military proponents of the idea could not articulate "strategic depth" beyond the notion of a secure and peaceful border in the context of the conventional threat on the eastern border.

Backing the Afghan Taliban could not be a viable option for Pakistan, not only because it would only embolden the Pakistani Taliban and extremists. The Taliban came to rule Afghanistan under peculiar circumstances of total collapse inside the country and indifference on the part of the international community, a scenario that is unlikely to be repeated. Even at the time, internal ethnic divisions and external attention on the part of Russia, India, and Iran had successfully prevented the Taliban from overrunning the country. These external actors have become far more vigorously involved and have a much stronger presence in the country now as compared to the situation in the early 1990s.

Even if some analysts in the Pakistani intelligence establishment are playing with the idea of a far-off post-U.S. scenario in Afghanistan, can they realistically believe in the return of Mullah Omar or of Gulbadin to Kabul? Jallaluddin Haqqani or his son Sirajuddin can be discounted because they were and, if they survive, would remain local leaders. An ailing, aging commander once lionized by both the CIA and the ISI, the elder Haqqani is known to be receiving treatment in Pakistan. Given the culture of intelligence agencies and local traditions, the ISI cannot hound him out of the country. He and his son retain their support base in Khost, Paktia, and Paktika and have staunch sympathizers among the tribes of Waziristan.

A Taliban resurrection in Afghanistan is an improbable prospect because opposition to the Taliban is now strong. Afghanistan is no longer the neglected, war-torn country of the mid-1990s. Under the gaze of the international community, the Taliban cannot conceivably launch military assaults on cities and maneuver their forces in the various regions, as they had been able to do in the 1990s. The non-Pushtun population and even some Pushtuns have no stomach for another Taliban rule. Furthermore, in the later years of their rule, the Afghan Taliban had become heavily dependent on the Pakistani Taliban, who are now viewed by the Pakistani public as a threat and by the Pakistani government as a challenge to its writ in the country. In a post-U.S. scenario, the Taliban could at best expect to wield local influence in a fragmented Afghanistan; they cannot hope to return to Kabul. As for Gulbadin, Pakistan could not succeed in helping him achieve his ambitions in the early 1990s under more propitious circumstances; his chances to rule Afghanistan in future are near zero.

Another view—that Pakistan is protecting the Afghan Taliban to exploit them in balancing Indian influence in the future—presumes that Pakistan would pursue factional politics in Afghanistan. This makes little strategic or tactical sense from Pakistan's point of view. Such a policy would only be a recipe for prolonging the turmoil in Afghanistan and thereby continuing to hurt Pakistan more than any other external player in the region.

In the soft and amorphous political environment of Pakistan, however, one cannot rule out contacts between the Afghan Taliban and some military individuals, especially retired personnel, who may have cultivated the Mujahedin and the Taliban in the 1980s and 1990s as part of state policy. These individuals, often described as "rogue elements" in the Western media, would have personal links within the intelligence organization, but they would not be acting at the behest of the agency. In the 1980s and 1990s, ISI behavior could be faulted, but it was consistent with the generally accepted policy of those years. As with the post-9/11 changes in Pakistan's policy, the ISI was required to reorient itself to implement the government's new agenda. As in the 1980s, the ISI after 9/11 developed close liaison and cooperative arrangements with the CIA and other foreign intelligence agencies. Any possible interaction between former intelligence officials with the Afghan Taliban or extremist elements that had once enjoyed official patronage cannot be confused with official policy. It is not uncommon that retired personnel from organizations such as intelligence agencies often cling to their beliefs and remain immune to change.

The widespread impression, partly promoted by the Pakistanis themselves, that the ISI behaves as an independent actor persists because at times some of the headstrong ISI chiefs, either in cahoots with army top brass or taking advantage of political leaders' proclivities or weaknesses, used the agency to meddle in internal politics. However, for most of the past three decades, during which the agency gained notoriety for manipulation and influence, Pakistan was under military rule. The ISI was acting in conformity with government policies when it served as Pakistan's interface with the Afghan Mujahedin groups in the 1980s and subsequently, in the 1990s, when it abetted the Kashmir Jihad, using religious elements. Zia ul Haq had decided to restrict the Afghan Mujahedin's contacts to the ISI for receiving supplies of arms, as, for good reason, he did not want to encourage independent Mujahedin weapons dealings with foreign governments. Nonetheless, despite the widely assumed military and ISI antipathy towards India, Zia was able to maintain his "peace offensive" towards India. Later, in 2004, Musharraf was able to push for normalization with India.

It can be argued that the ISI was more restrained under the military rule of Zia and Musharraf than during the civilian governments in 1990s. Then, its influence over policies relating to India and Afghanistan became more pronounced and excessive, particularly in practical dealings with the Afghan factions, and later the Taliban, or in supporting the Kashmiri uprising. Yet, this role was in sync with broad government policies. Like any institution, the ISI is not monolithic; but by and large, it did not act independently of the government of the day. Hawkish views on security and foreign relations often associated with the ISI and the military are, in fact, quite common within the Foreign Office and civilian establishment, partly owing to the long periods of military rule in Pakistan.

The opponents of Musharraf blame him for a U-turn on Afghanistan and for military action in the tribal areas, which they say intensified extremist violence in Pakistan. Musharraf's actions had become inevitable in view of the events that followed 9/11. Pakistan could not have stopped the U.S. military action or shied away from its responsibility to counter Al Qaeda and extremist militancy. It had no alternative strategic options. Tactically, in the tribal areas, the Pakistani approach showed accommodation. It tried peace agreements, despite Afghan and international objections. This course of action was dictated by ground realities and exigencies and sought to pacify the tribal population affected by militancy, rather than to keep the "Taliban option" open. Indeed, on the issue of combating militancy and Pakistan's participation in the "war on terror," rather than institutional differences within the government, there was a disconnect between official policy and public sentiment agitated over U.S. military intervention and wary of perceived U.S. interests in the region.

The 9/11 calamity affected Pakistan's official policy but not public sentiment. Relations at the human level between the Taliban and the Pushtun populations in the border regions did not dissolve, and the sympathy that had existed did not diminish but instead became heightened following the U.S. military intervention. The view of the Taliban and even of Al Qaeda among the Islamist elements within Pakistan was completely at odds with the official policy. A popular counternarrative to the official view emerged that 9/11 was a conspiracy hatched in the West against Muslims, and the Taliban were among its early victims. Conspiracy theories gained in strength with the Iraq invasion.[5] Official Pakistani policy, with its emphasis on Paki-

---

5. The popular view takes as truth the innuendos such as those in Thierry Meyssan's *9/11: The Big Lie* (Carnot USA Books, 2003), asserting that the Boeing 757 had not hit the Pentagon and that it was instead hit by a missile or a truck bomb, and in Michael Moore's documentary film *Fahrenheit 9/11,* which have served to strengthen the conspiracy argument. Though these works may not be familiar, arguments similar to those in the Meyssan book and the Moore documentary are frequently offered to substantiate the counternarrative, thanks to ubiquitous information technology.

stan as an ally in the "war on terror," became divorced from the broad public sentiment that turned increasingly skeptical of U.S. motives and believed that Pakistan had been sucked into America's war. The 2007 groundswell in this view owed in part to the unpopularity of President Pervez Musharraf following his dismissal of the chief justice and the Lal Masjid (Red Mosque) operation. Located in the heart of Islamabad, Lal Masjid became the scene of a showdown between the government and the mosque's militant clerics that ended in a bloody military action in July 2007. This development, which drew considerable international attention, will be discussed in the next chapter.

Within the Pakistani establishment the broadly shared view is that a stable Afghanistan is in the best interest of Pakistan and the region. It is assumed that such stability will depend on reconciliation among the country's several ethnic groups rather than political dominance by any one of them. Support for the Taliban government in the late 1990s was motivated partly by the expectation that the Taliban could bring stability to Afghanistan. Equally important were the obvious friendliness of the Taliban regime, which had little contact with the outside world, and its isolation, which made it somewhat dependent on Pakistan. Despite this apparent advantage, Pakistan demonstrated little ability to manipulate or influence the Taliban, as was the case when it dealt with the disparate Mujahedin groups then residing in Pakistani territory. The post-9/11 situation is far more somber for Pakistan, which now has minimal influence with Kabul. In the circumstances, Pakistani policymakers cannot conceivably contemplate the possibility of a pliant future government in Kabul. In Pakistan there is little desire to treat Afghanistan as an extension of Pakistan, a "fifth province"; instead, there is weariness caused by decades of conflict.

Trade Issues

The continuing conflict and turmoil in Afghanistan have largely dissipated earlier excitement about the anticipated opening of trade routes to Central Asia and about energy corridors transforming Pakistan into a gateway to that region. If, however, Afghanistan stabilizes and Pakistan overcomes its current spiral of violence, the economic potential is substantial. Economic relations between the two countries have long been a source of both strength and friction. Much of landlocked Afghanistan's trade has traditionally passed through Pakistan, regulated under a 1965 Afghan Transit Trade Agreement that allows transit to Afghan imports from all countries through the port of Karachi. The porous border has also been the site of flagrant smuggling activity involving the tribes on both sides. According to rough estimates, over two billion dollars' worth of goods subject to high Pakistani tariffs are brought into Afghanistan under the transit trade arrangement and then returned to be sold in Pakistani markets.[6] Close to a half million tons of wheat are smuggled into Afghanistan in addition to the roughly 600,000 tons officially exported to the country.[7] Smuggling is one of the main sources of funding for the insurgents as well as for warlords and criminal mafias operating in the area. Besides legal and illegal commerce, over 70 percent of the supplies to the U.S. and ISAF forces pass through Pakistan.[8] A major consequence of this activity is the emergence of strong transportation interests, largely in the hands of the Afghan and Pakistani Pushtun entrepreneurs.

The Afghan government has had persistent grievances against the Pakistani policy on transit trade, mainly in two areas: first, permission for Afghan trucks to drive to and from Pakistani ports for transportation of Afghan transit goods, and second, overland trade with India. Joint working groups set up from time to time to streamline procedures to remove impediments have been unable to offer solutions that satisfied the Afghan side. The main reservations regarding inland transportation by Afghan trucks have come from Pakistani transport interests. Nevertheless, the trucking problem has not been particularly severe, because Pushtun transporters from both sides of the border have controlled a large part of the business.

As for the second issue, Pakistan has allowed the use of the overland route from Torkham to Wagah only for Afghan exports to India of dry and fresh fruit. India could not use this overland route. Pakistan agreed to some flow of humanitarian or emergency consignments of Indian goods on a case-by-case basis, but insisted that India use the Karachi port for its ex-

---

6. The magnitude of smuggling can be gauged from the example of television sets. In 1996, when the Taliban ruled in Kabul and had banned TV viewing, Pakistan put TVs on the negative list under the transit trade facility. That year Pakistan's domestic production jumped from 72,000 to 288,000 sets. In 2005, when TVs were taken off the negative list, domestic production dropped from 795,000 to 534,000 sets and legal imports into Pakistan from 935,000 to 690,000. The problem is the differential in tariffs. On electronics, the Afghan tariffs are close to 5 percent whereas in Pakistan they are in the range of 35 to 40 percent. The same applies to items like tobacco and auto parts. Governmental working groups are examining various proposals, including narrowing the tariff gap.

7. These are Government of Pakistan estimates.

8. According to the *NYT,* March 4, 2009, Pakistan allows transit of 2000–3000 containers carrying NATO supplies every month.

ports to Afghanistan. The Afghan government complained that this restriction adversely affected Afghanistan's trade with India. Another problem was that Afghan trucks were not permitted to carry goods destined for India all the way to the Indian border. According to the existing practice, goods in transit are loaded onto Pakistani trucks in Peshawar and carried to Wagah, where the goods are transferred across the Pakistan-India border through a cumbersome process involving manual labor. Pakistan and India did not allow each other's trucks to enter their respective territories. These restrictions were ostensibly necessitated by security considerations. The resulting delays often caused damage to goods, especially fresh fruit.

On July 18, 2010, the two countries signed a "Note for the Record" in which Pakistan agreed to allow Afghan trucks to ply between Afghanistan and Karachi and Wagah carrying Afghan transit goods. At Wagah, Afghan trucks could transfer cargo onto Indian trucks and carry Pakistani goods on their return trip. Afghanistan in turn would allow Pakistani trucks through its territory to Central Asia. This understanding would firm into an agreement after cabinet approvals. The understanding attracted unwarranted criticism in the Pakistani media regarding a reference in the note that a "feasible proposal" for Indian exports to Afghanistan through Wagah "could be discussed at an appropriate time in the future." In practical terms, this did not amount to a commitment, yet the critics attributed it to U.S. pressure because the note was signed in the presence of the U.S. secretary of state and the United States had earlier prepared a study on the potential of overland transit trade.

The underlying considerations for disallowing overland trade to India have been twofold. At the political level, permission for such trade has been linked to full normalization of relations, which depends on progress toward the resolution of disputes, in particular on Kashmir. At the economic level, facilitating overland transit from India evoked Pakistani traders' fears of losing trade through competition. The issue was also linked to the larger problem of bilateral trade between Pakistan and India. In the meantime, India has partly overcome the handicap regarding access to Afghanistan by diverting its trade through Iran.

Pakistan's trade with Afghanistan swelled from a mere $70 million in the days of the Taliban to $1.2 billion in 2006. Pakistan was well placed to supply much of the construction material needed for reconstruction activity in Afghanistan after the U.S. intervention. President Karzai on many occasions referred to the trade benefits to Pakistan. He also made the political point that support of the insurgency might delay reconstruction or even provoke Afghan government retaliation and would hurt Pakistan. In the foreseeable future, trade between the two countries should increase with the anticipated intensification of Western military engagement and economic development aid envisaged under the new Obama policy.

Within its limitations, Pakistan has contributed to post-9/11 reconstruction in Afghanistan. It has provided $300 million for a number of projects, the most significant of which was the construction of the Torkham-Jalalabad dual highway. President Karzai joined Prime Minister Shaukat Aziz to inaugurate the road in 2007 and had words of high praise for the quality of the construction. Pakistan is working on setting up technical schools and medical facilities in Kabul and has offered a thousand scholarships to enable Afghan students to pursue studies at technical universities in Pakistan. Until 2006, the Afghan government had spurned the scholarship offer for the inexplicable reason that Afghan parliamentarians and concerned ministries were reluctant to accept Pakistan's help on education. They argued that Taliban elements operating from Pakistan were destroying schools inside Afghanistan, and that Pakistan should first restrain these elements. During Musharraf's visit to Kabul in September 2007, however, Karzai agreed to reconsider and later accepted the offer, which has since been doubled. Over the years, thousands of Afghans who have grown up in Pakistani cities have availed themselves of higher education facilities in Pakistan.[9]

Afghanistan is central to Pakistan's desire for access to Central Asia. Since the emergence of the post-Soviet Central Asian republics, Pakistan maintains as a declared policy goal to develop itself as the hub of economic activity, taking advantage of its geostrategic position and linking South Asia, Central Asia, and West Asia through energy, communications, and commercial corridors. The main obstacle to the realization of these possibilities continues to be the lack of transit access through Afghanistan, which remains hostage to the turbulence in that country. Pakistan built the Gwadar port, with Chinese assistance, on the western coastline of Baluchistan for the purpose of servicing commerce to and from Central Asia and to be a major energy port located just outside the Persian Gulf. So far the port remains dormant, attracting little business even as a transshipment facility. Plans for setting up a large oil refinery have also made no progress. The construction

---

9. According to Muhammad Sadiq, Pakistani ambassador in Kabul appointed in early 2009, more than 6000 Afghan students were enrolled in Pakistani universities and professional institutions in 2010.

of a prospective gas pipeline from Iran through Pakistan to India could have helped make the port operational. India pulled out of the negotiations in 2008, while discussions between Iran and Pakistan dragged on over the pricing formula, as oil prices kept shooting up during 2007–2008. Pakistan and Iran finally concluded an agreement in May 2010, when the shadow of international economic sanctions hung over Iran.

Pakistan's Regional Prospects

Regional developments have an impact on Pakistan's efforts to develop its potential as a transit country and hub for regional commerce. In addition to domestic stability and security, three factors are fundamental to the Pakistani objective: first, peace and stability in Afghanistan, highlighted in the preceding analysis; second, Pakistan's willingness to allow land transit through its territory to India; and third, the future development of China's Xinjiang region with a resultant export surplus, especially from the southern part of the province. Without any of these conditions materializing, Pakistan cannot develop into an economic hub for the region, and its potential to become so would diminish over time as alternative routes and communications are developed.

A proposal for a gas pipeline from Turkmenistan to India through Pakistan and Afghanistan gave rise to considerable speculation, prompted by hints of incipient rivalry for the pipeline project between Unocal (Union Oil Company of California) and Argentina's Bridas. The two companies tried to court the Taliban in Qandahar for the project in the early 1990s,[10] but it never advanced beyond an elementary interest. U.S. officials did not see a real chance that the pipeline would ever materialize, but they encouraged the idea in the hope that the prospect of shared pipeline profits might bring the warring factions to the conference table.[11] By the late 1990s, after a brief hiatus, Russia started reasserting its influence in Central Asia, while the newly independent Central Asian republics, controlled by old guard leaders from Soviet days, had no incentive to break away from Russia, especially because of their fear of radical Islam. Turkmenistan allowed the project to turn cold, while the Russian oil conglomerate GASPROM, with rights over gas reserves in the country, often dismissed it, hinting that the Turkmens had no gas to sell to Pakistan.

10. Rashid, *Taliban*, 145–46.
11. *The 9/11 Commission Report,* 111.

To gain access to Central Asia by circumventing Afghanistan, the Pakistan government tried to develop a northern route for commerce using the Karakoram Highway (KKH) through China and Turgut Pass to Kyrgyzstan and Kazakhstan. A quadripartite agreement was signed in March 1995, but modalities for transit of goods by trucks remained the subject of discussion in an effort to work out a plethora of bureaucratic procedures. Political interest in opening the route appeared to have dampened, especially after the rise of religious extremism in Pakistan. The KKH is open to bilateral overland trade with China, but its volume has not exceeded $200 million and that comprised mostly of Chinese consumer goods. Pakistan has officially offered the use of its port facilities to China and the other Central Asian countries, but the response, at least in practical terms, is tepid. At President Musharraf's urging, the Chinese agreed to upgrade the road to make it capable of bearing heavy traffic with forty-foot containers. Other ideas—for a rail link and oil and gas pipelines—are at best dreams for the future, for which the first requirement would be peace and stability in the area.

Pakistan's best hope from the activation of the KKH lies in the fast development of the Xinjiang region, which is rich in natural resources but remains one of the least developed regions of China. Development in this part of China would create demand for the use of Pakistani ports, which provide the shortest access to the sea. However, this route is an unlikely corridor for Chinese commerce originating from China's major manufacturing centers, located mostly on or near its eastern coastline. China's official drive to develop its western regions is focused on the provinces of Sichuan, Chongqing, Yunnan, Guizhou, and Shansi, technically part of West China but located in the geographical middle of the country, with land openings to Southeast Asia and India.

Pakistan's ambition to become a hub of economic activity would be difficult to realize without the opening of transit routes to India. When Pakistan initiated the idea of activating the KKH for commerce with Kazakhstan and Kyrgyzstan in early 1993, the two countries were enthusiastic. The Kazakh minister for transportation convened a meeting and invited both the Pakistani and Indian ambassadors based in Alma Ata.[12] He was disappointed to learn that India could not be included at that time, in view of tensions in relations between the two South Asian neighbors. The size of India's market creates the potential and generates the interest to enliven prospects for overland transit. Even for the prospective Iran-Pakistan-India gas pipeline, Iran was eager for Indian participation. For its part, Pakistan

---

12. The author was then the Pakistani ambassador in Alma Ata.

was ready to enter into a bilateral arrangement with Iran in case India did not join for ostensible reasons of pipeline security or plausible consequences for its nuclear deal with the United States.

Sensing a certain improvement in Pakistan-India relations, during the strategic dialogue the United States initiated with Pakistan in early 2006, the United States formally proposed the promotion of a Central Asia–South Asia axis for economic, trade and energy cooperation. The idea was not a counter to the Shanghai Cooperation Organization, as suspected by some analysts, because both Pakistan and India are observers at the SCO and seek formal membership in it. As always, the potential of such an arrangement would depend on improvement in Pakistan-India relations.

India

India has retained a steady influence in Kabul except during the brief Taliban interregnum, when it closed down its embassy and consulates in Afghanistan. Although India has taken advantage of the uncertainties in Islamabad-Kabul relations, it has never taken a formal position on the delicate issues of Pushtunistan or the Durand Line, the frontier of British India.[13] The historical relationship between India and Afghanistan dates to the Afghan dynasties that ruled India for centuries. The Anglo-Afghan wars of the late nineteenth century and Afghan King Amanullah's asylum in British India in 1929 are still recounted as part of the lore of the British Raj that was inherited by both successor states. Although no longer a neighbor, India has maintained and developed strong cultural links with Afghanistan, offering education facilities to a large number of Afghans. Indian films and TV programs popular among urban Afghans further enhance India's cultural influence. Many of the Afghan elite have personal links with India and in the turbulent times the country has faced since the Soviet military intervention have sent their families to live in India.[14]

13. An interesting remark is attributed to the Indian leader Mahatama Gandhi when he visited the Khyber Pass in 1946. On being informed that he stood at the northwestern border of India, Gandhi raised his finger to the north as if pointing to the Hindu Kush range and said, "No, the border lies there." This was told to the author by Sardar Shahnawaz, former foreign secretary of Pakistan.

14. President Karzai and many prominent Afghan leaders studied in India, and their families had lived in India. The same can be said about many other Afghan leaders, who, along with their families, also lived in Pakistan and continue to maintain establishments there.

India's ambivalence over the Soviet action did not draw any severe reaction from most Afghan expatriates except those residing in Pakistan and sympathetic to the Mujahedin groups. To the surprise of many, India abstained on the January 1980 UN General Assembly resolution that called for Soviet withdrawal, a position that it subsequently maintained. India also succeeded in building close trust with elements of the Northern Alliance, particularly during the 1992–96 period when Ahmed Shah Massoud controlled Kabul and was engaged in a deadly struggle first against Gulbadin and then against the Taliban forces. At the same time, Indian linkages with the Pushtun elite ensured that it did not earn their ire but rather retained their goodwill.

During the Taliban days, the Indian diplomatic profile on issues relating to Afghanistan remained low-key; it was not a member of the UN-sponsored "Six-plus-Two" group. However, the Indians maintained contacts with and assisted Ahmed Shah Massoud and other Northern Alliance leaders. In the post–9/11 situation, India has played an active role and has been part of every international conference and international initiative to advance the Bonn process and the reconstruction effort. By 2008, India had contributed $750 million for projects inside Afghanistan, in particular the 213-kilometer Zaranj-Delaram road,[15] inaugurated in March 2009. This road has strategic importance, as it will allow India to export goods to Afghanistan using the Iranian port of Chahbahar, bypassing Pakistan, and reduce Afghanistan's dependence on Pakistan for its trade. India is involved with a number of other infrastructure projects, including the repair of the southern parts of the ring road. In addition, India is constructing the new parliament building in Kabul and has undertaken projects in the health, education, power, telecom, and transportation sectors.

Over four thousand Indian workers and security personnel were at work in Afghanistan by 2008. Following incidents of kidnapping and attacks, especially on road construction sites close to the Pakistan border, the Indians brought in trained paramilitary personnel for security. India established a small base in Farkhor, Tajikistan, in support of its activities and personnel inside Afghanistan. Apart from signifying the rise in Indian influence in the country and a perceived corresponding loss for Pakistan, the presence of the Indians so close to its borders provokes Pakistan's sensitivities. In Pakistan, questions are raised about why the Indians choose to contract projects near the Pakistani border and in troubled areas when there is much they could do

---

15. Web site of the Indian Ministry of External Affairs, May 2008.

in the Afghan north. They could instead let others conduct projects in the south, although Kabul has the sovereign right to let any country engage in reconstruction in any part of the country. This activity by India, coupled with reported visits to the area by RAW operatives and the presence of the Indian consulates there, has been a constant sore point, especially in the Pakistan intelligence community. The Indians, on the other hand, suspect a Pakistani intelligence hand in the attacks on Indian personnel. Indian National Security Advisor M. K. Narayanan accused the ISI of instigating the July 2008 suicide attack near the Indian embassy in Kabul that resulted in the death of the Indian military attaché.[16]

In 2006, before the Mumbai commuter train blasts, the composite dialogue between Pakistan and India was proceeding relatively smoothly, and the Indian side informally suggested discussing possible cooperation in helping Afghanistan to settle down. It looked to Islamabad like another Indian approach intended to soften Pakistan on the transit issue, which Pakistan had linked to progress towards resolution of bilateral disputes and normalization. At that point Pakistan had made only one exception to this linkage, in the case of the gas pipelines from Iran and Turkmenistan to India through Pakistan. The suggestion to cooperate on Afghanistan evoked an ephemeral interest in Islamabad that was soon to be lost in the downturn in relations.

However, the Indian suggestion was substantive. The Obama administration's Af-Pak approach also recognized the need to involve India in a strategy to address regional issues. Given the two countries' inextricable influence on Afghan factional politics, some understanding and cooperation between Pakistan and India could have a positive impact on the Afghanistan situation. To that extent, normalcy in Afghanistan depends on easing of relations between Pakistan and India.

India and Iran have a convergence of interests and an incipient partnership in relation to Afghanistan. Apart from historical relations, politically both countries' influence in Afghanistan owes in good measure to their consistent support for the Northern Alliance leaders. There are nuanced differences of emphasis in this support; for example, the Iranians sheltered Ismael Khan and Gulbadin Hekmatyar and have a sectarian interest in protecting the minority Shia interests. But these interests do not give rise to a divergence in approach from that of India.

16. *Daily Times* (Lahore, Pakistan), July 13, 2008.

On the economic plane, the convergence is striking. Iran desires to develop commercial routes through its territory to Afghanistan and Central Asia, while India has the same interest in reaching out to the region through routes that bypass Pakistan. Almost the entirety of India's commerce with Central Asia now passes through Iran. The Zaranj-Delaram link will further lessen the critical importance of Pakistani land routes for access to landlocked Afghanistan. Not surprisingly, Pakistan views such developments in a zero-sum context as a corresponding loss of Pakistan's trade in the area.

Iran

As a neighbor, Iran has a long and intertwined history of relations with Afghanistan and its people. Much of modern-day Afghanistan had been part of the Persian empires of antiquity. In more recent times, Herat and Qandahar had been under the control of the Safvid dynasty until Ahmed Shah Durrani consolidated his rule by rallying the Afghan tribes. Tajiks speak Dari, the classical form of Persian that is the predominant language spoken in Kabul. As with Pakistan, Afghan relations with Iran have their share of mutual misgivings and suspicion. Throughout the 1980s, Iran remained mired in its conflict with Iraq. Apart from providing help to over two million Afghan refugees, it kept a low profile regarding the Afghan resistance and the diplomatic process that sought Soviet troop withdrawal. Pakistan kept Iran informed about the Geneva negotiations, and Iran voted for the Pakistan-sponsored resolution in the UN General Assembly, but with an explanation that implicitly blamed the United States for interference in Afghanistan.

The Iranians began focusing on Afghanistan as the Iran-Iraq war reached a stalemate in the late 1980s. At that time, the Iranian thinking had a distinctly sectarian cast, which was opposed by the Peshawar-based Mujahedin leaders, especially the hard-line groups of Gulbadin, Sayyaf, and Yunas Khalis. Another issue was the Iranian influence with the Shia community in the FATA area, especially the Kurram Agency, where a firebrand Shia cleric, Allama Arif ul Husseini, who had once studied in Qom, had a running quarrel about the passage of weapons through the Parachinar salient and the growing influence of the Mujahedin in the area. There were incidents of his interdicting weapons going into Afghanistan and reports that he was trying to acquire Stinger missiles to pass on to the Iranians. Arif al Husseini was assassinated in Peshawar in June 1988, the fateful year that also saw the death in August of President Zia ul Haq in a plane crash. During 1990–91, the Iranians sought Pakistani cooperation to ensure a certain percentage representation for the Shia groups in any interim arrangement. At the same time, Iran put together a group of nine Shia parties in Tehran as a counterpart to the Islamabad-based seven Tanzeemat, actively promoted Shia Hazara parties,[17] and forged closer ties to the Dari-speaking Tajiks who had rallied around Burhanuddin Rabbani and Ahmad Shah Massoud.

The rise of the Taliban was a challenge to the Iranians because of the anti-Shia creed the Taliban had developed at madrassas operating under the Saudi Salafi influence. The killing of the Iranian personnel in Mazar e Sharif in 1998, most probably at the hands of Pakistani anti-Shia elements in the ranks of the Taliban, created an unbridgeable divide and led to implacable Iranian hostility towards the Taliban. Iran's concern for return of the Iranian bodies and captured personnel and investigation of the incident dominated subsequent "Six-plus-Two" meetings. Iran also fully supported the Northern Alliance with weapons and funds, as the Osh incident revealed.[18] Iranian antipathy to the Taliban could be gauged by Iran's offering asylum to Gulbadin Hekmatyar when he was obliged to leave Pakistan at the Taliban's insistence. As soon as the Taliban were dislodged from Kabul, the Iranians pushed him back into Afghanistan. The American intervention in Afghanistan that caused the Taliban's ouster proved to be a windfall for Iranian interests, despite their public opposition to the U.S. presence in the country.

The Taliban period also benefited Iran indirectly. In the early 1990s, the Central Asian republics were wary of the Iranian revolutionary regime and its religious rhetoric. Such concerns faded with the emergence of the Taliban and produced instead a coincidence of views about the common threat posed by the Taliban. Meanwhile, Iran developed a rail link connecting Mashed with Ashgabat at the Sarakhs crossing point on the Iran-Turkmenistan border, thus providing the Central Asians a vital access to the Arabian Sea.

Tehran maintains a degree of cordiality in its relations with Kabul despite worries over the presence of the U.S. forces. U.S.-Iran hostility had

17. Iran supported Karim Khalili, Mohaqeq, and Mazari, but was suspicious of Sheikh Asef Mohsini, whose group was the first to resist the Soviets and had nominally become part of Yunas Khalis's Hisb e Islami to receive arms from Pakistan.

18. In October 1998, on inspection in Osh, Kyrgyzstan, a railway freight train was found loaded with Iranian military equipment bound for delivery into Afghanistan.

spawned speculation, but no evidence, on Iranian complicity in allowing Al Qaeda elements to cross into Iraq. Similarly, the early U.S. charge of linkage between Al Qaeda and Saddam Hussein turned out to be without justification. By 2003, much of Al Qaeda had already fled Afghanistan to hideouts in the Pakistan-Afghanistan border regions where both ISAF and Pakistani forces have since pursued it. Iran, on the other hand, has concerns about U.S. encouragement to dissident Iranian groups and criminal elements operating in western Afghanistan, in particular the Jundullah group led by Abdul Malik Regi, whom the Iranians were able to capture in March 2010. The group has been blamed for terrorist bombings inside Iran. The Tehran government desires close liaison with Islamabad to counter Jundullah activity and movement, as well as close coordination to curb drug trafficking.

The Iranians appear to understand U.S.-Pakistani military cooperation in the Afghan context and have avoided making it into an issue in bilateral dialogue with Islamabad. Pakistan, however, remains sensitive to U.S.-Iran hostility and is particularly uneasy over the prospect of U.S. strikes against Iranian nuclear installations and the consequences for the region. During late 2006 and early 2007, because of noticeable escalation in the Bush administration's threatening rhetoric, the subject came under discussions between the Pakistan and Iran, including during Musharraf's brief visit to Tehran in early 2007 to explain his initiative for a Middle East peace process.[19] The Iranian leadership seemed confident of coping with any eventuality.

As the United States pressed Pakistan to back down from the Iran-Pakistan-India pipeline project, mostly at the technocratic level, Pakistan defended its deep interest in the project, in view of its growing energy needs. Pakistani officials argued that if the United States wanted to be helpful, instead of raising objections to the IPI pipeline it should assist Pakistan with the Turkmen pipeline project by interceding with the Russians, who appeared to control the Turkmen gas reserves.

---

19. In early 2007, Musharraf traveled to Iran, Turkey, Indonesia, Malaysia, Saudi Arabia, Egypt, Jordan, and Syria in an effort to develop a Middle East initiative that would address three major issues: Palestine and the Arab-Israeli conflict, the Iraqi problem, and the rising Iran-U.S. confrontation. Apart from basic ideas on each of these problems, the initiative was aimed at forming a group of important Islamic countries not direct parties to the various issues that would play a role with the United States and the EU in particular. The effort was abandoned after March 2007.

The politics underpinning the energy corridors suggested that neither Russia nor Iran could be sanguine about a north-south pipeline through Afghanistan and Pakistan. The Russians acquiesced in the Baku-Tbilisi-Ceyhan oil pipeline at a time when Moscow was preoccupied with domestic change. Turkey signed the agreement with Azerbaijan in March 1993, immediately after the emergence of the CIS. The pipeline, more than 1,000 miles long, became operational in 2005. Tehran, for its part, has an interest in developing its own resources and the use of its Chahbahar port as an outlet for Central Asian commerce and, possibly, energy. On the face of it, this Iranian interest conflicts with the development of an alternative route through Afghanistan and Pakistan. Yet it would be stretching the case, as Iran's critics often do, to argue that Tehran would want to keep the pot boiling in Afghanistan until its own north-south corridors to Central Asia are fully established.

Despite the theocratic disposition of its government, Iran's policy in the region, including its Afghanistan policy, has been largely pragmatic and circumspect. It has been able to build relationships of confidence with the Central Asian states and has succeeded in putting at rest their fears about the export of Iran's revolution. Toward Afghanistan, Iran has pursued a security-oriented policy, but with a partisan emphasis in support of the Shia and non-Pushtun groups. It recognizes the moderate Pushtun base of the Karzai government and has shown little agitation over the presence of U.S. troops in Afghanistan. Iran has cooperated with the Bonn process, something even the United States recognized.[20] Taking advantage of the ascendancy of the Northern Alliance, Iran secured important representation for all pro-Iran elements in the Kabul government. Pro-Iranian Karim Khalili has been one of the vice presidents, and Yunus Qanooni became the speaker of the Parliament's lower house. Shia Hazaras have a greater share in the government institutions than ever before. The Iranian contribution to reconstruction in Afghanistan until 2008 was estimated at $660 million. Iran has also succeeded in repatriating most of its Afghan refugees, applying some pressure and aided by the relative calm in northwest Afghanistan, where stability is critical for Tehran.

20. U.S. envoy to Afghanistan James Dobbins acknowledged that his instructions were to press for "a broadly based representative government," and the word "democracy" was introduced at the recommendation of the Iranian delegation (Philip Kurata, "Former U.S. Envoy to Afghanistan Reviews Bonn Agreement," http://www.America.gov, October 6, 2005).

Saudi Arabia

Saudi Arabia's impact on the region has been complex, multidimensional, and deep, particularly on the Pakistani and Afghan societies since the 1980s, when the oil boom coincided with the Afghan Jihad and the Iranian revolution followed by the Iran-Iraq war. Al Qaeda's presence in the region, the Taliban's outlook and orientation, and the rise of religious extremism in the region have been inextricably linked to Saudi Arabia, though not as the objective of the Saudi government or a product of its deliberate policies. These phenomena are mostly the unintended consequence of Saudi Arabia's enormous oil wealth and the austere but harsh Wahabi, or Saudi Salafi, theology[21] and culture that this wealth has helped to propagate.

This is not to say that Pakistan and Afghanistan have not benefited from the oil largesse of the Saudi kingdom. Over one million Pakistanis and close to one hundred thousand Afghans have found gainful employment in the country. Saudi Arabia has major investments in Pakistan and has helped Pakistan financially at critical junctures, in particular through concessional terms on oil supply following Pakistan's 1998 nuclear tests and resulting U.S. sanctions. The Saudis were among the principal contributors to helping over three million Afghan refugees residing in Pakistan since the early 1980s. Saudi wealth also fueled the Afghan Jihad, matching dollar for dollar what others contributed for covert assistance for the Afghan resistance against the Soviets. And although Saudi generosity has helped Pakistan, unintentionally it has contributed to the growth of obscurantism, which in combination with regressive influences at home and external circumstances has sapped the country's ability to develop its full potential for progress.

Saudi Arabia has a schizophrenic quality to its persona, embedded in the alliance forged by the founder of the kingdom, King Abdul Aziz Al Saud, between the dynasty he established and the Wahabi orthodoxy. Respectively they control the state structure and the spiritual authority in the country. The

---

21. The terms Wahabi and Saudi Salafi are used interchangeably. Salafi, in Arabic meaning "from predecessors or ancestors," is a generic term for revivalist movements in Islam that emphasize returning to the practices of early Islam or the times of the holy Prophet's companions and the two succeeding generations. Salafis also call themselves Ahl e Hadith (people of the tradition) or Ahl e Towheed (people who believe in the Unity of God). Wahabism and the Saudi Salafi creed go back to Muhammad ibn Abdal Wahhab, the eighteenth-century reformer from Nejd in the Arabian Peninsula. The later revivalist thinkers such as Muhammad Abduh, Jamaluddin Afghani, and Rashid Rida founded the Egyptian Salafi revivalist movement in the nineteenth century.

Saudi ruling family maintains a strong alliance with the United States, based on assurances of security guarantees in exchange for U.S. access to Saudi oil. The Wahabi orthodoxy, on the other hand, has been the effective protagonist of Jihad against Western interests in the last two decades and a powerful inspiration for the angry "jihadist" elements, including Al Qaeda.[22]

The Saudi government acted largely in tandem with the U.S. government in helping the Afghans with material resources to fight the Soviets. The Saudi foreign minister was the first to weigh in for a stronger resolution against the Soviets at an emergency OIC meeting in January 1980, calling for de-recognition of the Soviet-installed regime in Kabul and condemnation of the Soviet intervention. The Saudi intercession was believed to be coordinated with the Americans, especially in view of Pakistan's preference for a milder version put forth at the preceding meetings at the United Nations. Unlike the United States, however, the Saudi government's interest in Afghanistan continued beyond the exit of the Soviet troops; it actively tried to promote conciliation among Afghans, especially after the Mujahedin takeover of Kabul in 1992. Saudi Arabia's anticommunist orientation and concerns provoked by the Iranian revolution initially accounted for its activism in Afghanistan, but it was later spurred by Saudi interest in stabilizing the war-ravaged country. The Saudi government distanced itself from the Taliban when they refused to hand over Osama bin Laden.

The Saudi religious establishment and charities, operating in parallel with the government but independently of it, have had a profound impact on Afghanistan and the region. Rabita al-Alam al-Islami and the educational and relief organizations affiliated with it were the most prominent Saudi-based semiofficial Islamic charities. As noted in chapter 2, Maktab al Khadmat was among the most significant Saudi private organization that raised funds for the Afghan Mujahedin groups fighting the Soviets. Its leader, a Palestine-born radical Islamic scholar, Sheikh Abdullah Yusuf Azzam, encouraged a large number of Arab youth to visit Peshawar to help the Afghans. One of the first to authoritatively pronounce the Afghan struggle

---

22. "Jihadist" Islam needs to be distinguished from "political" or "radical" Islam. "Jihadist" is normally applied to the Islamic militant groups with a commitment to global jihad against the interests of the West and its perceived allies in the Muslim world; they are quintessentially defined by Al Qaeda. Initially, Al Qaeda's agenda was limited to evacuation of U.S. and allied forces from Saudi Arabia and Palestine. "Political" or "radical" Islam is a broader description that applies to essentially political Islamist movements indigenous to many Islamic countries that focus on local agendas rather than an international agenda.

as an "obligatory jihad," he believed in creating a vanguard for a jihad to liberate all Muslim lands under foreign occupation. Following Azzam's assassination in 1989, Osama rose to prominence and created his own militia of Arab youth to fight in Afghanistan, the precursor of Al Qaeda.

In addition to fostering the Arab jihadists, the Saudi charities' other significant contribution was the mushrooming in Pakistan and Afghanistan of madrassas teaching the Saudi Salafi version of Islam. The Saudis saw a challenge in the rise of Shia theocracy in Iran, which spawned a Sunni-Shia rivalry that deeply affected Pakistan and the region. Sunni clergy of the Deobandi tradition, which had a philosophical affinity with Wahabi religious doctrine,[23] developed a strong bond with the Saudi religious sheikhs and philanthropists, leading to the establishment of thousands of madrassas that later fed the ranks of religious militancy in Pakistan and Taliban in Afghanistan. Oil wealth and religious zeal, buoyed by the collapse of the Soviet Union, extended the Saudi Salafi influence, partly through its Pakistani adherents, as far as the newly independent Central Asian states.

The Saudi government washed its hands of the Taliban after the September 1998 showdown between Mullah Omar and Prince Turki over the Osama issue. The Saudis downgraded their presence in Kabul and withdrew their direct assistance to the Taliban. But this development did not affect the private Saudi involvement through religious circles and charities and the flow of private funds to the Taliban and the madrassas. The events of 9/11 had shaken the Saudi rulers out of their complacency towards the extremism and violent anger gestating within the Saudi society, caused in part by Salafi sheikhs' routine advocacy of jihad and their largely xenophobic attitude towards other cultures, especially those of the West. Saudi Arabia also generated massive funding for madrassas in other Islamic countries that propagated the same philosophy, with disastrous consequences.

On the domestic front, the Saudi government has moved onto a war footing, arresting suspected extremists and Al Qaeda members and initiating a major program for their reform and rehabilitation, using "learned clerics" who understand the message of peace and tolerance in Islam.[24] However,

---

23. Both traditions followed a puritanical doctrine that emphasizes the Quran and the Sunnah as the only authority and guidance for a Muslim and rejected *bida* (innovation) in religious practices. In comparison with Deobandi tradition, which accommodates a cultural range, Wahabism is culturally far stricter and narrower, especially on the seclusion of women in the society and the status of minorities.

24. In explaining the Saudi policy on reforming the extremists, the Saudi ambassador in Islamabad, Ali Awadh Asseri, once enthusiastically endorsed a comment by the

there are no parallel Saudi efforts to reach out and reverse the violent creed instilled by the Saudi Salafi madrassas outside the Saudi Kingdom or any effective measures to control the flow of private funds to these institutions. The Saudis can play an important role in reforming the Salafi madrassas, especially in helping Pakistan to bring them into the mainstream of the country's education system. Similarly, the Saudi government and its religious establishment can help counter extremist religious tendencies that have been partly sustained by Saudi funds and Wahabi inspiration in many parts of the Muslim world, particularly in Pakistan and Afghanistan.

Leaders from Saudi Arabia and the other Gulf Cooperation Council (GCC) countries have often underscored the importance of Pakistan for the security and stability of the Gulf region. They look at the country as a significant factor in the regional balance of power. Its geographic proximity, the region's demographics, and the presence of nearly two million Pakistani expatriates in the GCC countries appear to validate this assessment. In the past, many of these countries had relied on Pakistan to help organize their security forces, and many Pakistanis form part of their security apparatus and have a reputation for loyalty to the host country. There is significant ongoing cooperation in the military field, including exchanges, training programs, and deputation of personnel, even though, broadly, Pakistan pursues a policy of neutrality in intra-Arab disputes. In addition to its strong economic and trade relations, Pakistan has a vital stake in the stability of the Gulf region. Saudi Arabia, the United Arab Emirates, and Kuwait are among Pakistan's principal oil suppliers and largest investors in wide-ranging sectors of the Pakistan economy, including energy, agriculture, infrastructure, and telecommunications.

The United States

Past U.S. relations with Afghanistan have been largely ad hoc and mostly reactive to events and developments of strategic importance. Since 9/11, though, the United States has publicly declared a long-term commitment. But the United States shifted emphasis towards Iraq while the Afghan situation remained unsettled, necessitating U.S. engagement with no letup. The

---

author, made only half seriously, that perhaps Pakistanis did not correctly understand Islam and Pakistani extremist elements were beyond reform because they did not understand Arabic.

diversion of U.S. attention to Iraq was reminiscent of the early 1990s, making it appear that the United States was in the habit of walking away and leaving the job unfinished.[25] The Bush administration assigned clear primacy to the Iraqi theater. In December 2007, in testimony before the U.S. Congress, the chairman of the Joint Chiefs of Staff, Admiral Mike Mullen, put it plainly: "In Afghanistan, we do what we can. In Iraq, we do what we must."[26] The Obama administration has brought the focus back on the conflict in Afghanistan with a succession of policy reviews. It recognized that the situation in the region had deteriorated since the early success of the U.S. military intervention, and now both Afghanistan and Pakistan required sustained U.S. attention.

Despite adjusting the objective, narrowing it to the elimination of Al Qaeda–related militancy, and indicating a drawdown in troop levels beginning in mid-2011, the U.S. military presence in Afghanistan and Operation Enduring Freedom are likely to continue in the foreseeable future. Al Qaeda is intertwined with several layers of local militancy and violence in the region, and rooting it out will entail a complicated, protracted effort. The Afghan Taliban and Pakistani extremist groups had primarily local agendas and motivation; however, association with Al Qaeda and the multinational jihadist presence in Afghanistan has imparted an appreciation to some of these elements of the relevance of striking at targets beyond the region. The continuing violence and extremism in the region thus have implications for U.S. homeland security. In this age of globalization, allowing a region to become a safe haven for Al Qaeda–like groups with an international outreach presents a clearly unacceptable risk.

Until the late 1970s, Afghanistan hardly figured in the U.S. strategic vision. It was relegated to the backwaters of Asia or presumed to lie within the Soviet sphere of influence. Soviet economic assistance to Afghanistan was several times greater than that from the United States. For their part,

25. In a jointly written op-ed article appearing in the *New York Times* of October 5, 2004, former U.S. Secretary of State Madeleine Albright and former British Foreign Secretary Robin Cook stated that "the United States–led coalition and the international community need to do what we failed to do after the overthrow of the Taliban. We must formulate and implement an integrated strategy for recovery that does not skimp on manpower, resources, or forces; one that takes into account the full gamut of threats rather than addressing some challenges at the expense of others." The film *Charlie Wilson's War* laments the messing up of the "end game," which applies equally to the post-9/11 U.S. military intervention in Afghanistan, where the job was again left unfinished.

26. *Washington Post,* January 13, 2010, op-ed by Lawrence J. Korb quoting Admiral Mike Mullen.

the Afghan government and ruling elite were complacent about the sea change that had materialized in the regional balance of power with the exit of the British and the emergence of the successor states of Pakistan and India. Afghanistan had lost the safety of its erstwhile status as a buffer between two empires. In the new circumstances, Afghanistan chose to associate itself with the amorphous but essentially weak grouping of the Non-Aligned Movement, which was suspect in the eyes of the United States but wooed by the Soviet Union. Within Afghanistan, the influence of left-leaning groups continued to build, with the encouragement and steady interest of Moscow, culminating with the murder of a leftist leader, Mir Akbar Khyber, and the April 1978 Saur Revolution. The violent revolt, brought about by the active involvement of leftist elements within the army, did not cause even a ripple of concern in Washington or London.[27]

The Soviet military intervention in December 1979 shook the United States, as did a quick succession of setbacks to U.S. interests within the same year—from Kampuchea to Iran in Asia, Ethiopia and Angola in Africa, and Nicaragua in Central America. For the next ten years, Afghanistan remained a focus of U.S. strategic thinking. However, the situation changed with the exit of the Soviets and the great transformation of the late 1980s and early 1990s in Eastern Europe. Once again, Afghanistan slipped into a blind spot.

The congressional intelligence hearings of the 1990s reveal an absence of references to Afghanistan. The new concerns and threats were articulated in terms of proliferation of nuclear, biological, and chemical weapons, loosely lumped together as weapons of mass destruction (WMDs), and state-sponsored terrorism, with specific reference to Iran and individual acts of terrorism, with frequent mention of Ramzi Yousef. They also included narcotics, organized crime, information warfare, and, significantly, a certain nervousness about the rise of China and its expanding relations in west Asia. The same trend persisted in the early years of the Taliban. In the late 1990s, the U.S. intelligence community had started recognizing the threat from loosely affiliated groups operating in Afghanistan and from Osama bin Laden as a financier of terrorist elements, with possible links to the June

---

27. The Pakistan foreign secretary at the time, Sardar Shahnawaz, who belonged to the exiled branch of the Afghan royal family, was deeply disappointed after briefing the U.S. ambassador and British chargé d'affaires in Islamabad about the events of the Saur Revolution. He wondered about the two powers' geopolitical sensibility, as his interlocutors seemed disinterested and indifferent to the event. To be fair, Shahnawaz belonged to a generation that still talked about the three wars the British had fought in Afghanistan in the nineteenth century.

1996 attack on the Khobar Towers. The 1998 bombing of the U.S. embassies in Kenya and Tanzania brought about a quantum leap in the level of U.S. concern about Al Qaeda activity inside Afghanistan and the group's close alliance with the Taliban. Correspondingly, after late 1998, the tone of official U.S. statements, especially regarding the human rights situation under Taliban rule, became increasingly harsh.

As the circumstantial evidence grew, U.S. officials in the security establishment became increasingly convinced of Osama's complicity in the embassy bombings and agitated over the Taliban's refusal to hand over or expel Osama. The United States tried but failed in its efforts to capture or eliminate Osama. In May 1999, the United States imposed sanctions against the Taliban and effectively designated the regime an FTO (foreign terrorist organization) for harboring Al Qaeda. The UN Security Council later applied similar sanctions. Sanctions and designation as a "state sponsor of terrorism" are the coercive tools of diplomacy that the United States has resorted to against perceived errant states, especially after the end of the Cold War. Pakistan itself received veiled threats during the 1990s of a possible designation. According to the *9/11 Commission Report,* in 1999 the counterterrorism bureau of the U.S. State Department had even sent a formal memo, citing Pakistan's support to the Kashmiri insurgency and its nuclear proliferation activity, which the secretary of state withdrew as an inadvisable measure.[28] It is debatable whether such measures yield the desired results. Nonetheless, regardless of the merit, this form of coercive diplomacy betrays U.S. hubris and, in the nomenclature of "sponsors of terrorism," a presumption of moral high ground and rectitude.

The post-9/11 U.S. intervention in Afghanistan had strong domestic and international support. The Bush administration had little difficulty in building an international coalition and consensus within the United Nations, which later helped propel the Bonn process. In the Islamic world, by and large, there was understanding of why the United States had to launch Operation Enduring Freedom. That sentiment changed, however, as the United States prepared to intervene in Iraq, disregarding the clear opposition of Islamic countries, especially Iraq's neighbors. The U.S. military venture in Iraq compounded the United States' problems in Afghanistan and, at a different level, complicated its relationship with the Islamic world. The stated U.S. objectives for both countries had been nation-building, based on a democratic polity. In Afghanistan, the goals included reconciliation and re-

---

28. *The 9/11 Commission Report,* 124.

construction. Neoconservative theology justified the intervention in Iraq as part of a grand design to transform the Middle East. In the event, the U.S. engagement in both countries remained mostly focused on the military effort. Even for the sole superpower of the day, this two-front military engagement proved an overextended enterprise.

The new rhetoric in the United States appeared to be infused with an evangelical spirit, and the discussion of the challenge, described as a "global war on terror," often conflated terrorism with Islam. "Islamic rage" was seen as directed at the freedom, liberal democracy, culture, and lifestyle espoused by the West. Following the collapse of the Soviet Union, it seemed as if ideologues within the United States were groping for a new security-threat paradigm, which was eventually provided by 9/11. Portraying terrorism as a "civilizational threat" and a "clash between value systems" may appear overdrawn, but doing so has spawned a huge antiterror and security industry, with concomitant vested interests. The 9/11 disaster also brought out extremist impulses within the United States that seem rooted in a deep faith in American exceptionalism and a belief that unassailable U.S. power is essential for the good of the world.

Although Bush himself was careful and respectful in his references to Islam, his unfortunate use of the phrase "crusade" for the "war on terror" reverberated in the Islamic world. Persistent reference to the clash of value systems and the perceived authoritarian character of Islamic societies, together with right-wing talk of "Islamo-fascism," raised suspicions and questions in Islamic countries about "real" U.S. objectives in the region. Exhortations on democracy had the ring of an imperialist power on a civilizing mission. The characterization of Iraq and Iran as part of an "axis of evil" was, in ideological terms, the equivalent of declaring war against these countries. The initial sympathy and understanding for action against Al Qaeda and the Taliban in Afghanistan were swept away by the opposition to the U.S. war in Iraq, which was widely perceived as unjust. This questioning of U.S. motives for the Iraq war contributed to the rise in anti-American sentiment.

There is an irony in the turn of events since the fateful 11th day of September 2001. Al Qaeda's vicious orientation and violence have disrupted the life and social fabric of its host countries and raised levels of anxiety around the world; yet its tenacity, partly sustained by the Iraq war, has brought home the sobering lesson of the limitations of power in international affairs. The relentless ambition of the neoconservatives to refashion the Middle East and assertions that the world needed the transformational power of the United States—the doctrine of unilateralism and the opportunism reflected in the imprudent assertion of U.S. military power—are on the wane. The post-Bush United States is veering towards diplomacy, dialogue, engagement, and multilateralism with an admission that "the burdens of a young century cannot fall on American shoulders alone."[29] But sadly, the hopes for a better world, which had emerged at the end of the Cold War and which provided a unique leadership opportunity for the United States with a moral accent, have been extinguished. Powerful influences in the United States remain attached to a worldview largely preoccupied with the familiar paradigm of confrontation, conflict, and fear reconfigured around a "war on terror."

The U.S. military engagement in Iraq and Afghanistan figured prominently during the 2008 presidential election campaign in the United States. The campaign debates brought out a clear preference for returning to Afghanistan, where the problem of Al Qaeda and the Taliban was located and had become more complicated, spreading to Pakistan with the passage of time. Following weeks of review and consultations in March 2009, the Obama administration opted for a narrower but more practical approach shorn of the "war on terror" cliché. The objective was to "disrupt, dismantle and defeat," or to eliminate and deny space and safe haven to Al Qaeda and jihadi groups with similar designs on attacking U.S. interests worldwide.

Failure of the Bush policy in Afghanistan, apart from its ideological undertone and undiscerning rejection of the Taliban, primarily lay in the implementation of what had been its professed aims, especially those of building an "ethnically balanced" Afghan army, reviving the Afghan economy, and promoting reconciliation. The resources committed to pursue these goals fell short of the requirement, and the strategy lacked focus, largely because of the distraction caused by the intervention in Iraq. The same challenges continue for the Obama administration, and much will depend on success and achievement on the multiple fronts of economy and politics. Military force is required to ensure insurgency attrition and denial of space to the militants and to help the Kabul government and political forces allied to it assert their authority and presence in the diverse regions of Afghanistan. The minimum objective demands the elimination of ungoverned spaces sought by Al Qaeda and the irreconcilable Taliban, as well as by drug and criminal mafias operating in the region.

---

29. President Obama's introduction to the first national security strategy released under his administration on May 27, 2010. See report by *NYT* of May 28, 2010.

Propelling the Obama administration's Af-Pak policy is an assessment that the conflict inside Afghanistan is inextricably linked to forces of extremism and religious militancy inside Pakistan. This realization had dawned on the Bush administration as the conflict dragged on; but it was primarily concerned with the Afghan Taliban's "sanctuaries" within the Pakistani tribal areas rather than with militant elements indigenous to Pakistan and their links with the Afghan Taliban. There has been U.S. distrust of the Pakistani army and doubts about its willingness to fight the Afghan Taliban. These misgivings partly reflected the suspicions that permeated the broader U.S.-Pakistan relationship. They also stem from different expectations. The tactics the Pakistani army deployed were largely designed in accordance with its own operational requirements and assessment of the threat in the Federally Administered Tribal Areas.

By the time the Obama administration took over, perception of the threat had undergone a change owing to the intensity of the militancy within Pakistan. Coordination and consultation between the two militaries also improved, somewhat attenuating mutual misgivings and reflecting a better recognition that efforts to strengthen Pakistan's capacity to address the challenge of militancy would not be effective unless they took into account Pakistani sensitivities and concerns.

The events of 9/11 had underscored the importance of Pakistan for Washington beyond the context of the "war on terror." There was a realization in Washington that letting its relations with its erstwhile Cold War ally Pakistan degrade and abandoning Afghanistan following the Soviet troop withdrawal were mistakes. During the 1990s, Pakistan-U.S. relations nose-dived with the U.S. imposition of sanctions. At the same time, U.S. policy institutions saw an opportunity in a transformed global political landscape to forge a strong "natural" alliance with India, which was fast readjusting to the new situation that had made its nonaligned rhetoric irrelevant. By the end of the decade, U.S.-India relations had acquired considerable depth and resonance. Shared values were rooted in strong formal and informal institutional linkages and an increasing commonality of interests following the end of the Cold War. U.S. relations with India and Pakistan pursued separate trajectories. The return of the spotlight on Pakistan following 9/11 did not presage a return to the "hyphenated" U.S. approach to the two countries in previous decades. But the event brought home Pakistan's significance for the stability and protection of U.S. interests in the region. In almost every high-level meeting, the U.S. leadership and senior officials would try to assure their Pakistani counterparts that the United States desired to build "long-term, broad-based, and strong" relations with Pakistan and described the country as a major non-NATO ally.

In March 2006, during the visit of President George W. Bush to Islamabad, the United States offered Pakistan an institutionalized, regular strategic dialogue,[30] which was intended to set a long-term trajectory for bilateral relations. The U.S.-Pakistan strategic dialogue, notwithstanding the high-sounding terminology, was due partly to a genuine U.S. desire to place the relations on a broader long-term basis and partly to an effort to bring a semblance of balance vis-à-vis what Bush had initiated in New Delhi before landing in Islamabad. The United States had offered India a civilian nuclear deal that signified a qualitatively new phase in bilateral relations and a recognition of India's status as a de facto member of the Non-Proliferation Treaty (NPT) nuclear club and an emerging global player.

The U.S.-Pakistan dialogue envisaged regular wide-ranging discussions at the foreign secretary level. The United States also identified four areas for cooperation to be discussed and promoted as part of the "strategic dialogue," namely, financial and economic cooperation, education, energy, and science and technology. Agriculture was later added at Pakistan's request. Progress over 2006–2008 was unsatisfactory, largely because the relevant institutions on both sides did not have funds to support the projects they initially proposed for cooperation. The projects were also modest, comprising mostly training programs and technology transfer in limited areas. The United States was unable to respond to Pakistani interest in better access to the American market. Pakistan could not conclude a bilateral investment treaty, because of difficult legal implications. Partly for this reason, the strategic dialogue in the economic sector made no meaningful progress towards a free trade or preferential trade arrangement between the two countries. U.S. economic support to Pakistan remained largely restricted to the assistance program that was extended and expanded under the 2009 Kerry-Lugar Bill.

The strategic dialogue was resumed in March 2010 under the Obama administration after a hiatus of nearly two years. The timing was important, as the United States had embarked on a new strategy for its war in Afghanistan, while the Pakistani army had concluded successful operations in Swat and South Waziristan. There appeared to be better coordination between the Pakistani army and the coalition forces on the ground. The resumed dia-

---

30. Pakistan-U.S. joint press communiqué issued on March 4, 2006, following President Bush's visit to Islamabad.

logue was elevated to the foreign minister level and included heavy top-level participation on both sides, especially the seniormost military level. The sectors for cooperation and dialogue were expanded to ten in number. Even if the results in the economic sector, which is purportedly the primary focus of the dialogue, fall short of expectations, the high-level discussions on security matters and the expected intensification of cooperation between the two sides would be important, especially in the context of the continuing U.S. engagement in Afghanistan.

Despite the mutually expressed desire to build a strong relationship and expand cooperation beyond the conventional arena of security, U.S. interests in Pakistan remain essentially linked to the Afghan conflict and the rise of extremism in Pakistan, which is increasingly perceived as the epicenter of the terrorist threat to the West.[31] The difficult and fickle nature of the "strategic partnership" was highlighted once again by the abortive attempt to bomb Times Square by Faisal Shahzad, who reportedly received training in North Waziristan. Even though Pakistan's ability to prevent such plots is at least as limited as the U.S. ability to detect them before they mature, disastrous consequences for bilateral relations would have ensued if Shahzad's plan had resulted in mayhem. Even if sober minds understand these limitations, in the event of a recurrence, media and public opinion would exert enormous pressure on the U.S. administration to act by hitting targets in Pakistan. Circumstances would prevail over reason. Accordingly, Secretary of State Hillary Clinton lost no time in cautioning Pakistan that any future terrorist attack against the United States traced to Pakistan would have "very severe consequences" for bilateral relations, and she echoed the familiar demand for Pakistan to "do more."[32] Pakistani policymakers should not misread any sugarcoating language in the statement and underestimate the sharpness and gravity of the underlying message, which was graphically emphasized by the U.S. national security adviser and the CIA chief that Obama especially sent to Islamabad for this purpose in mid-May 2010.[33]

Clearly, the U.S.-Pakistan relationship revolves narrowly on Pakistan's cooperation in fighting militants and extremists who threaten the United

---

31. Commenting on the Times Square bombing attempt, Fareed Zakaria referred to Pakistan in an op-ed article as "Terrorism's Supermarket," *Washington Post,* May 10, 2010.

32. *The News* (Islamabad), May 9, 2010.

33. Bob Woodward, *Obama's Wars* (New York: Simon and Schuster 2010), 365.

States. Success in this arena would be the necessary condition for the development of broad-based bilateral relations and improved political understanding. From this perspective, the relationship is prone to accidents, suspicion, and the vicissitudes of circumstance. Historically, at times, the U.S.-Pakistan relationship was fairly strong at the top but remained weak at the public and institutional level. This anomaly persists because Pakistan-United States relations generally converged on one specific agenda such as the Cold War or the Soviet intervention in Afghanistan or the war on terror. During periods of convergence, the leadership-level understanding and cooperation largely remained limited to the military and the establishment elite and was not backed by any sustained institutional interaction. Unlike India, Pakistan has not been able to engage the informal institutions of American democracy, in particular civil society organizations, the media, and academia. The more recent rhetorical emphasis on forging a "long-term, strategic partnership," a strategic dialogue, or Pakistan's status as a major non-NATO ally have not removed the vulnerabilities of this hitherto largely episodic relationship.

The premise of the Obama administration's Af-Pak policy—that the Afghanistan situation cannot be effectively addressed without taking into account the situation inside Pakistan—had initially also conceded that problems inside Pakistan could not be divorced from tension between Pakistan and India. The Kashmir issue has spawned militancy and radicalism in the region. Any comprehensive strategy to help the region towards normalcy will have to push Pakistan and India to work for solutions of their mutual problems. India, however, is highly sensitive to any outside intercession to address its problems with Pakistan, with the exception of terrorism-related issues. President Obama's remarks, made first in an MSNBC television interview on September 25, 2008, in the context of challenges to U.S. policy in South Asia, underlining the need for the United States to use its diplomatic resources to facilitate resolution of the Kashmir dispute drew negative comment in India. The Pakistani reaction, by contrast, was appreciative of those remarks and of a subsequent indication that the scope of Af-Pak policy could be broadened to include U.S. diplomatic engagement to address India-Pakistan tensions. Daunted by India's rejection of any discussion of Pakistan-related bilateral issues, U.S. special envoy Richard Holbrooke did not pursue the idea. Notwithstanding this reticence, the strategic relationship forged with India should allow the United States room for diplomatic maneuver, even if only through subtle nudging, to play a constructive role in solving problems between the two South Asian neighbors, thereby reducing tension in the region.

Russia, the Central Asian Republics, and China

Russian interests in Afghanistan have a long history dating back to the Tsarist era of the nineteenth century; but it was the unfortunate ten years of Soviet intervention that have most contributed to shaping a succession of tragic developments in Afghanistan. Following the collapse of the Soviet Union in December 1991 and the emergence of the Commonwealth of Independent States (CIS), Russia, now a pale shadow of its former persona, maintained a low-key attitude towards Afghanistan. For the next several years Russian diplomacy was concentrated on consolidating the CIS and renewing Russian influence with the components of the erstwhile Soviet Union. Russia took over primary responsibility for the security and monitoring of the former Soviet borders and thus maintained a military presence along the Amu Darya. Russia shared a deep suspicion along with other Central Asian states of the rising Islamist threat, heightened by the troubles in Chechnya, the religious orientation of the strife in the Balkans, and the internecine conflict in Tajikistan.

During the intra-Mujahedin conflict in the early 1990s, the Russians favored Ahmed Shah Massoud, with whom they had dealt even in the days of the Afghan Jihad in the 1980s. In late 1992, Kabul returned Russian prisoners in Massoud's custody. Russia also kept a close liaison with Iran, and both supported the Northern Alliance. The emergence of the Taliban further deepened the concerns of Russia and the Central Asian neighbors as well as Iran. Along with Afghanistan's neighbors and the United States, Russia participated at the "Six-plus-Two" meetings, which became increasingly critical of the Taliban.

While Russia and the Central Asian neighbors supported Ahmed Shah Massoud and his allies, the Taliban-controlled parts of Afghanistan provided shelter to Islamists escaping repressive measures in these countries. The growth of the Islamist movement was attributable in part to the participation of a large number of youth from Central Asia in the 1980s' Soviet-Afghan war. It also benefited from large contributions, mainly from the Gulf states, used to set up Saudi Salafi madrassas to revive religion, which had been actively discouraged under the communist system. Juma Namangani and Tohar Yoldashev, who together had started the Adolat (Justice) movement in 1992 to introduce Sharia in the Ferghana Valley of Uzbekistan, were forced to move to Tajikistan in the mid-1990s following Uzbek president Islam Karimov's crackdown against the Islamist movement.[34]

Tajikistan was going through an internal struggle between President Emomali Rakhmonov and elements of the Islamic Renaissance Party, led by Said Abdullah Nuri. In 1997, through the intercession of the Russians, Nuri agreed to a power-sharing deal with the government. This development obliged Yoldashev and Namangani to move to Afghanistan, where they launched the Islamic Movement of Uzbekistan (IMU). Yoldashev had earlier stayed in Peshawar at the invitation of Jamat e Islami and had developed contacts with Al Qaeda and the Taliban leadership. The location of the IMU in Afghanistan attracted a large influx of Uzbek militants, who had been forced to flee Fergana and other areas in the region in 1999, following Islam Karimov's second major crackdown after a series of bomb blasts attributed to the IMU. Hundreds of Uzbek youth escaped to Afghanistan and became part of the Taliban forces operating in the north, especially after the 1998 capture of Mazar e Sharif. The IMU suffered as a result of the post–9/11 U.S. military action in which Namangani was killed. The remnants of Uzbek fighters, and reportedly Yoldashev, moved to Waziristan, where they formed part of the most ruthless militant elements operating in alliance with Al Qaeda and Baitullah Mahsud forces.

The Russia-Taliban mutual hostility could be readily grasped, as the Taliban were the only government to recognize Chechnya as an independent state and, in January 2000, allow it to open an embassy in Kabul. This was the period when the ambitious Islamist Chechen leader, Shamil Basayev, under Saudi Salafi influence, had ill-advisedly sent his militia into Dagestan to try to help a local Islamist shura enforce Sharia in Chechnya and Dagestan and evict the Russians from the two republics. This gave Moscow the opportunity to scuttle its August 1996 peace treaty with Chechnya, concluded at the end of the first Chechen war.[35] The treaty had promised a referendum for independence at the end of a five-year period. Eventually, Moscow, now led by President Vladimir Putin, was able to install a pro-Moscow government and eliminate a number of separatist leaders, includ-

34. The terms "Islamist movement" and "Islamist elements" are used to describe those political influences that demand the strict enforcement of Sharia law.

35. Khasav-Yurt Accord, signed on August 22, 1996, by President Boris Yeltsin's security advisor, Alexander Lebed, and Aslan Muskhadov, who later assumed the presidency of Chechnya.

ing the moderate President Aslan Muskhadov and the radical Basayev. The second Chechen war was more ruthless than the earlier 1994–96 conflict, in part because the Russian military could act without restraint, since by 1999 the international presence in the republic, including foreign media and NGOs, had been pushed out under pressure from Salafi militant elements. A large number of Chechens made their way to safe haven in the Taliban's Afghanistan, only to be displaced again by the U.S. military action.

Other Islamist dissident elements to find refuge in the turbulent and isolated Afghanistan under the Taliban included Uighur insurgents from the neighboring Xinjiang Province of China. The independence of the Central Asian states in 1991 and an apparent reassertion of religion across the region had given rise to Islamic ferment in Xinjiang, which already had a history of dissidents, many of whom had once found refuge in the former Soviet Union. A large number of pilgrims to Mecca used to travel from Xinjiang through Pakistan to Saudi Arabia and returned with influences from outside. The first reports of violence by radical Islamic elements in Xinjiang and the formation of the East Turkestan Islamic Movement (ETIM), led by Hasan Mahsum, appeared in the early 1990s. The Chinese action against the militants pushed them into Central Asia and then to Afghanistan. Many Uighurs captured during the U.S. action in 2001 landed in Guantánamo Bay, and others escaped to Pakistan, including their leader Mahsum, who was killed by the Pakistani army in October 2003. Chinese concern over religious militancy, especially ETIM, was one factor that militated against their recognition of the Taliban and underlay continued support to the Rabbani representation at the United Nations.

The presence of these Islamist groups in Afghanistan added to the hostility towards the Taliban of the neighboring countries and Russia and their interest in the regime's removal. While in Afghanistan, these groups forged linkages with one another and with Al Qaeda and other extremist groups. This amorphous coalition remains part of the core of irreconcilable militancy that troubles Pakistan and Afghanistan. This is also why the U.S. military intervention evoked no adverse reaction, including from Russia, China, or the Central Asian republics, and why there was a sense of relief on their part at the ouster of the Taliban. They all welcomed the Bonn process and participated in international conferences convened within the Bonn framework, especially for reconstruction. These nations have a common interest in the stabilization of Afghanistan.

The cooperation among Russia, China, and the Central Asian states in combating terrorism, however, has a somewhat narrow context. Each country is mainly concerned with the particular separatist militant group that poses it a direct threat. In the long term, however, Russia and China are bound to keep a wary eye on the U.S. military presence in the region and would not like to see its consolidation beyond the objective of fighting terrorism and curbing religious extremism. These two major powers and the United States compete for influence and a share of the region's energy and other natural resources.

There is a parallel between Russian policy towards the Central Asian states and its sensitivity to the expansion of NATO influence closer to its western periphery. Russia has acquiesced in the advance of NATO to the East European states but has drawn a line where the borders of the former Soviet Union begin; it has opposed NATO efforts to bring within its fold the former Soviet republics currently part of the CIS. This may explain the termination of the U.S. base in Uzbekistan in July 2005 and reports in early 2009 of pressure on the Americans to close down their base at Manas in Kyrgyzstan, even though Bishkek remains supportive of NATO's presence in Afghanistan. The United States negotiated the Manas air base facility immediately after 9/11 to supplement facilities agreed with Pakistan. Under obvious pressure from Russia, Kyrgyzstan declared its inability to continue the arrangement beyond 2009. In February 2009, the Kyrgyz Parliament voted to discontinue the base. The United States was able to renegotiate the agreement to retain the facility, but it will have to remain mindful of Moscow's interest in the region. There is no such concern in Russia about the U.S. bases in Afghanistan, where NATO is seen as fighting a common enemy. Russia allows transit of NATO's nonlethal equipment through its territory to Afghanistan. The route could assume importance if for any reason transit through Pakistan should become difficult.

Beyond Central Asia and Afghanistan, Russia's relations with Pakistan and India are colored by historical experience, particularly in the Cold War period. In comparison with India, Russia's dealings with Pakistan will always be placed on a second pedestal. The same would apply to Afghanistan, provided Kabul is not ruled by religious zealots threatening to stoke the fires of religious uprising across the Amu Darya. But these nuances do not inject rancor. Both Pakistan and Russia have made efforts to develop bilateral cooperation, especially in the economic area, still constricted by limited capacities in trade and investment, apart from difficult access resulting from the instability and conflict in Afghanistan. The summit-level contacts during the post-9/11 period between Musharraf and Putin were cordial and free of any reserve on political grounds. Earlier, when Pakistan backed the

Taliban, Moscow supported the Northern Alliance, but it did not nurse hostility towards Pakistan as it had done in the 1980s. In the prevailing circumstances, Moscow shares the world's anxiety over the growth of religious extremism and the presence of Al Qaeda in Pakistan, but these are points of convergence rather than divergence during official exchanges between Islamabad and Moscow.

Given the long-standing tradition of consultation and cooperation between the two countries, Pakistan has taken a sound measure of China's concerns and interests. Pakistan is fully sensitive to Chinese concerns about ETIM and related problems in Xinjiang. And Chinese interest in the stabilization of Afghanistan and success in the fight against extremism and terrorism is quite apparent. In bilateral Chinese-Pakistani interaction, China has shown no signs of anxiety about the presence of NATO troops in Afghanistan or the U.S. use of Pakistani facilities. Chinese officials understand the dynamic of Pakistan-U.S. relations and at times have hinted that they wanted them to remain positive and on an even keel; tension between Pakistan and the United States could easily turn into a liability for China. The official Chinese line repeated at the government and Chinese Communist Party levels invariably points to the forces of terrorism, extremism, and separatism as the main threat to China. At the academic and think-tank level, there are expressions of possible U.S. complicity in stoking the fires of separatism; but such suspicion is in the context of China's general concern over such tendencies in Xinjiang and Tibet and Chinese irritation with American rhetoric over human rights and democracy.

A remarkable initiative that brings China and Russia together with the Central Asian republics in an arrangement for security and economic cooperation is the Shanghai Cooperation Organization (SCO), founded in June 2001 on the basis of its precursor, the Shanghai Five, formed in 1996. The SCO has placed special emphasis on antiterrorism cooperation and has established a separate bureau for this purpose in Tashkent. The SCO arrangement is also a bulwark against U.S. military ingress into the Central Asian space that was part of the former Soviet Union. The initiative became possible because of an early push by China to conclude agreements with the newly independent states of Kazakhstan, Kyrgyzstan, and Tajikistan on the existing boundary demarcation, which, in the days of the Soviet Union, Beijing had contested as a product of unequal treaties imposed by the expanding Tsarist Russia[36] on decadent imperial China. Russia followed China's

36. Initially, Moscow resented that the Central Asian republics had concluded the

example, and an agreement delineating principles to resolve the boundary issue was concluded in 2004. Another agreement, demarcating the entire border of more than four thousand kilometers, was completed in July 2008. These boundary agreements have brought about an environment of trust that could sustain the cooperative arrangements envisaged under the SCO.

China is a major economic player in Central Asia and has already indicated interest in the development of mining in Afghanistan, in addition to being willing to contribute to its economic reconstruction. The earliest projects initiated by China following the independence of the Central Asian states were the development of road and rail links with Kazakhstan and Kyrgyzstan and an oil pipeline from the Caspian Sea to Xinjiang. A rail link through the Druzhba-Alataw Pass (Alashankou) was completed by 1992 and inaugurated in early 1993, linking Urumchi and Alma Ata. Today, much of the 3 billion dollars' worth of trade and nearly 7.5 million tons of cargo exchanged between China and Kazakhstan is carried through this railway link. The Chinese and the Kazakhs have also agreed to upgrade the rail link to carry a cargo of 40 million tons and to make it a Eurasian railway line that would branch off into Iran and Turkey. In 1992 when the American oil giant Exxon started negotiations with the Kazakh government to develop energy resources in the Caspian Basin, Beijing began discussing with Alma Ata a 3000-kilometer pipeline project from the Aktube oilfields to Alataw Pass; a formal agreement was signed in 2004 and two main segments of the pipeline have been completed. China has shown strong interest in investing in Afghanistan, with China Metallurgical Group bidding for development of the Aynak copper deposits along with power generation and a rail link. Across the border in Pakistan, Chinese companies have already developed the Saindhak copper mines. However, progress on the Aynak copper fields will depend on political stability in Afghanistan.

The growth of the Chinese economy, its appetite for energy, metals, and minerals, and its expanding economic interaction have caused speculation about its rivalry with other powers in the region, in particular with India in the Indian Ocean region. China's help to Pakistan for the construction of a deep-sea port at Gwadar has generated a good deal of speculation that the port would serve as a long arm of China's navy to protect its energy supplies from the Gulf. According to this speculation, Pakistan would offer an alternative energy corridor to China that would bypass the Strait of Malacca,

---

boundary accords without Russia, which had its own residual dispute over two islands located at the confluence of the Amur and Ussuri (Heilungjiang and Wusulijiang) rivers.

a choke point that could possibly be blocked in a future confrontation involving China.

Some in India worry about encirclement by China as it develops ports and interests on the coasts of Pakistan, Sri Lanka, and Myanmar.[37] These are sensational scenarios essentially rooted in anxiety about China's rise as a global player. The prospect of a blocking of the Malaccas is purely hypothetical and has nothing to do with the development of Gwadar. The problems posed by the congestion of the Malaccas have already engaged the countries in the region, and there is a feasible proposal for a navigable canal across the Isthmus of Kra in Thailand. Similarly, China and Myanmar are interested in developing an overland oil pipeline linking Myanmar's ports to southern China.

Mention of these future plans involving neighbors of Afghanistan and Pakistan, especially in energy, communications, and commerce, underscore the point that the turmoil in the two countries has not blocked progress and development in the surrounding regions. They also reveal the hollowness of the rhetoric mindlessly repeated by Pakistani leaders and analysts in the 1990s that Pakistan was the gateway to Central Asia. Furthermore, these plans lend strength to the argument that early opening of transit routes would mainly help Pakistan and Afghanistan, while undeniably bringing some benefit to the region.

As for Gwadar, China helped to develop this small fishing port into a commercial port at Pakistan's specific request to serve the Central Asian hinterland and Pakistan's own growing needs. Contrary to speculation, there is neither a naval base nor plans for a naval base to service any Chinese naval ships. The port does provide an additional docking facility for the Pakistan navy, but beyond that its sole purpose is commercial shipping. For the time being, the port is being used for transshipment and import of food grain for the country and is operated by a Singaporean company. De-

---

37. The location of Gwadar outside the Strait of Hormuz has been the inspiration for much of the speculation that the port could serve China's interest in gaining naval influence in the Indian Ocean. A U.S. Army War College Strategic Studies Institute July 2006 report by Christopher J. Pehrson, "String of Pearls: Meeting the Challenge of China's Rising Power in the Asian Littoral States," counted Gwadar among the string of facilities being developed by China to strengthen its naval presence in the area. Indian commentators also raised concerns over the strategic potential of a port so close to the oil lanes. Much of this speculation about the port, which Pakistan had conceived primarily as an economic project, has now died down, especially after the management of the port was given to a Singaporean company.

pending on the situation in the region, there are plans to develop it as an energy port with an oil refinery and possibly an energy pipeline terminal from Central Asia that would avoid the Strait of Hormuz. If these plans materialize, a pipeline from Gwadar to Xinjiang, across the Karakorams, could become a viable proposition. At present, China's focus is on the far more feasible options of building oil pipelines from the Caspian Basin and from Siberia, for which China has already signed agreements with Kazakhstan and Russia, respectively, and work on both projects is well along.

In the Indian Ocean region, rather than big power rivalries or confrontation, the headache for all major powers is the safety of the shipping lanes threatened by piracy and insecurity, resulting from destabilization of countries on the Indian Ocean rim. A cooperative effort to address the problem of piracy and terrorism in the Gulf of Aden has taken shape in the Combined Task Force–150, a naval force contributed by the United States, the Europeans, Canada, and regional countries, including Pakistan. A similar and larger cooperative effort is at hand along the coast of Somalia. Nations located around the Indian Ocean and beyond have major economic interests at stake in the region. Most of them are likely to cooperate rather than try to manipulate and monopolize the shipping lanes to one another's exclusion. The competition in trade would speed up regional economic development. The emergence of China and India will lessen American preeminence in the Indian Ocean region, but the United States will remain a significant player in the same way that its role in the Asia-Pacific seaboard has not declined, despite the emergence of China, Japan, South Korea, and Southeast Asia as creating together a great economic powerhouse that has transformed the global economy during the past quarter century.

This chapter has attempted to focus on the Afghanistan-related interests and concerns of neighbors and other external major powers. Afghanistan and Pakistan lie at the center of the tremors caused by extremist and militant forces produced by the region's history and its problems. At present the U.S. military presence looms large in the region. But this is a temporary phase, and future U.S. engagement will be determined by the long-term U.S. interests in the region. However, beyond this presence and the conflict and violence that have gripped Afghanistan and Pakistan, the powerful contemporary forces of globalization, regional economic integration, and the technological development of major Asian population centers are transforming the larger Asia. These transformational currents appear to have bypassed Afghanistan and Pakistan, keeping them in a virtual time warp of economic stagnation.

Extremism and terrorism pose a threat to fast-developing and modernizing societies, but they inflict the greatest harm on the societies that become their breeding ground. While inextricably fused with the past three decades of developments in Afghanistan, the extremist violence and militancy in Pakistan have their own complex history and multiple motivations. The rise of this phenomenon in contemporary Pakistan and its antecedents will be the focus of the next two chapters.

Part II

The Pakistan Context and the Challenge of Extremism

5

The Challenge of Religious Militancy and Extremism in Pakistan

The Afghanistan conflict has deeply impacted Pakistan's polity and society. Until September 11, 2001, and the U.S. military intervention, the phenomena of Talibanization and Taliban-related militancy had been largely concentrated in war-ravaged Afghanistan and were generally viewed in Pakistan as a product of the Afghan Jihad and subsequent warfare in Afghanistan. Nonetheless, within Pakistan a number of radical militant groups emerged supporting the Afghan Jihad and the uprising in Indian-held Kashmir that flared up in 1989. A combination of religious motivation, madrassa education, Afghan-related and later Kashmir-related rhetoric, and official patronage instigated and imparted momentum to religious militancy.

The Zia years had witnessed the growth of a culture of religious zeal in Pakistani society, especially among the middle and lower middle classes, the bureaucracy, and the armed forces. Under Zia, religious influences favoring Islamist orthodoxy became firmly entrenched in Pakistani politics. The sectarian dimension of religious militancy also became acute during this period, the result in part of the intense Arab-Iranian rivalry following the Khomeini revolution in 1979 that also played out within the soft, open, and susceptible Pakistani society. However, it was the Pakistani Sunni militant groups that developed contacts with the Afghan Mujahedin groups and were later influenced by the rise of the Taliban in Afghanistan and by Al Qaeda. Members of these groups participated in the Taliban military campaigns. The official patronage enjoyed by groups like Lashkar e Tayaba during the 1990s was linked to the Kashmiri insurgency. Public sentiment, especially in urban areas, was sympathetic, shaped by self-serving rhetoric. Forcing the Soviets out of Afghanistan inspired a sense of triumphalism, and the travails of Muslims in the Balkans, the Caucasus, Palestine, and

Kashmir fostered a deep sense of grievance. Religious groups and political parties openly collected funds to help jihad in Kashmir, Bosnia, Chechnya, and Afghanistan. Nonetheless, the jihadi groups avoided violence within Pakistan even though they contributed to an increasingly intolerant environment within the country. The incidence of religious violence inside Pakistan, sometimes targeting Americans and Europeans, was largely related to sectarian tensions.

Throughout the 1980s and 1990s, Afghanistan remained the storm center of conflict and militancy in the region, first because of the Soviet intervention and later as a result of the relentless internal power struggle, with its overlay of religious fanaticism associated with the Taliban. Afghanistan provided a haven and a breeding ground for extremists and militants, with sectarian and jihadi motivations and links to groups and agendas beyond Afghanistan. The U.S. military intervention altered the location of the militancy, pushing it to the border regions of Pakistan, but not before many Pakistani militants perished in the initial confrontation, especially in northern Afghanistan and Kabul. Those who survived returned to Pakistan along with elements of Al Qaeda and many Afghan Taliban. Despite the rout, their ideological motivation and deep indoctrination remained intact. During debriefing sessions by Pakistani security authorities, many of those who had barely escaped death inside Afghanistan and whom the Red Cross repatriated to Pakistan wanted to go back to join their "fortunate" martyred brothers to enjoy blessings in paradise.

References to Pakistani jihadi groups and extremist militant groups require clarification. Jihadi groups are those motivated by the Afghan Jihad of the 1980s and the Kashmiri uprising that began in the late 1980s. Following the Soviet troop withdrawal, jihad lost its full meaning in Afghanistan, though the conflict persisted. The Afghan Taliban attracted to their ranks religious militants from Pakistan, including elements of the Kashmiri jihadi groups. They often described their military campaigns as jihad, but that was a perversion of the concept, because the Afghan Taliban campaigns were part of a struggle for power and political control in Afghanistan. Altruism, if it had ever underpinned the Taliban's original motivation, was drained over the years in the internecine Afghan conflict, which also became a training ground for elements from Pakistani jihadi and militant groups. After the 2001 U.S. military intervention, the Pakistani militants—and also the Al Qaeda and Afghan Taliban elements fleeing Afghanistan—gravitated to the FATA. There they joined forces with local insurgents and began to see in their coercive power and capacity for violence a means for wresting political power and control. Whatever their early motivations, these groups became the perpetrators of extremist militancy and violence in Pakistan, which is the focus of this chapter.

The Afghan Taliban have once again invoked jihad against the foreign military presence in Afghanistan. The call resonates among some conservative religious circles. Nonetheless, it is noteworthy that the rise of Al Qaeda and an assortment of similar groups with extremist ideology and violent disposition has influenced debate and mainstream religious thinking within Muslim societies to veer away from careless usage of the term "jihad" and to reject the right of individuals and disparate groups to proclaim jihad.

Main Strands of Religious Militancy in Pakistan

The shock and scale of 9/11 obliged the Musharraf government to reverse policy on the Taliban, although it made an effort to convince Mullah Omar to be responsive to the UN demand on Osama bin Laden. Pakistan also hunted Al Qaeda members who had taken refuge in Pakistani cities where they had contacts; subsequently they retreated to the safety of the ungoverned border regions. Initially, the Taliban forces appeared to be fatally damaged. Slowly, they started recovering; militancy spread and intensified in the bordering FATA regions.

Meanwhile, by 2004–2005, Pakistan-India relations started to improve, and Musharraf saw in the process an opportunity to address the long-standing Kashmir dispute. The pursuit of this objective required, down the road, measures to restrain the Pakistan-based militant elements that aided the Kashmiri insurgency across the line of control inside Indian-administered Kashmir. The new policy had its skeptics, critics, and opponents, including some within the government and army establishment. More important, the policy provoked militant groups committed to the Kashmir Jihad, who then turned against the government.

The three broad domestic strands of religious militancy were represented by those elements who later styled themselves as local, Pakistani Taliban; those supporting the Kashmiri insurgency; and those with a domestic sectarian agenda. The loose alliance among these groupings and with Al Qaeda and insurgents in the FATA posed a grave and increasing challenge to the writ of Islamabad. The violence by these militant groups preoccupied the

Musharraf government throughout most of its tenure after 2001. Accordingly, under the vaguely defined rubric of the war on terror, the policy addressed three main areas: first, countering Al Qaeda and other foreign and homegrown militant groups; second, handling the situation in the FATA border regions; and third, addressing the growing extremism in the country.

Al Qaeda had its origin among the Arab youth attracted or brought to Afghanistan. They had developed a Middle East–oriented internationalist agenda to target Western interests as well as governments in their home countries that were generally viewed as pro-West. Al Qaeda needed a new base once Afghanistan had been virtually denied to it by the American invasion. The other foreign elements who descended in the thousands into the FATA from Afghanistan were the Central Asian and Chechen fighters. During the 1990s, they had been forced to flee their countries and found refuge in Afghanistan. Without any clear agenda, these angry men were driven by desperation to become ruthless fighters on behalf of their new paymaster, Al Qaeda. The Afghan Taliban, who crossed into Pakistan with the same ease as Afghan refugees had done after every convulsion in their country, were more focused on wresting back their lost authority inside Afghanistan and fighting the new intruder, the United States and its allies in NATO/ISAF.

The Arabs had been operating in the area for almost two decades. They had developed relationships and support both in the FATA staging grounds for the Afghan Jihad and in urban centers of Pakistan, where jihadi outfits had enjoyed official patronage in the context of Afghanistan and Kashmir. Until 1992, Peshawar had attracted a large number of Arabs wanting to help the Afghan Jihad, especially with funds. In late 1993, because of increasing problems with the locals, the provincial authorities evicted several hundred Arabs from Peshawar. Most shifted to Afghanistan, as they could not return to their own countries.

Prominent among the Pakistani-based militants were the Kashmiri jihadi groups, since they had the backing of the Pakistani military, who regarded them as an important instrument of the strategy to compel India to negotiate a reasonable Kashmir settlement. The Kashmiri uprising in the late 1980s was seen as an opportunity. The prevalent view within the Pakistani establishment was that, absent outside support, the "indigenous movement" would not be able to withstand Indian coercion. India maintained close to half a million military and paramilitary forces in Indian-administered Kashmir. To reinforce the argument for support, Pakistani military analysts would draw historical parallels with national liberation struggles, such as in Vietnam and Zimbabwe, which had succeeded with material support from outside powers. This thinking was essentially an analysis designed to fit a strategy. It ignored the necessity for a powerful political leadership in control of its militant wings to achieve success in any indigenous freedom movement. In Afghanistan the schismatic Mujahedin leadership, with autonomous Mujahedin commanders, had only led to turmoil and torment.

Another motive often ascribed to the Pakistani military is that by supporting militancy, Pakistan will have succeeded in tying down a large part of the Indian Army in the Indian-held Kashmir. Such an assumption, besides knocking out the moral basis of the Pakistani position on Kashmir, does not make sense in view of the conventional and nuclear deterrence that has existed between the two countries since the late 1980s. Such a tactical consideration could be part of a short-term wartime strategy, but it cannot be the basis for a long-term policy, which, in the case of Pakistan, has to be based on the premise of a reasonable settlement of the Kashmir dispute rather than prolongation of the conflict and suffering in that territory.

In late 1987, after a long hiatus of relative calm, the Kashmiri discontent had erupted in reaction to repressive measures taken by the Indian authorities to subdue Kashmiri protests following controversial elections in Kashmir. The Kashmiri agitation gained marked momentum after the assassination of the well-respected Kashmiri leader Mir Waiz Muhammad Farooq in Srinagar in May 1990. The indigenous militancy grew under the umbrella of Hizbul Mujahedin, which first emerged in 1989. The group had close links to Jamat e Islami in the Indian-administered Kashmir and enjoyed the support of anti-India political groups: the pro-independence Jammu and Kashmir Liberation Front (JKLF) and pro-Pakistan All Parties Hurrieyat Conference (APHC). Violence increased in 1993 after the Indian military action against militants who had sought refuge in the Hazrat Bal and Cherar Sharif mosques. During the siege, the Cherar Sharif mosque, an old wooden structure, was completely gutted.

In Pakistan, the main supporters of the Kashmiri militancy at the early stages were Harkatul Mujahidin, led by Fazalur Rahman Khalil, who had broken away from the precursor group, Harkatul Jihad al Islami, formed in 1985 to support the Afghan Jihad. Two other groups that emerged in 1990–1991 with Pakistani encouragement were Harkatul Ansar, an offshoot of Harkatul Mujahidin, with Maulana Masood Azhar as its secretary-general, and Lashkar e Tayaba, led by Hafiz Muhammad Saeed. All three leaders shared strong pan-Islamist views and were committed to the cause of jihad in Afghanistan and Kashmir; two were alumni of the Binori Masjid Darul Uloom. In January 2000, immediately after the Indians released him to end the hijacking of the Air India flight 814 that had been taken to Qandahar, Masood Azhar formed a new militant group, Jaish e Muhammad, which sent its recruits both to Afghanistan and Kashmir and maintained close ties with Al Qaeda.

Following a split in Hizbul Mujahidin, its leader, Syed Salahuddin, based himself in Azad Jammu and Kashmir, the Pakistani-administered part of the state. Later in 1994, he became the head of an umbrella organization for the Kashmiri jihad, the Muttahida Jihad Council (United Jihad Council) based in Muzzafarabad, the capital of Azad Jammu and Kashmir. The Council acted as an important interface with the Pakistani authorities, loosely representing the mainstream of Kashmiri jihadi elements. Hizbul Mujahidin suffered further internal dissension when its top commander in Indian-administered Kashmir, Abdul Majeed Dar, offered the Indians a conditional cease-fire in July 2000. Syed Salahuddin endorsed the cease-fire at first but within one month, allegedly under pressure from Pakistan's ISI, retracted his support of Dar. The cease-fire offer might have resulted from debate and confusion within the Kashmiri Mujahedin leadership, first, over the positive turn in Pakistan's relations with India evident in the February 1999 Lahore summit and, then, over its reversal as a result of the Kargil crisis.

These militant groups did not have a rigid discipline or firm outside control; the violent dynamics of militancy gave rise to internal dissensions and virulent autonomous splinter factions. This degeneration of the Kashmiri jihadi groups became evident when Al Faran, a splinter group of Harkat ul Ansar, abducted five European tourists and beheaded one of them in July 1995. That incident changed the perception in the West of the Kashmiri uprising, which had previously evoked some international sympathy.[1] Al Faran's act, allegedly committed to bargain for the release of Masood Azhar, was condemned by Harkatul Mujahidin, but it revealed the breakaway tendency of militant groups not controlled by strong political leadership.

The Kashmiri militant groups began posing a direct problem for Pakistan in 2004 when Musharraf opted to initiate a peace process with India, something that was becoming an imperative. Changing global circum-

---

1. The European Parliament's resolutions relating to Kashmir marked a sharp change in their sentiment following the Al Faran incident. Before 1995, the resolutions were sympathetic to the Kashmiri agitation and called for respect for human rights. Subsequent to the incident, terrorism became the main focus in these resolutions. However, extremist groups are often impervious to such international censure.

stances and pressures for development necessitated a certain modicum of normalcy in Pakistan-India relations, which had come under stress following the December 2001 attack on the Indian Parliament. India had accused Pakistan-based jihadi organizations for the attack, in particular Lashkar e Tayaba, which the Indians described as an "infrastructure of terror" that threatened India. For over one year, tension between the two countries remained high and over one million troops, from both sides combined, faced each other in a virtual "eyeball-to-eyeball confrontation." The countries came close to the brink but avoided a conflict, thanks to international concern and, more important, keen awareness that they both possessed nuclear weapons. Strategic deterrence had worked to prevent a clash. Meanwhile, the Musharraf government kept insisting on de-escalation, reduction of tension, and dialogue.

The situation began to thaw by late 2002. In mid-2003, Musharraf offered a cease-fire along the line of control dividing the Pakistani-administered and Indian-administered parts of Kashmir. This was significant, because the Indian side had consistently alleged that Pakistan provided fire cover to enable Kashmiri militants to cross the line of control. In early 2004, Indian prime minister Atal Bihari Vajpayee attended the much-delayed summit conference of the South Asian Association for Regional Cooperation summit conference held in Islamabad. During the course of the summit, Musharraf and Vajpayee signed the January 4, 2004, declaration that committed the two countries to restarting the peace process to resolve Kashmir, and Pakistan stated that it would not allow "territories under its control" to be used for acts of terrorism inside India.

The Kashmiri jihadi organizations resented the declaration and the policy direction it had set out. For the credibility of the peace process and to make any progress, these organizations had to be effectively demobilized and restrained from continuing militant activity inside India and Indian-administered Kashmir. This effort proved more difficult than anticipated. First, the militants of the Jihadi organizations were highly motivated, making it difficult to change their mind-set. Second, many of them had known no vocation other than "the Jihad." As the Kashmir front cooled down, many of them drifted to the FATA and Afghanistan, joining the Afghan Taliban and even turning their guns against the state of Pakistan.

The sectarian militancy became active in Pakistan in the 1980s, after the Iranian revolution. Until then, Pakistan had witnessed ethnic violence but virtually no sustained sectarian militancy based on Shia-Sunni divisions.

Sectarian tensions, normally confined to the Ashura days, were managed by local administrations.[2] The other source of sectarian problems was the Qadiani (Ahmadiya) issue that had simmered in the Punjab since the turn of the twentieth century. The Qadiani sect was widely regarded as heretical, because of its founder's claim of prophethood, which provoked common Muslim sentiment.[3] Tehrik Tahafuz e Khatam e Nabuwat (Movement for Protection of the Finality of Prophethood), joined by activists from several political and nonpolitical religious parties, pushed for excommunication of the Qadianis. The movement turned to violence in 1953, which the government suppressed by imposing martial law in many cities of Punjab. In 1974, when the tension erupted once again, the government of Prime Minister Zulfikar Ali Bhutto deferred to the Parliament, which declared the Qadianis non-Muslim. The decision averted violence by the Tehrik activists but gave rise to a host of human rights issues and excesses that the state has been unable to address. The declaration gave a boost to orthodox and fringe religious elements in the forefront of the Tehrik. These elements were able to make the ruling Pakistan People's Party, a self-proclaimed secular political party, concede to their demand for ex-communication of the Qadianis.

The virulent form of sectarian violence witnessed since the 1980s owed its origin partly to the Iranian revolution and the impact on Pakistan of the Arab reaction to it and partly to the policy of "Islamization" pursued by Zia ul Haq, which had an orthodox Sunni stamp. The Iranian revolution activated Shia clergy inside Pakistan, where the Shias, roughly 15 to 20 percent of the population, lived in relative, but at times precarious, peace with the majority Sunni population. Shia sentiment had become strained because of Zia ul Haq's military takeover and the subsequent hanging of Zulfikar Ali Bhutto, who was generally known to be of the Shia persuasion. Shias were wary of Zia's attempt, beginning in 1979, at Islamization based on the Sunni

2. Until the 1970s there was no particular prejudice in Pakistan towards its Shia minority. Many Pakistani leaders, including the founder of the nation, Muhammad Ali Jinnah, belonged to Shia families. In rural central and southern Punjab, there are pockets where influential Shia families owned large feudal holdings. This fact was exploited by the area's militant Sunni clerics from poor or lower middle class backgrounds who became active in the 1980s.

3. The founder of the Qadiani sect, Mirza Ghulam Ahmed (1835–1908), started as an Islamic scholar who, like the earlier eminent reformer Sir Syed Ahmed Khan, advocated cooperation with the ruling British. Ghulam Ahmed proposed to suspend the tenet of jihad. However, it was his later claim to prophethood that challenged the consensus Muslim belief system.

Hanafi Fiqh,[4] especially the introduction of the compulsory deduction of Zakat (Islamic charity tax, a religious obligation to help the poor), although the government revised the regulation to exempt the Shias from its application. The same year also saw the Soviet military intervention and the subsequent forging of an alliance between Pakistan and the United States. The Iranian theocrats openly and harshly accused Zia ul Haq of being a lackey of the Americans and hung his caricature, along with those of Anwar Sadat and Menachem Begin, on the gate of the U.S. embassy in Tehran, where the U.S. diplomats were held hostage.

Zia ul Haq was generally indifferent to and dismissive of the Iranian diatribes and did not show any personal bias against the Shias. Several of his close advisors and confidants were Shia. However, within the country, sectarian sentiment began to intensify. Shia activism and latent Shia-Sunni tensions took a sinister turn with the emergence of hostile sectarian groups, in particular the Tehrik e Nifaz e Fiqh e Jafaria [TNFJ, movement for the enforcement of Jafaria (Shia) jurisprudence], and Sipah e Sahaba Pakistan (SSP, army of the companions), a breakaway group of Jamiat Ulema e Islam, a mainstream Sunni political coalition with Deobandi inclination. The two sectarian groups spawned other, more violent offshoots, Sipah e Muhammadi (Shia) and Lashkar e Janghvi (Sunni). In addition, a number of sectarian groups that had splintered from the original SSP and TNFJ and operated under new adopted names continued to wreak havoc in the country after the parent organizations and their well-known offshoots had been officially proscribed in January 2002.

In the early 1980s, the Pakistani sectarian groups started receiving overseas funds. There is evidence of early support by Iran to a firebrand TNFJ leader, Allama Arif al Husseini, who was murdered in 1988. A cache of arms discovered at the Iraqi embassy in Islamabad was reportedly meant to be handed over to anti-Shia SSP, whose leader, Haq Nawaz Janghvi, met a violent death in 1990. Saudi funds became available to leaders of Sunni political and religious movements that were close to Wahabism, in particular the Ahl e Hadith and Deobandi schools. The same period saw the growth of madrassas with Saudi Salafi orientation, which further accentuated sectarian tensions in society. Sectarian violence and murders had begun in the mid-1980s.

---

4. The overwhelming majority of Sunnis in Pakistan adhere to the Hanafi Fiqh, one of the four schools of jurisprudence in Sunni Islam.

The violent Sunni groups had organic linkages with political and religious parties demanding that Pakistan be declared a Sunni state, and with Jihadi groups active in Afghanistan and Kashmir. Most of these groups had Deobandi and Saudi Salafi inspiration, which permeated the madrassas mushrooming in Pakistan during the 1980s and 1990s, with large donations raised locally and from the Gulf, especially from Saudi Arabia. Since the late 1980s, numerous efforts to bring about sectarian harmony through calls by the mainstream sectarian parties have helped reduce sectarian violence, but these efforts have fallen short of eliminating sectarian hatred and militancy. They have not prevailed upon the extremist sectarian groups that have wreaked violence on several areas in Pakistan, especially the Kurram Agency in the FATA, southern and central Punjab, and Karachi.

The sectarian tensions in the Kurram Agency continue to erupt intermittently, because first the Afghanistan conflict and later the Afghan Taliban and Al Qaeda interests impacted the sectarian dimension of the local demographics. Kurram has a significant Shia population with a history of friction with the Afghan Mujahedin groups, and, subsequently, the Afghan Taliban. The Shia population resented the rise of the radical Sunni influence and activities in the area in the 1980s, when the agency had become one of the important staging bases for the Afghan Jihad and a conduit for the supply of arms to the Afghan Mujahedin.

The homegrown militancy, both sectarian (Sunni) and jihadi, developed informal but close linkages and cooperation with Al Qaeda. Harkatul Mujahidin and Jaish e Muhammad recruited volunteers to help the Taliban in Afghanistan, had a declared agenda to fight in Kashmir, and enjoyed close linkages with Al Qaeda. Harkat leader Fazalur Rahman Khalil was one of the first to condemn the August 1998 U.S. missile attack targeting Osama that killed among others Harkat militants being trained at the Al Qaeda base. Harkat was the first to be banned after 9/11 for its linkages with Al Qaeda. Investigations into various incidents of bombings, including the attempts to assassinate Pervez Musharraf, revealed that extremist militants often had multiple affiliations with Lashkar e Janghvi, Jaish e Muhammad, and Al Qaeda[5] and contacts with members of religious parties, mosques, and madrassas. Such linkages and collaboration also came to light in the confession by Omar Saeed Sheikh, who was associated with Masood Azhar and

---

5. Details of linkages between the various Pakistan-based extremist groups and Al Qaeda are brought out in the accounts of the Jihadi groups by Amir Mir in *The True Face of Jihadis* (Lahore, Mashal Books, 2004), 49-65.

found to be an accomplice in the kidnapping of *Wall Street Journal* correspondent Daniel Pearl in late January 2002. According to Omar Saeed, while Jaish members carried out the kidnapping, Daniel Pearl was murdered by Khalid Sheikh Muhammad, one of the alleged masterminds of 9/11 and a strategist for Al Qaeda.[6]

The Sunni fringe groups responsible for sectarian violence were at times intermingled with jihadi organizations. Religious militancy thus acquired a dual persona, complicating Pakistan's task of rooting it out. Pakistani governments in the 1990s as well as the early Musharraf government saw the problem but addressed it in a largely selective and compartmentalized fashion. For example, throughout the 1990s, while sectarian violence was seen as a bane and steps were taken to counter it, the jihadi groups, regardless of their Sunni sectarian affiliations, were cosseted by the military as assets in support of the uprising in Kashmir. Lashkar e Tayaba and Jaish e Muhammad were known to enjoy such backing. Generally, until the late 1990s, the government and the military establishment remained complacent about the extremist threat and oblivious of its potential to destabilize and challenge the government's writ. They thought that militant groups, especially those linked to Kashmir, would do their bidding and would not cross the line to turn against the state. Their experience with the hard-line Afghan Tanzeemat either had not registered or was unlearned.

Before 9/11, the army viewed religious militancy mostly in the narrow context of sectarian violence and primarily as a law-and-order issue that ought to be addressed by the civilian political and administrative authorities, who remained equally smug about the phenomenon. Local civilian authorities, including the police, sometimes hesitated to take action against Sunni militants because of the popular notion that they had links with intelligence agencies operating under the army or the federal interior ministry. The police were mainly focused on the sectarian problem, which the leadership of the main Jihadi groups tried by and large to avoid. In the early 1990s, the government of Benazir Bhutto remained focused on the ethnic violence in Karachi, which at that time had overshadowed even the sectarian problem.

6. Khalid Sheikh Muhammad was captured in 2003 from the house of a member of Jamat e Islami living in Rawalpindi. A similar connection was revealed when in March 2010 Pakistani security forces demolished the house of a member of Jamat e Islami and former member of the national assembly, Haroonur Rashid, in Bajaur for sheltering TTP and Al Qaeda members.

Besides ambivalence and lack of attention on the part of successive governments in the 1990s, at a different level the spread of religious militancy in Pakistan was aided by depressed socioeconomic conditions, with growing poverty, unemployment, and demographic pressures and the increasingly volatile religious environment that together kept feeding militant groups with new recruits. The religious parties provided a powerful source of political support. They were generally sympathetic to the professed goals of the jihadi groups, even when disagreeing with their violent methods and tactics. These groups also often blended a jihadi agenda with a commitment to public service. The Muslim League under Nawaz Sharif, which was part of Pakistan's mainstream politics, carried with it strong influences inherited from the days of Zia ul Haq. The party strongly opposed sectarianism but viewed the jihadi groups with equanimity.

The 9/11 shocks and the Pakistan-India standoff following the attack on the Indian Parliament, allegedly carried out by Lashkar e Tayaba activists, affected the outlook of Pakistan's top army echelon. These came on the heels of the changes Musharraf had engineered in forcing the exit of generals known for pro-Mujahedin views. The military leadership became sensitive to rising religious and extremist militancy and the danger posed to the country by the jihadi groups. However, by this time, the problem was growing partly concealed and partly with nebulous official connivance and began to emerge with a vengeance. The danger had already assumed monstrous proportions that could not be contained simply by proscribing extremist groups and pursuing individuals responsible for acts of terrorism. The jihadi and other militant extremist groups, riled up over the perceived U-turn in policy over the Afghan Taliban and the hunt for Al Qaeda, targeted Musharraf. His moves towards normalization with India initiated in early 2004 further accentuated their vitriolic attacks against the Musharraf government.

As the extremist threat to the state gradually unfolded, the Musharraf government failed to deal with it firmly. Instead, the government took piecemeal actions such as proscribing the militant groups, partly in compliance with Security Council requirements, and pursuing those involved in acts of violence. The intermittent military operations focused on the FATA, in the context of the peculiar conditions in the area and developments next door in Afghanistan. Many within the government believed that the ideological fervor and zealotry of the jihadi militants, especially those weaned away from involvement in Kashmir, would fade away with time. However, developments continued to exacerbate the problem. These militants gravitated towards the FATA and joined with tribal insurgents, local religious and extremist groups, and foreign and Al Qaeda elements to undertake militant activity inside the FATA and across the border in support of the Afghan Taliban. Their agendas often depended on their affiliation with various tribal insurgencies. Many of those hailing from various parts of Punjab had been part of the Afghan Taliban military campaigns before 2001 and were known as "Punjabi Taliban." Later, in 2007, many of these disparate elements and tribal insurgents rallied under the umbrella of the Tehrik Taliban Pakistan (TTP) led by Baitullah Mahsud. They claimed allegiance with but were distinct from the Afghan Taliban, who, after the collapse of their rule, remained mainly focused on regaining influence inside Afghanistan.

Efforts by Successive Governments to Control Militancy

The governments of Nawaz Sharif and Benazir Bhutto had moved against sectarian extremist groups in a tentative manner. In the early 1980s, in order to cut into the PPP influence in Sindh Province, Zia ul Haq had encouraged ethnic and linguistic–based politics, which led to the formation of the Muhajir Quami Movement (immigrant national movement). The MQM was built around perceived grievances of the Urdu-speaking population in urban Sindh, especially Karachi, that had migrated to Pakistan at the time of partition. Benazir's first term (1988–90) was mainly preoccupied by action against MQM violence. The resulting ethnic tensions gripped Karachi for years. In the early 1990s, the intelligence agencies had reportedly worked to split MQM and succeeded only in compounding the problem. The harsh tactics, including extrajudicial killings, apparently sanctioned by PPP's interior minister, Naseerullah Khan Babar, however, succeed in reducing violence. Later, the MQM became a mainstream political party, with a change in nomenclature to Muthehida Quami Movement (united national movement), and entered into alliances with other political parties, including the PPP.

In the late 1980s and early 1990s, the government still viewed sectarian violence as a sporadic and containable problem. Towards the late 1990s, the sectarian violence escalated. In early 1997, Lashkar e Jhangvi even targeted and killed Iranian cadets training in Pakistan and the Iranian consul general in Lahore, obliging the government of Nawaz Sharif to proscribe and move against the group. Nawaz Sharif himself became the target of the group in 1999. The public reacted with abhorrence to the sectarian violence, which included bomb blasts and targeted killings.

In January 2002, in the wake of the attack on the Indian Parliament building, allegedly by Lashkar e Tayaba militants, Musharraf took firmer action by formally banning five militant groups—Sipah e Sahaba Pakistan, Tehrik Nifaz Fiqh e Jafaria, and Sipah e Muhammadi, as well as the two pro-Kashmir jihad groups, Lashkar e Tayaba and Jaish e Muhammad. The sense of urgency was for taking action against the two Kashmiri militant groups; but for the optics and to defend the action publicly, it was thought advisable to lump them together with the three sectarian militant groups. The members of these groups went underground, changed affiliations, or, in the case of Lashkar e Tayaba, regrouped as a charity organization, Jamat ud Dawa. Jaish tried to reconstruct itself as Khudam ul Islam. But most of the Jaish and SSP elements dispersed, morphed into more violent groups, and established linkages with Al Qaeda. They became hired guns for the Taliban in Afghanistan as well as for the insurgent groups in the FATA. Extremists originally affiliated with Jaish and SSP masterminded many of the suicide attacks.

The violence perpetrated by the extremist, sectarian, and jihadi groups were not exclusively the result of religious indoctrination. Criminal elements had lodged themselves in the sectarian groups in particular. Riaz Basra and Akram Lahori, erstwhile leaders of Lashkar e Jhangvi, were hardened criminals involved with scores of murders and terrorist attacks against Shias, security personnel, and foreigners. Banned, and driven by anger and desperation, Jaish e Muhammad turned virulent and justified its violence against the government. The loosely administered FATA had long attracted criminals, convicts, and fugitives escaping justice. In addition, successive governments tolerated open smuggling and dealings in arms and other contraband in the area. Many of such elements were part of the Pakistani Taliban and other militant outfits operating in the FATA and were known as Charsi Taliban (drug-peddling Taliban). Masterminds who have been the mainstay of Pakistani Taliban, recruiting and brainwashing young boys for suicide bombings and slaughtering hostages and captured personnel are not entirely motivated by some perverse ideology; some are certainly psychopaths and hardened criminals. Thus religious extremism, zealotry, and militancy had become mixed up with criminal, smuggling, and drug mafias. Along with the extremist religious groups, these unholy alliances needed ungoverned and troubled spaces for survival.

Immediately after 9/11, the Musharraf government zeroed in on Al Qaeda. The intelligence and security agencies, as well as the army, did fairly efficient work in capturing some of the top leadership, in particular Khalid Sheikh Muhammad, Ramzi bin al Shibh, Abu Faraj Al Libi, Abu Zubeida,

Walid Bin Attash, Ahmed Khalfan Ghailani, and Omar Saeed Sheikh, as well as hundreds of minor Al Qaeda operatives.[7] Even though the top two leaders, Osama bin Laden and Ayman Al Zawahiri, had eluded capture, the government's early successes prompted Musharraf to claim to visiting foreigners that Al Qaeda's back had been broken and its lateral and vertical lines of communications effectively disrupted. The assertion proved to be premature; Al Qaeda has survived, and its ideological appeal and militancy continue to afflict many Islamic countries besides Pakistan.

Al Qaeda has been a loose organization with a hard core of affiliates. With the important exception of the two top leaders, most have been captured or killed. Al Qaeda's resilience can be traced to its potent message, which has resonated with many alienated youth in the Muslim world. In one sense, Al Qaeda has turned into a franchise; disparate cells, either loosely affiliated with Al Qaeda or using its name, could become active without instructions from a central command or a structured organization. By early 2003, the organization had been severely damaged. But it found in Iraq a new theater of conflict and opportunity to revive itself. The Iraq war drew new recruits, especially from Saudi Arabia, and provided a new justification for Al Qaeda's violent opposition to the United States and pro-U.S. regimes in the Islamic countries.

Osama and Al Zawahiri were no longer required to plan and micromanage operations carried out in the name of Al Qaeda. They only needed a safe refuge and, from time to time, an opportunity to stoke passions through messages relayed through the globalized technology of diskettes and cyberspace. For example, in March 2004, al-Zawahiri released a video message to Al Jazeera TV launching a focused attack against Musharraf in which he argued that the army's action in the FATA was America's war and not Pakistan's war. This argument, and the corollary that the extremist violence was linked to the U.S. intervention in Afghanistan and to Pakistan's complicity with the United States, were becoming key points in Pakistan's debate on terrorism that continued to dominate the print and electronic media. In Pakistan, particularly in the FATA, Al Qaeda depended for its survival on the disturbed environment created by the violent activities of extremist groups and the Pakistani Taliban, which challenged the state writ and destabilized the country.

Action by the Pakistani army against Al Qaeda and Pakistan's alliance with the United States in the "war on terror" stoked terrorist activity inside Pakistan involving elements from the banned extremist Sunni outfits. Some

7. Amir Mir, *The True Face of Jihadis,* 225

high-profile attacks targeted the corps commander Karachi, Ahsan Hayat Saleem, in June 2004, and later in the year President Musharraf and Prime Minister Shaukat Aziz, when Aziz was campaigning for election. The army's deployment in the FATA also complicated the local situation where the sentiment was supportive of the Afghan Taliban. The military action to fight Al Qaeda and to interdict the Afghan Taliban and other foreign elements was resented by the tribes, especially in North and South Waziristan, which had received the largest influx of Afghan Taliban and Al Qaeda that had been flushed out by the American military intervention, in particular the bombings of Tora Bora in early 2002.

The ruffled Pushtun sentiment over the perceived return of Kabul to non-Pushtun control was one of the factors in the election victory of the religious alliance Mutaheda Majlis e Amal (MMA) in NWFP and Baluchistan in the September 2002 elections for national and provincial assemblies. The MMA success also owed to the formal coalition of the main religious parties, including Jamat e Islami and the factions of Jamiat Ulema e Islam, while the main opposition political parties, namely the PPP and Pakistan Muslim League (Nawaz) [PML(N)], were handicapped because their respective leaders, Benazir Bhutto and Nawaz Sharif, were in exile. It is also widely believed that the army actively helped the religious parties counter the PPP and PML(N) vote strength. MMA had agreed to endorse Musharraf's Seventeenth Amendment to the constitution that, inter alia, allowed him to continue as both president and army chief.

MMA formed governments in the border provinces of NWFP and Baluchistan, which were the most affected by the American action. These provincial governments did not support Musharraf's alliance with the United States in the "war on terror" and were sympathetic to the Afghan Taliban. In this environment, the Pakistani army soon discovered that it was less than prepared to meet the escalating scale of the local militancy and tribal insurgency mixed with Al Qaeda and other militant extremist groups. The situation in the FATA continued to deteriorate, with the army taking large casualties, which by 2008 had exceeded 1500 in number.

Government Engagement in the FATA

Before 2001, the army had started a program of welfare projects in the FATA and worked towards integrating it into the rest of the settled districts in the province. Since 1947, when the tribal elders had formally agreed to accede to the new state with an understanding that the autonomous status of the area would be respected, the FATA had remained virtually ignored. Successive governments in Islamabad paid little attention to the longer-term necessity of integrating the area with the rest of the country. They were even unable to extend to the FATA the political parties' act of 1962 to encourage normal political activity. Meanwhile, in the 1980s, the FATA had turned into a staging ground for the Afghan Jihad. The rise of "warrior mullahs" weakened the traditional structures of governance through the system of local elders (Maliks) and political agents. The institution of the political agents that operated under the authority of the federally appointed governor of the province lost much of its authority.

In 2000, the army started a program for the development of roads, schools, and health clinics that was well received by the local tribes; but it came to a halt after the 9/11 and its aftermath. The army was now required to weed out Al Qaeda and interdict the Afghan Taliban. The main theater of action shifted to North and South Waziristan, where initial successes gave way to stalemate, as more foreign elements, including Al Qaeda Arabs, Uzbeks, Chechens, and other Central Asians, escaped from Afghanistan into the area. Local tribal mullahs and elders already having contacts with these elements offered them shelter, invoking religious causes as well as time-honored tribal customs. The new foreign military intervention and turmoil in Afghanistan and now what was perceived as the hostile Pakistani army presence in the FATA also brought out the local tribes' traditional antipathy and well-known defiance to the presence of regular armies in their midst.

A turning point in the army operations came in mid-March 2004, when a major operation was launched in the Wana Valley in South Waziristan. According to intelligence reports, a large number of Al Qaeda and other foreigners were present, protected by area locals, pointing to the possibility that a high-value target, most likely Al Zawahiri, was holed up there. Initially carried out with the Frontier Corps, the operation started on the wrong foot when a number of FC troops were trapped in an ambush. When negotiations for their release, through tribal jirgas, did not produce results, the army launched a major operation involving six thousand troops; but most of the foreign elements were able to break the Army cordon and escape. Almost seventy Pakistani army troops lost their lives as did about as many militants. Operations were later launched in the Shakai Valley, again with mixed results. The casualties suffered by the army and the militants were almost equal in number. But the inevitable collateral damage that accompanied the military action, especially the use of the air force, caused an outcry locally and in the media.

The army's realization that it was faced with a determined adversary that enjoyed local support led to efforts for piecemeal agreements with local militia leaders through local jirgas. Following the Shakai operation, a high-profile but controversial agreement was signed in April 2004. To indicate his seal of approval, the Peshawar corps commander, Lt. Gen. Safdar Hussain, met the new rising militant leader Nek Muhammad. Later, in February 2005, another agreement followed at Sararogha. Although these agreements did not hold, others followed, interspersed with military action and deployments. These dubious peace moves gave rise to considerable controversy.

Throughout mid-2005 and early 2006, Musharraf and the army were preoccupied with the deteriorating situation in Waziristan. The large numbers of foreign and local Taliban fighters and the terror tactics they deployed against government supporters were the subject of frequent meetings at the Presidency and the Army Headquarters in Rawalpindi to explore the range of possible options. Since these hostile elements were mingled with the local population, major military operations against towns and villages were ruled out for reasons of collateral damage, especially civilian casualties. The meetings considered deployment of commandos from the Special Service Group for covert operations against the foreign elements, but lack of specific information and the large numbers of the foreign elements and their sympathizers made this option seem infeasible. In one meeting in late 2005, Musharraf was impressed, after watching a video, by the training and toughness of the militants, remarking that they could climb a hillside like "mountain goats"; yet he continued to underestimate their fanatical motivation and ruthlessness as fighters.

The Al Qaeda and militant response to these sporadic military operations had been to hit selected targets severely. In the FATA, the militants resorted to brutal tactics against those suspected of siding with the government. More than two hundred Maliks were slaughtered in places where the army withdrew after military action. The militants began spreading into other tribal agencies. Elements from the banned groups, in particular Jaish e Muhammad and Lashkar e Jahgvi, now aligned with Al Qaeda and local insurgents, spread violence to cities and towns outside the FATA. They escalated suicide bombings, targeting the country's urban centers to shake the people's confidence in the government's ability to enforce its writ.

Apart from the army, the government's thin administrative presence had practically disappeared in many parts of the FATA, especially those affected by the militant activity and army operations. The tribal insurgents, the newly emerging Pakistani Taliban, and Al Qaeda recruited the unemployed and mostly uneducated local youth to bolster their ranks. The local population, which had always lived under a tenuous administrative control, saw safety in supporting the militant coalition rather than standing with the army and facing reprisals when the troops redeployed elsewhere. For its part, the army could not keep a permanent presence; it complained that after it had cleared an area, the local administration or (nonexistent) police ought to take responsibility. But this would require advance planning and coordination between the provincial authority and the federal government. Both conditions were missing, in part because the provincial government was controlled by MMA, the coalition of religious parties that did not support the military action in the FATA, even though it was not directly responsible for the area. By now militancy had also gained the support of criminal elements engaged in extortion, kidnappings for ransom, and drug trafficking.

Al Qaeda, the Pakistani Taliban, and other militants scored an important propaganda success in characterizing the Pakistani army's actions as undertaken at the behest of the United States and its puppet and proxy, the Pakistan government. The propaganda was so strident that in some instances local mullahs refused to say funeral prayers for soldiers or others who died in action against the militants. In the face of this multidimensional challenge of profound gravity, the Pakistan government was ill prepared, lacking the resources and ability to take coordinated and focused action. The MMA government in NWFP was less than cooperative. Soon, the militancy spread to the Provincially Administered Tribal Areas (PATA) and to settled districts in NWFP.[8]

In late 2005, the policy towards the FATA tried to combine selected military action and continued military presence with attempts to gain peace through tribal jirgas and agreements. The new provincial governor, Lt. Gen. Orakzai, now retired from the army and himself from the tribal areas, favored mixing a political approach with military operations by involving the tribal elders instead of directly reaching out to militant commanders. He was the one mainly responsible for the controversial North Waziristan agreement with tribal elders, religious leaders, and local Taliban negotiated over several months and concluded in late August 2006. Orakzai's efforts were not unprecedented. Before him, in his capacity as corps commander Peshawar, Lt. Gen. Safdar Hussain had cut a peace deal with Nek Muhammad. Peshawar experts in Pushtun affairs later criticized Safdar's decision in 2004 to meet and have direct talks with Nek Mohammad as based on lack

8. PATA in NWFP includes the Districts of Chitral, Dir, Swat, Kohistan, and parts of Mansehra District. In Baluchistan Province, PATA includes the districts of Zhob, Loralai, Dalbadin, and Marri, and Bugti tribal areas.

of knowledge of the history and culture of the tribal areas. They viewed the meeting as a gesture that emboldened militants and raised the stature of a militant tribesman in the eyes of the local people, conferring respectability on insurgent activity.

Orakzai involved local tribal elders and jirgas in negotiations with the local Taliban, instead of dealing directly with them himself. He also tried somewhat disingenuously to argue with these elders, who believed in the rightness of the jihad against the Americans, that if they wanted to see the back of the Americans from the region then the only way was to stop the militancy and Taliban activity across the border and help promote peace in Afghanistan. Nevertheless, the Waziristan Accord was faulty in the same way as its precursors; it placed the government of Pakistan and the local tribal jirgas at the same level and accorded a degree of respectability to the insurgents. The title of the accord, which was in the Urdu language, described it as an accord between the government of Pakistan and the Aqwam (meaning nations or nationalities) of Uthmanzai and the Taliban and Ulema of the area.

The main points of the accord included a cease-fire and a hold on Pakistani army operations, a halt in militant activities inside Afghanistan launched from across the border in Waziristan, and amnesty for all foreign elements such as Arabs, Uzbeks, and Chechens in the area who renounced violence and gave up their arms. One of the clauses required the tribal elders not to allow the (Afghan or Pakistani) Taliban to cross the border for armed activity inside Afghanistan. The agreement led to a short-lived uneasy calm in the area. Soon, the militants resumed their activity. The Taliban did not cease crossing the border; they simply did so from other agencies, thus "keeping their word" with the North Waziristan tribal elders. The Taliban and militants' sympathizers blamed U.S. drone attacks for the collapse of the Waziristan agreement. Even General Orakzai later felt that the agreement was not given enough serious consideration or time for its implementation. However, despite slim prospects of the success of the agreement, it was understandable that General Orakzai could not have ruled out a peaceful approach to avoid bloodshed when dealing with his own tribal kinsmen.

The tribal insurgents and foreign elements never abandoned violence, which increased towards mid-2007, as Baitullah Mahsud formally launched the Tehrik Taliban Pakistan (movement of Pakistan Taliban).[9] Baitullah Mah-

9. Before the formation of the TTP by Baitullah Mahsud, insurgency in Waziristan was led by Abdullah Mahsud, who was released from Guantánamo Bay in March 2004. Later the same year he was involved in the kidnapping of two Chinese engineers, one of whom was killed in a botched rescue attempt. Abdullah Mahsud was killed in Zhob on July 24, 2007.

sud belonged to the Mahsud tribe from South Waziristan. His star had risen after the death of Nek Muhammad in a missile attack in June 2004 and the subsequent eclipse of his cousin, Abdullah Mahsud, who briefly led the Waziristan insurgency and was eventually killed in July 2007. Baitullah was not part of the Waziristan deal. He continued to target progovernment Maliks in the area and orchestrated kidnappings for ransom and as bargaining chips for release of the Tehrik (TTP) militants. By late 2007, Baitullah Mahsud boasted that he was in command of thousands of local Taliban and foreign fighters and hundreds of suicide bombers.[10] This coalition of tribal insurgents and religious militants with links to Al Qaeda aimed at nothing less than wresting political power for themselves in Waziristan and beyond. In this pursuit they had no qualms about resort to brutal methods.

Baitullah Mahsud launched a full-scale effort to destabilize Pakistan. The TTP was bolstered by the assault against the Lal Masjid (Red Mosque) in Islamabad in July 2007 and the killing of over one hundred militants and one of the chief clerics of the mosque, Abdur Rashid Ghazi. (The Lal Masjid crisis will be discussed later in the chapter.) Many of the madrassa students from in and around Islamabad and other areas, especially southern Punjab,[11] moved to Waziristan and operated under the umbrella of the TTP. The TTP claimed responsibility for most of the suicide attacks in Pakistani cities in 2008 and 2009, including army targets, police personnel and training centers, and the provincial center of the Intelligence Bureau in Lahore. Baitullah Mahsud was a suspect in the assassination of Benazir Bhutto. He declared an autonomous "Emirate of Waziristan" and openly professed alliance with Al Qaeda and Mullah Omar, whom he regarded as Amir ul Momineen (commander of the faithful). In 2008, TTP activities spread to other tribal agencies. Kurram was the scene of sectarian mayhem caused mostly by the TTP and its allies. Khyber and Bajaur agencies witnessed strife and regular attacks on the ISAF/NATO container trucks carrying supplies into Afghanistan.

In Khyber and Bajaur, the government tried to organize tribal lashkars (militias) to contain the TTP, but these created new law and order problems, distressing the local population. Local militias could hardly be expected to

---

10. According to a *NYT* report of July 27, 2009, TTP has 10,000 to 12,000 fighters, with 4,000 foreigners, who are paid $60 to $80 per month. In February 2008, the TTP kidnapped Pakistani ambassador to Kabul Tariq Azizuddin and demanded a large ransom in addition to the release of certain extremists, including a mastermind involved with indoctrination of suicide bombers.

11. Adbur Rashid Ghazi and his brother Abdul Aziz belonged to Dera Ghazi Khan in southern Punjab.

act on behalf of the state for law enforcement. Instead, they gave rise to new militant groups such as the one led by Mangal Bagh in Khyber. These groups developed ambitions for autonomy and wanted to create their own space, exploiting local resentment and resorting to violence and extortion to generate funds. The tribal areas have a tradition of forming lashkars under the authority of local jirgas for specific agreed purposes under joint command of the tribe(s), but not to serve as a standing force led by any local fortune seeker.

In Waziristan, the army's tactic of pitching Maulvi Nazir, a Waziri tribal leader and local commander, against Baitullah Mahsud did not work. Maulvi Nazir had a tribal feud with Baitullah, but ideologically they were on the same wavelength. When in May 2009 the army launched a full-scale operation to clear the Taliban from Swat, Maulvi Nazir and Baitullah Mahsud announced that they would shed their differences and join hands to resist the army. Local rivalries among militant groups generally allied to the Afghan Taliban and Al Qaeda have remained largely contained. These otherwise disparate groups betray a mutual interest in each other's survival, and there is little evidence that their differences could be exploited to any meaningful advantage.

Pakistan Faces Difficulties on the Ground and in Public Debate

During 2006, difficulties in coping with the rising militancy in the FATA and terrorist violence in the cities assumed a serious dimension; yet the Musharraf government maintained a certain complacency and confidence about its ability to contain and deal with the problem. There was worry but no panic. The government could not concede the army's failure to neutralize the insurgency in the FATA and a loss of writ in the area. Musharraf felt that short of a full-scale army action, a combination of political, administrative, economic, and military measures could control the militancy. The government saw the military setbacks in Waziristan, where the tribes were notorious for their fiercely free spirit and rebellious traditions, as temporary and able to be overcome with training and better equipment. The successive deals and agreements with local tribes were considered expedient and suitable tactics to bring peace in areas that were traditionally under loose federal control. The government faced criticism for allowing the situation in the FATA to deteriorate, with increasingly louder voices placing the blame on Musharraf's alliance with Bush's "war on terror." However, until early 2007, Musharraf's hold on the country and politics appeared secure and without any visible threat.

Internationally, pressure on Pakistan to "do more" had been building, particularly through stories by Kabul-based foreign media blaming Pakistan for tolerating Taliban safe havens in the FATA and allowing Mullah Omar to hide in Quetta. The government kept refuting the charge and tried to deflect pressure by pointing a finger at failures of Kabul and the coalition and by proposing measures along the border such as fencing and mining, discussed in chapter 3. In Washington rumblings of concern followed the Waziristan agreement, but these seemed manageable. Furthermore, a certain fatigue was affecting government attitudes towards criticism in the international media, which relentlessly repeated similar themes. At the official level, this criticism was routinely dismissed with a set of familiar counterarguments and charges.

The year 2007 proved to be a watershed period. The militancy and violence and an unanticipated political crisis began spinning out of control, with the focus of international concerns shifting to Pakistan. Musharraf became embroiled in a judicial crisis that started in March 2007 with the lawyers' protest movement over the unceremonious dismissal of the country's chief justice. The protest became politicized and paralyzed the increasingly beleaguered Musharraf government. Almost simultaneously, a violent situation erupted in Islamabad with an audacious challenge to the writ of the government by extremist madrassa students. Two brothers, clerics in the Red Mosque, the Lal Masjid, located in the heart of the capital, led the students' challenge. The Red Mosque standoff persisted for four months before it was ended in July 2007 by forceful military action that resulted in considerable trauma and bloodshed. These developments encouraged the FATA-based TTP militants, who began to expand their activities beyond the tribal areas into settled districts. The cities suffered an increasing incidence of bomb blasts and terrorist violence at the hands of extremist groups. The year ended with the assassination of the former prime minister and chair of the PPP, Benazir Bhutto, in a suicide attack.

The turmoil of 2007 brought into full view the weaknesses of the government and its intelligence and administrative systems for handling extremist violence in the country and the TTP challenge in the FATA. Public support plummeted for Musharraf and his allied ruling coalition, in which the Pakistan Muslim League (Quaid e Azam), PLM (Q), had been cobbled together with breakaway elements of the PPP and Nawaz Sharif's Muslim

League. In addition, an important debilitating factor handicapping the Musharraf government was the negative public discourse opposing the "war on terror," which print media and interminable talk shows on dozens of private TV channels led and intensified.

Musharraf believed that military action by itself was not the answer to the growing militancy in the FATA. His government had abandoned the pre-9/11 plans to gradually integrate the tribal areas through development and administrative reform. In the changed post–9/11 circumstances, the thinking turned to resurrecting the old system of tribal Maliks and political agents and to reinforcing local paramilitary forces, the Frontier Corps (FC) and Frontier Constabulary, and police to help the local administration. In 2004, twelve new FC wings were planned to triple the Corps' strength. The progress was slow for want of funds; by late 2007, Pakistan had raised only half of the planned addition to the FC, which still needed training and equipment. The building of a FATA police force raised problems similar to those faced in Afghanistan and Iraq, where new recruits became the target of militant attacks and suicide bombings, resulting in large desertions. As for FATA development, especially in relatively calm agencies, the government's plans continued to languish for lack of funds, bureaucratic inertia, and the increasingly deteriorating law-and-order situation.

Meanwhile, as time passed, the militants continued to gain strength and became increasingly ruthless in asserting their hold on the tribal populations, especially in South and North Waziristan. The Baitullah-led TTP insurgency targeted and assassinated progovernment Maliks and forced progovernment elements and hapless local officials to simply leave the area. Without defeating the militants, it was impossible to resurrect a system seriously undermined by the Jihad of the 1980s and the subsequent troubles in Afghanistan, which had given rise to autonomous actors in tribal areas. These had little allegiance to the provincial government or the federal authority reposed in the province's governor. The central government was mistaken in underestimating the gravity and scale of the problem and thus doing too little too late in terms of military action and deployments. Nevertheless, as the situation deteriorated, the government increased the number of troops in the FATA from around 80,000 in late 2005 to over 100,000 by 2007. It was the persistent and flagrant defiance by religious extremists, Pakistani Taliban, and insurgents that eventually propelled the Pakistan state machinery, including the army, to take strong military action against these forces, such as was witnessed in 2009.

In addition to the Lal Masjid showdown in Islamabad, the capital city, during 2007, Pakistani cities, especially in the provinces of Punjab and

NWFP, saw a sharp rise in terrorist incidents, including bomb blasts and suicide bombings. Punjab was relatively quiet in 2006, with less than 10 incidents, increasing to 25 in 2007 and 30 in 2008. NWFP saw an increase from
16 incidents in 2006 to 131 in 2007 and 157 in 2008.[12] According to another
estimate, such incidents resulted in 216 deaths in 2005, surging to over
25,000 by 2009. The escalation came in 2007, when 3,447 people died in
terrorist-related violence. The figure reached 7,997 in 2008.[13] Baluchistan
and Sindh, in particular Karachi, had long suffered target killings and subversive activity. The major suicide attack on Benazir Bhutto's convoy in
Karachi on October 18, 2007, resulted in more than 140 fatalities. The TTP
openly threatened to strike the cities with hundreds of suicide bombers it
had in readiness.

The violence exposed the weakness of the country's administrative structure, which had suffered deterioration over the years. A variety of factors, including military and political interference and experimentation by successive
governments, had eroded the quality and proficiency of the administration.
Local administration was no longer capable of the much-needed monitoring
and controlling of extremist groups and tendencies. The problems were compounded by Musharraf's well-intentioned reforms aimed at a devolution of
power by replacing the federally or provincially appointed bureaucrat with an
elected head at the district level. The elected district head could hardly be
expected to use force in his electoral constituency, even if necessary to curb
extremist violence. The new system thus could not effectively use police or
mobilize local intelligence to counter militancy and extremism. By training
and tradition, local police could not initiate action, which was an administrative prerogative. In addition to their lack of authority and erosion of professional standards, the police had no training in counterterrorism, and their
weaponry and skills often proved no match for the militants and extremist operatives, hardened by training and battles in Afghanistan.

The centrally controlled intelligence agencies were mostly busy trying
to track down the perpetrators, the handlers, and the masterminds behind
various suicide bombings and other terrorist incidents, and their approach
largely missed the forest for the trees. Successes in resolving a number of

12. These figures have been gleaned from data compiled by the South Asia: Terrorism Portal Web site. According to Pakistan Ministry of Interior data, Punjab suffered 41,
44, and 47 incidents in 2006, 2007, and 2008, respectively, while in the same years the
figures for NWFP were 55, 216, and 244 and for FATA 256, 228, and 199. There is considerable discrepancy in some figures, depending on the tabulation of reported incidents.

13. Figures cited in an article by Robert Fisk published in *The Independent* (London), April 6, 2010.

cases, especially the attacks against high-profile targets, were ephemeral triumphs in combating terrorism, while the bigger picture of emerging convergence and coordination among militant groups and organizations escaped attention that might have compelled the top decision makers to take urgent and difficult steps. Before 2007, the government spent considerable energy in countering Cassandras and denying Pakistan's blame for the troubles in Afghanistan.

The question is why a forceful and sustained operation such as was seen later in 2009 in Swat and South Waziristan was not initiated in 2006 and 2007, when the government, along with intermittent military action, continued toying with peace agreements or using local tribal lashkars against local Taliban and militant groups. The government's first preference was to pacify the Pakistani Taliban through selective and limited military operations and peace deals instead of promptly resorting to a fight-to-the-finish military action. The additional complication was that the army was now pitted against its own people. There were genuine concerns that the ordinary soldier would be reluctant to fire at militants who looked like Mujahedin with religious bearing. Accordingly, the military operations were piecemeal, reactive, and incremental, corresponding to the growth of militancy. Planning for operations evolved as the militancy grew, instead of being based on a full grasp of the nature and gravity of the threat. That the area was generally regarded as lawless contributed a further degree of procrastination.

In dealing with the jihadi militant elements when they were proscribed in 2002, Pakistan's state machinery did not show the same firmness as it had against Al Qaeda. That these jihadi groups had once been officially encouraged and even empowered during the 1990s helped account for the initial Pakistani tolerance towards them. While the policy and thinking of the government and the army on jihadi activity was changing under the force of new circumstances, there was hesitation to direct military action against the jihadi groups, especially those linked to Kashmir. The preference was to deny these groups free rein and wean them away from militancy. However, the jihadi groups, a product of past policy and now on the wrong side of the drastically altered regional and global circumstances, resisted change. Having a strong motivation, many members and leaders of these groups went underground and gradually braced themselves to direct their violence and fury towards the government and Musharraf, whom they saw as an accomplice of the U.S.-led coalition.

Another important psychological factor that weakened the ability of the government and the army to take forceful action was the loss of clarity within

Pakistan regarding the nature of militancy. Endless media and public debates inhibited recognition of the gravity of the problem. The discourse intensified during 2007 as Musharraf's political position faltered. The political transition in 2008 was also marked by confusion and bickering among the political parties, obscuring the challenge of militancy. Internationally, the Bush policies on Iraq and terrorism began to be questioned and discredited. Musharraf's policy on terrorism and deployment of the army in the FATA against its "own people" came under vocal public criticism. The religious elements and Musharraf's political opponents challenged the notion of the "global war on terrorism" and his early assertion that Pakistan was an ally in this war. In the critics' interpretation, Pakistan was fighting the U.S. war and paying a terrible price in the hostility of elements that did not engage in violence against the country before 2001. The change of nuance in official statements since 2005, emphasizing that terrorism and extremism were first and foremost the gravest threat to Pakistan itself, went virtually ignored or were drowned out by the din of the opposition point of view.

The controversy over the government position on the "war on terror" was further fueled by the *suo moto* (on its own motion) judicial enquiry started by the Supreme Court in mid-2007 to look into the cases of missing persons, who it was alleged had been transferred to the United States.[14] Ironically, critical U.S. comments also damaged the government position. The refrain that Pakistan should "do more" undermined the Musharraf government's effort to convince public opinion that terrorism was primarily Pakistan's own problem.

Because of the growing judicial and political crisis in the country in 2007, the credibility of the government position had so plummeted that de-

---

14. Figures vary on the number of missing persons. According to *Daily Times* (Lahore), August 21, 2007, the chairperson of the Pakistan Human Rights Commission gave the figure of 173 cases, of which 95 were still missing. The *Daily Times* (Lahore) of April 10, 2009, reported that the acting chief justice stated that 101 persons had been recovered or traced. The government claimed that those still missing may have been individuals gone to Afghanistan with jihadi groups. All Guantánamo Bay inmates of Pakistani origin had been picked up by the Americans in Afghanistan. The Musharraf government also maintained that no Pakistani was handed over to the Americans. The handing over of Amal Kansi and Ramzi Yousef to the Americans predated the Musharraf government. The circumstances of the oft-quoted case of Dr. Afia Siddiqui and how she entered Afghanistan are murky. A Pakistani delegation visited Guantánamo Bay to secure the release of Pakistanis held there. Those released included Abdullah Mahsud. Dissident leaders from Baluchistan allege hundreds of disappearances and blame the government for political victimization.

spite good evidence, most commentators refuted the government version of Baitullah Mahsud's involvement in the assassination of Benazir Bhutto. Commentators in the Urdu print media preferred to give prominence to a TTP disclaimer of responsibility for the act, which asserted that the group did not target women. In these circumstances, Musharraf or the government in transition were in no position to rally the people against the dangers posed to the country by the extremists and the TTP. Meanwhile, as the activities of the Pakistani Taliban and extremists continued to spread beyond Waziristan, by early 2008 the Swat District, located next to the Bajaur Agency, flared up with a separate brand of religious militancy, to be discussed later in this chapter.

Following Musharraf's exit in 2008, the army wanted the political leadership to embrace the policy of using military force and owning responsibility for military operations against the rising militancy. When the military top brass briefed the leaders of the major parties in early May 2008, the politicians could not agree on a decision to endorse military action or a continued military presence in the FATA or in Swat, where troops had been sent in early 2008. According to some reports, the PML(N) initially favored withdrawing the troops from the tribal area to bring peace. The party changed its position and agreed to support the continued troop deployment only when the army clearly conveyed to Nawaz Sharif that, once withdrawn, the army should not be asked to move back to the area again, reminding him of the earlier experience of withdrawal that had allowed the militants to return and kill many government supporters.

For almost two weeks in mid-October 2008, the newly elected Parliament debated, mostly in camera, the issue of terrorism and the army's involvement. The debate was preceded by army briefings, later dismissed as operational details by Chaudry Nisar Ali Khan of the PML(N), the leader of the opposition benches in Parliament. Chaudry Nisar criticized the government for simply continuing the policies of Musharraf. Maulana Fazal ur Rahman, who represented the moderate religious view, called for dialogue with the Pakistani Taliban. There was almost unanimous condemnation of the U.S. drone attacks, which had become a frequent occurrence, with significant civilian casualties in each attack. The Parliament ended up adopting an omnibus resolution that allowed both dialogue and use of force against militancy and a reference to the responsibility of the government to protect the country's sovereignty against attacks and incursions, an indirect reference to drone operations. The resolution called for dialogue with all elements willing to abide by the constitution of Pakistan and rule of law, and called for the expulsion of foreign militants. It also indirectly accepted the role of the military by calling for its replacement only where competent civilian law enforcement agencies existed to make it possible.

The parliamentary debate took place at a time when militants operating under Maulvi Fazalullah, firebrand son-in-law of cleric Sufi Muhammad, were actively harassing and targeting villages and towns in Swat, especially landowners and government officials. A major operation against the militants launched by the army was in progress. To sustain such action, the army needed full backing by the political leadership rather than calls for dialogue. The parliamentary debate therefore posed a dilemma for the army. Politicians wavered because of the consequences of harsh military action in the shape of civilian casualties and flows of internally displaced persons. Procrastination over tough decisions was inescapable in such circumstances. Meanwhile, the continued U.S. drone attacks further agitated public opinion and stirred media and parliamentary debates criticizing the alignment of Pakistan's policy with that of the United Sates. On the ground, the TTP and foreign militant elements who had become active in the Bajaur agency were ready to spill over into the neighboring Swat District to join hands with Maulvi Fazalullah's militant elements.

The Rise of Militancy in Swat

The malfunctioning justice system and the absence of speedy justice engender a serious malaise that afflicts Pakistan generally and forms part of the failure of the country's institutions of governance. In Swat, the militants exploited the local population's long-standing grievance against the slow and corrupt justice system. Prior to the merger of the former princely state of Swat with NWFP in the 1970s, the system in force in the state, a mix of Sharia and local customs, had been far more efficient. The grievance against the successor justice system became the rallying point for the local cleric, Sufi Muhammad, to launch a movement, Tehrik Nifaz e Shariat Muhammadi (TNSM—movement for enforcement of Sharia). In 1994, Prime Minister Benazir Bhutto had agreed to reinstate the old system and give the provincial government the privilege of appointing the Qazis (judges). A slightly modified version was accepted later in 1998. But the system, called Nizam e Adl (system of justice),was not implemented.[15]

_____

15. For a succinct but detailed background on insurgency in Swat, see a report by

Against the backdrop of the rise of the Taliban in neighboring Afghanistan, TNSM gained in strength with an increasing disposition towards militancy. After 9/11, Sufi Muhammad led several thousands of his followers to fight on the side of the Afghan Taliban. Most perished inside Afghanistan. In 2002, with a few hundred of his devotees, Sufi returned to Pakistan through Parachinar, where he was arrested.[16] By early 2006, his son-in-law, Maulvi Fazalullah, a cable car mechanic at a ski resort turned religious leader, organized his own militant group. He incited the local madrassa youth through FM radio messages to rise against the local khans, or feudal landowners, and advocated imposing the Taliban-style system for quick dispensation of justice in the district. Promising to distribute land and orchards in the valley, Fazalullah rallied support among poor sections of the population, especially economically depressed gujjars, herdsmen who lived in villages on mountain heights.

The MMA government in Peshawar remained reluctant to permit military action in the district,[17] which encouraged Fazalullah militants to start attacking video stores and barbershops and girls' schools. By late 2007, the militants also started terrorizing the local notables and religious persons who opposed Fazalullah. His tactics had a distinctive appeal of class struggle by the have-nots against the rich. An incentive for his followers was the distribution of land and orchards to the landless when the landowners fled Swat. The army, which was operating against the local Taliban in neighboring Bajaur Agency, moved into Swat following the February 2008 elections. The situation in the district suddenly deteriorated, with local Taliban and militants from Bajaur and other areas joining the ranks of Fazallulah. The provincial government, now led by the secular Awami National Party (ANP), requested military action.

Following six months of effort, the army was able to push the militants out of the district headquarters, Mingora, and other towns of Swat. Using helicopter gunships and infantry, the army forced Fazalullah to vacate his stronghold in Matta. Again, the army faced the problem of consolidating administrative control because of the absence of local administration and

---

Khalid Aziz, *Swat: The Main Causes of the Breakdown of Governance and Rise of Militancy,* published in June 2010 by the Regional Institute of Policy Research and Training, Peshawar.

16. According to a widely accepted version, Sufi Muhammad did not return directly to Swat for fear of reprisal by relatives of the young men who had lost their lives in Afghanistan and chose instead the circuitous route of entering Pakistan from Parachinar, where he "offered" his arrest in exchange for the safety of his person.

17. Swat is part of PATA, the Provincially Administered Tribal Areas.

police. The military action had also created more than one hundred thousand refugees, leading to protests, mostly orchestrated by the religious parties and their political supporters, who had been defeated in the elections and were sympathetic to the local Taliban.

The new government in Islamabad became embroiled in other political problems, especially the issue of reinstating the Chief Justice deposed by Musharraf in November 2007. The army's gains began to dissipate, with the army unable to act effectively in an environment of political vacillation about how to address the Taliban presence in Swat. Sufi, who by now had been released, activated his movement for the implementation of Nizam e Adl. He successfully rallied people around the old demand, bringing thousands onto the streets of Mingora. The provincial government caved in and by April 2009 agreed to enforce Nizam e Adl, provided Fazallullah and his militants gave up violence. In fact, the provincial government accepted demands that went beyond the issue of Sharia.

According to the agreement the provincial government accepted, the Qazi courts to be established were to be autonomous, and appeals against their verdict would lie within the local Taliban-dominated system and not with the provincial high court or the Supreme Court of Pakistan. A good deal of confusion resulted from the statements made by Sufi Muhammad, who asserted that a Taliban shura to be nominated by him rather than the provincial government would appoint these judges. He further made it clear that the agreed Nizam e Adl had immunity against the application of the law of the country and that the Taliban could not be tried under the law for their past actions. He demanded compensation for those who had suffered on account of the military action. The provincial government chose to overlook Sufi's humiliating interpretations but kept defending the deal as a move in the interest of peace.

President Zardari referred the agreement to the Parliament, which endorsed it, with opposition from MQM and a few individual voices. Zardari tried to assuage the fears of many, within and outside the country, who saw in the deal a dangerous precedent. He claimed that Nizam e Adl was not Sharia and that it would be reviewed if peace did not return to Swat. Voices critical of the existing legal system dominated the print and electronic media. They urged respect for the long-standing legitimate demand of the people of Swat, as demonstrated by the rallies in Mingora and other district towns. The parliamentary debate was devoid of focus on the violence perpetrated in the area by the Taliban and the ruthless tactics they employed to terrorize the people and consolidate their control.

The deal, nevertheless, raised a host of constitutional and legal issues for the government, aside from its dubious impact on the security situation in Swat. It was because of difficulties in dovetailing the system in Swat with the system in force in the rest of the country that there had been delays in implementing the 1994 agreement and the subsequent 1998 modified formula. The relevant larger question was how to resist any new demands for the enforcement of Sharia, as interpreted by any self-styled mullah or leader with political ambitions. Politically, the provincial government's decision to reach an agreement with Sufi Muhammad had clearly undermined the gains made by the military action, which was stopped midway.

The supporters of the decision justified it as an effort to give peace a chance by removing a long-standing grievance; but many critics saw the decision as one taken from a position of weakness, when the militants appeared to be holding out against the army. This pattern could easily repeat itself in parts of the FATA, and then even in settled districts where the authority of the government was weak. The Swat deal materialized while the local Taliban were continually gaining ground and madrassas, especially in areas affected by extremism, were producing indoctrinated young men from poor families to fill the ranks of religious militants and to do the bidding of the extremists and zealots leading the Taliban movement in Pakistan. Swat was thus not an issue of settling an old demand to bring peace in this disturbed district; instead, it was part of the challenge of creeping Talibanization faced by Pakistan. Loss of Swat to the Taliban sank into the psyche of urban Pakistan. Unlike the isolated and lawless badlands of Waziristan and much of the tribal area, Swat was familiar to most Pakistanis from Punjab and Sindh, and its verdant valleys attracted thousands of domestic tourists, from Peshawar to Karachi.

The Swat deal encouraged the militants, but they quickly overreached themselves. The Fazalullah militants and TTP fighters returned to Mingora and the towns from which they had been evicted by the military. They interpreted the agreement to imply complete withdrawal of the military from the district and any military movement in Swat to be subject to permission by the shura under Sufi Muhammad. Fazalullah's men blocked the movement of one of the regiments. Sufi Muhammad made a couple of inflammatory speeches declaring both democracy and the judicial system in Pakistan as un-Islamic, which drew a sharp reaction even from sympathizers of the Taliban and Sufi's movement. Qazi Hussain Ahmad, the chief of Jamat e Islami, had to say that Sufi Muhammad did not understand Islam.

Within days of their return in April 2009 by virtue of the deal, the militants resumed their oppressive actions and targeted government personnel.

Two incidents, however, had a deep impact in turning public opinion and the media and forging a broad national consensus for action against the Taliban. First, human rights activists released to the media a video, filmed on a cell-phone camera, that showed a young girl being lashed under the Sharia law for the purported moral dereliction of stepping out of the house unaccompanied by a close male relative, an incident that had taken place three months earlier in February. More than the Taliban's reported brutal slaughter of four policemen in Mingora's public square, this act captured on video created a furor and drew countrywide condemnation of the act as a vile insult to Islam. The only defense by some pro-Taliban commentators was to dismiss the video as a fabrication designed to malign the Taliban. The other development that could not be denied was the Taliban's move to advance beyond Swat to the Buner District only ninety kilometers from Islamabad.[18] The move raised concerns internationally and domestically, reinforcing the reversal of public opinion. The deal with Sufi Muhammad for Nizam e Adl could no longer be viewed as redress of a long-standing local demand. The Taliban were clearly using it as a pretext to reestablish control over Swat and as a stepping-stone to assert their influence beyond Swat.

Taking advantage of the change in public opinion, in May 2009 the government backed strong military action against the Taliban in Buner and Swat. The Pakistani army chief stated that "victory against terror and militancy will be achieved at all cost," and that "operational pause" in Swat was meant to give talks a chance and was not a concession to the Taliban.[19] This time the army operations were carried out on a large scale, involving 40,000 troops and use of airpower. To avoid civilian casualties, people were asked to vacate villages and towns, often at short notice, creating an unprecedented exodus of between two million and three million internally displaced people. There was criticism of the government for not anticipating and preparing to deal with the problems of IDPs, and agitation among human rights groups and relief agencies about their plight. Nonetheless, this time there had been no domestic voices against the military action and its severity.

The experience of the October 2005 earthquake had been helpful in organizing relief assistance to the displaced people,[20] but this 2009 program was of short duration, as the army operation could not have stretched over a long period without a negative reflection on the army's ability to address

---

18. *NYT* editorial, "Sixty Miles from Islamabad," April 27, 2009.

19. *Daily Times* (Lahore), April 25, 2009.

20. The head of the relief operations, Lt. Gen. Nadeem Ahmad, has also been the head of the earthquake reconstruction and rehabilitation program since 2007.

the challenge of the Taliban. While most of the displaced persons have returned, the Swat situation will be settled only when operational police and administration have improved the law and order situation. It will be a protracted effort, since the TTP and Fazalullah followers in Swat will continue their attacks to harass the population and keep the local administration off balance. The government plans to raise a large police force with a component of retired army personnel. Another idea under active consideration is to devise a system of local neighborhood committees to ensure local security. The confidence of the people is likely to remain shaky as long as Fazalullah and his lieutenants remain at large.

The army expected the tenacity of Fazalulluh's militants and other TTP elements but did not anticipate their possession of sophisticated arms and equipment. One of the intelligence failures had been the inability to trace and block sources of funding and weapons supply to the extremist militant groups operating in the FATA and Swat. Funding sources include drug and ransom money and smuggling, apart from overseas donations, but the sources of arms supplies continue to pose unanswered questions. There is a presumption of the involvement of hostile intelligence agencies, in particular RAW, ISI's Indian counterpart, and the Afghan and other intelligence agencies. The availability of arms to the militants has deserved greater focus and collaboration between the coalition and Afghan and Pakistani military and intelligence. The frustration at difficulties in containing militancy and extremist violence feeds suspicions of external conspiracy and the habit of overlooking the domestic circumstances and impulses that are the principal causes underlying the problem.

The Continuing Challenge in Waziristan

The other major challenge for the army continued to be Waziristan, which by any measure would prove to be a far tougher operation than Swat. The terrain is difficult and the militants are deeply entrenched in the local population. The army launched the new phase of its operation in South Waziristan in late 2009. The TTP responded to the operation by escalating bomb blasts and suicide bombings targeting government installations, including an unprecedented attack on army general headquarters in Rawalpindi, as well as markets and other public places. This time there was no interruption of the operation halfway. The government and the army again took advantage of the turn in public opinion against the Pakistani Taliban after Swat. The

Taliban's erstwhile vocal supporters from religious political parties could no longer publicly support the Taliban creed, even though they continued to blame the U.S. presence and influence in Afghanistan and Pakistan for instability in the area. By early 2010, the army was able to clear much of South Waziristan, allowing General Kayani to claim in February that the "Myth of South Waziristan"—that no one could control this unruly region—had been broken. He correctly observed, "If we turned back, we would have destroyed the credibility of the army."[21] The consolidation of administrative control and rehabilitation would, however, continue to pose a major challenge.

The army's 2009 operations underscored the magnitude of the problem, which was not restricted to Waziristan, Swat, and Bajaur. Extremist militancy afflicts not just the tribal agencies; it is rooted in many parts of the country, in particular southern Punjab. Proscribed militant groups that enjoyed public support and army backing in the past, such as Lashkar e Tayaba and even the sectarian Sipah e Sahaba, are capable of taking out processions in the cities in a show of force. Understandably, it would not be possible for the government or the army to take on all these groups at once. An incremental approach appears prudent. The army is already overstretched, with nearly one-third of its strength deployed in the north. It needs to consolidate the cleared areas for police and other security forces and local administration to become functional before shifting or expanding the theater of operation.[22]

Musharraf's View and Strategy to Counter Extremism

For most of his rule, Musharraf was preoccupied with the problem of terrorism and extremism. Over the years, he developed his views and discussed them with many of his interlocutors, including foreign visitors. He linked the problem in the region to the Afghan war as well as to the festering Kashmir dispute and socioeconomic underdevelopment. He also believed that in Pakistan the moderate and enlightened segment of the population that understood Islam and its message of peace and moderation had abdicated the

21. *The News* (Islamabad), February 13, 2010.
22. Explaining to the NATO high command in Brussels in February 2010, the Pakistani army chief, General Ashfaq Parvez Kayani, indicated that the army had reached close to its optimal level of deployment in the FATA area, on the basis of the operational principle of one-third deployment on each of its two fronts and the rest needed as operational reserve for rotation and internal security.

religion to semiliterate clerics who did not understand it in the present-day context. He also likened terrorism to a tree, where the handlers and the mastermind were manipulating the individual perpetrators of terrorism. Taking out the perpetrators was like plucking the leaves, while eliminating the handlers and the mastermind was like cutting the branches. But the tree would continue to produce branches and leaves until it was struck at its roots, which in the case of the Muslim world lay in the unresolved problems such as Palestine and Kashmir, poverty and illiteracy. Extrapolating these ideas, Musharraf had developed a concept of "enlightened moderation" as a strategy to counter terrorism and extremism in Islamic society.

Musharraf's enlightened moderation was conceived as a two-pronged strategy. The first prong was to be delivered by the West's helping the Islamic world resolve some of the outstanding problems, in particular Palestine. Musharraf stated on several occasions that much of militancy and the impulse for terrorism would die down if the Palestinian issue were resolved. He also initiated an ambitious plan to establish a small group of significant Islamic countries to promote dialogue among the principal parties involved in the complex Middle East issues, ranging from Palestine to Iraq to the tension in the Gulf. In February 2007, Musharraf even undertook visits to several Arab and non-Arab Muslim capitals. The effort, as expected, proved futile. It tapered off with the adoption of an anodyne declaration at the conclusion of a meeting of foreign ministers from Saudi Arabia, Egypt, Turkey, Jordan, Indonesia, Malaysia, and Pakistan, held in Islamabad in March 2007.

The second prong of enlightened moderation was supposed to be for the countries of the Islamic world to take responsibility to make reforms that would counter extremist tendencies. In many of his speeches, Musharraf would lament the backwardness of the Islamic world, citing figures of literacy, numbers of PhDs in sciences, GNP, and per capita incomes as compared to the natural resources available in these countries. This concern, however, was only partially reflected in his own government's priorities and allocations for socioeconomic development.

The assumption that the West would help with the resolution of problems afflicting the Islamic world was simplistic, if not naïve. In the West, the discourse on extremism and terrorism had moved away from recognizing political problems as the root cause and towards the articulation of a clash of values between authoritarian systems and free and democratic systems. The fact that the festering Palestinian problem spawned terrorist violence was generally acknowledged and figured briefly in commentaries seeking to explain the horror of 9/11. But soon a powerful counternarrative was promoted linking the motivation to a difference in value systems. Even without these polemical assertions, the idea of the West helping to resolve outstanding disputes, coming from the head of state of Pakistan, appeared to be just one more attempt to internationalize the Kashmir issue. The West and many other nations viewed terrorism as a strategic threat and wanted it countered without linking the effort to any other issue.

On the strategy's second prong, it was difficult to expect unity among the Islamic countries on the issue of reform or a common approach on how to address the various political issues and terrorism. Musharraf also wanted to invigorate the Organization of the Islamic Conference on a platform of reform and common action to address challenges and problems facing the Muslim *Ummah* (community). and he supported revision of the OIC charter. A revised charter was adopted in early 2008 in Senegal, but it was virtually a recast of the older version with little change that could inject potency into the organization.

Failed Madrassa Reforms and Systemic Weakness in Countering Extremism

Musharraf made a distinction between terrorism and extremism. He believed that while terrorism had to be handled with force, extremism was a state of mind to be addressed through a policy of reform. The main pillars of his policy to counter religious extremism and the plethora of related problems included madrassa reforms, mosque reforms, and banning of militant sectarian groups. Given the enormity of the challenge posed by their numbers and mode of education, reform of the madrassas was the centerpiece of the policy to counter extremism. Madrassas were the traditional institutions of learning in the Islamic world. In the Middle Ages, madrassas of Baghdad, North Africa, and Central Asia had earned great renown as centers of both religious and temporal learning. In recent centuries, with the decline of sciences in Muslim societies, madrassa education became limited to imparting religious subjects, in particular jurisprudence. These madrassas exist in all parts of the Islamic world and are often linked to different sects and schools. Most of the Taliban and Sunni political movements in Pakistan have been linked to either the Deobandi or the Saudi Salafi tradition.

The Deoband School, founded in 1867, was established in northern India at a time when the British had already consolidated their rule, having ousted the last Mughul king after defeating the great Indian rebellion in 1857. Deoband was part of the revivalist movement defined in reaction to defeats and loss of power the Muslims suffered in India. Deoband Ulema have been reformists in the orthodox tradition and, like the Wahabi School, rejected *bida,* or innovation, and focused on teaching classical religious curricula of the Quran, *hadith,* and *fiqh* (jurisprudence). Unlike Wahabism or the later Saudi Salafi movement, Deobandis accepted the main schools of Sufism (Silsila e Tariqat), which had strong followings among the Afghans and the Muslims of India. Also, the founding Ulema recognized the need for coexistence and even cooperation with the majority Hindu community to stand up to the British rulers. This sentiment lost relevance in Pakistan where, since independence, Deobandi Ulema have been politically active with various factions of Jamiat Ulema e Islam (JUI), which are part of mainstream Pakistani politics. Madrassas that were the inspiration for the Taliban were affiliated with the more conservative Deobandi tradition in Pakistan.

The madrassas have no centralized institutional hierarchy. A large majority of madrassas, close to 75 percent, are affiliated with an umbrella of five associations, Wifaq ul Madaris, which broadly regulates curricula and examinations. The five associations of the Wifaq are the Deobandi, Barelvi, Ahl e Hadith, Jamat e Islami, and Shia schools. Most of the madrassas under the Wifaq follow teaching close to the Deobandi tradition.[23] A large majority of *khatibs* (Muslim chaplains) attached to army regiments are educated in these madrassas. The various other sects run their own madrassas, imparting essentially religious education in accordance with their own denominational emphasis. Pakistan saw a phenomenal increase in the number of madrassas during the Afghan Jihad of the 1980s, with official patronage and Saudi funds. For Afghan refugee children in camps and the poor sections of the Pakistani population, madrassa was often the only avenue for education. From a few hundred with around 7000 students in the late 1970s, by 2001 over 16,000 madrassas were operating in the country with nearly two million students.[24]

---

23. Stephen P. Cohen, *The Idea of Pakistan* (Washington: Brookings Institution Press, 2004), 180, mentions that Deobandis control 65 percent of madrassas in Pakistan.

24. Two articles on "The Madrassa" by Ikram Sehgal appearing in *The News* (Islamabad), May 20 and 27, 2010, citing data maintained by the Ministry of Religious Affairs, place the number at over 10,000 madrassas, including 448 for girls. The figure of over 16,000 was mentioned by the Ministry of Interior in an official meeting. The higher number accounts for those not registered with the Ministry of Religious Affairs. The articles place the number of madrassa students at roughly two million, 3 percent of all students in schools in Pakistan. Ikram Sehgal also suggests that 18 percent of madrassas, almost all unregistered, have a "jihadist trend."

The curricula of almost all madrassas are strictly limited to religious teaching and in some ways are more orthodox and rudimentary than the standard introduced at Deoband more than a century ago or than the Dars e Nizami conceived in the late eighteenth century and followed by many non-Deobandi Sunni madrassas. Since the Afghan Jihad, the curricula, especially in the Deobandi and Salafi madrassas and those belonging to militant groups like Sipah e Sahaba, brought in political overtones by emphasizing jihad and a worldview that encouraged xenophobia. While a good many of the madrassas rejected subjects associated with Western and science education, the large number of madrassas affiliated with the Wifaq have been ambivalent, placing little emphasis on teaching science. As a result, apart from obtaining a position in private sector businesses, graduates from the madrassas can enter into low clerical positions in the government, get absorbed in religious organizations, become imams in mosques, or drift towards jihad. They do not possess the qualifications to fit into the economic and developmental sectors.

Since Zia ul Haq's time, the government has allowed the expansion of madrassas without giving any thought to the future employment of madrassa-qualified youth. Most of the students belong to poverty-stricken families with many children. Poor parents who found it difficult to educate or feed these children were happy to send them to madrassas, where they got religious education and free board and lodging and even a small stipend. Madrassas in turn received generous contributions from charities within Pakistan as well as substantial funds from private donations and charities operating in the oil-rich Gulf countries.

Every year, scores of thousands of young men graduated from madrassas operating across the country. Apart from feeding the ranks of the Taliban and other militant groups, this phenomenon reinforced sectarian divisions in the country. Mosques belonging to various sects mushroomed. The religious political parties developed a strong vested political interest in the madrassas, as they derived clout and support from madrassa youth, as well as an economic interest in the huge donations received to run the institutions.[25] It was not surprising that efforts to mainstream madrassa education and reform the institution met stiff resistance.

The Pakistani public commonly view madrassas as good charity organizations; Musharraf and many government functionaries would describe

---

25. There are reports of coercive methods of collecting donations by some madrassas. For example, it was known that shops doing good business in Islamabad paid fixed monthly donations to madrassas run by the Red Mosque clerics.

them as the best NGOs functioning in the country. Quite often, senior bureaucrats who sent their own children to high-profile private schools defended the madrassa system as being comprised of charitable institutions,
overlooking and obfuscating the need to provide proper education as a right
of every child in the country. This view was also a sad reflection on successive governments, including the Musharraf government, for abdicating
the country's educational system to the private sector. The failure of the
government system had created vast space for private sector activity that
was filled by either the expensive English medium schools or the madrassas dependent on private donations.

The other pervasive misconception about the madrassas is that only a
handful teach intolerance and emphasize jihad. This is a simplistic notion,
inasmuch as the unemployed madrassa graduates, having learned no skills,
tend to gravitate towards militancy, whether as jihad or in defense of sectarian interests. Even if the religious education imparted by madrassas were
entirely benign, Pakistani society could not absorb the graduates in such
large numbers. The youth qualified as *alim* (scholars) from these institutions
are bound to suffer frustration and anger. An important objective of mainstreaming the madrassas through reform was to impart normal education
and vocational skills along with the emphasis on religious teaching. The
effort launched by the Musharraf government, however, by and large remained a failure.

The madrassa reforms announced in early 2002 required both administrative and academic changes. The program called for madrassa registration, including identification and regularizing of foreign students by obtaining permission from their respective governments, and a declaration of
the madrassas' sources of income. On the academic side, the madrassas
were promised government funding for teachers and facilities and teacher
training needed to introduce science subjects. They were also required to
cleanse the religious curricula of hate material, especially the type that incited violence on a sectarian basis. The madrassas were asked to adopt part
of the standard curricula recommended for government-controlled schools
and to agree to examinations through the government-established boards.
For its part, the Ministry of Education undertook a major exercise to revise
the curricula to be introduced in government schools for the first twelve
years of schooling. Much of the valuable work done in this area has remained unimplemented. The provincial governments, which are responsible for primary and secondary education, found it difficult to introduce the
revised curricula for lack of trained teachers.

The Ministry of Religious Affairs in coordination with the Ministry of Education would implement the madrassa reforms for mainstreaming madrassa education, with the Ministry of Interior responsible for administrative reforms, including the issues of registration and foreign students. At the early stages, Musharraf was given the impression that enforcement of the reforms would be easy, since almost 75 percent of the madrassas, close to 11,000 in number, were part of the Wifaq ul Madaris. When it came to implementation, little was achieved beyond the registration of foreign students studying in madrassas under the Wifaq. These were regularized in most cases, with appropriate permission from their countries of origin. However, the mainstreaming of madrassas remained stalled and much was lost in an interminable wrangle between the Ministry of Education and the Ministry of Religious Affairs, which nominally maintained liaison with Wifaq ul Madaris. The remaining madrassas, anywhere between 3,000 and 4,000 madrassas scattered all over the country, especially in NWFP and southern Punjab, remained oblivious of the new government regulations or reforms because of their remoteness or the absence of government implementation machinery. These schools continued to operate outside official oversight.

Wifaq ul Madaris could not agree to render accounts to the government for their sources of income, since according to the Wifaq, these were largely private donations and madrassas should not be required to provide accounts for funds that they did not receive from the government. Wifaq was agreeable to introducing "secular" subjects such as mathematics, physics, and chemistry; however, it could not accept the conduct of examinations by the government board and insisted on recognition of their own board for the purpose. Wifaq argued that the government had accepted independent boards, such as the Agha Khan Board for educational institutions run by the Agha Khan Foundation and examination systems from outside Pakistan for teaching Ordinary or Advanced Cambridge School Certificate levels by the English medium schools. The ad hoc growth of private sector education thus became an obstacle in the effort to reform the madrassas. This was partly the result of long neglect of education by successive Pakistani governments. Their disinterest in educational reforms debilitated public sector education in the country and relegated this important social responsibility to the private sector, accentuating imbalance, polarization, and stratification in the society.[26]

26. Private schooling in the form of madrassas and English medium education represented polarization not only in the economic sense, with madrassa students belonging

The government plan to run parallel model madrassas providing free board and lodging for students belonging to poor families did not take off. It ended up with only three such functioning institutions by 2006, a meaningless result given the scale of the challenge required. Ijaz ul Haq, son of President Zia ul Haq and minister for religious affairs in the Musharraf government, regarded madrassas as his personal constituency and opposed any ostensible discrimination under the proposed reforms. On the curricula, Wifaq explained its own system of screening and denied preaching violence or hate, a largely correct statement. The problem related mainly to madrassas beyond the jurisdiction of Wifaq that were influenced by the jihad culture and received the bulk of their private funding from the Gulf countries. They carried the Saudi Salafi influence and its sectarian bias.

Musharraf's argument—that board examinations and standardized curricula would enable madrassa students to apply to colleges and universities and that Pakistan would thus successfully integrate religious and public schools—was lost in a good deal of discussion among the ministries and the Wifaq, while little progress was achieved on the ground. His reform program failed to make headway ostensibly because of disagreement among the ministries and the Wifaq over technical issues of procedure and form. The deeper problem was the resistance of the madrassa establishment to allowing government or outside interference and control.

Sadly, reluctance to reform the antiquated curricula has been a perversion of a religion that insists on "seeking knowledge even unto China" and on the obligation of every man and woman to receive an education. As the madrassas have become a political constituency for religious parties and their leaders, mainstreaming threatens to unravel this support base,[27] not-

---

to the poor strata of society and those studying in English medium schools coming mostly from the upper-middle and rich classes. The system also spawned two different cultures. Madrassa learning was restricted to theology, Urdu rhapsodic eloquence, and early Muslim history and traditions, with little about contemporary issues. In contrast, until Zia ul Haq introduced Urdu as a compulsory subject, the English medium graduates could hardly read or write in Urdu and had little knowledge of Islamic history but could recite English verse and cite Western literature and thinkers.

27. The author can recall his personal experience with the concern of madrassa authorities to keep their students insular and protected from new ideas. I was posted in Islamabad at the Foreign Office from 1998 to 2002. Between 1998 and early 2001, Col. Imam (real name, Amir Sultan Tarar), who had retired from the ISI and earned fame for training thousands of Afghan Mujahedin during 1980s, was Pakistan's consul general in Herat. A few times, when he came to the Foreign Office, Col. Imam dropped by for a conversation with me. Rarely would he take a cup of coffee or tea, as on most occasions

withstanding the huge cost to the country in the loss of human resources even if these madrassa graduates do not drift to militancy.

The government approach was less than focused and at times even naïve.[28] The efforts continued under the new government have paid some dividends. In October 2010, the education ministry and the Wifaq reached an agreement[29] that recognized the five Wifaq boards in exchange for the Wifaq's agreeing to include "compulsory contemporary subjects" in their secondary and higher secondary–level curricula. A "regulatory body," including representatives of the Ministry of Education, was to ensure uniformity of curricula and examination standards. This will be a challenge, in addition to that posed by the large number of madrassas operating outside the Wifaq. In any event, the experience with the reform process showed that the madrassa authorities accepted introduction of science subjects as part of the curricula not out of conviction but as an unavoidable compulsion.

Government efforts aimed at countering extremism through social reform faced similar problems. As a follow-up to his banning of extremist sectarian organizations in early 2002, Musharraf announced a set of measures that included a ban on the writing, publication, printing, sale, or distribution of hate material in various forms; monitoring the misuse of loudspeakers in mosques to spread hatred and incite violence; and review of all school curricula to re-

---

he was fasting during the day. Our conversation normally related to the Taliban and their governance, which he admired for security and a certain moral austerity that the Taliban had brought about. On a couple of occasions, I argued that the Taliban were living in a time warp; they offered no model for governance of Muslim societies who needed modern education, science, and technology and interaction with other societies, giving examples from historical experience. Once when listening to me he asked if I could speak to students of a madrassa near Islamabad, as he felt they (faculty and students) should be aware of such views. I agreed. Col. Imam did not run a madrassa but was associated with a number of them. Afterward, twice he telephoned me from Herat, inquiring if somebody had contacted me. The third time, after a lapse of two months, on learning that I was still not invited, he remarked that the madrassa authorities were "very careful" in exposing students to "outsiders" and that this time he would press them to get in touch with me. However, I told Col. Imam not to put any such pressure.

28. Once, the government looked at the Turkish training of khatibs, the Hatip schools, as a model for reforming madrassas, without realizing the qualitatively different nature of the problem. Hatip schools had been established in Turkey to train a few hundred religious scholars to be appointed to mostly government-controlled mosques. In Pakistan the issue is how to provide proper education and training to over two million madrassa students so that they can become useful members contributing to the socioeconomic progress of society.

29. For the text of the agreement, see *The News* (Islamabad), October 8, 2010.

move materials that spread religious or sectarian hatred and to inject material that instilled a message of peace and humanity in the Islamic faith.

Musharraf intended to initiate a national discourse on Islam that would engage enlightened religious scholars to educate and influence the minds of the people, whom he thought were fundamentally moderate in their outlook but ignorant of the real spirit of Islam and often misguided and confused by semiliterate clergy. This was an ambitious agenda for which the government, which was soft and largely inept when it came to implementation, lacked both the political will and the intellectual and administrative capacity. Even the effort to oversee the Friday sermons in the mosques in Pakistan was, by any measure, a difficult undertaking. To monitor clerics who made incendiary speeches or the distribution of inflammatory material by mosques and sectarian groups required local intelligence and administrative action using the police. However, the administrative structures at the local level were inherently weak and incapable of monitoring and arresting religious extremism.

The government reform programs initiated to address extremist tendencies in society evoked barely any public enthusiasm, nor were they given the attention they deserved by the largely private, though increasingly powerful, print and electronic media. Public revulsion and media reaction concentrated mostly on sectarian violence, bombing of places of worship, and targeting of religious personalities and helped efforts to bring Ulema of different sects together to arrest sectarian violence. But when it came to the politics and ideological underpinnings of extremism, the public was ambivalent. The media reinforced this ambivalence by giving considerable space, in the interest of balance, to sympathizers and spokesmen of militant and extremist points of view, including those of the Taliban. These exponents of religious extremism and support for the Taliban were quite often eloquent and articulate, with a mastery of rhetoric in Urdu and local languages. In contrast, those with a moderate voice and contemporary outlook were at best well versed in English and often incoherent or bland in their expression. Official statements justifying the reforms were few and characteristically uninspiring, even defensive. Spokesmen of the moderate political parties lacked conviction when speaking about the dangers of religious extremism and militancy.

Public relations campaigns promoting reforms to counter extremism were virtually nonexistent. Musharraf used to make reference to the program and its importance in his speeches, but members of the ruling party, PML(Q), hardly underscored the urgency of countering extremism and only appeared to pay lip service to the significance of the reform initiative. The same disconnect was discernible between Musharraf and his political allies with respect to the madrassa reforms, giving the impression that it was Musharraf rather than his political partners pushing the reform agenda. The level of motivation, commitment, and conviction required to ensure success of the reform program was simply absent in the government.

Lal Masjid (Red Mosque) Debacle

Musharraf had inherited a difficult situation, with obscurantism, extremism, sectarian violence, and jihadi and madrassa culture well entrenched in the society. The U.S. action in Afghanistan and Pakistan's inevitable about-face on the Taliban brought these elements into full play, disrupting peace within the country and threatening its security and development. The Lal Masjid (Red Mosque) episode that came to a boil and shook the country in July 2007 exemplified the nature and enormity of the threat. At the same time, the episode brought to light the complexity of the problem of extremism and the confusion that swirled around it. Located in the heart of the capital, Islamabad, Lal Masjid over the years became a center of jihadi activism and militancy. Its potential as a threat grew largely unnoticed by the government. In early 2007, as the crisis unfolded, it revealed the difficult choices the government faced and the reactions it provoked, especially in the aftermath of the eventual military action.

Maulana Muhammad Abdullah, an adherent of the Deobandi School, was appointed by the government in the mid-1960s as chief cleric of Lal Masjid, which was built around the same time that Islamabad began to take shape as a new city. Maulana Abdullah had a significant following among the lower-middle bureaucracy housed in sectors around the mosque. His criticism of the elite bureaucracy for the country's ills and for their un-Islamic conduct and lifestyle often resonated with these followers. Such criticism was a staple of many mosque sermons.

Maulana Abdullah's ascent started with Zia ul Haq's rule and the Afghan Jihad. He helped the Jihad with recruiting mujahedin, for which he enjoyed government patronage. Later, domestic and Saudi financial contributions enabled him to start two madrassas in Islamabad affiliated with the mosque, namely Jamia Fareedia for boys and Jamia Hafsa for girls. Both madrassas were built on encroached land, which city authorities ignored because of the influence Maulana Abdullah enjoyed. He also became a link with the

Kashmiri jihadi organizations once the Kashmir situation was stirred up in the late 1980s. In 1998, Maulana Abdullah was assassinated by assailants suspected of sectarian motivation, and Abdullah's equally zealous sons, Abdul Aziz and Abdur Rashid Ghazi, took charge of the mosque .

The two brothers, though part of a government-supported mosque, were stridently opposed to the post–9/11 policy identified with Musharraf and agitated in their Friday sermons about the government's abandonment of the jihad. Abdul Aziz even issued a fatwa against giving Islamic burial to army personnel who died fighting the Taliban. The crisis point came in early 2007 when female students from Madrassa Jamia Hafsa, run by Umm e Hassan, Adbul Aziz's wife, occupied and refused to vacate an adjacent children's library. The action by the Jamia Hafsa students was triggered by a notice from the Capital Development Authority (CDA) to vacate the land encroached by the mosque, including that on which the girls' madrassa was built. Similar notices were served to several other mosques that had been constructed without the required CDA permission. In the following weeks, hundreds of madrassa students, especially from Jamia Fareedia, gathered and remained on the mosque compound with the purpose of defending the clerics and the girls' madrassa against any official action. The clerics started taking matters into their own hands to cleanse the neighborhood of immoral activity by encouraging vigilante missions.

The Jamia Fareedia students kidnapped a couple of police personnel and an alleged prostitute from the neighborhood. They started closing down music and video shops and temporarily detained workers of a Chinese health clinic reputed to be a massage parlor. They frequently broke police cordons, and Abdur Rashid Ghazi openly confirmed to the press reports of arms and suicide bombers inside the mosque. This activity, in the full glare of the press, with scenes of veiled female students as well as male madrassa students carrying sticks and some even being seen with firearms, was causing deep embarrassment to the government. Several meetings of senior civil and military officials, chaired by Musharraf and including the prime minister and senior ministers, were convened to discuss how to deal with this open defiance of government authority in the capital. It was evident that there could be no police or army action without bloodshed, something the government wanted to avoid.[30]

---

30. The author had attended a couple of early meetings in March–April 2007, which ended with a decision to try as far as possible nonmilitary options for a solution in order to avoid bloodshed.

Attempts by the government to reach a nonviolent resolution of the crisis involved the Imam of the holy Ka'aba, who flew in from Mecca, as well as local political and religious notables, in particular Chaudry Shujaat Hussain, leader of the ruling Pakistan Muslim League (Q) party, and Minister of Religious Affairs Ijaz ul Haq. The Imam of Ka'aba abandoned his effort, describing the two brothers as fanatical. Government ministers who were part of the negotiations held the same view. Towards the end of June when the situation had become highly tense, the ISI even brought in Fazalur Rahman Khalil, the erstwhile leader of the proscribed Harkatul Mujahedin, disregarding his obvious link with an organization that many in the West had declared a terrorist group. None of these efforts persuaded the two clerics to ask the militants to vacate the mosque and allow the area to return to normalcy.

A few skirmishes occurred between the militants and the police and paramilitary Ranger Force deployed around the area who wanted to prevent some madrassa students from entering the mosque compound. The government delayed action in an effort to seek a violence-free resolution of the situation, especially when it was preoccupied with the internal judicial crisis. Meanwhile, the media and liberal groups were clamoring for action and accusing the government of failing to control the situation. Inaction while letting its authority be challenged in the capital, they insisted, would only encourage religious militants elsewhere.

Meanwhile, evidence surfaced of contacts between the Lal Masjid clerics and Baitullah Mahsud. Thousands of Taliban militants in Bajaur demonstrated in support of the Lal Masjid clerics on July 9, chanting anti-Musharraf, antigovernment, and anti-U.S. slogans. Finally, at dawn on July 10, 2007, after agonizing over the situation for nearly four months, Musharraf ordered army action that lasted almost two days. According to official figures, close to one hundred militants, including Abdur Rashid Ghazi, died. A few days before the military action, Rashid's elder brother, Abdul Aziz, and his wife, Umm e Hassan, left the Jamia Hafsa compound along with hundreds of the barricaded girl students. The government claimed that the tactics deployed ensured that all the female students and most of the sympathizers who had gathered at the mosque premises were able to escape. According to military sources, the loud booms heard all over Islamabad were detonations without explosives meant to scare any remaining girl students or other individuals to compel them to leave the compound. As evidence, it was argued that there were no claims of missing girl students after the action. With Umm e Hassan, the firebrand head of Jamia Hafsa, leaving the compound, her disciples were unlikely to stay behind, a circumstance that appeared to validate the assertion.

The aftermath of the crisis, however, presents a case study in the difficulties the government faced in taking tough action against militants, even when dealing with blatant defiance of the law. The religious and right-of-center political parties and elements erupted in virulent criticism of the action, lamenting the massacre of hundreds of girls and other madrassa students. Even liberal opinion attacked the government for the heavy-handed tactics and delay, which complicated the problem. For days, TV channels kept showing the debris and the burned-out Jamia e Hafsa. This outburst coincided with the groundswell of negative public opinion sparked by the popular lawyers' movement against Musharraf's ill-advised dismissal of the Supreme Court chief justice, Iftikhar Muhammad Chaudry, earlier in March.

More than one thousand madrassa students picked up from the Red Mosque and Jamia Fareedia compounds were detained and released after debriefing. Most came from poor families from NWFP, FATA, and areas in Kashmir that literally depended on the largesse of the madrassa for sustenance and were quite ready to answer the call of Maulana Abdul Aziz. Detained under charges for inciting violence, Abdul Aziz was released on bail in early 2009 by the Supreme Court, almost six months after Musharraf was forced to resign and one month after the deposed chief justice was reinstated. Lal Masjid became a watershed. The blowback was severe, even though it took a few months for the militants to organize and escalate their attacks on military, police, and government targets. Lal Masjid could have been handled more prudently, although there could have been no avoidance of military action. After the breakdown of the negotiations with the Lal Masjid clerics, time should have been allowed to assure the public that only hardcore militants were left in the compound and that other sympathizers, particularly women, had left the venue. Officials did make this claim following the action. which was undertaken the night the negotiations reached a deadlock. A few days' gap could have lent credibility to the government position that it had exhausted all avenues for a peaceful surrender by Abdur Rashid Ghazi.

The Lal Masjid episode brought into sharp relief the trend among the extremist religious groups to act autonomously in defiance of the government to enforce their view on society through violence. Extremism in Pakistan now boasted the muscle of madrassa youth and a spiritual motivation resulting from a mix of orthodox and jihadist views of Islam and the world.

The Afghan conflict, spanning three decades since 1979, and the festering Kashmir issue contributed to the growth of the extremist phenomenon in a sympathetic environment and culture—a sociopolitical impulse generated by depressed economic circumstances, marked by narrowing opportunities, rising unemployment, increasing demographic pressure, and the widening class divide in the country. Swat was first to see the economic undercurrents of the extremist rhetoric, with Fazalullah instigating the poor against the established land-owning families. The same undercurrent is evident in southern Punjab, where religious extremists claim they can bring about economic justice and equity. These rumblings, with the TTP, Al Qaeda, and religious and other militants challenging the government and the sociopolitical system in the country, have created conditions suggestive of civil war. Such conditions could reach a definitive and fateful denouement, either in the gain of one of the antagonists or in the rout of both.

This situation must be arrested and reversed for the survival of the state and its future progress. The military operations currently under way are critical in reversing the tide of extremism and religious militancy in the country. Beyond military action and political and economic measures, addressing this enormous challenge to achieve a functioning and robust society and state demands intellectual clarity about the twenty-first century imperatives of universal modern education, good governance with a justice system that inspires public confidence, and socioeconomic and technological development.

The next chapter will discuss the inspiration and sources of intellectual discourse in Pakistan that signify a confusion conducive to the growth of obscurantism and extremism resistant to modernizing currents in the society. The failure of political institutions and governance has further distorted the picture and exacerbated polarization among a people looking for certitude in their lives and a future for the state.

6

Pakistan: A Case of Intellectual Crisis and Weak Governance

The preceding chapters have focused on the spread of conflict in Afghanistan, its impact on Pakistan and the region, and the rise of religious extremism and militancy, particularly in Pakistan. The discussion has often referred to the public discourse in Pakistan that showed ambiguity about the threat religious extremism posed. The intellectual and psychological environment that surrounds this discourse not only sustains and tolerates religious extremism and obscurantism; it is resistant to modernizing currents in the society. To understand this environment and how it developed over the years requires revisiting the past to look into the thinking, circumstances, and colonial experience of the Muslims of colonial British India that affected Pakistan's genesis and conditioned the subsequent search for its identity and role in the contemporary world.

The tumultuous political history of the new country and its inability to build strong political institutions and systems of governance further distorted the picture to accentuate confusion and polarization among a people looking for certitude in their lives and the future of their state. This chapter steps back to highlight the sources of Pakistan's religious and political impulses and discourse that cloud a clear understanding of the challenges the country faces. A sampling of popular perceptions and mind-sets reveals an intellectual confusion. The chapter also presents a brief survey of the checkered politics of Pakistan that weaken the country's institutional capacity to provide effective governance.

Since its inception more than six decades ago, Pakistan has been a crucible of contending ideas and experiments in governance. Protection and defense of the interests of the Muslims of British India underlay the Pakistan movement, which was led by men schooled in the British educational system rather than the traditional seminaries and who professed a modernist outlook. Pakistan's founding father, Muhammad Ali Jinnah, had used the Muslim identity issue and reached out to orthodox Ulema to advance political objectives in the final phases of the Pakistan movement; but he rejected the idea of Pakistan as a theocratic state on the eve of its independence.[1] Again addressing a public meeting at Dhaka on March 20, 1948, he declared unequivocally, "Pakistan is not a theocracy or anything like it."

The majority of orthodox Ulema, including many belonging to Jamiat Ulema e Hind, and Maulana Syed Abul Ala Maududi, the most influential South Asian theologian and scholar of Islam, had generally opposed the idea of Pakistan; after its creation many of them became active protagonists for shaping Pakistan into a model Islamic state.[2] In the absence of a forceful arbiter such as Jinnah, who was ailing and died in September 1948, the issue of the orientation and identity of the new state became the subject of a continuing debate, especially in the drafting of the state constitution. The issue was how to reconcile the Ulemas' demand for introducing Sharia law with the inherited body of laws and institutions of governance, which included a system based on parliamentary democracy that, despite its colonial antecedents, was contemporary in character and suited the ruling elite of the country.

1. For a detailed reference to the thinking of Muhammad Ali Jinnah, see a brief but important profile of the founding father of Pakistan by Aitzaz Ahsan in his work, *The Indus Saga and the Making of Pakistan* (Karachi: Oxford University Press, 1996), 327–38. In Jinnah's address to the Constituent Assembly on August 11, 1947, he stated: "You are free. You are free to go to your temples, you are free to go to your mosques and any other place of worship in this state of Pakistan. You may belong to any religion, caste or creed—*that has nothing to do with the business of the State.* . . . Now I think we should keep that in front of us as our ideal and you will find that in the course of time Hindus will cease to be Hindus and Muslims will cease to be Muslims, not in the religious sense, because that is the personal faith of each individual, but *in the political sense as citizens of the state.*" Emphasis has been added.

2. Maududi had opposed the creation of Pakistan, first, because a nation-state was contrary to the idea of *Khilafat* and an Islamic state encompassing the entirety of the Muslim community; and second, in view of the demographic complexion of the proposed Pakistan, it could not possibly transform itself into an Islamic state, nor could it safeguard the interests of all Muslims living in British India, an objection shared with several other leaders of the Muslim community in India. Postpartition, he accepted Pakistan as a reality and joined other religious elements in demanding an Islamic character for the new state's constitution. As a result of the transfer and exchange of populations, which had not been anticipated before partition, he argued, Pakistan was predominantly Muslim, and an Islamic system of governance was feasible and needed to be enforced.

The new state had a weak political and administrative structure, an anomalous geographical configuration and, in the western wing, which comprises today's Pakistan, a largely tribal and feudal society with only a few urban centers and almost no industrial base. At the same time, the new country had a strong agricultural base, a reasonably developed network of communications and railways, and a relatively strong army institution.[3] The country's potential for development, despite a few spurts of rapid economic growth, remained largely constricted because of its preoccupation with a security threat from India, an unsettled political system and leadership, and experiments with civil and administrative institutions that instead of reform led to their weakening.

At the intellectual level over the years, particularly after the separation of the eastern wing in 1971 and Zia ul Haq's coup in 1977, ground was ceded to conservative Islamic thinking essentially resistant to adapting to the imperatives of twentieth-century socioeconomic and political progress. Islam has always been part of the popular ethos in Pakistan and a factor of unity and identity. Since the 1980s, however, attempts at Islamization and the promotion of religiosity and jihad have increased divisiveness and intellectual impoverishment in the country. The roots of the current turbulence in Pakistan lie in the systemic problems of weak leadership and institutions of governance and a deepening intellectual crisis, reflected in confusion over the identity and purpose of the state, its Islamic outlook, and its relationship with the present-day regional and global environment.

Though the 1979 Soviet military intervention proved fateful for Afghanistan, it also made a profound impact on Pakistan. The invasion touched off a protracted conflict that destroyed almost every institution in Afghanistan, and now the country depends on powerful outside intervention for its revival and reconstruction. The events in Afghanistan became a catalyst for the increasing destabilization of Pakistan, a prospect that can have incalculable consequences for the region and beyond. While the conflict in Afghanistan has transformed Pakistan, today both countries have become mutually reinforcing centers of conflict.

---

3. The British developed an extensive railway system in the northwestern regions of their erstwhile colonial empire in India, which were regarded as vulnerable to the expanding Russian Empire in Central Asia. Northern Punjab was the main recruiting ground for the British army in India, headquartered at Rawalpindi.

Reactions to Western and Modernizing Influences

Conflict and religious militancy also go to the heart of the struggle of both societies, each with its distinct historical experiences, to adjust to modern times. In many ways, the conflict represents quintessential resistance to modernity in the context of two essential attributes: progression in the development of the human condition, and tolerance of pluralism. These two attributes define modernity purely for the purpose of this chapter. In a broader sense, these attributes underpin the creativity and innovation associated with modernity and the evolving concept of human rights, including those germane to gender and minority issues. Modernizing societies have imbibed these characteristics in varying degrees.[4]

Since modernity has been popularly associated with Western political and philosophical thought and socioeconomic and scientific development, modernization, especially in Islamic countries, has often been a cultural synonym for Westernization. Globalization has compounded the confusion, as it is a vehicle for the spread of modernizing influences along with Western culture, which tends to overpower and dominate local cultures everywhere. The following discussion focuses on the context of the debate in Muslim societies, particularly in South Asia, agitated by their experience of domination by the West. It does not analyze the response of Islamic scholars and institutions to the inexorable currents of modernity. This overview will explore the antecedents of the confusion and contradictions that permeate the Pakistani mind-set when dealing with the issues of extremism and religious militancy.

The fusion of religion and politics in Islam has a strong tradition and intellectual foundation that goes back to the early days of Islam, when the holy prophet had established the state of Medina and the four pious caliphs, who combined the temporal and the religious authority. How to reconcile this tradition with the emergence of dynastic rule, which claimed the title of *Khilafat* (Caliphate) barely half a century after the advent of Islam, has long preoccupied Muslim thinkers, in particular the Fuqaha, authorities in Is-

---

4. An important contribution of the Maoist revolution in China has been in changing the outlook of Chinese society by breaking its traditionally static cyclical view of human history and instilling it with a confidence in the constant improvement in the social condition. The new mind-set readily accepted the later program of Four Modernizations initiated by Deng Xiaoping to bring about the great contemporary transformation of China.

lamic jurisprudence and law. Traditionally, *Khilafat* has referred to the Islamic governance of the *Ummah* (generally connoting the entire Muslim community) by Sharia law, under the authority of *Khalifa* (or Caliphs, literally meaning successor, representative, or vice-regent).[5]

The issue has been important to political discourse in Muslim societies during the last century, when the institution of the *Khilafat* had already disappeared and a large part of the Muslim *Ummah* was under alien non-Muslim rule or divided into nation-states. Many orthodox Muslim scholars reject the idea of the nation-state, one of the objections to the idea of Pakistan held by Maulana Maududi, the founder of Jamat e Islami. Maududi has greatly influenced Islamic political thought in South Asia, particularly Pakistan. The transnational impulses of many of the contemporary Islamic revivalist movements reflect a subconscious yearning for the *Khilafat* and a strong belief in the unity of religion and politics.

Except in the brief early period, much of Muslim history includes a tradition of somewhat overlapping but distinct spheres of governance and religious authority. Autocratic rulers were the final arbiters of state affairs, with their authority sanctified by the Ulema, the custodians of jurisprudence and moral standards. The implicit alliance worked in the largely agrarian society and decentralized governance of Muslim societies. Facilitating it were the spiritual and intellectual traditions of *taqlid* (imitation), as well as exegesis of early authoritative jurists who accepted the ruler and abhorred *fitna* (rebellion, anarchy, and political discord).[6] By the eleventh century, Mutazelite thinking[7] had declined and scholars rejected the application of a philosophical critique to religion and divine law. Dominant Islamic thought settled on closing the door of *Ijtehad* (interpretation as source of Islamic law) and clung instead to the orthodox interpretation of Sharia, based on the four schools of fiqh in Sunni Islam, which represented the grand con-

---

5. According to Maulana Maududi and recent revivalist views such as those held by Hisb ut Tahrir, the Khalifa has to be chosen by the *Ummah* on the criteria of wisdom and piety and should be assisted by a shura of men selected on the same basis. Traditionally, however, Muslim jurists believed that the Khalifa is chosen by Providence and must be obeyed as long as he enforces Sharia. This approach, most notably supported by Imam Tammaya, was an adjustment to dynastic *Khilafat,* established successively by the Ummayad, Abbasid, Fatimid, Almohad, and lastly the Ottoman rulers.

6. Anwar Hussain Syed, *Pakistan: Islam, Politics and National Solidarity* (New York: Praeger Publishers, 1982), 13–24, discusses the issue in detail.

7. Mutazilli was a ninth-century rationalist school that emphasized the obligation of reasoning in interpretation.

sensus.[8] The consequent rigidity in thought, combined with uncritical acceptance of authoritarian governance, produced a coercive environment that stifled creativity and led to inertia and stagnation similar to that existing in other Eastern societies.

The past two centuries have witnessed Eastern, including Islamic, societies' reactions and attempts at adjustment to the advent of Western imperial domination and colonization and to the compelling force of modernity. Defeats at the hands of European powers shook the Muslim societies. In contrast to Japan and later China, where the reaction came mainly from the elite ruling classes, Muslim reaction came from both the elite and the clergy, with differing overtones. The process gave birth to the reformist political and secular movements that swept across Turkey and Egypt and found resonance in Iran and Afghanistan in the early twentieth century, mainly to modernize by adapting Western ways. At the intellectual level the religious response varied widely, from revivalist orthodoxy, to a new discourse for renewal and reform in religious thought, to a defense of selectively adopting modern European ways and thinking in worldly matters. The revivalist tradition in South Asia is often traced to the great eighteenth century theologian and reformist Shah Waliullah, who considered that deviation from pure Islam had led to decadence in Muslim societies.

One of the most respected voices for reform and reawakening of Muslim societies emerged from Afghanistan in the person of Syed Jamaluddin Afghani (1838–97), a scholar, linguist, and reformist who traveled extensively in Europe and the Middle East and influenced Islamic reformist movements at the turn of the twentieth century. In his view, Islam was compatible with the requirements of modern progress and that the malaise afflicting Muslim societies arose from fatalism and corruption of the faith. He ardently opposed European imperialism and believed that, to progress, Muslim societies must first rid themselves of European enslavement.[9] In Cairo, one of his disciples was Muhammad Abduh, who blamed Muslim intellectual decadence for distorting Islam. Abduh believed that "every good modern concept" of ethics and humanism could be derived from a rational interpretation of the Quran and Hadith.[10] His exegesis for rational reform

8. Shia Islam has a distinct tradition of structured clergy and the concept of Vallayat e Faqih, who is the authority for continuing *Ijtehad.*

9. Rafiq Zakaria, *The Struggle within Islam: The Conflict between Religion and Politics* (London: Penguin Books, 1988), 165, states that in India, Jamaluddin Afghani chastized Syed Ahmed Khan for cowering before the British.

10. Ibid., 167.

within the framework of Quran and Sunnah appealed to both conservative Islamic scholars and those exposed to Western education who were looking for answers for Muslims' backwardness and dire predicament. Muhammad Abduh became the inspiration in particular for Ikhwan al Muslemin (the Muslim Brotherhood), founded by Hassan al Banna in 1928 and forerunner of various present-day Islamist movements representing political or radical Islam. These movements glorified Islam, adhered closely to the conservative interpretation of Sharia, and accepted modern education to the extent necessary for material advancement, while rejecting its essentially Western ethical underpinnings.

The impact of British colonization on the Muslim psyche in India was especially strong. Indian Muslims felt that not only had power been wrested from them, but they were also in danger of being relegated by the colonial power to a lower status than that of the rival Hindu community. South Asia was the only region where Muslims ruled a population that was majority non-Muslim and had done so for nearly eight centuries. The Muslim rulers by and large were prudent and did not apply Sharia in its entirety in the manner interpreted by the orthodox clerics, who at times resented this fact and the coziness of the rulers with the Hindu elite.[11] The measures taken by the last great Mughal emperor, Aurangzeb, to enforce a strict form of Sharia continue to generate controversy to the present day.

The colonial subjugation produced a new dilemma for the clergy and Muslim thinkers in having to accept non-Muslim rule. Two distinct reactions came from Syed Ahmed Shaheed Barelvi, who called for jihad, and from Syed Ahmed Khan, who advocated conciliation with the colonial power and the need for modern education and reform in religious thinking. Syed Ahmed Shaheed's jihad in the early nineteenth century has been the inspiration for subsequent militant religious movements with the same purported aim of enforcing Sharia. His effort foundered in the treacherous politics of the Pushtun tribes, who had joined him at first to fend off pressure from the expanding Sikh kingdom in the Punjab. The tradition of calls for the enforcement of Sharia, however, survived in the Pushtun and Afghan tribal culture. The late-nineteenth-century rebellion by Mullah Hudda of Ghazni and the early-twentieth-century Fakir of Epi uprising presaged the post–Soviet intervention calls for the creation of an Islamic state in Afghan-

---

11. Dr. Mubarak Ali, *Almiah Tarikh* (Lahore: Fiction House Publishers, 1993), 9–33, elaborates this point.

istan by the Mujahedin. Regardless of the differences in the politics and circumstances of these uprisings and conflicts, the Taliban had similar religious undercurrents and inspirations.

Against the backdrop of Britain's brutal suppression of the Great Rebellion of 1857, which brought to a violent end the Muslim rule in northern India and the last vestiges of the Mughal Empire, Syed Ahmed Khan emerged as a major Muslim thinker and reformer who considered a Muslim renaissance vital for the socioeconomic progress of the community. A rationalist who defended Islam as divine faith, he reasoned against superstition and decadent rituals that had encumbered its practice. He rejected literal interpretation and favored critical understanding of popular dogma and beliefs. He argued in his works that the Quran rested on appreciation of reason and natural law and encouraged Muslims to engage in scientific inquiry. He remained undeterred by the verdict of *Takfir* (apostasy) for his views, rendered by the conservative Ulema hostile to modern influences.

Syed Ahmed Khan's modernist approach was epitomized by his singular achievement in establishing the Mohamadan Anglo-Oriental College at Aligarh (later Aligarh Muslim University) in 1875. The institution became a beacon for the Indian Muslim elite who sought to progress in life and was the alma mater of many Muslim leaders in the struggle for the rights of the Muslims of the subcontinent. However, the institution was primarily aimed at preparing the Muslim elite to become part of the new ruling class. Syed Ahmed Khan's efforts, despite his stature as a bold thinker on religious issues, were not primarily aimed at reform or renewal of religious thought among Muslims. The impulse and movement for such renewal came from within the orthodox tradition antithetical to Western learning and influences.

This third reaction to colonial subjugation came from thinkers who maintained an uneasy acceptance of alien rule as a temporary condition. They advocated, as a priority, the cleansing of centuries-old religious thought, practices of corruption, and *bida* (innovation or deviation), and instead advocated promoting a puritanical form of Islam. This attitude was reflected in the Deobandi tradition, as well as in the prolific writings of Maulana Maududi, which shaped the thinking of many educated Muslims in South Asia. Works by Maududi and the Jamat e Islami, the party he founded, represent an important development in the Muslim awakening in South Asia, similar to the Ikhwan movement in Egypt. The later Islamic Salvation Front (FIS) in Algeria, Hamas in Palestine, and similar influences in the Muslim world imbibe the same tradition.

The central theme of Maududi's exegesis was the unity of politics and religion, with Islam as a complete way of life superior to the social philosophies and systems offered by Western thinkers. He based his approach on logic and reason and attempted to provide the blueprint for an Islamic state based on the Quran, the Sunnah, and enforcement of Sharia. In his view, sovereignty belonged to Allah, and man was required to establish His sanctioned system in the world (*Khalifat ul Ard*) based on justice (*Adl*) in accordance with the "Supreme Law" of Quran and Sunnah.[12] There was room for individual freedom to progress and for *Ijtehad* and *Ijma* ("interpretation" and "consensus" as sources of Islamic law), the two most cited dynamic principles in Islamic theology for necessary reform; but these must be practiced within the *Hudud* (limits) prescribed by the Quran. In the interpretation of *Hudud,* Maududi was a literalist in the tradition of scholars of the text, affirming Quran as the law rather than as a source of law.

Apart from the number of problems that this interpretation can bring up in the practical functioning of a government, Maududi's rigorous logic raised two difficult issues: the position of minorities under an Islamic state[13] and the obligations of Muslims in a non-Muslim state. He argued that non-Muslim minorities under an Islamic state could not be treated equally and therefore he rejected the plurality principle of modernity. The prescription for Muslim minorities was even more rigorous, as every Muslim was obliged to establish Allah's sovereignty on earth. Maududi's logic absolved a Muslim state of responsibility towards Muslims in a non-Muslim state unless they are persecuted. However, he made it incumbent on the Muslim citizens of a non-Muslim state to do all they can (peacefully) to enforce Allah's law.[14] He also believed it an obligation of Muslims, when strong enough, to liberate all lands that had once been under Muslim control.[15] Accordingly, Muslims and non-Muslim societies could not coexist in harmony, a proposition that is untenable in today's world.

The orthodox revivalist tradition represented by Maududi and Deobandi schools in Pakistan opposes a secular approach because it relegates religion to the periphery, even if the approach is culturally inclusive of religion. The Islamic system, in contrast, places religion at the center as the source of

12. Syed Abul Ala Maududi, *Khilafat aur Malukiat* (Ichra, Lahore: Idara e Tarjuman al Quran, 1966), 22–33.

13. Maududi, *Islami Riyasat* (Lahore: Islamic Publishers Limited, 1962), 483–87, 575–83.

14. Maududi, *Jihad fil Islam* (Ichra, Lahore: Idara Tarjuman al Quran, 1988), 91–92, 101–2, 119.

15. Ibid., 63.

legal and ethical principles. It allows no room for a plurality of political parties, but recommends, through proselytization or call (*Dawa*), the formation of a party of the religiously pious, who have the right to enforce the Islamic system. This approach essentially runs contrary to the norm of tolerance for pluralism.

Furthermore, this revivalist tradition is predicated on the premise that a perfect system had already been established in the early days of Islam. The objective ought to be to reestablish that system, with some adjustment through *Ijtehad* and *Ijma* necessitated by the contemporary environment. The premise thus does not permit evolution or change; it rejects the notion of continuing progression in human affairs. The orthodox revivalist school in Pakistan also assumes *a priori* that the perfect system of Islam is ordained to be established and that it is the obligation of Muslims to dedicate themselves towards that goal, irrespective of whether they are part of a broadly Muslim or non-Muslim society.

In theological terms, Maududi saw a secular division of religion and state as antithetical to the idea and purpose of Pakistan. He rejected the democratic process of elections and multiparty politics. In Islam, he maintained, there could be no parties, and governance was the right of a select group of pious and capable individuals (*Ullul Amr*). But he compromised when he supported Fatima Jinnah, sister of Muhammad Ali Jinnah, against President Ayub Khan in the 1965 elections, ostensibly to get rid of the greater evil.[16]

Prior to this compromise, Maududi rejected inclusiveness and a pluralistic approach in an Islamic polity. In his writings he conceded that his concept of an Islamic system of leadership selection was closer to National Socialism and Marxism.[17] According to his interpretation, a democratic process of elections could apply in selecting men of character and piety, the *Ullul Amr,* only if the entire Muslim society were to be both conversant with and observant of Islamic injunctions.[18] Jamat e Islami applied strict criteria for its membership. This thinking often surfaced among the hard-line Afghan

---

16. In conformity with orthodox interpretation, Maududi opposed rule by a woman, but he modified his position to say that it was acceptable under the circumstances, though not desirable. Maududi, *Islami Riyasat,* 379.

17. Ibid., 137. See also, Maududi, *Islam ka Nazriah e Siyasi* (Islamic Political Concept) (Ichra, Lahore: Markazi Maktaba e Jamat e Islami Pakistan, 1955), 36.

18. Zia ul Haq's Majlis e Shura, the Parliament revived in 1985, was elected on a non-party basis and introduced a criterion that candidates be Muslims with good character. A separate electorate was introduced for election to reserved non-Muslim seats. Party-based elections were reintroduced in 1988 after the death of Zia ul Haq, and Musharraf reversed the separate electorate provision under protest from religious parties.

Mujahedin factions. However, moderate religious groups and parties in Pakistan, including Jamat e Islami, have reconciled to the inevitability of a multiparty system in a democratic dispensation. This adjustment is more a consequence of bending to popular sentiment, perhaps a form of *Ijma,* than the result of deliberations for *Ijtehad.* Jamat e Islami has had an important influence in Pakistani politics and in shaping the religious outlook in Pakistan.

Colonial constraints did not permit Muslims in India the kind of modernist response initiated from the top by political leadership, such as occurred elsewhere in the Islamic world. The Kemalist paradigm in Turkey went to the extreme in embracing secular and Western values and systems; the approach adopted by Khadiv in Egypt, Reza Shah in Iran, and King Amanullah in Afghanistan was comparatively circumspect. Each country experienced a backlash and has since evolved *sui generis.* In Afghanistan, King Amanullah, who had introduced reforms especially aimed at the education and emancipation of women, was ousted as a result of a revolt led by the orthodox and conservative tribal confederacy, abetted by the British.[19] An echo of the same episode was discernible when, in the wake of the 1978 Saur Revolution, similar reforms by Hafizullah Amin triggered a similar turn of events.[20]

Syed Ahmed Khan had witnessed the carnage of 1857 and was convinced of the superior organization and technological capabilities of the British. He advocated cooperation with the colonial rule and modern education for Muslims so that they could advance as a community. Nationalists castigated him as a traitor and a camp follower of the British. But under the circumstances, his vision was clearly intended to rehabilitate the Muslims, who were powerless and in decadence and for whom confrontation with the colonial rulers could only cause them further ruination. The Aligarh movement played an important role in energizing the Muslim elite in India to make a position for themselves in the British colonial power structure and in shaping their political thinking in defense of their rights as a community. The movement targeted the Muslim elite, instead of the masses, for its appeal, and Aligarh-educated men became the vanguard of the Indian Muslim League and of other campaigns for Muslim political activism, such as the *Khilafat* movement to help besieged Turkey in the aftermath of the First World War.

19. Tariq Ali, "Afghanistan: Between Hammer and Anvil," *New Left Review* (London), March–April 2000.

20. Riaz M. Khan, *Untying the Afghan Knot: Negotiating Soviet Withdrawal* (Durham, N.C.: Duke University Press, 1991), 9.

The Aligarh movement is sometimes viewed as a precursor of the Pakistan movement, and there is some truth in this premise. Nonetheless, the modernizing influence generated by Syed Ahmed Khan for a Muslim renaissance lost its vitality in Pakistan, where traditional tribal and feudal interests and religious orthodoxy were strong and politically well entrenched. An urban and business middle class grew fast after independence, but it largely fell under the influence of Maududi and Deoband.

Muhammad Iqbal, revered as the poet philosopher of Pakistan, is another towering influence in the intellectual discourse that preoccupies Pakistani intellectuals today. The power and rhythm of Iqbal's poetry and its message of awakening and change had a universal appeal for the Islamic world and made an impact beyond the Muslims of India, especially in the Persian-speaking Muslim populations of Afghanistan, Iran, and Central Asia. He lamented decadence and inertia (*Jumud*) in Muslim thought and society and, through his poetry, invoked the dynamic principle of change and movement as central to nature and the spirit of Islam, which he eulogized as a liberating and life-giving force.[21] His seminal philosophical work is contained in a series of lectures he gave in Madras, Hyderabad, and Aligarh in 1928–29. Besides articulating the nature of religion and the spiritual focus of Islam, in two of the lectures he discussed legal principles, emphasizing the requirement of *Ijtehad* and a critical attitude for rejuvenating Islamic societies. He recognized that "the growth of republican spirit and the gradual formation of legislative assemblies in Muslim lands constitute a great step in advance. The transfer of power of *Ijtehad* from individual representatives of schools to a Muslim legislative assembly . . . is the only possible form *Ijma* can take in modern times."[22] Yet, he also worried that an assembly may make "grave mistakes" in their interpretation of law.[23]

21. The dynamic principle of social change is not new to Islamic scholars. Ibn Khaldun has been one of its prominent exponents.

22. Allama Muhammad Iqbal, *The Reconstruction of Religious Thought in Islam* (Lahore: Iqbal Academy Pakistan, 1986), 138. Also see discussion by Dr. Muhammad Khalid Masud in his chapter "Islamic Modernism," in *Islam and Modernity: Key Issues and Debates*, edited by Muhammad Khalid Masud, Armando Salvatore, and Martin van Bruinessen (Edinburgh University Press, 2009), 247–48. Dr. Masud mentions that Iqbal believed that "a universal *Khilafat* was no longer possible" and that political sovereignty belonged to the Muslim people and not to a specific individual.

23. Iqbal, *The Reconstruction of Religious Thought in Islam,* 139. Muhammad Sohail Umar, *Khutbat e Iqbal: Naye Tanazur Mein* (Lahore: Iqbal Academy Pakistan, 1996), 194, argues that Iqbal's view on giving the right of *Ijtehad* to a parliament or elected body was highly circumspect.

Iqbal shied away from discussing specifics. He spoke of an Islamic state, but did not dwell on issues such as the institutions of governance, rights of women and minorities, issues of economy, and relations with non-Muslim states that a modern Islamic state must address and which must be the subjects of contemporary *Ijtehad*. Maududi set limits on *Ijtehad;* Iqbal was ambivalent about its scope and modality.

Iqbal veered towards a fusion of religious tradition and morality with the evolution of Muslim society along modern lines. He did not foresee the enforcement of an Islamic system that required a definition such as offered by Maududi and a popular consensus that could hardly be possible, given the diverse religious schools and sects. He was dismissive of the Western polity and material progress as devoid of a spiritual, religious content that provided, in his view, the essential core of collective ethics and morality in a society. He appeared to overlook the power and capacity of material progress to affect improvement in the human condition and the inherent ability of societies to evolve social ethical norms independent of a structured religion.

A survey of the entirety of Iqbal's poetic, philosophical, and political writings would reveal grey areas and even contradictions. He was a powerful exponent of the unity of the Muslim *Ummah,* while on the other hand, as a practical politician, he conformed to the idea of a nation-state by proposing self-governance for the territories that roughly comprise today's Pakistan. He supported King Amanullah's reforms in Afghanistan, but his ideas on the role of women in society leaned towards conservatism. At the intellectual plane, his concept of a perfect man could hardly help to delineate a perfect society. His forceful poetry appeared to be dismissive of *Aql* (intellect), reason, and rationalism, and instead emphasized *ishq,* a metaphysical state of love and passion, for experiencing the subliminal quality of religion that improves and enriches life.

Like some of his contemporary thinkers, who witnessed the height of European imperial power and the devastation of the twentieth-century European wars, Iqbal predicted the decline of Western civilization in its unfettered avarice and moral corruption and rejected Western philosophies, especially materialism and liberalism. Some of his verses are even dismissive of Western democracy. He saw human salvation in a revitalized Islam. These thoughts have been treated delicately and with due circumspection in his philosophical lectures. Iqbal admired many facets of Western societies, especially their discipline and creativity. Today, at the popular level in Pakistan, there is a perversion of the understanding of Iqbal, and conservative, religious polemicists often invoke his verses to baldly reject Western thought and rationalism, constricting his influence as a modernizing force. This is ironic, because in practical politics Iqbal was closer to Jinnah, a modernist, and endorsed his leadership of the Muslim League.

Among today's Muslim states, Pakistan shows a strong transnational impulse, nurtured by a romantic notion of the Islamic *Ummah* and its unity. At the state and policy level, this is reflected in the expressed attachment to Islamic causes and in endeavors for greater cooperation among the Islamic countries, within the framework of the Organization of the Islamic Conference. Most of the Islamic religious parties espouse a pan-Islamic view, and all jihadist groups go a step further in showing scant regard for national boundaries. Many of these parties and groups justify their support for jihadist activity in other Muslim lands—and in the case of Afghanistan the cross-border activity—by asserting that within the Islamic world there ought not to be any artificial boundaries. The Taliban found this argument to be politically convenient to deflect any Pakistani suggestion for recognition of the Durand Line.

The idea of Islamic *Ummah* as a transnational entity encompassing the entire Muslim community is ingrained in Muslim thinking but is especially pronounced among Muslims of South Asia, who appear to have drawn comfort from being part of a much larger community instead of being a minority in India. The Indian Muslims were vocal advocates for the restoration of *Khilafat* when Kemal Atatürk formally abolished it as an irrelevant legacy of the decadent past. The present-day proponents of *Khilafat,* such as Hisb ut Tahrir, are largely of Pakistani or South Asian origin. Transnational identity resonates in Pakistani popular culture for yet another reason. Many prominent families trace their origins from outside Pakistan or have affiliations with Sufi saints who came from Central Asia or the Middle East and were responsible for conversions to Islam in the area. Nevertheless, transnational identity has often proved to be a brittle veneer that falls apart in practical state-to-state politics. In the case of Pakistan, transnational proclivities did not transcend its national interests when dealing with Afghanistan, whether on the border issue or on economic interests.

Ceding Space to Religious Parties

The ideological underpinnings of the Pakistan movement, including the nebulous but politically potent two-nation theory, had already ensured space for religious parties and groups that began to form and assert themselves politically after 1947, in particular in the shaping of the new country's constitution. The political elite dominated by the Muslim League leadership, the bureaucracy, and the landed class in West Pakistan needed religious elements as political allies[24] in their internal political maneuvering. But they were status quo–minded in their outlook on governance and administration and had no inclination to supplant the existing system with the introduction of Sharia, as demanded by the religious parties. The ruling elite viewed Muslim nationalism more in a cultural than an ideological sense. The different social complexion of East Pakistan, with a substantial religious minority, worked in favor of continuing with an essentially secular model based on the continuation of the institutions inherited at the time of independence.

The 1956 constitution, adopted after a good deal of debate and tribulation, was drafted along the lines of the Government of India Act of 1935, preserving the same judicial, legal, and administrative structures. To accommodate the Ulema as well as in recognition of the widely acknowledged ideological moorings of the Pakistan movement, the country adopted as its name the Islamic Republic of Pakistan. Additionally, the preamble included the Objectives Resolution, moved by the first Pakistani prime minister, Liaquat Ali Khan, in the Constituent Assembly in March 1949, and the broad Islamic precepts of the resolution were invoked as the guiding principles in the formulation of the constitution. The constitution also stipulated that no law would be adopted inconsistent with the Quran and Sunnah.

The religious elements, in particular the Jamat e Islami, however, rejected the 1956 constitution. The military coup by Ayub Khan in 1958 led to the abrogation of the 1956 constitution and the adoption in 1962 of a new constitution as secular in character as its precursor. In fact, the word "Islamic" was dropped in the designation of the country. The new constitution also broadened the composition of the Pakistan Council on Islamic Ideology, an advisory body, to include scholars and legal experts other than Ulema, a step resented by the latter.

The third constitution, adopted in 1973, was the result of deliberations of an all-parties committee operating under the changed circumstances of a dismembered Pakistan, the interim presidency of Zulfikar Ali Bhutto, and the political ascendancy of the People's Party and its slogan of Islamic socialism. Mollified by the invitation to participate in its formulation, many

---

24. Husain Haqqani, *Pakistan: Between Mosque and Military* (Lahore: Vanguard Books, 2005), 20.

religious parties welcomed the new constitution, especially restoration of the designation of the country as the Islamic Republic, and the provision that "no law shall be enacted that is repugnant to the injunctions of Islam." Jamat e Islami maintained its fundamental objection, which did not make a material difference in the new constitution's acceptability. Jamat influence had been kept in check, and the party, like its counterpart, the Ikhwan in Egypt, was at times treated high-handedly during the Ayub and then the Bhutto period. In 1985, when Zia ul Haq decided to introduce a democratic form of government, he restored the 1973 constitution with a major amendment that included the Objectives Resolution as an integral part of the constitution and introduced elements of his policy of Islamization, in addition to investing new powers in the office of the presidency. Until the Zia ul Haq coup in 1977, Pakistan's constitutional history had demonstrated a measure of continuity in a pragmatic and modernist rather than ideological approach to state affairs. But there were other areas where the ruling elite bent under the pressure of the religious groups.

Encouraged by local politics in Punjab, the religious groups launched a violent anti-Qadiani movement in 1953, which got out of control and led to the imposition of martial law and deployment of the military in many cities. The report of the inquiry commission headed by the chief justice of the Supreme Court, Munir Ahmed, considered an important document on religion and politics in Pakistan, highlighted the lack of agreement among Ulema of different schools on who qualifies as a Muslim. More than twenty years later, the same intellectual integrity could not be maintained when once again riots broke out on the Qadiani issue. This time a religious question was decided politically by the Parliament's turning itself into a committee of the whole to deliberate on the issue. An earlier significant gain in the assertion of religious politics in Pakistan had been made in the early 1960s, when religious groups were able to compel President Ayub Khan to ease out the first chairman of the Council on Islamic Ideology because of his views on compatibility between Islam and modernity, as reflected in the 1962 family laws the council had drafted.

In Pakistan, religion could not be separated from political debate. Powerful religious interests and influences were an integral part of the political and social fabric of a society steeped in tradition and orthodox conservatism. Besides the Jamat, the religious parties fell largely into the two main religious schools of Barelvi and Deobandi traditions, represented respectively in two coalitions, Jamiat Ulema e Pakistan (JUP) and Jamiat Ulema e Islam (JUI). The Barelvi School represents a broad tradition of religious

Sufi orders and Pirs (spiritual guides) associated with influential religious families and the ritualistic cultural aspects in Islam that are dismissed as *bida* by the orthodox Ahl e Hadith and Deobandi School. The religious parties were vocal in politics, but their vote bank remained limited and they could only manage 5 to 10 percent representation in successive parliaments, with the exception of the 2002 elections when they had significant showing in NWFP and Baluchistan, partly because of the events in neighboring Afghanistan. While Jamat e Islami has an urban middle-class base, JUI has a rural base especially in southern districts of NWFP. Led by Maulana Fazal ur Rahman, a pragmatic political personality[25] and religious scholar, the party was founded by his father, Mufti Mahmud, who also established the madrassa Darul Uloom in Dera Ismail Khan.

Another nonpolitical yet powerful religious movement that has impacted the intellectual and cultural environment in Pakistan has been the Tableeghi Jamat, founded by Maulana Illyas in 1926 as a pacifist voluntary movement that eschewed politics and differences of fiqh in Sunni Islam. This populist, voluntary association emphasizes proselytizing, observance of religious obligations, and moral cleansing to secure better rewards in the hereafter; its ethos is dismissive of worldly achievement. Tableeghi Jamat activities gained momentum in Pakistan in the late 1960s, when it began focusing on educational institutions. Attracted by its austere approach, which appeared to transcend divisions of sects and *maslak* (schools of religious dogma), hundreds of thousands of youth and working professionals, including members of the civil bureaucracy and the army, devote their time to preaching and persuading mostly fellow Muslims to join the effort to earn grace and salvation. The cumulative effect on society over the years has been significant; the Tableeghi activity brings together people of diverse backgrounds, including highly placed, politically motivated individuals, creating an informal network that generates political undercurrents. Tableeghi Jamat has served as a catalyst for building the dense religious environment that conditions popular orientation and intellectual discourse in Pakistan.

---

25. In a conversation with Maulana Fazal ur Rahman in early 2007, the author gathered the impression that the Maulana was deeply anxious about the strength of extremist religious and other fanatical groups in Waziristan, which adjoined his constituency in Dera Ismail Khan. He had doubts about the willingness of the core leadership of these groups to change course towards reconciliation and renounce violence; and he felt that the government had a better chance of success with efforts to isolate them by winning over the foot soldiers and the outer layers of the leadership.

As a political party, Jamat e Islami survived the hostility of the Ayub and Bhutto governments in the 1960s and 1970s. As the only cogent articulation of an Islamic political system, Maulana Maududi's works continued to influence minds of that section of the intelligentsia, middle class, and students who sought answers for political ills in Islamic values and teachings. Among all religious political parties and movements, Jamat e Islami has been the most tenacious, organized, active, and influential in shaping the religious thinking of the urban middle class in Pakistan. Maududi's well-reasoned concept of an Islamic state establishing a society based on Sharia and the Islamic principles of social justice, altruism, and civic responsibility appealed to the literate sections of the urban population, in particular the youth in colleges and universities with middle and lower middle class and rural backgrounds. Its youth wing, Jamiat e Tulaba e Islam, was similarly motivated and active. In organizing the party, its youth wing, and its modus operandi, Maududi appeared to have been influenced by the disciplined, ideologically oriented, contemporary European movements.

During the 1960s, in universities and other higher educational institutions, Jamiat e Tulaba e Islam was the main contender for intellectual space with the left-leaning influences of the times. Jamiat had an advantage; its members had cultural affinity with the large body of students belonging to middle and low-income classes in the society. In contrast, left activists were often identified with upper classes and exposed to left ideological influences during their stay at university campuses abroad. They advocated theories of a classless society but could not relate to their peers from lower income and cultural strata.

The Beginning of Religious Vigilantism in Pakistan

As the students belonging to Jamiat grew stronger in numbers and organization, their conduct gave rise to the early instances of religious vigilantism on the campuses, especially those with coeducation. Jamiat students were known to agitate against teachers and students whose thinking and demeanor did not subscribe to perceived Islamic values. Debate over sensitive subjects, especially religion, began to diminish.

At this point a short digression is needed to look into the intellectual underpinnings of Islamist vigilantism. A scholarly review in December 2003 by Dr. Muhammad Khalid Masud, chairman of the Pakistan Council on Islamic Ideology, assessing the curricula of the International Islamic University of Malaysia, traced the first justification for individual action to Abdul Qadir Awda, a second generation Ikhwan al Muslimin scholar. Awda's teachings set the trend to "privatization" of jihad and implementation of Islamic law. He had opined that *Hudud* was an obligation for the Muslim *ummah* as a whole and not only for the state. If courts in a Muslim country could not sentence a person for violating an Islamic law, then these courts could not also have the authority to punish a person who acted within the requirements of Islamic law. Sayed Qutb carried forward the same thinking; both men were executed following Egyptian President Gamal Abdel Nasser's clampdown on the Ikhwan, the first standard bearers of radical (fundamentalist) political Islamist movements.[26]

In Pakistan, Maulana Maududi's religious discourse did not explicitly approve individual action independent of the state. He emphasized the concept of an Islamic state implementing the Sharia law, notwithstanding the proclivity of its youth wing to veer towards vigilantism. The 1980s Afghan Jihad was unique in the sense that it enjoyed universal recognition and support within the Islamic world, even though it was not formally waged by any Islamic state. Rather, it enjoyed popular recognition and support as jihad within the Islamic world and appealed to myriad Islamist groups. The violence accompanying the Afghan Jihad, mixed with the severe Wahabi, Deobandi, and *Takfiri* thought, spawned both the Taliban's narrow interpretation of Sharia and the ideologues with a confrontational worldview who championed global jihad.[27]

Within religious political parties, including Jamat e Islami, there is debate on the responsibility for law enforcement and punitive action, which is generally agreed to be the prerogative of the government of the day. Most

---

26. Fundamentalism is a complex phenomenon. In a generic sense it applies to religious movements and thinking of different shades that emphasize commitment to religion in its puritanical form. Citing Richard T. Antoun's *Understanding Fundamentalism: Christian, Islamic and Jewish Movements* (Oxford: Altamira, 2001), Dr. Muhammad Khalid Masud has identified common themes in fundamentalist ideologies to include: the quest for purity, the search for authenticity, totalism and activism, the necessity of certainty, selective modernization, and centering the mythical past in the present. In the 1950s in the Middle East, the West encouraged Fundamentalist Islamist movements as a counter to Nasserism and other left-political influences that dominated the Arab lands.

27. Dr. Muhammad Khalid Masud, "Rethinking Islamic Fundamentalism in Pakistan," a paper presented at a conference in London on November 30, 2002, organized by Leicester University's Institute of India-Pakistan Relations. The paper discusses in detail the jihadist exegesis of Maulana Masood Azhar, the head of Jaish e Muhammad, predicated on permanent struggle between Islam and Kufr.

Ulema agree that individuals or individual groups cannot arrogate to themselves the right to enforce *Amr bil Maroof wa Nahi al Munkir* (commanding good and forbidding wrong, or, by another interpretation, to seize good and to shun wrong) without regard for the interpretation of this Quranic and well-known eclectic principle in human affairs. However, as the application of *Amr bil Maroof* under the Afghan Taliban rule showed, the spirit of this principle has been lost and its meaning has been reduced to enforcement of ritual and form.

In 2006, the MMA government led by Jamat e Islami made the only serious attempt in Pakistan to institutionalize *Amr bil Maroof wa Nahi al Munkir* at the official level, through a proper legislative process, by moving a Hisba Bill in the NWFP provincial assembly. The idea was to establish a government institution similar to the one that had functioned under the Taliban, headed by a Mohtesib (ombudsman) responsible for monitoring *Amr bil Maroof.* The bill partly explained its objectives, such as ensuring Islamic ethics and etiquette at the provincial level, controlling the media to make them conform to Islamic values, and instructing provincial functionaries not to do anything inconsistent with Sharia. The bill also included under the special responsibilities of the Mohtesib progressive measures for prevention of social evils such as child labor, honor killings, begging, and cruelty to animals.[28] The Pakistan Council on Islamic Ideology examined the bill. Along with a number of technical observations, the council made an important comment related to imprecision in, or absence of definition of, *Amr bil Maruf* that could open the application of the bill to abuse and confusion. The bill was dropped after the MMA government lost the elections in 2008.

Returning to the discussion on politicization of educational institutions in Pakistan, the Jamat influence increased in 1973 with the nationalization of the education sector. This action affected a large number of colleges and schools that were privately managed, in some cases by Christian missionary organizations, which had a long tradition of maintaining discipline, efficiency, and educational standards. The 1970s saw regular clashes on university and college campuses between the youth wings of Jamat e Islami and the Pakistan People's Party. Under Zia ul Haq, Jamiat e Tulaba e Islam

---

28. These are examples of a few enlightened elements introduced in the bill that showed sensitivity to the Pakistani environment. There was no such element in the Taliban-enforced *Amr bil Maroof* in Afghanistan. Nonetheless, there is nothing to bar invoking this eclectic principle to reject contemporary evils such as environmental degradation, rampant consumerism, and waste.

gained the upper hand, and campuses became a strong base for Jamat and a breeding ground for religious radicalism. Later, the Muslim Students' Federation, the youth wing of the Nawaz Sharif's Muslim League, and similar but more parochial student groups joined the fray to the further detriment of the educational system. The campuses became a battleground for jostling for political influence. In the process they suffered as institutions of learning with declining educational standards. Campuses all over the world, including Pakistan, had witnessed a great ferment in the late 1960s. Within the span of a few years, most of those campuses returned to normal academic discipline. In Pakistan, it has taken several decades and the reintroduction of private institutions of higher learning to partially free the campuses from the stranglehold of political parties.

The campus vigilantism of the 1960s and 1970s in Pakistan persists and, with the rise of religiosity in society, has contributed to a stifling cultural environment. But it would be wrong to assume that this phenomenon was a precursor of the religious or extremist violence witnessed since 1990s in various parts of Pakistan. This violence owed to the rise of extremist militant religious groups of both sectarian and jihadist character, such as Sipah e Sahaba and Jaish e Muhammad, respectively. Accentuating the violence was the insurgency in the tribal areas fueled by post–U.S. intervention developments in Afghanistan.

Militant groups such as Sipah e Sahaba and Jaish e Muhammad commonly resorted to threats to browbeat opponents. A perverse form of religious vigilantism was evident in the violence directed against individuals and religious minorities over alleged incidents of blasphemy. Low-level police officials and even lower court judges felt harassed or dealt with cases under pressure from fanatical religious groups. The mainstream religious parties such as Jamat e Islami, JUI, and JUP opposed such violence. However, their politics and the outlook and attitudes they promoted created an environment susceptible to religious extremism.

The ascendancy of religious orthodoxy and Jamat e Islami and Deobandi politics began with the military rule of President Zia ul Haq in 1977 and the Afghan Jihad in the 1980s. Zia ul Haq came from a modest, middle-class religious background. He was personally devout and built up a religious constituency, partly out of conviction and partly to prop up his political position.[29] The head of the Jamat, Mian Tufail Muhammad, was a close advi-

---

29. Zia ul Haq also attracted revivalist Islamic scholars from the Middle East; Dr. Hassan Al Turrabi of Sudan and Sheikh Abdullah Nazeef of Rabeta al Alam al Islami were frequent visitors, both in the context of the Afghan Jihad and Pakistani Islamization.

sor to Zia; the two men shared an additional affinity, having had the same hometown, Jallundhar in East Punjab, before their families migrated to Pakistan. Zia's patronage of the Jamat helped it to position itself firmly in the country's politics. In particular, Jamat was able to consolidate its influence in the critical education sector by placing professionals affiliated to it or like-minded bureaucrats in key education departments. Jamat influence ran deep in the revision of the curricula, especially at the primary and secondary levels, giving them a narrow ideological orientation, with a reduced emphasis on science, world history, and civics. In the teaching of the Islamic tenets, an emphasis was placed on the concept of jihad in the defense of oppressed Muslims. This new emphasis in education resonated with the growing nationalist and patriotic sentiment and was readily accepted. Pakistani society, like other societies with a similar predisposition, already had a glorified view of Islamic history as romanticized in popular literature.[30]

The Policy of Islamization and the Decline of Rationalism

Zia ul Haq's declared policy of Islamization, against the backdrop of international support and approbation for the Afghan Jihad, gave rise to a culture of religiosity and an environment of somewhat superficial and coercive self-righteousness that diminished space for secular thinking and free discourse. He acted as a man in a hurry. Under the rubric of Islamization, he introduced measures without debate and deliberation on such fundamental issues as introducing an Islamic system of justice that he called *Nizam e Mustafa* (the system of the holy prophet). This experiment, which was carried out virtually in parallel with the extant system of justice based on Anglo-Saxon law, did not bring reform but rather led to confusion and abuse.

The main planks of the Islamization policy included the introduction of the Islamic punishments under the *Hudud* Ordinance; establishment of Sharia benches in higher courts; the blasphemy laws, *Toheen e Risalat* (insulting prophethood); further restrictions on the Qadianis regarding their religious practices; and other economic measures such as introducing interest-free banking and compulsory deduction of Zakat (the Islamic charity tax).

---

30. A case in point is the powerful historical novels of Nasim Hijazi about Muslim conquests and setbacks that have been a staple reading and source of inspiration for young people in their formative years. Urdu literature has a genre of romanticized writing with historical perspectives, highlighting Muslim character and attributing Muslim defeats to corruption and deceit, rather than backwardness.

The policy and the official patronage increased the influence of clerics, especially the Deobandi clerics who had become involved with the Afghan Jihad. In his personal behavior, Zia exhibited a modest, courteous, and sincere demeanor,[31] which was quite unlike that of Bhutto, who was brilliant but arrogant. Nonetheless, for maintaining his political hold, Zia was no less ruthless, as evident from his suppression of protests in Sindh, ignited by the 1983 Movement for Restoration of Democracy the political parties launched. Zia's Islamization, even if driven by altruistic motivation, was equally a vehicle of politics for the legitimacy of his rule, which ended up promoting dogma rather than reason and gave rise to religious bigotry in the society.

Zia's Islamization policy did not improve governance. It exposed the weakness and incompatibility of attempts to implement Sharia in its literalist interpretation with the present-day requirements of governance in a large, diverse society such as Pakistan's. Moreover, the mixing of politics with the invocation of religion produced cynicism and confusion in the country. The introduction of a nonparty Shura had suited Zia ul Haq's interest in diluting the influence of the People's Party; yet the step was publicized as conforming to the spirit of Islam that disapproved parties and divisions. Despite the pious requirements of good character for the candidates, those elected to the new Shura in 1985 were familiar political faces with party affiliations. In 1988, when Zia dismissed the government of his handpicked prime minister, Muhammad Khan Junejo, for political reasons, he announced that the step was necessitated by lack of progress towards Islamization, in addition to deteriorating law and order and economy. Within one month, Zia enunciated an ordinance extending the jurisdiction of the Shariat courts to financial and constitutional matters in addition to their appellate authority. With this ordinance, he declared that he had com-

---

31. Mushahid Hussain, a prominent Pakistani politician, described it as a kind of "double handshake and warm embrace." After the dismissal of the Junejo government, Zia decided to move me (the author) from the Afghanistan desk in the Foreign Office and place me in charge of external publicity. Zia asked me to his office in Rawalpindi and spoke about his intention, saying that he wanted someone with experience of interacting with foreign journalists, especially those who did not understand his policy of Islamization. I demurred, saying that while I had been dealing with Afghanistan issues, on Islamization "either I did not understand his policy or I had a different opinion." He disarmingly remarked, "Riaz, you should say to them (the foreign journalists) what comes from the heart. That will make an impact. You are not serving Zia ul Haq, you are serving Pakistan."

pleted the process of Islamization. The ordinance lapsed after Zia died. His successor, Ghulam Ishaq Khan, decided to hold party-based elections.[32]

At the practical level, the introduction of Sharia courts, in parallel with the existing civil courts, did little to improve the justice system in the country. Many of the *Hudud* punishments were abandoned. Public floggings caused revulsion at home and abroad; no medical doctor was prepared to undertake amputation of a hand, a Sharia punishment for theft. The enforcement of the compulsory deduction of Zakat drew protests from the Shia community, obliging the government to make modifications that only encouraged people to make false declarations. Furthermore, the application of *Hudud* under the *Zina* (adultery) Ordinance and the introduction of blasphemy laws, for which there is no clear Quranic basis, led to gross and blatant abuse. An obvious lacuna had been the absence of the rigorous requirement of evidence as prescribed under the Sharia, which is difficult to apply in a society rife with corruption. The blasphemy laws became an instrument for unscrupulous individuals, including clerics, to persecute opponents and members of minority communities. The abuse of these laws and the *Zina* Ordinance gave rise to indefensible and irrational situations. The emphasis on *Hudud* was partly the consequence of the pronounced reference to the immutability of *Hudud* in the writings of Maulana Maududi.

The other inspiration for the Islamization policy was the Saudi system. Saudi Arabia is the only Islamic country that claims to implement the *Hudud* punishments. The Saudi example could hardly serve as a model for Pakistan, given Saudi Arabia's differences, with its vast oil economy, relatively much smaller and less diverse population, and the unique alliance between the House of Saud and Wahabi clergy. The puritanical Saudi dogma could not be divorced from its regressive, eighteenth-century Nejd cultural outlook, especially its obsessive seclusion of women.

---

32. There is considerable evidence that Zia dismissed the Junejo government because of pressure from army generals upset over demands for a parliamentary inquiry into the Ojeri camp incident, in which over one hundred people were killed as the ammunition dump meant for the Afghan Mujahidin blew up in the heart of the twin cities of Islamabad and Rawalpindi. Following the dismissal of the Junejo government, Brig. Siddique Salik, the president's speechwriter, who died with Zia in the Bhawalpur crash, mentioned to the author, then director general for external publicity, that "Zia was totally unprepared to take such an action." Zia asked Salik to prepare a draft for him to address the nation to explain the action and was annoyed when Salik asked for guidance, saying, "Have you not prepared draft speeches before?" Salik remarked to me that he drafted a "formula speech," which the president read out without any significant alteration.

An old issue in Islamic jurisprudence has been that of adjusting social norms with legal norms. The Saudi Salafi creed has a tribal temperament and appeals to a tribal mind. It had failed to inspire the established Arab centers of Islamic learning and civilization for nearly two centuries, until Saudi oil wealth helped its proselytization, partly as a counter to Gamal Abdel Nasser's secular Arab nationalism. The events of 9/11 impelled the Saudi ruling elite to revisit the autonomy it had allowed the clergy and push for reform and reeducation. However, the Saudi Salafi creed, with its aggressive and xenophobic traits, has taken root with the Taliban and the madrassas, impacting the largely poor and tribal segments of the otherwise far more complex Pakistani society.

Under Zia ul Haq, a combination of factors, ranging from the policy of Islamization to the growing Saudi political and financial influence in Pakistan attributable to the Afghan Jihad and the large presence of nearly one million Pakistani expatriate workers in the kingdom, built acceptability and respect for the Saudi system and for its Salafi doctrine as the correct interpretation of Islam. The large number of Saudi-funded madrassas reinforced the trend over time. The *Hudud* punishments became the hallmark of Zia ul Haq's Islamization policy and thereby debased instead of elevating the project. The policy would have gained in respect and stature if instead of *Hudud* it had adopted a more thoughtful approach of building a welfare state, emphasizing Islamic values of social justice and compassion and addressing the bane of a poor work ethic, corruption, lack of a sense of civic duty, absence of basic civic amenities, socioeconomic underdevelopment, and low achievement in the society. The great early jurists and even Maududi had emphasized that Sharia and *Hudud* could be applied only after ensuring welfare in the society.

The decade of Zia ul Haq's rule and the rhetoric of the Afghan Jihad, which had boosted Pakistan's international profile, served to fuse ideas of security, religiosity, and patriotism to create a mental makeup that suited the interests of the military, the clergy, the pro–status quo feudal classes, and the religiously inclined urban middle classes. The same period also saw a depletion of courage and intellect in the country and erosion of the capacity to withstand and counter the spreading obscurantism and bigotry. Subsequent governments failed to grasp the gravity of the trend and redress the situation. The 1990s witnessed a succession of political wrangles. They drifted at a time when it needed a strong, focused, and prescient leadership to understand and arrest the dangers that had resulted from the policies of the previous decade and that were increasing in the changed regional and global environment. The military encouraged the Kashmiri Jihad without a clear idea of its direction or denouement.[33] The intelligence agencies supported the jihadi groups and linked militias, comfortable in the false belief that these could be influenced and manipulated as and when required.[34]

Civil society elements and human rights activists constantly protested the abuse of blasphemy laws and called for review. But the clergy and interest groups linked to Zia ul Haq's politics were strongly entrenched and dismissive of these calls as originating from Westernized liberal elements out of touch with Pakistan's Islamic identity and ethos. Efforts of human rights activists helped secure the release of scores of women wrongfully incarcerated under the Zina Ordinance.

The abuse of blasphemy laws presented a glaring aspect of the intellectual crisis and growing insensitivity to obscurantism perpetrated in the name of religion. Pakistan faced international criticism, but even as broad-minded and Western-educated a prime minister as Benazir Bhutto could do little to review the laws, which were often defended on the basis that similar laws existed in the statutes of the United Kingdom.[35] The international embarrassment was illustrated by one personal experience of the author in 1997 in Brussels, when four members of the European Parliament came to meet him to make a demarche. The leader of these MEPs said that as Europeans they could not agree with the law, but understood the sovereign right of Pakistan to enact any law and prescribe capital punishment for its violation. But, he continued, "What kind of law is this that on the evidence

33. For most of the 1990s, there was a lack of clarity about the policy of support to the Kashmiri Mujahedin, and the policy remained in a state of drift, waiting for an opportunity for a Kashmiri settlement. In late 1998, in a meeting with the army chief, Jehangir Karamat, an astute general with a sound worldview, I (the author), having returned from assignment in Brussels as ambassador to the EU and exposed to international criticism of Pakistan's support to jihadi elements in Kashmir, expressed doubts about the success of the policy. I suggested that a policy must be thought through and judged on the basis of the weaknesses and strengths of the protagonists and the opposition and a road map for progress. Jehangir Karamat appeared confident in terms of comparative strengths, but agreed that the policy required a periodic review to determine where it was heading.

34. This false premise was reflected in the attitude of General Akhtar Abdur Rahman, head of the ISI in the 1980s, who was confident that the Afghan Mujahedin leaders would accept Pakistani advice regarding dialogue and broad-based government, if and when there was a need to move in that direction. When the opportunity came in the late 1980s, this premise proved to be false.

35. Such laws did exist in British statute books but had been moribund for over a century.

of a single person the accused is put behind bars and the government justifies this unbailable imprisonment to be in the interest of the personal safety of the accused. What kind of intolerant society have you created?"

In early 1999, the Pakistan Foreign Office moved a proposal for review of the procedure subjecting registration of cases under the law only after initial screening at the district administrator's level to minimize abuse. Several meetings were held involving senior officials from the ministries of foreign affairs, law, and religious affairs. In one discussion, reacting to a remark that the law needed scrutiny for its soundness from an Islamic legal point of view, an official from the Ministry of Religious Affairs cautioned that such observations could only be made in the "safety of these (Foreign Office) walls; outside, these could cause lynching." Finally in a meeting in September 1999 at the ministerial level, the religious affairs minister, Raja Zafarul Haq, a devout person of moderate temperament who had served as secretary general of the Rabita al-Alam al-Islami, agreed to the Foreign Office proposal, saying that he had studied 171 cases and not more than a half dozen should have been registered under the law. The joint recommendation was put to the Nawaz Sharif government in late September 1999. After a delay of a few months following the October 1999 military coup, Pervez Musharraf, who had taken over power, approved the recommendation. But shortly thereafter, he was forced to overturn the decision when, on his arrival from a tour of Central Asian states, he was informed at the airport that the decision had caused much anxiety among the "ranks." Later, instructions to exercise care in registering cases under blasphemy laws were issued in a low-key manner without publicity.

The episode underscored the influence of the clergy and their opposition to reviewing any provision, howsoever irrational, introduced under Zia's Islamization policy.[36] The issue was essentially political. They feared that any

36. There is no exact parallel to blasphemy laws in other Islamic countries, since they do not have a Quranic sanction. The British had introduced these laws in view of the communal situation in the Indian subcontinent. According to some scholars, clergy had put pressure on Zia to introduce a law for apostasy with capital punishment. Zia resisted introduction of an apostasy law but agreed to capital punishment for blasphemy. In 1997, the author once asked the Egyptian ambassador in Brussels, Muhammad Chebane, about any similar laws in his country. In Egypt, he said, a crime similar to blasphemy that threatens public order is punishable by a maximum of a few years' sentence, and the case is dropped if the accused denies culpability or seeks *Tauba* (contrition). Articles 98(f), 160, 161, and 171 of the Egyptian Penal Code criminalize and prescribe sentences for "ridiculing or insulting a heavenly religion or a sect," disturbing religious rituals, "blasphemy," "profanity of graves," or abetment of such crimes. The punishment

apparent retreat on what they had secured under Zia would amount to attrition and unraveling of their authority and influence in the society.

Such fears are common to the mind-set of fundamentalists, who are averse to admitting any challenge to their doctrinaire approach. Pakistani society has thus become susceptible to unreasonableness in its internal discourse and suffered emasculation of its pluralistic, inclusive, rational, and pragmatic outlook.

Both religious and political parties have drawn on religion and ideology as an instrument of politics to retain and increase their influence and gain prominence. Issues that provoke religious sensitivities are employed for agitation, not necessarily for seeking resolution or as the best recourse to address the issues but to advance political interests in the domestic context. For example, there could be some justification for the protest rallies over the Danish cartoon issue to send a signal to European governments; but the violent agitation seen in Pakistan that resulted in loss of life and property was politically motivated.

The preceding paragraphs have detailed and analyzed the developments and environment that made the Pakistani society susceptible to unreasonableness in its internal discourse and governance and tolerated and condoned religious militancy and Talibanization. These are the outward symptoms of an intellectual confusion and decline that have weakened the capacity of the society to gather intellectual strength and courage to exercise scrutiny and rectify an obvious wrong simply because it had the dubious sanction of a hastily conceived Islamization policy pushed by a politico-religious authority, partly in a struggle for political power and partly in a struggle for the soul of the country. Zia ul Haq was at the center of this struggle, buoyed by the Afghan Jihad and driven by his personal convictions, which did not have to face the test of the ensuing Mujahedin strife, Taliban excesses, and extremist violence in the name of religion.

The problem preceded Zia ul Haq. His predecessors had failed to address the banality of the feudal and tribal prejudices evident from the neglect of education. They could not reconfigure the security paradigm of the state that drained resources meant for socioeconomic development; nor did they

---

is imprisonment "not exceeding five years." In Pakistan the offense has been made unbailable and carries capital punishment. In most cases punishments have been overturned by higher courts, but the accused are often targeted by fanatics, who also reportedly harass lower court judges hearing such cases.

withstand the tenacious challenge of traditional orthodoxy, with its regressive temperament, to incrementally gain political space. Zia's predecessors ignored the polarization within the society, its intellectual persona torn between the pulls of an antiquated religious outlook and the demands of a fast-changing world, where survival of societies depended on sustained progress, expanding knowledge, and constructive engagement with the world community. Pakistani leadership and intellectuals failed to develop consensus over basics for a new society capable of keeping in step with the challenge of the times.

Zia ul Haq's successors, on the other hand, were far too preoccupied by the vagaries of politics. Benazir, with her international outlook and exposure, was hamstrung by uncertain politics and her caution in dealing with the army. She did not consider it prudent to take on the religious constituency and extremist groups that had emerged as part of Pakistan's support for the Jihad in Afghanistan and then in Kashmir. Nawaz Sharif belonged to that segment of the business elite who believed in Islamization, without scrutiny of its minutiae. Initially, his political rise also owed to the support of Zia ul Haq and rightist elements within the army and intelligence community, and he valued political support of the clergy and the Jamat. Musharraf was secular minded but cautious in taking measures that could touch upon the army's sensitivities, especially on Kashmir, or ruffle religious orthodoxy and radical groups. It was only after 9/11 that he could push for his reform program to counter extremism and religious militancy.[37]

The society's disorientation, confusion in its domestic discourse, and its failures of governance and institutions will be this chapter's next focus.

Elements of Confusion in Public Discourse

The discussion on the intellectual crisis in Pakistani society has so far related to the consequences of the Islamization policy and support to jihad in Afghanistan and Kashmir. It is relevant to look as well at the behavior and

---

37. In April 2000, I had an occasion to raise the issue of support to jihadi groups with General Pervez Musharraf, then chief executive, on the occasion of the Havana G-77 summit, in the company of Foreign Secretary Shamshad Ahmed and National Security Advisor Tariq Aziz. I argued that Musharraf could not realize his economic agenda for development without giving up support for jihadist groups, who were spawning an environment hostile to foreign investment and economic growth. Musharraf disagreed and placed the blame for economic ills on corruption. When I persisted, he literally closed the argument with a remark that what I was suggesting could bring an end to his government.

patterns of thinking that have become pronounced in Pakistani society in the past few decades and contributed to the confusion in public discourse on national policies, priorities, politics, and vision. The patterns are discernible, in varying degrees, in the electronic and print media debates and analysis and, more importantly, in the thinking of policymakers and politicians. None of these elements is unique to Pakistani society; only the extent to which they preoccupy the Pakistani mind and form part of the popular ethos makes them noteworthy.

Over the years, public discourse has become increasingly angry and even violent, intensifying polarization in the country and giving rise to distrust and suspicion in the society. Political commentators, especially in the Urdu press, use harsh and disparaging language routinely. As a result, people look at issues and personalities in black and white. In political discussions, words such as traitor, unpatriotic, and betrayal are used lightly and loosely. Mutual accusations of perfidious conduct are commonplace. Consequently, the capacity to develop a balanced perspective on challenges and problems and, thus, a clear analysis and judgment has suffered a certain decline. The anger and severity in the tone of public discourse result partly from historical experience, in particular the unstable political institutions and systems of governance, insecurity, a weak rule of law, and deprivation caused by lack of sustained progress in addressing socioeconomic problems.

Broadly, the Pakistani intellectual has been reduced to a polemicist. Analysis and arguments are mostly deployed to serve an activist point of view or political agenda. The recent growth of electronic media has accentuated this tendency, making the public discourse noisier and no less polemical. With their often-dramatic tone, the electronic media have injected a certain stridency in national debates around the world. Media are unquestionably powerful and perhaps the defining element of the present times. Their role, however, is not altogether benign, and they have a great capacity to reinforce prejudice, disinformation, and distorted perceptions. Vitriol and anger in the media and the incredibly dynamic cyberspace are potentially dangerous. In Pakistan, too, sound bites, sensationalism, and grandstanding reveal a taste for the extreme. These new media favor those who make their case aggressively and advocate a self-righteous popular view, instead of those inclined to make a serious but understated and, if necessary, bitter and unpopular evaluation. The hope is that with time the media will develop as a force for stability and not just change, while maintaining their watchdog role.

On regional and global issues, Pakistani reactions and commentaries often betray a besieged mentality verging on a persecution complex. In addition to an appetite for outlandish conspiracy theories, the political culture of the country shows a proclivity to look for extraordinary explanations, in particular for failures. Political changes in the country have often been attributed to foreign machinations rather than to mistakes committed at home. The national psyche is partly rooted in the colossal political and military debacle of 1971, when Pakistan was dismembered. There has been no serious attempt to explain that dark chapter in the country's history, a failure that has given furtive encouragement to conspiracy theories.[38] None of the high-profile assassinations in the country's history has ever been resolved, deepening public distrust of the government and of perceived internal and external enemies of the state. Instead of explaining adversity and setbacks in terms of weaknesses or failed or ill-advised policies, commentators, in particular in the print media, often resort to externalizing the blame in a show of patriotic emotionalism. Conspiracy theories have warped Pakistani thinking and popular political culture. Disinformation and propaganda have added to the confusion, reinforcing delusion on the part of the instigators and distorted perceptions among the public.

Politics and media have encouraged a culture of accepting views and even rumors uncritically as long as these fit a subjective perception or popular prejudice. Outrageous and outlandish theories find ready supporters. The tendency has accentuated distortion and imbalance in analysis and thinking, which have impacted the popular worldview especially. In a similar vein, the society shows an increasing tendency to accept dogma and tradition uncritically, especially if peddled in the name of religion. A certain degree of parochial prejudice exists in every society and is often linked with pride in one's distinctiveness. But excessive credulity and an obsession with conspiracy theories in the public discourse stifle the spiritual, intellectual, and physical well-being of the society.

In the more immediate context, doubts about the linkage of Al Qaeda with 9/11 are widely shared among the intelligentsia in Pakistan. Instead, 9/11 is seen as part of a CIA or Mossad conspiracy to create a pretext for the Americans to militarily occupy Afghanistan and Iraq or harm and malign Muslims. Yet, the same protagonists of these theories shy away from condemning the terrorist act itself and its perpetrators, the suicide bombers, who according to these theories acted as instruments of the two Western agencies.

---

38. The only serious effort was the establishment of a commission headed by Justice Hamoodur Rahman with a restricted mandate to "ascertain the facts." The commission's report was completed in October 1974 but never officially released.

Specific to developments in the FATA, there has been confused thinking regarding the source of funds and arms for the Taliban and insurgents in the area. Some analysts point a finger at India and the United States and speak about the long-term objective of destabilizing Pakistan and eliminating its nuclear assets. Every print media story in the West that casts doubts about the safety of these assets and their falling into the wrong hands, or even a lone speculative research paper published in the West redrawing the map of the region, can trigger local reaction providing grist to conspiracy mills. The apparent differences in the Pakistani and U.S. approaches in dealing with militants in Waziristan have further generated speculation and innuendos.

Since the TTP heightened its violent activities before his death, there had been frequent expressions of suspicion in the press that Baitullah Mahsud might be enjoying U.S. or Indian patronage. Even after Baitullah was killed by a U.S. drone attack, an editorial of August 11, 2009, in the widely read Urdu daily *Jang,* while strongly criticizing the failure of intelligence agencies to trace the sources of his funds and weapons, concluded on the note that these agencies must remain alert regarding the schemes of outsiders to damage Pakistan. Again, the curious aspect of such musings has been the absence of denunciation of Baitullah Mahsud and the Pakistani Taliban for acting at the behest of Pakistan's adversaries.

Similarly, speculation persists about suspected sponsorship of the foreign Al Qaeda elements by outside intelligence agencies without placing any responsibility on the local or Afghan Taliban, who were host to these elements. Many see a "foreign hand" behind the violence and suicide bombings and assert that such acts could not be the work of Muslims. They ignore claims of responsibility for numerous such acts by the TTP and other extremist groups and their boastful statement of having hundreds of suicide bombers in reserve. They overlook fatwas by extremist clerics promising paradise to suicide bombers, their families, and their victims, or by *Takfiri* militants who condemn the victims as accomplices of infidels. There is little public or media pressure on the government to disclose findings of investigations, especially the background and affiliations of scores of those arrested for terrorist violence.

A contrary, mirror-image view is also prevalent, though rarely mentioned in print or electronic media. This conspiracy view accuses the Pakistani intelligence of complicity with the Taliban and insurgent elements and an assortment of extremist and militant groups, notwithstanding the army action in Swat and elsewhere and the large casualties that army personnel have suffered. Typically, there is little scrutiny of the premise of such theories and attitudes, and the contrived logic is considered enough for their assumed validity.

A siege mentality is also manifest in aggressive patriotism and narrow nationalism. The sentiment is especially evident among retired midlevel officials, both military and civilian, and religiously inclined middle class citizens, who have imbibed suspicion towards the West, hostility towards India, and pride in a culture of patriotic self-righteousness typical of middle classes in many societies. This mentality induces further stress in an environment of anger, suspicion, dissension, and delusions in which extremist tendencies breed and thrive.

Yet another concern is a regressive tendency Pakistani thinking has shown towards an easy resort to denial. This habit has its roots in the convenient myth of noninterference in Afghanistan's affairs Pakistan maintained during the period of the Afghan Jihad in the 1980s.[39] At that time, however, such a stance elicited understanding from much of the international community. The Soviet intervention was largely seen as a violation of international norms and Pakistan's help to the Afghan resistance as justifiable. In the 1980s, the classic case of denial related to Pakistan's pursuit of its nuclear program as necessitated by the 1974 Indian test. Pakistan came under relentless American pressure to abandon the program until 1979. Then it became convenient for the United States to accept the denial in the interest of cooperation against Soviet military intervention in Afghanistan. In the 1990s, Pakistan found it expedient to maintain denial of its support to the Kashmiri Mujahedin, describing their struggle, which Pakistan regarded as just, to be entirely indigenous.

These were issues of high national policy on which all states adopt positions in conformity with their national interests. However, issues of lesser import such as the presence of Osama or Mullah Omar or cross-border ac-

---

39. A poignant example of this mode of denial was President Zia ul Haq's response to President Reagan in early 1988, when the Geneva negotiations came to a head. Sensing that Zia ul Haq was uncomfortable with the Geneva texts, as these were predicated on commitments of noninterference, Reagan sent his top national security advisor, Frank Carlucci, to Zia to convey that the United States could refuse to be a guarantor and thus scuttle the negotiations and take the blame. Zia responded that the negotiations had gone very far and that the Geneva Accord could be signed, but Pakistan would continue to provide material support to the Afghan Mujahedin. When Zia's response was conveyed to Reagan, he reportedly remarked that Zia would probably continue to lie as he did on (Pakistan's) nuclear program. Finally at Geneva, an arrangement based on positive symmetry stretching the definition of material support to both Afghan sides was agreed to facilitate signature.

tivity by Afghan Taliban from the Pakistan side did not warrant such categorical denials as were initially maintained in official statements. A matter-
of-fact or noncommittal position, taking into account the peculiar condition
of the border regions, could do no damage, politically or diplomatically. Another damaging effect of the attitude is the government's denial of problems
relating to the domestic situation, either by deflecting responsibility or by
refusing to recognize them. When such denials become untenable, they result in loss of credibility, a situation that ought to be avoided. Again it bears
repetition that a state of denial is not peculiar to Pakistan. It is a question of
degree and loss of credibility, to the point where even the denial of fairy
tales becomes suspect.

Pakistani strategic thinking and perspectives are inclined, furthermore, to
construct seductive but realistically questionable doctrines and assumptions.
The previous chapters have discussed the idea of seeking "strategic depth"
in Afghanistan; to this can be added such dubious concepts as "strategic
defiance" and "leveraging negative potential." Incidentally, when the then
army chief first propounded it in early 1990, many in Pakistan perceived Saddam Hussein to be the paragon of "strategic defiance." These are dangerous
concepts when they preoccupy military minds for their glitzy appeal. They
detract from objective analysis in the same way as did the pre-1971 military
doctrines that "the best defense lies in offense" and that "the defense of East
Pakistan lies in West Pakistan," which proved so badly mistaken.

Of lesser import is a familiar political and public insistence on "negotiations with honor," especially in the context of India, as if negotiations can
be thrust on a country without mutual interest. The insistence is often a euphemism for objections to negotiating process *per se.* The lure of the cliché
resonates with Pakistani ideologues, who are fond of describing Pakistan as
"the fortress of Islam" and equate patriotism with the defense of its ideological frontiers. Instead of providing the intended glue for unity and integration, these notions and catchphrases have served to deepen intellectual
confusion in the society.

The debate on identity relates to the Islamic persona of the country that
is germane to the genesis of the Pakistan movement and the concomitant
"two nation" theory and has since been at the heart of the country's political evolution.[40] The issue did not fade away with the separation of East Pak-

---

40. The issue of identity is not the subject of this study. The purpose here is to point
to it as one of the peculiar aspects of national discourse in Pakistan. There have been

istan, which appeared to demonstrate that Islam alone could not be the basis for preserving the new nation state. Some ideologues argue that the "two nation theory" remains the basis of Pakistani ideology. Invoking historical experience, they place Pakistan in a permanent antagonistic juxtaposition to India. Defining identity, even partially, in such terms with reference to another nation state is fundamentally flawed.

Many analysts in Pakistan believe that identity is one of those unsettled issues that are at the heart of problems and of an inner angst in the country. This is an exaggerated view, as the religious militancy, violence, and extremism that pose a grave threat to the country cannot be treated as the product of an identity crisis. Nevertheless, the question of identity has distorted perceptions about governance and the business of the state. To start with, the multiple ethnicities, languages, and local cultures have required a more inclusive approach to refurbish Pakistan's persona, of which Islam is an essential ingredient. Instead of pulling these diverse subidentities together, Zia ul Haq's policy of Islamization injected further divisions into the society. The aggressive advocacy of Islamization and Islamic identity engendered fears of marginalization among the adherents of minority sects and religions.

The pan-Islamic impulse that is part of the identity issue has also blurred Pakistan's role and interests as a state, and the narrow interpretation of its identity has constricted the appreciation of Pakistan's rich history and culture.[41] Within a diverse society such as Pakistan, what generates a strong

---

endless debates on the "two nation" theory, the inevitability or otherwise of the partition of British India, and how this has been among the significant issues in the contention for political space by religious and political parties in Pakistan. From the point of view of a practitioner of politics or diplomacy, however, it is important to take the establishment of Pakistan, like the emergence of so many nation states, as a fact of history and a point of departure for discussing and shaping state affairs for the common benefit and welfare of its people and setting out its external relations, bearing in mind its geography, its varied historical experience, its interest in peace, security, and development, and its aspirations, which must be sensitive to present-day imperatives and compulsions.

41. A personal experience could illustrate the seriousness of this denial of Pakistan's pre-Islamic history. In 1988, during a short tenure as director general for external publicity, the author had proposed the publication of a coffee-table book on Pakistan that, in addition to the country's magnificent landscape, would portray its over six thousand years of rich history as the cradle of the Indus River and Gandhara civilizations. When the proposal was discussed with the well-educated but devout head of the Information Ministry, he objected to the inclusion of the pre-Islamic history. The discussion remained inconclusive. The project was not pursued, because after the death of President Zia the author returned to the Ministry of Foreign Affairs. He revived the idea and completed

bond and cohesion, inspires confidence, and reinforces a sense of collective identity is often achievement, especially in the socioeconomic sector, and a common stake in the preservation and strength of the country.

In the past three decades, Pakistani attitudes have begun to betray a degree of mental reserve toward scientific and material progress, which many among the religious-minded tend to dismiss as an attribute of the West. Since the 1970s, Pakistan's drive towards development and modernity, which had been pronounced in the 1960s, has slowed down and even suffered a regression. The political setback of 1971 and the subsequent nationalization of the economy and educational institutions in 1973 were shocks that disrupted the momentum for development but yet did not impact the mind-set towards progress and modernization. The rise of religiosity in the urban population, the jihad rhetoric, and growth of madrassas with Saudi Salafi influences has encouraged the development of an antimodernity streak in popular thinking, even though no disciple of Maududi or any other established religious school of thought ever argued against scientific teaching and development.

There have been subtle indicators, however. With the increased influence of Jamat e Islami in educational institutions in the 1980s, science teachers were asked to explain all causation as acts of God, before stating whatever theory science had to offer. Under Zia, religious orientation became a factor for advancement in addition to professional qualification. In discussions, an emphasis on science and development was at times countered with the argument, especially by adherents of the Tableeghi Jamat, that in the sciences Muslims would never be able to compete with the West; where they could forge ahead of the West was in the arena of religious ethics and morality. The erosion of professionalism in Pakistan has been an unintended consequence of rising religiosity, despite the belief of Jamat e Islami and its founder in the value of professionalism and work ethics.

In the 1960s and early 1970s, Pakistanis had a fairly good reputation as competent professionals among the developing countries. The deterioration started with the nationalization of the economy and the tampering with the

---

the book when he headed the ministry from 2005 to 2008. This episode illustrates an ideological effort that gained momentum under Zia to obscure the cultural diversity and rich history of the country under the construct of an identity based on Islam, the "two nation" theory, and a negative, albeit less pronounced, assertion of antipathy towards "Hindu India."

educational system under Zulfikar Ali Bhutto.[42] Since then, the political and religious elite has shown little comprehension of the critical importance of scientific education and professionalism in national development and the rigor these demand for maintaining quality and standards.[43] Making matters worse, the Gulf oil boom drew hundreds of thousands of skilled and unskilled Pakistani laborers to the region. This phenomenon impacted Pakistan's value system, setting a trend for seeking employment in the Gulf and degrading the pursuit of professional excellence in Pakistan, which did not bring comparable monetary reward. The trend was accelerated in the society with the acceptance of the madrassa system, neglect of the education sector, and reduced emphasis on modern scientific learning.

A low level of scientific education and professional standards generally afflicts, in varying degrees, all Muslim societies, which remain largely the consumers and not the producers of the fruits of technology and modern creativity. The prosperity boom in the Gulf region instilled a false sense[44] of development, power, and modernization. When exposed, as in the Arab experience with Israel or in the Gulf Wars, it produced a mixed reaction of resentment against the West and dependence on its support. Paradoxically, the oil earnings brought prosperity to many Muslim countries; but they did not correspondingly engender scientific education, a progressive outlook, or professional ethics and habits. This is one reason for their backwardness in industrial and technological development in comparison with other major societies.

42. Some educationists argue that the setback to the educational system began under the Ayub government in the early 1960s, when the entire secondary education system was centralized and placed under provincial control, removing district and local oversight and management. This led to a deterioration of standards, as the provincial center was far removed from scores of thousands of schools, especially those located in remote districts. Nationalization by the Bhutto government produced a setback to educational standards at the college and university level, particularly because of the increased politicization of these institutions as a consequence of nationalization.

43. The Pakistani governmental structure normally has separate portfolios for education and for science and technology. Political governments often assigned low priority to these ministries, in particular the latter. At times, the ministries were headed by second-ranking politicians with no experience in the area. The author can recall two occasions when the ministers in charge of science and technology were heard commenting that they had accepted the portfolio only as an ad hoc stopgap arrangement and were waiting for a more meaningful ministry.

44. This false sense in the power of oil wealth was reflected in the claim made in remarks to the author by Gulf country diplomats in the 1980s that Saudi Arabia had emerged as the third superpower beside the United States and the Soviet Union.

Pakistan had a comparatively better start, which accelerated in the 1960s, when the country could be counted as the most technologically advanced within the Islamic world. Today, it has fallen behind Turkey, Iran, Malaysia, and Egypt in industrial growth. These countries are now placing serious emphasis on scientific and technological education. However the oil-rich Gulf countries, including Saudi Arabia, have only established a few showcase technical institutions, such as the King Abdullah University in Jeddah with barely one thousand students, and have yet to promote a scientific culture.[45]

The attitudinal changes and growing religiosity in the Pakistani urban middle class, bureaucracies, and business community have led to loss of the scientific outlook so necessary for contemporary living within expanding urbanization. There is increasing resort to an ad hoc approach, especially in government planning, a trend aggravated over the years by political instability. The loss is also reflected in day-to-day life, from controversy and commotion over sighting of the new moon for celebrating the Eid festival to the rejection of population control, with the argument that "God has endowed every human with two hands to work and one mouth to feed." The resulting failure of population planning has given rise to unmanageable population growth and urban sprawl that are turning into ecological disasters.

Another facet of the same mental habit is the lessening inclination to scrutinize facts or to adopt a measured tone in discussion and debate. This is highly pronounced in the media in general and the Urdu press in particular. The op-ed pages of the Urdu press only sparingly focus on technical subjects, and even these are hardly ever examined on their merit to offer a view that is without exaggeration or political and ideological spin. Today, poetic flourish and passionate argument generally pass for good writing in the Urdu press, a trend far removed from the simple logical prose of such greats as Syed Ahmed Khan or Maududi or the measured writing style of Pakistan's early decades.

The support for the madrassa system as charity institutions regardless of the nature and quality of education is yet another example of misplaced religiosity replacing sensitivity to common sense and the need for proper

---

45. In 1997, in Brussels, during a discussion on the need for the promotion of science and technology, Saudi ambassador Nasser Alassaf remarked to the author that in Saudi Arabia the religious sheikhs (Ulema) exhort the people that their only obligation is to pray and thank God because He had blessed them with something that foreigners take away and in return bring them (the Saudis) all kinds of "gifts."

planning. Pakistanis have a tradition of community service and philan-thropy. Much of the effort goes into charity works, including hospitals, maintenance and building of mosques and madrassas, and orphanages, which also offer religious education. In addition, the financially well-to-do families and politicians have a competition for performing *Umras* (praying at the holy Ka'aba) for well-being and forgiveness. Only a little of private donations goes for creating scientific and research institutions.

The Muslim reaction to the dominant Western culture in South Asia has found a reflection in the confusion and antipathy surrounding contemporary ideas of secularism, modernization, and liberalism. In addition to the asso-ciation of these ideas with the colonial experience, religiously minded scholars often debated them to prove the superiority of Islamic precepts, es-pecially in regard to protection of individual and collective rights.

The most important influence, once again, is the genius of Maulana Maududi. In Urdu he popularized the translation of "secularism" as *La Diniyat,* "anti-religion creed" or "negating religion." This interpretation spawned a natural prejudice against the concept in popular view. In Arabic, because a number of Arab countries had adopted secular philosophy in their political systems, the translation is *Alamaniyat,* "system based on worldly knowledge or reason."[46]

"Modernization" in Urdu has been popularized as a synonym for West-ernization, once again evoking an inherent bias that is also mixed up with the colonial experience.[47] To highlight the resulting confusion over this im-portant contemporary phrase, the example of the distinction made in the Chi-nese language would suffice. In Chinese, there are two different words for modernization and Westernization, namely, *Xiendai Kanfa* and *Xifang Kanfa* respectively. *Kanfa* is used for "outlook, orientation, or method"; *Xiendai* means "contemporary or of the present," and *Xifang* means "of the West." Such clarity has been denied to the Pakistani mind on concepts so germane to progress and development in present times. The resulting confusion has

---

46. Dr. Khalid Masud, chairman of the Pakistan Council on Islamic Ideology, men-tioned to the author that the root of *Alamaniyat* is *Alam,* or the world; but the author has also come across a reference by Ali A. Alawai in *The Crisis of Islamic Civilization* (New Haven, Conn.: Yale University Press, 2009), 91, suggesting *Ilmaniyya* as the Arabic equivalent of secularism, with *Ilm,* or knowledge, as the root, a far cry from *La Diniyat.* Some Saudi Salafi and Egyptian Ikhwan scholars use *La Diniyat,* taken from Maulana Maududi.

47. Masud et al., *Islam and Modernity,* 241.

been a disservice done to the Pakistani society by intellectuals who claim to be the custodians of the country's ideological persona and Islamic culture and traditions. Young Pakistani minds have to contend with these troublesome ambiguities as they try to understand the world around them.

"Liberalism" is yet another much maligned term in the vernacular sentiment and is translated as *Azad Khayal,* which is close to "free thinker (on religion and morality)" or a "libertine" in one connotation. Since Urdu is an assimilative language, most of these concepts are adopted in their phonetics and used in that fashion in print media and literature; but the commonly attributed meaning is loaded and unsavory in popular perception. The phrase has fallen prey to the severely polarized debate in the country about the "war on terror." Some popular Urdu commentators describe the critics of orthodoxy and the advocates for liberal (Western) values and rights as "liberal fascists," an oxymoron that exemplifies Pakistan's polemical diatribe.

Over the years Pakistani thinking has become susceptible to xenophobic tendencies, though with contradictory undercurrents. Pakistanis have been generally known for their extroverted temperament, as evident in the large expatriate community that numbers well over six million, including large communities in the West. Pakistan generally sought close relations with the West, and large numbers of Pakistanis continue to travel and seek businesses and education in the West. Nonetheless, there has long been a latent but circumspect anti-West sentiment, in part a throwback to the past colonial experience. Much of the anti-West feeling today is directed against the United States, which suggests the political underpinnings of the trend. Anti-Americanism has seen a sharp increase since the early 1990s, when Pakistan came under U.S. sanctions, discussed later in this chapter.

The rise of fundamentalist and obscurantist tendencies in Pakistani society contributed to anti-West sentiment. It also stoked old anti-West civilizational prejudices, a mirror image of Islamophobic thinking evident among far-right elements in the West following 9/11. The 1990s also saw a growing alienation among the expatriate Muslim communities in Europe, including the large Pakistani community in the United Kingdom, because of the lack of integration and employment opportunities. Since these communities maintained strong links with the home country, the growing conservative religious influences there were readily transferred to expatriate Pakistanis, whose disaffection and inability to integrate locally served somewhat to intensify the anti-West sentiment.

Common anti-West undertones in individual attitudes have caused a certain diffidence, loss of confidence, and fear of exposure to Western cultural influences. The midlevel Pakistani businesses have lost the aggressive competitiveness that is a hallmark of international trade. As compared to the earlier generation, Pakistani students on Western campuses today show a reserve and tendency to withdraw into close circles of compatriots; and the same behavior has become pronounced in Pakistani expatriate communities living in Europe and North America.

A poignant example of the contradictory undercurrents of Pakistani anti-West sentiment has been the vociferous Pakistani reaction to Samuel P. Huntington's hypothesis about the clash of civilizations. In its baldest interpretation, notwithstanding its nuances and merit, the hypothesis posited that the "authoritarian" Islamic and Sinic (Confucian) civilizations were on an inexorable collision course with "democratic" Western civilization and culture. Huntington's concept was based on the premise that with the demise of communist ideology, the new fault lines for a global confrontation ran along cultural lines. Though the thesis presaged the apparent post–9/11 resurfacing of dormant cultural and religious prejudices, it was widely commented upon and rejected by an array of Pakistani intellectuals and academics, including those who reveled in an essentially anti-West worldview that blamed the West for every mischief on the planet. Yet, they would not agree with Huntington and argue in favor of harmony between the West and Islam.

The factors identified above have contributed to and are symptomatic of the deepening intellectual crisis and confusion at the national level reflected in the current domestic debate on Talibanization. More importantly, this conflicted and diffuse debate limits the society's capacity to resist and overcome the challenge that has to be met at the cerebral and ideological level, as well as through counterinsurgency measures. The condoning of the Taliban and Al Qaeda excesses and violence as simply a consequence of the U.S. and foreign military presence in Afghanistan is glaring evidence of the intellectual confusion that pervades the public debate. There have been frequent instances in the public discourse of indifference to the antiquated ways of the Taliban and complacency towards their brutal methods of terrorizing the population, blowing up girls' schools and video shops, and slaughtering men in public squares. Public sentiment did undergo a change following the Taliban advance beyond Swat, when a transformed public opinion made strong army action possible. But a return to nebulous thinking on the issue or persistence in efforts to externalize the blame for the situation would be a relapse into a state of denial—an escape from realism in facing a threat that is grave and destabilizing.

The Growth of Anti-Americanism

Anti-Americanism is a worldwide phenomenon, prompted by diverse impulses and shaped by local circumstances and historical experience. The sentiment has undergone changes and has been ameliorated considerably in today's China and India, as compared to the Cold War days. In both societies, the earlier tendency to externalize their problems and blame the United States for many of their difficulties has greatly diminished. Through development, education, and attuning themselves to the demands of globalization, these two large nations show confidence in their dealings with the United States and the West.

Broadly, three influences have affected anti-Americanism in Pakistan over the years. In the early days, the left-leaning political groups, inspired by Marxist ideology and Moscow, resolutely opposed Pakistan's alliance with the United States. Left-of-center politicians believed that the Americans instigated Zia ul Haq's military coup against Zulfikar Ali Bhutto, allegedly because they were upset by Bhutto's commitment to pursue Pakistan's nuclear option. The second influence on opinion developed with the 1979 Khomeini revolution in Iran, which made a deep impact in particular on Pakistan's large and intellectually vibrant Shia community. Many admired Iran for its "independence and defiance" of the United States, ignoring that without Iran's oil and with its own troubles in the region, Pakistan could ill afford such luxury in its foreign relations. Pakistan has to exercise due care when its interests require opposing U.S. positions. The third and perhaps most potent factor in the present context has been the Sunni Islamic fundamentalist hostility towards the United States, exacerbated by the U.S. military interventions in Afghanistan and Iraq.[48] Reinforcing this hostility is the vexed Pushtun sentiment in Pakistan, which holds the U.S. intervention responsible for the Tajik control of Kabul and the diminution if not elimination of Pushtun influence in the Afghan capital.

48. Stephen P. Cohen, *The Idea of Pakistan* (Washington: Brookings Institution Press, 2004), 175, argues, "Most of the Islamist political and revolutionary groups are anti-American, not only because of Washington's support for Israel, but because of its support for successive moderate Pakistani governments over the years, including those dominated by the army."

Anti-Western sentiment has roots in the colonial experience and the role the British played at the time of partition. Regardless of merit, in popular perception, the Kashmir dispute is synonymous with British injustice to Pakistan and to Kashmiri Muslims. The other parallel that subsists in the Pakistani mind is the West's role in the creation of Israel in the Palestinian Mandate, causing anguish equally to Islamic revivalist thinkers and to pro-West reformers and elite. The Palestinian issue continues to agitate Muslims everywhere. The popular political culture of Muslims in South Asia, as reflected in the *Khilafat* movement, the thinking of conservative Ulema, the writings of Maulana Maududi, and even the powerful poetry of Allama Iqbal, carried a distinctive anti-West political undertone.

In the recent context of the 1980s Afghan Jihad, the hard-line Mujahedin groups entertained suspicions about possible U.S. designs in support of the "moderate" groups or in favor of King Zahir Shah. Zia ul Haq's plane crash, which was generally believed to be the result of sabotage, came to be attributed by Islamist groups to the CIA, supposedly to foil Zia's plans for Mujahedin victory in Afghanistan and the spread of the Islamic insurgency to Central Asia. They viewed U.S.–Western support for the 1990 coup in Algeria that thwarted the anticipated landslide victory of the FIS, an Islamist political party, as a sign of determined U.S.–Western opposition to the ascendancy of Islamic politics or the enforcement of an Islamic system, as espoused by the Islamist groups.

Religious political parties contributed to the anti-American and anti-Western sentiment as they began to perceive, with some justification, that the West was the major obstacle to their political ascent. This view was reinforced by U.S.–Western antipathy towards Hamas in Palestine and, importantly in the context of Pakistan, towards jihadist groups operating in Kashmir. The United States in particular opposed Pakistan's backing of the Kashmiri militants and threatened to characterize it as supporting terrorism. The first Gulf War and the U.S. military presence in Saudi Arabia shaped Al Qaeda, which reflected the deep hostility that had already infused the radical Islamist and jihadist movements, only to be reinforced by the U.S. military interventions in Afghanistan and Iraq.

One segment of opinion viscerally portrayed the United States as the villain of the piece in the region. The search for demons in the conspiracy-prone Pakistani society invariably ended up in Washington. More broadly, however, anti-American public sentiment in Pakistan owed in good measure to the vicissitudes of the Pakistan-U.S. relationship over the decades and a feeling of being jilted that the Pakistani establishment had commonly nursed. In the early years, Pakistan had sought to be part of U.S. alliances to augment its security and obtain a settlement of Kashmir. Failure to leverage the alliances to put pressure on India for a settlement and the U.S. overtures to India in the wake of the Sino-Indian tensions frustrated Pakistani policymakers. Somewhat naïvely, Pakistani policymakers had tried to persuade a superpower to their point of view instead of understanding its interests and disposition in the region. On the other hand, when Pakistan readjusted its policy by opening to China, it caused chagrin in Washington. The experience of the 1965 conflict with India built the popular perception that the United States not only did little to rectify the historic injustice on Kashmir but also did not stand by the side of its ally at a critical juncture.

Particularly hurtful was the egregious application of the 1990 Pressler Amendment immediately after the Soviet withdrawal from Afghanistan. Pakistanis viewed as unjustified and excessively hostile towards an erstwhile ally the U.S. refusal to return the funds Pakistan had already paid for an F-16 aircraft, whose delivery was halted, and U.S. confiscation of military equipment that had been sent for retrofitting and repairs. This grievance was reinforced by the wide public perception that the United States had acquiesced in the 1974 Indian nuclear test while it relentlessly opposed the subsequent Pakistani nuclear program in pursuit of its security. Pakistanis see the U.S.-India nuclear deal of 2008 as discriminatory, and indeed a similar access to civilian nuclear technology under safeguards facilitated by the United States could help in good measure to reduce anti-Americanism in Pakistan.

The sharp downturns experienced in Pakistani-U.S. relations as a result of sanctions bruised the Pakistani psyche at both government and public levels. In contrast, especially since the 1990s, the Pakistani establishment and intelligentsia have watched with a certain unease the growing strategic convergence in U.S.-India relations, with India assuming the status of a "natural ally" in the region. This qualitative change in U.S.-India relations owes partly to the transformed global situation and partly to the strong linkages between democratic institutions and people-to-people contacts forged between the two countries over the years. Indians are among the strongest expatriate communities in the United States, with growing influence in academia, financial institutions, the corporate sector, and politics. Pakistan had an opportunity to take advantage of its special relationship in the 1950s and '60s and again in the 1980s, but it had few measures aimed at the long-term development of relations. For example, Pakistani governments made no plans to send students on a large scale, as the Indians and the Chinese have done, nor did they pay attention to the value of expatriate communities in contemporary global political and economic interaction. Pakistani governments have rarely demonstrated such foresight or vision.

There is a common perception that the United States interferes in and controls Pakistani politics. This impression partly reflects the lack of public confidence in political leaders and partly the malice that is rife in Pakistani politics. Over the years, instead of admitting their mistakes, political leaders have blamed their failure and downfall on the machinations of a "foreign hand," a euphemism for the United States. Even seemingly pro-U.S. leaders, unsure of their domestic political support, have been generally nagged by the suspicion that the United States could engineer their downfall. The intrusive activist tradition of U.S. diplomacy of trying to keep in touch with the entirety of a country's political spectrum and myths about CIA machinations feed doubts on the part of these leaders.

At the same time, there have been several instances of political leaders allowing U.S. and other foreign diplomats to become involved with domestic politics. The latest example was the involvement of U.S. and British officials in efforts to promote an understanding between Musharraf and Benazir Bhutto in 2007. In hindsight, this made little material difference on the ground. The course of events was determined by domestic political realities, including the desire of the two leaders to reach an understanding to advance their own political interests. Domestic changes in Pakistan, contrary to the popular view, owed to the leadership's decisions, and often mistakes, rather than conspiracies hatched in any foreign capitals.

Generally, the access to Pakistani political leadership that foreign diplomats and visiting officials and representatives have enjoyed is beyond all norms of diplomatic propriety or governmental etiquette[49] and in its optics verges on a solicitous behavior that is unwarranted and yields no political dividend. WikiLeaks revelations do not bring to light any compromises on vital policies by Pakistani leaders but only instances of wholly unnecessary and gratuitous frankness on their part, apparently in an effort to build trust with American officials. Besides diminishing these

---

49. The first time a foreign diplomat or official played a high-profile mediatory role in Pakistan's domestic politics occurred in 1977, during the last days of Prime Minister Zulfikar Ali Bhutto. Bhutto encouraged Saudi ambassador Riyad Al Khatib to facilitate an understanding with the Pakistan National Alliance (PNA), a coalition of the political opposition that had joined hands to launch a countrywide protest movement.

leaders in the public eye, the revelations could serve to strengthen the pervasive but mistaken popular view of American ability to influence Pakistani politics.

Many Pakistanis believe that the United States has always sided with military regimes in Pakistan. The fact is that Pakistan's relations with the United States have been episodic, and interests often coincided when military regimes governed Pakistan for more than half the time since its inception. U.S. administrations were cool towards both the Zia and Musharraf regimes in their early years, before unexpected and momentous developments obliged the United States to reach out to Pakistan for partnership.

The political opposition in Pakistan is in the habit of criticizing the government for bending under U.S. pressure, to discredit it by exploiting anti-American public sentiment. However, a good part of the criticism is mere political posturing and populist rhetoric. The perception that Pakistani policies are "designed" in Washington is essentially polemical. It is belied by major policy decisions taken at critical times by various Pakistani governments in open disagreement with the United States. A country of Pakistan's size and complexity is essentially governed by its internal dynamics, within the constraints of international and regional politics.

Failure of Governance: The Leadership and Institutional Crisis

A discussion of Pakistan's contemporary difficulties and its turbulent history requires reference to the weakness of its institutions of governance, at times graphically described as the leadership and institutional crisis. This chapter has attempted to throw light on the intellectual confusion, lack of clarity in national priorities and vision, and absence of broad consensus on Pakistan's role as a state in the life of its people and in the world. The ambiguities prevalent in the national thinking and the failure to build a stable political system have impeded socioeconomic development and the shaping of a progressive outlook in the society. Effective leadership, which is inseparable from strong political institutions, is also an essential ingredient for national motivation, work ethic, and morale. Failures of leadership have thus taken a corresponding toll on Pakistani society. Here follows a brief examination of the weak political base Pakistan inherited, its political and economic development, and arbitrary experimentation over the years with the country's constitution, administration, and economy.

Political and Constitutional Vicissitudes

The problems of leadership and politics in Pakistan can be traced back to the predicament of the political party that led the Pakistan movement and that was responsible after the creation of the new state for nation-building and development. In India, the Congress Party had a clear objective of pursuing self-rule and independence and thus developed both a concept and a strategy of post-independence India. The inner workings of the Congress Party had matured over time. In contrast, the Muslim League was for the most part pursuing protection of the interests of the Muslim minority in India within the post-independence framework. The concept of Pakistan came late; and until the state emerged on the map, even its physical features were unclear.

The League was led by the towering personality of Muhammad Ali Jinnah, who did reflect on the nature of the new state in his famous address to the Constituent Assembly on August 11, 1947; but he was unable to set the direction for the new state, as he was already debilitated by age and ailment and barely lived for one year after independence. No other leader in the party could match his authority. With the assassination of Pakistan's first prime minister, Liaqat Ali Khan, in October 1951, the League lost another figure of influence and authority, aggravating the problem of effective leadership in the early years for the new state, which had yet to agree on a constitution. The Muslim League failed to develop a strong political culture that trained its leadership and cadres, and it splintered within a decade of independence. The significant successor political parties developed since the late 1960s, whatever their agendas and support base, have been largely personality or family oriented. An important exception is Jamat e Islami, which adheres to a disciplined, egalitarian political culture and practice within the party as set by its founder.

With the decline of the Muslim League, governance in the new state suffered. Pakistan's political landscape was further complicated by its anomalous geographical configuration, comprising two culturally and politically dissimilar and disparate wings separated by a thousand miles of hostile India. The leadership void created by the League's failure was filled by opportunistic bureaucrats and diminutive political parties led by feudal, tribal, and parochial interests in the West and nationalists and ideologically left-leaning political parties in the East. By 1958, the internal squabbling created room for long-serving army chief General Ayub Khan to step in. By his own account, he had watched with anxiety the disarray and infighting among incompetent politicians.

Ayub abrogated the 1956 Parliament-based constitution and introduced, under the 1962 constitution he promulgated, a partyless system of "basic democracy," a presidential form of government based on indirect election and a Parliament with a largely legislative role. Despite his firm control, in the 1964 elections held under the new constitution he faced a tough challenge from Fatima Jinnah, the sister of the founding father of Pakistan. She was supported by most of the political parties that existed but could not participate as parties in the election. The 1964 election underscored the Pakistani political culture's latent disposition towards a multiparty dispensation, which survives as a legacy of the colonial experience in South Asia, reinforced by its apparent success in India.

Ayub's "basic democracy" experiment died with his exit in 1969, because he himself chose to hand over power to the military chief instead of to the speaker of the national assembly as the 1962 constitution required. Whether the system introduced by this constitution would have survived in a geographically contiguous Pakistan, as it emerged after 1971, is moot. The demise of "basic democracy" was another example of failure to build political institutions in Pakistan following abrogation of the 1956 constitution and the political shenanigans earlier in the 1950s.

Yahya Khan's interregnum was marked by the direct, party-based elections of 1970 and the East-West political divide, made acute by economic disparities, which finally split the country in two—a tragedy, a political failure, and a military defeat that is etched in the Pakistani psyche. The arrangement of the two geographically distant wings was politically unworkable within the framework of a federation; yet the parting, with or without formal linkages, could have materialized through an act of political realism and prudence. But that would have required a political leadership of wisdom and stature.

Zulfikar Ali Bhutto took over in circumstances of a deep crisis resulting from the trauma of Pakistan's breakup. He faced the grave challenge of restoring the morale of a defeated nation and had a momentous opportunity to lead the people, who had rallied around him as never before around any leader since the days of the Pakistan movement. He overcame the challenge, but squandered the opportunity. A brilliant, charismatic leader with fatal contradictions, he rallied the political parties and contributed to the consensus constitution of 1973, accepting a parliamentary form of government when his own temperament was inclined to a presidential system.[50] He skillfully negotiated the return of Pakistani prisoners of war and astutely handled diplomatic recognition of Bangladesh, which touched raw nerves in the dismembered Pakistan.

On the other hand, he left unfulfilled the progressive agenda and secular outlook that he eloquently professed. Many of his long-standing political companions, who espoused leftist idealism, broke away from him in dismay. Despite his professions of "Islamic socialism" and commitment to democracy, in his style of governance Bhutto was an authoritarian leader, with a feudal streak that became increasingly pronounced in the later days of his rule. He bent to religious pressures on the Qadiani/Ahmadiyya issue and later unsuccessfully tried to assuage the religious constituency when faced with political agitation over the controversial elections in 1977 that led to his overthrow by Zia ul Haq in a military coup in July the same year.

Lacking legitimacy, President Zia ul Haq depended on the military and religious orthodoxy for his political survival and strength. The Soviet intervention in Afghanistan was an unexpected development that bestowed international prominence on him and on Pakistan. Zia focused his politics on Islamization and the Afghanistan Jihad. Like Ayub Khan, Zia also experimented with the country's political system of the country. Every military ruler in Pakistan realized that he could not rule with martial law indefinitely and that the country had to return to some form of civilian democratic rule. The elections Zia had promised to hold within ninety days of the coup were finally held on a nonparty basis eight years later, in 1985, to constitute a Majlis e Shura (parliament) and choose a prime minister.

The restored 1973 constitution was modified, through the Eighth Amendment, to give the president the power to dismiss the parliament and the prime minister. Zia's handpicked prime minister, Muhammad Khan Junejo, however, soon started asserting his authority as the chief executive, setting a precedent for an uneasy diarchy at the top. He demanded and secured the restoration and functioning of the parties, which led to the return of Benazir Bhutto, Zulfikar Ali Bhutto's daughter, in late 1986. In May 1988, Zia dismissed the Majlis e Shura and Junejo in response to strong demand for a parliamentary inquiry into the explosion in the Ojeri camp, located in the midst of the twin cities of Rawalpindi and Islamabad. The inquiry was

---

50. Following the debacle of 1971, when army generals decided to hand over power to Zulfikar Ali Bhutto, the winner of 1970 elections in West Pakistan, he assumed for himself the title of Chief Martial Law Administrator and President of the country.

bound to implicate the generals responsible for the camp for negligence or ineptitude.

By dismissing Junejo and the Shura, Zia ul Haq destroyed the system he had created, bringing to an end another experiment in Pakistan's tumultuous political life. Three months later, Zia died in the mysterious Bhawalpur incident. Apart from Islamization and jihad, his political legacy survived in the shape of the Eighth Amendment to the 1973 constitution, which continued to remain a controversial and destabilizing element instead of striking a balance in the powers of the prime minister and the president. Zia's successor, Ghulam Ishaq Khan, held party-based elections in November 1988, once again resurrecting Pakistan's politics with the return of the People's Party, this time headed by Benazir Bhutto.

Benazir's two terms in office as prime minister, interspersed by her rival Nawaz Sharif's two terms in the same position, represent a period of political instability and drift. The rivalry reflected the divide that had set into Pakistani politics as a consequence of Zia's hanging of Zulfikar Ali Bhutto, following a highly controversial court trial and verdict, an event that remains seared in Pakistani politics, creating deep division. The instability also had much to do with misrule and corruption. The army chiefs repeatedly interceded between the president and the prime minister whenever the politicians tied themselves in knots. Generally, however, the army was content with its share in the budget and its grip on issues of importance to it, in particular the policies related to Kashmir and Afghanistan.

The 1990s witnessed frequent changes of government, each lasting barely three years, leaving them largely dysfunctional and incapable of anticipating, planning for, and addressing the emerging challenges of Pakistan's getting embroiled in jihadi dynamic and rising religious militancy. The general weakening of the government also created space for radical Islamist organizations to expand their influence. By engaging in welfare work and managing charities, these organizations gained approbation in an environment with a failing education system, widespread illiteracy, increasing poverty, uncontrolled population growth, and intense ideological rhetoric. The two democratic leaders of the 1990s simply could not grasp the challenges and address them by rising above their mutual distrust and political infighting.

The decade of democratic but politically chaotic interregnum ended with Musharraf's coup in October 1999. His eight-year rule left a mixed legacy and coincided with a period when the previous two decades' policy of support to the jihadi groups came to haunt Pakistan, especially in the wake of

9/11. Like Pakistan's earlier military rulers, Musharraf was bedeviled by the issue of legitimacy. To keep his hold on power, which also relied essentially on the army's support, he had to tamper with the constitution and reconstitute the political dispensation. The Supreme Court gave him three years' reprieve before he was required to hold elections. When the 2002 elections were held, the heads of the two major parties, Benazir and Nawaz Sharif, were in exile.

The 2002 elections were unique in that, for the first time, religious parties, which had merged in a coalition, Muthaheda Majlis e Amal (MMA), did well, enabling them to form governments in the two provinces bordering Afghanistan. At the federal level, a ruling coalition was forged together with elements that split away from the PPP and Nawaz Sharif's Muslim League. As part of a political deal, the new ruling coalition and MMA agreed to amend the constitution (Seventeenth Amendment) to allow Musharraf to hold the offices of both president and army chief of staff and provided for the restitution of the president's power to dismiss the Parliament. The amendment also barred any individual from holding the office of prime minister for more than two times, an obvious move to disqualify Benazir and Nawaz from holding the post again. Later, MMA, in particular Jamat e Islami, opposed Musharraf for his policy on the "war on terror" and his continuing to hold the two offices.

Musharraf espoused a liberal view of Islam and emphasized development and moderation in his speeches. But, as with his dealings with the religious parties, he found it expedient to overlook official encouragement of the jihadi groups, until he was obliged to reverse the policy after 9/11. In his first three years, he initiated a forward-looking reform process to empower women and minorities.[51] His later progressive policy initiatives included a reform program to counter extremism and reorient madrassas. However, the challenge of religious militancy and the tenacity of the orthodoxy proved too strong for meaningful success.

Since the days of Zia ul Haq, Pakistani society has increasingly embraced religious conservatism. In Pakistan, religious conservatism and secular thinking have more cultural than class underpinnings. Religious conservatism cuts across all classes, whereas secular thinking is confined to educated

---

51. Under the Seventeenth Amendment, women were allocated sixty reserved seats in the Parliament. Also, the joint electorate system, along with reserved seats for minorities, was reintroduced to discontinue the separate electorates for the minorities. At the grassroots level, one-third representation was assured for women in local bodies.

middle and upper middle classes in urban centers. Religious militancy and Talibanization are mostly rooted in the poor strata of the population.

Musharraf's nemesis came in the shape of an unexpected judicial crisis, beginning in March 2007 when he dismissed the country's chief justice, Iftikhar Muhammad Chaudry, on the basis of a government "reference" listing corruption charges. The underlying motivation was his government's unease with the judicial activism the chief justice had initiated and Musharraf's own overweening interest in securing without legal wrangles his election as president for a third time, scheduled for the end of the year. Political parties took advantage of the hamhanded treatment of the chief justice, which sparked countrywide protests by lawyers and the civil society, sustained by animated media that had turned hostile to the government. By the middle of 2007, the crisis had begun to unravel the Musharraf government, which was further shaken by the Lal Masjid episode. The resulting political turmoil once again left Pakistan mired in weak governance and economic doldrums against a backdrop of rising insurgency and religious militancy.

The February 2008 elections resulted in the return of the two major parties, the PPP and the Nawaz Muslim League, to the top, giving rise to the hope that this time they would cooperate in addressing the enormous challenges facing the country. The party leaders were expected to have learned the hard lesson that their past misfortunes were mainly caused by infighting and misrule. However, after a brief honeymoon, political tensions emerged over the issue of restoration of the chief justice, the fate of the National Reconciliation Order (NRO) negotiated between Musharraf and Benazir Bhutto before her assassination, and the powers of the president under the controversial Seventeenth Amendment. These powers were now concentrated in the hands of Asif Ali Zardari, the widower of the slain PPP leader, who assumed leadership of the party and, through political maneuver, ousted Musharraf and got elected to the top position in the country.

Nawaz Sharif opposed the Seventeenth Amendment and the NRO as contrary to the Charter of Democracy that he and Benazir Bhutto had signed to launch a joint movement aimed at curtailing the president's powers and restoring parliamentary democracy consistent with the 1973 constitution. Once again, the two parties fell into discord, impairing public confidence in the political leadership. On its part, the PPP government failed to build credibility and has been tainted by corruption.[52] Its rule may prove to be yet an-

---

52. According to the 2010 Transparency International Report, Pakistan had slipped six positions, as compared to 2009, to the forty-second most corrupt country. An egre-

other uneasy interlude of continuing political instability in Pakistan, although there is broad public sentiment that the restored democratic system must be allowed to settle down and not be derailed for any reason.

The balance of power between the offices of the president and the prime minister formed the focus of the major changes in the 1973 constitution sought by Zia and then Musharraf through the Eighth and Seventeenth amendments. They wanted to ensure continuation of their position and authority, while making a transition to parliamentary democracy, and were not motivated by desire to reform the system or enhance the representational quality of governance, or by a genuine need for balancing authority or powers flowing from the constitution. Essentially, these amendments were prompted by specific and narrow political interests. Zia's introduction of the Islamization provisions, even though a category apart, had similar motivation. The Eighteenth Amendment, adopted in April 2010, has largely restored the parliamentary character of the 1973 constitution; but it retains the religious aspects of the earlier amendments and discards modifications aimed at injecting democratic procedures within the political parties. This latest amendment generated controversy in the media. Though the amendment by itself is no guarantee of political stabilization, many politicians celebrated it, nonetheless, as an achievement of consensus-based polity.

Repeated suspensions of the constitution and long periods of military rule have had an unintended but sinister consequence in the unsettled relations between the center and the provinces. Provincial grievances over time have assumed particular gravity in Baluchistan. The feeling of deprivation and alienation, which could have been ameliorated through an inclusive democratic polity ensuring participation of local politicians and tribal chiefs, could not be assuaged by the well-meaning but halting efforts of military leaders aimed at development and reform in the province. Baluch nationalist sentiment and dissidence have become violent and endemic, adding to the country's woes.

Pakistan's turbulent political history over six decades is a consequence not only of constitutional wrangling but also of the failure of leadership, an inability to rise above narrow interests, and the ambition to pursue and monopolize political power. This malaise lies at the heart of the dysfunction and weakness of the institutions of governance and policy. One manifestation of this dysfunction is the friction and disequilibrium between institu-

---

gious form of corruption noted was the absence of a tax culture, particularly the wealthy ruling classes' dismal record, with virtually no contribution to the national exchequer.

tions, with each institution trying to overstep its jurisdiction. In addition, over the years, incompetence, corruption, and mismanagement have seriously undermined public confidence in the government's ability to bring about improvement and reform. For this dismal predicament, considerable responsibility rests with the political leadership.

Most of the public representatives and leaders who filled the parliament chambers or headed ministries and government institutions remain largely the creatures of local politics, displaying considerable cunning but bereft of vision and understanding of contemporary issues of governance and development. They are people mired in the politics of personal or party interests. Pakistani politics is by and large short on institutional or individual foresight, on gravitas, and on capacity to grasp issues and implement solutions. The breakdown in governance has been glaringly evident in the deteriorating security environment, provincial discontent and discord, slow economic development, and neglect of the social and education sectors. This sorry state of governance also facilitated the growth of extremism and militancy in the society and a credulous submission to religious obscurantism. Political leadership and government failed to anticipate and analyze these dangerous tendencies and take effective action in time. Years of misrule have pushed Pakistan, a country of considerable potential, to endemic instability and diminished it internationally.

Politicization of the Administrative Bureaucracy,
the Judiciary, and the Army

One facet of the institutional breakdown in Pakistan has been the politicization of the bureaucracy. In the early years, in the absence of strong political leadership, the bureaucracy and the administrative machinery, mainly the elite civil service inherited from the colonial period, became inordinately powerful. Rising from the ranks of the bureaucracy, Ghulam Muhammad, the third governor general, and Iskander Mirza, the country's first president, illustrated the authority and role played by the bureaucracy, first curtailed during the Ayub government. Bhutto brought about a major change. Instead of making the bureaucracy accountable to the political institutions, he weakened the bureaucracy through large-scale purges and numerous political appointments, mostly of PPP loyalists, thereby taking away the sense of security that bureaucrats had enjoyed. This practice became a traditional part of the country's political culture and reduced the professional quality and integrity of the civil service.

Zia ul Haq began his military rule by installing military officers to oversee and control bureaucratic functions, thereby further damaging the morale of the civil services. The military officers were withdrawn from civilian duties after a few years, but meanwhile the intelligence agencies gained in authority, in particular the ISI because of its involvement with the Afghan Jihad. The weakened civil services and law enforcement agencies, the police in particular, showed indifference, if not deference, to the growth of religious activism and early signs of religious militancy.

The political rivalry between Benazir and Nawaz Sharif led to further deterioration of the country's administrative and law enforcement structures that verged on becoming a system of spoils. Every change of government would bring about a change of administrative and police officials and new, politically motivated recruitment, which shook the law enforcement structure. The deterioration was across the board. The tax and revenue collection administration, for example, was never strong, nor was it ever known for maintaining high standards of integrity; but over the years the system had become so rife with corruption that lucrative posts were literally on sale or reserved for appointments as political bribes. Musharraf's rule again installed army personnel on a large scale in the administration and in government-owned enterprises and corporations. This time the military officials were not withdrawn but held permanent jobs.

Musharraf also experimented with a new administrative system through devolution of administrative and magisterial powers to Nazims, the elected heads of local bodies at the district and municipality level. The idea was to empower people at the local level by transferring responsibility for administration and economic management to representatives, including the Nazims, chosen through partyless elections. Nazims supplanted the old system of government-appointed civil servants heading district administration.

In theory, devolution was a sound idea, but in practice it weakened administration in the districts, as Nazims would find it impossible to apply coercive measures in the interest of law and order or to use police against people who were their constituents and voters. Furthermore, Nazims could not act as neutral players in an environment steeped in party and clan politics. The new system was inherently unsuited for dealing with the problems of extremism and militancy at the local levels through monitoring and firm action against those inciting violence and hatred. Yet again, an experiment apparently carried out in good faith had served to weaken the institutional administrative structure at a time when it was needed to play a critical role.

Over the years, the judicial system, the third pillar of the state, suffered a gradual decline in quality, efficiency, and integrity. At the national level, judgments in high-profile cases that challenged the imposition of martial law damaged the reputation of the highest court in the land. Instead of upholding the high principle of defending the constitution that had been violated, the court offered justification of the act on the basis of the law of necessity. Zulfikar Ali Bhutto's sentence was widely seen as a politically motivated verdict and a judicial murder. The Supreme Court of Pakistan upheld the dismissals of Benazir Bhutto on successive occasions, but reversed the dismissal of Nawaz Sharif, which was viewed in political and ethnic terms. The mob assault on the court in December 1997, allegedly prompted by the ruling party against Chief Justice Sajjad Ali Shah, was a low point in the mistreatment of the superior judiciary similar to the Musharraf government's dismissal of Chief Justice Iftikhar Muhammad Chaudry.

There has been a tradition of independent-minded judges in the superior courts. The judgment in the case of Prime Minister Zulfikar Ali Bhutto was a split decision, with three out of a bench of seven judges recording dissent. During every period of martial law or when enforcement of constitutional changes required new oaths on the part of the judges, a number of them preferred to stay away and relinquish their position. Such decisions reflected the motivation of some of superior court judges to maintain the independence and autonomy of the judiciary as an institution.[53]

The success of the lawyers' movement in the restoration of Chief Justice Iftikhar Chaudry was an unprecedented and unique development, but it was essentially political. However, by itself this development is unlikely to reform the judicial system, which suffers from systemic problems as well as from widely alleged inefficiency. Another manifestation of the weakened judicial system has been the application of the laws promulgated under the Islamization policy, in particular the blasphemy laws and the *Hudud* Ordinance, which gave rise to cases of clear abuse of the law. The lower courts often could not provide redress because of the pressure and even threats from extremist religious groups.[54] In many cases, the higher judiciary over-

53. Apart from these instances where judges of the superior court demonstrated their independence, some of the judges were admired for their integrity and high caliber. The report of the commission under Justice Munir to look into the issue of apostasy in the case of the Ahmadiyya sect is widely cited as an authoritative and important view on a religious issue.

54. In October 1997, a retired justice of the Punjab High Court, Arif Iqbal Bhatti, was murdered by a fanatic for having earlier acquitted two accused Christians, Rehmat Masieh and Salamat Masieh, who were then taken out of the country by human rights groups.

turned the verdict of the lower courts, but the suffering of the victims was never recompensed. These laws by themselves need to be rationalized, which demands bold *suo moto* action by the supreme judiciary, as the issue relates to the compatibility of law and justice with common sense and reasonableness. Failure to rectify flawed laws introduced and maintained in the name of religion is no less than a continuing disservice to Islam.

The Pakistani army inherited strong traditions of professionalism and discipline from the days of the British that it still retains within its ranks. However, the top levels have been politicized because the country has been under military rule for nearly half of its independent life. The army chief is viewed as one of the principal poles of power in the country. As noted, army chiefs have intervened in the past to resolve deadlocks between the president and the prime minister and to avert political crises in the 1990s during the patchy periods of democracy. The ISI has maintained a separate wing to monitor domestic affairs. In September 1988 it encouraged and abetted formation of the Islamic Jamhoori Ithehad (IJI, Islamic Democratic Alliance) to oppose the PPP in the elections. Musharraf tried to formalize the army's role in governance by establishing the National Security Council, which included the top civilian and military leadership and was supposed to address issues of high national importance. Musharraf defended the council as an assurance against the need for the army to intervene or impose martial law in the future, but it was disbanded with his departure.

Another important change within the army related to the orientation of its officers. The army expanded considerably after the 1965 war with India, drawing heavily on the induction of officers with middle class and conservative backgrounds. This coincided with a period in which Pakistan-U.S. relations began to lose their former closeness, shrinking opportunities for new officers to be exposed to the West. Under Zia, transforming society's culture accelerated in a way that promoted a religious orientation, especially in the expanding middle class, the bureaucracy, and, importantly, in the armed forces. Against the backdrop of the Afghan Jihad, *Jihad fi Sabeel Illah,* Jihad in the way of Allah, and *Jihad, Taqwa* (piety), and *Iman* (faith) became central mottoes of the army. The increasing tendency among officers to have beards and attend collective prayers reflected the official encouragement of religious conduct. Khatibs and Imams at the regimental level gained importance. In addition, during the 1990s, the army and the ISI encouraged and backed militant groups that claimed to be helping muja-hedin in Kashmir, oblivious of the militancy and violence that they spawned within Pakistan. The involvement of low-level air force officials as accomplices with extremist groups targeting Musharraf in 2003 revealed that the ranks of the armed forces were not immune to extremist influences. However, the operations in Swat and South Waziristan demonstrate that the army disposition remains nationalistic and its discipline largely intact.

Apart from denying constitutional stability, military rule deeply impacted Pakistan's political development and outlook. Lack of participatory politics impacted the working of the federation and aggravated systemic problems of governance. With army cadres exercising considerable authority in managing administrative and corporate sectors, the growth of political and civilian state institutions remained stunted. These institutions did not develop the necessary maturity and balance in their functioning and failed to induce confidence or promote a broad consensus in national thinking.

More important, the long periods of military rule and influence induced a security orientation in state thinking, creating a justification for high expenditures to maintain military preparedness against perceived threats. Security became the central strategic concern. This view was so well entrenched that, following the nuclear tests and overt establishment of deterrence and strategic balance with India, the suggestion to divert resources from defense immediately drew a counterargument that conventional balance was also necessary in order to keep the nuclear threshold high.[55] The influence of the military elite on the polarized and often unstable politics did not allow civilian political leaders to shift the governance paradigm from its emphasis on security to one that addressed the complex issues of welfare, development, and political cohesion.

By training, the army rank and file, as well as the top brass, have difficulty with nuanced views and approaches. They are used to thinking in black and white, trained to deal with situations that define enemies and friends and attuned to discussions in an opinionated and didactic style. Military culture generally imbibes patriotic bravado and confidence and often looks at compromise and circumspection as akin to defeatism. Under military rule, this institutional disposition influenced public thinking and even policy options. Mistrust of India is part of the Pakistani army's institutional culture, which can be softened but not completely changed. This perhaps applies

---

55. On nuclear issues, Pakistani analysts remain preoccupied by the U.S.–USSR model, albeit in the South Asian regional context. They overlook the example of China, which for decades maintained nuclear deterrence at a minimal level and conventional forces with modest technological prowess, even when, after the upheavals of the Cultural Revolution, the Chinese economy experienced rapid growth during the 1980s and 1990s.

equally to the Indian army, whose concerns are mostly Pakistan-centric. Suspicion of India remained deep even when, under Zia, Pakistan maintained normal relations with India and, after 2004, when Musharraf actively sought confidence building between the two countries.

Despite the high-profile army training institutions developed since the early 1970s that serve as think tanks to study a wide range of national and international issues and matters of strategy and tactics, the senior levels of the army cadres show a certain naïveté in their understanding of the global correlation of forces and of international opinion. The army top brass is susceptible to misreading international circumstances, just as they misjudged or failed to anticipate the international reaction to the Kargil operation.[56] Miscalculation by such a powerful institution in evaluating either the external or internal situation can be costly for a country like Pakistan.

Experimentation with the Economy

A brief reference to Pakistan's economic trajectory is relevant to this chapter's theme, which mainly focuses on the lack of clarity and absence of broad consensus in intellectual discourse within the Pakistani society. Had the country remained on the path of economic growth, as it appeared to be in the 1960s under Ayub Khan, economic development would have generated modernizing impulses and prevented the backward drift towards obscurantism and antiprogress extremism. Socioeconomic transformation could have fused the demands of modernity with the country's popular cultural and religious ethos, a synthesis that did not materialize in the society at the intellectual level.

Ayub Khan's ten years of military rule provided stability and the most sustained economic growth in the country's history. During this period Pakistan's economy grew by an average of 6 percent annually, and Pakistan was often cited as a model for economic growth among developing countries. Textile, pharmaceutical, basic consumer industries, and financial sectors saw remarkable development. The hydropower sector developed partly as a result of the Indus Water Treaty with India, which required massive projects for redistribution of water. This period also saw the increase in qualified

---

56. Besides any tactical problems relating to the sustainability of the Kargil operation, the ostensible purpose of raising the profile of the Kashmir dispute and that of the Kashmiri Mujahedin was based on a misreading of the expected international reaction.

technical professionals who became the backbone of industrial growth and in the skilled expatriate community, especially medical doctors and engineers. Even though economic growth was uneven and had led to interprovincial grievances over economic disparity, especially in East Pakistan, Ayub's policies had put Pakistan on the path of economic growth, setting modernizing trends, including urbanization.

Zulfikar Ali Bhutto's most fateful step was nationalizing the entirety of the industrial sector. It is debatable whether his nationalization policy was prompted by a revolutionary vision or by a banal perceived threat arising from the powerful new influence industrial entrepreneurs had injected into the country's feudal-dominated politics.[57] Nevertheless, when Bhutto visited Beijing in January 1972, no less a person than the Chinese premier, Zhou Enlai, tried to dissuade him from taking the step. When Bhutto spoke eloquently of the people's revolution in Pakistan and his plan to nationalize industries, Zhou recalled that after the 1949 Chinese revolution, the Chinese government had to appeal to former owners to run the nationalized industries. Pakistan's nationalization was followed by labor reforms that strengthened labor unions. These steps built an enduring labor constituency for the Peoples' Party, especially in urban Punjab, but they stifled industrial productivity and growth.

Zia ul Haq did not reverse Bhutto's nationalization, but he encouraged the entrepreneurial class to restart investment. On the whole, his economic policies remained conservative and oblivious of the new opportunities emerging as part of the phenomenon of globalization. Large remittances from the Pakistani expatriate community working in the Gulf countries partly sustained the economy. At a personal level, Zia ul Haq remained preoccupied with the policy of Islamization and the Afghan Jihad, which had brought international focus on Pakistan as a key country in this last front of the Cold War. In general, with the exception of Ayub Khan, leaders of the first four decades of Pakistan's national life showed a remarkable lack of understanding and concern about global economic trends and the strategic relevance of economic strength in global affairs.

---

57. Around the time of the 1970 election, surveys by a respected young economist, Mahbul Haq, to show that the nation's wealth was concentrated in the hands of twenty-two families had helped to provide an emotional impetus for Bhutto's socialist agenda for nationalization. Soon after the nationalization of major industries, the policy was applied so thoroughly that it even covered flour mills, cotton-ginning mills, and rice-husking factories that were sprouting in rural areas, giving rise to an entrepreneurial class viewed as a challenge by the local feudal interests.

In the 1990s, Nawaz Sharif took a few initiatives that energized economic activity, partly because of his good economic instincts as scion of a major business house and because he was attuned to the interests of the business community, an important part of his political constituency. One significant step he took was to allow a free flow of currency, which instilled confidence among potential investors. However, the impact of the nuclear tests during his second tenure and the unfortunate decision to freeze foreign exchange accounts dealt a heavy blow to the economy. During the 1990s, economic growth remained far from stable because of the tenuousness of politics and the lack of an overall framework, with each government barely lasting three years. The same period saw the rise of religious militancy and Pakistan's increasing embroilment with the jihadi dynamic.

Under Musharraf, with international support following 9/11 and relative political stability after the 2002 elections, economic growth resulted from the emphasis on liberalization, deregulation, and privatization steered by Shaukat Aziz, who served as finance minister for four years before taking over as prime minister in late 2004. Nonetheless, foreign investments remained below their potential because of frequent bomb blasts and the worrisome security situation in the cities. The economic downturn came with the political crisis in 2007, which coincided with an unprecedented global spike in oil and wheat prices, adding to the woes of the Musharraf government. The successor PPP government, while blaming the economic malaise on its predecessor, is banking more on outside help to salvage the country's deteriorating economic plight rather than adopting any thoughtful and well-considered approach to mobilize domestic potential.

Pakistan is among the few countries to miss out on the opportunities offered by globalization. In a sense, the seeds of this failure were sown in the fateful decision to nationalize industries, years before the country was sucked into the Afghan Jihad and developed its own jihadist inclinations. If Pakistan had persisted on the path of economic development set out in the 1960s, or had it not become the frontline state in the final episode of the Cold War, it had a good chance of economic and sociocultural transformation and intrinsic resistance to religious extremism and militancy. At present, however, bad governance, corruption, and extremist violence are stifling Pakistan's economy, thereby dangerously compounding economic disparities and sociopolitical problems.

One must question whether the post-Musharraf, democratic dispensation has demonstrated the intellectual clarity and strength needed to build a broad national consensus to overcome the extremist militancy. The early behavior of the political leadership, which included both the ruling party and the opposition, was reminiscent of the tentativeness of the 1990s' democratic polity in grasping the challenge posed by religious extremism. In Swat, the newly elected government first opted to placate the militants and agreed to a loosely negotiated accord that compromised the government's writ in the district. More than the efforts of the elected government to address the issue with a clear conviction, it was the mistimed ambition of the Pakistani Taliban, in the wake of the agreement, to move beyond Swat and the brazen hubris they demonstrated—in attacking and killing security personnel stationed in the area and denouncing the country's democratic and justice system—that sensitized the public to the danger of "creeping Talibanization." The subsequent firm action initiated by the army in Swat and later in South Waziristan was facilitated by this public reaction and was not the result of determination and clear guidance on the part of the political leadership.

Part III

Perspectives and Options

7

Conclusions

The preceding chapters have attempted to provide an overview of developments relating to the Afghanistan conflict since the Soviet forces exited more than two decades ago. This study has explored the roots and nature of religious radicalism and violence and the rise of extremist militancy in Pakistan and the region. It provides historical perspective on these overarching developments and the challenges they pose to Afghanistan and Pakistan. The study has also examined the impact on the two countries and the region that the American military presence and other external interests have made. The preceding chapter sought to explain the intellectual confusion that pervades the Pakistani mind and national discourse about these developments. To overcome the challenge of extremism, stabilize the region, and align Pakistan's development with the contemporary currents of modernization, clarity is essential. The discussion has given rise to a number of questions, many of which have been addressed in the course of this analysis of events. This concluding chapter will make an effort to shed light on the opportunities that may have been missed to influence events in a more salutary direction; the nature of the current challenges in Afghanistan and Pakistan; and the stakes involved for the two countries, the region, and the world. Lastly, it will also offer reflections on the way forward.

Afghanistan and Pakistan form one of the two poles of the "arc of crisis" covering Central Asia, South Asia, and the Middle East, with Palestine and Iraq forming the other pole. The persistence of two of the oldest festering disputes in the region, namely Palestine and Kashmir, coupled with the conflicts in Afghanistan and Iraq and the related rise in extremist and terrorist violence, have defined and shaped much of the post–Cold War global security threat. The inconclusive nature of the U.S. interventions in Afghanistan and Iraq, despite initial quick but Pyrrhic victories, will have long-term consequences that will shape future security paradigms already manifest in the limitations on the use of military power and the increasingly clear emergence of a multipolar world. The conflicts and military interventions in this "arc of crisis" have soured the promise of global peace and the dividend briefly held out by the end of the Cold War and removal of the global confrontation threat from the erstwhile bipolar world.

In the past, imperialist interventions had a pattern of disrupting settled situations, however anachronistic, leading to long periods of readjustment, often accompanied by bloodshed. The earlier Soviet and subsequent U.S. interventions in Afghanistan are no exception. Readjustment will take time, and the Afghans themselves, by and large, will have to accomplish it. Blaming Pakistan for providing sanctuaries to the Afghan Taliban and the Karzai government for fecklessness and corruption is to deny this more fundamental reality of Afghanistan. Yet the blame game is also understandable. As the United States begins extricating itself from an unpopular and difficult military engagement, it is frustrated because even the minimal goals remain elusive after sacrificing many hundreds of American lives and limbs and spending hundreds of billions of dollars.

The conflict and political vacuum in Afghanistan have sucked in numerous outsiders—the Soviets in the 1980s, then Pakistan, Iran, and Al Qaeda in the 1990s, and finally, since 2001, the Americans and NATO. Absent a modicum of a functioning political system, a working economy, or security, the country could easily draw in regional forces, in particular those of Pakistan, Iran, India, and Russia, to fuel fires of conflict as the Americans begin to withdraw. That would be unfortunate. Therefore a special responsibility lies with the regional countries to contain their rivalry and help Afghanistan to stabilize.

The experience of the past two decades has underscored the relevance of stabilization in Afghanistan and equanimity in Pakistan for the future of the region and for global peace, and, most important, for the security and economic development of the two countries. The greatest responsibility for moving in that direction lies with the Afghan and Pakistani leadership and opinion makers, including the media and the intellectual elite. They must comprehend the dangers and help their societies reorient themselves to the imperatives of modern times through improved governance and progress in education, science and technology, and socioeconomic development. And the world community cannot afford to disengage itself and repeat the mistakes of the early 1990s. The protracted turmoil and conflict in Afghanistan teach us that it is difficult, in today's globalized world, to completely insulate a conflict situation or to immunize adjoining regions or the world from its noxious fallout.

Because the destinies of Afghanistan and Pakistan are so intertwined, their impact on each other and on the region must make them more careful in dealing with each other and not allow whims and drift to determine the course of their relations. Pakistan is a major player in the region, with substantial demographic and military strength. Developments within Pakistan, whatever internal or external variables may shape them, will be pivotal for the future stability and peace of the surrounding regions.

Missed Opportunities

For the past three decades, the Afghanistan story appears to play out like a Greek tragedy, with a good deal of predictability and no dearth of good intentions, relentless ambition, or players, both internal and external. Overall, it is mostly a history of failures. A few occasions have presented the illusion of light at the end of the tunnel or of perhaps fleeting opportunities. Though referring to these possibilities may be wholly academic, doing so is relevant to this discussion and to better appreciate what is needed to develop approaches and perspectives for the future.

As the narrative of the previous chapters suggests, certain critical junctures had the potential of becoming turning points for stabilizing Afghanistan; but various factors prevented such a turn, as shown in the following examples.

- The siege of Jalalabad in April 1989 was such an opportunity, lost in part because of disinterest and weak commitment on the part of some Mujahedin leaders and commanders, who kept their sights on Kabul and considered Jalalabad a distraction. More importantly, it was the lack of guidance from Pakistan's ISI, as evident in the absence of coordination among the Mujahedin fighters on the ground and the massacre of defectors, that led to the failure of the Jalalabad operation. It should not have been undertaken without adequate preparations. The fall of Jalalabad in 1989 could have forced cohesion among the Mujahedin, offering an alternative political arrangement to the Najibullah regime and the possibility of an effective transition in early 1992, when the regime collapsed immediately following the demise of the Soviet Union.

- A good deal has been written about the abandonment of Afghanistan following the Soviet withdrawal. Substantive international engagement at that time or immediately after the exit of Najibullah could have made a difference. The incentives of help and robust political initiatives at the international level could have forced a better dispensation in Kabul and contained the internecine strife. At that stage, only Pakistan, Saudi Arabia, and to a certain extent Iran tried to get involved; but the donor community and the United Nations, which for a long time had been attentive to Afghanistan, held back, literally writing off Afghanistan as a failed state beyond redemption. The focus of the world community had almost entirely shifted to Eastern Europe and Russia, which was ironic considering that the Afghan resistance to the Soviet military intervention had contributed to the surge of freedom in Eastern Europe. Russia alone received more than $50 billion from major donors in assistance and balance-of-payments support in the first five post-Soviet years (1992–97). In contrast, there was no assistance for Afghanistan, apart from the dwindling UNHCR and World Food Program humanitarian aid.
- The further isolation and ostracizing of Afghanistan following the advent of the Taliban gave Al Qaeda and other radical and extremist elements, each with their individual agendas, the opportunity to influence the narrow-minded, cash-starved Taliban leadership. Had foreign embassies continued their presence in Kabul after the Taliban takeover of the city in 1996, and had the Taliban received some financial assistance, Al Qaeda might not have gained the influence it did over Mullah Omar. Osama could have been extradited to Saudi Arabia through effective diplomacy. But the Saudis scuttled the effort in a fit of anger in 1997, never to revive it. International assistance and presence in Kabul were unlikely to reform or moderate Mullah Omar, but perhaps they would have prevented the 9/11 catastrophes and the destruction of the Bamiyan Buddhas. Over time, the Taliban might have begun to mend their ways. Sanctions are a double-edged sword that can easily lead to the hardening of the targeted regime in ways that triggered the sanctions in the first place.
- In the post–9/11 situation, treating the Taliban leaders as terrorists along with the Al Qaeda leadership blocked an important avenue of reconciliation. By reaching some of the reconcilable Taliban leader-

ship at that time, the coalition could have weakened the Taliban and narrowed the prospect of their subsequent revival. Blurring the distinction between the Taliban and Al Qaeda was both misreading the ground reality and imprudent. Al Qaeda, with its implacable anti-West agenda, not the Taliban, was responsible for attacks on U.S. targets. The Taliban, while guilty of hosting Al Qaeda, were not accomplices in such attacks and had in fact tried to keep channels open with the West. They had a local, Afghanistan-specific focus and enjoyed a modicum of support among the abysmally poor rural population of the southern Pushtun belt of Afghanistan, who were deeply conservative and wedded to old tribal customs and a harsh interpretation of religion. For this population, the Taliban rule was no more severe than the earlier rapacious control by the warlords. As General Stanley McChrystal's analysis conceded eight years later, a certain "nostalgia" persists about security and justice under the Taliban rule.[1] Lumping the Taliban together with Al Qaeda turned out to be a mistake, which was compounded by insensitivity about the need for keeping ethnic balance in the government and restoring the country's security apparatus. General Muhammad Fahim of the Northern Alliance was put in charge of rebuilding the national army, which he did by recruiting Tajiks and non-Pushtuns. This mistake was recognized in the 2006 Afghanistan Compact put together at the London donors' conference, but the delay had already helped the Taliban preserve and revive their appeal among the Pushtuns.

- An additional factor that favored the Taliban was the failure of the reconstruction effort in southern and eastern Afghanistan. Both military and economic efforts had suffered in Afghanistan because of the diversion of attention and the bulk of the resources to Iraq. Within Afghanistan, the southern and eastern regions saw minimal economic activity under assistance programs because of unrest and conflict.
- The possibility of capturing Osama and most of the Al Qaeda membership was lost by weak planning and absence of coordination. When most of Al Qaeda was holed up in Tora Bora following a somewhat un-

1. See "Lack of Human Security" under subtitle "Strategic Situation" in *Integrated Civilian Military Plan for Afghanistan, August 10, 2009* (http://www.politico.com/static/PPM130_civ-mil_plan_afghanistan_090907.html), a "sensitive but unclassified" document signed jointly by General Stanley McChrystal and Karl W. Eikenberry, U.S. ambassador in Kabul. The document noted, "While most Afghans rejected Taliban ideology, key groups have become nostalgic for the security and justice Taliban rule provided."

expected retreat and dispersal of the Taliban from Kabul, the United States had no ground forces to seal the Tora Bora area and left the task of interdicting Al Qaeda to Northern Alliance troops and local warlords. Northern Alliance troops had not even fought the retreating Taliban in the north. To expect them to operate and fight in the southern Pushtun territory was at best naïve. There was a similar lack of coordination with the Pakistani army. As a consequence, Al Qaeda was able to escape to the mountainous border region of Pakistan. A number of Al Qaeda elements that sought refuge in Pakistani cities were subsequently captured.

- Whether justified or not, the Iraq war diverted resources from the Afghanistan theater where they could have made a difference because the U.S. action was broadly accepted internationally and within Afghanistan. The United States committed several times more resources to its Iraqi military effort than what it could afford for troops and reconstruction in Afghanistan. Moreover, the Iraq diversion provided a much-needed reprieve to both Al Qaeda and the Taliban, allowing them to regroup in the bordering regions of Pakistan and Afghanistan. More important, the U.S. misadventure in Iraq provoked a strong popular reaction within most parts of the Arab and Muslim world. This popular sentiment breathed new life into Al Qaeda, attracting new recruits for its ranks from Iraq's Arab neighbors. Iraq has exhausted the United States, draining its stamina for an enhanced and long-term military presence in Afghanistan.

Stabilization of Afghanistan and Exit Strategy

The security situation in Afghanistan remains uncertain as the U.S. military effort, the longest war in U.S. history, has visibly entered a closing phase. No neat wrap-up is expected; bitterness and discord will likely linger on as part of the war's legacy, as often occurs when foreign military intervention gets entangled with an internecine conflict. The best hope would be that Afghan politics may work out a balance that would consolidate with time. The Bonn process produced a political and governmental structure, but actual governance remains fragile, especially in the conflict zones of south and southeastern Afghanistan.

Two points deserve to be underscored in the context of stabilizing Afghanistan and U.S. strategy for that purpose. First, it is the long-term international and U.S. political and economic engagement, rather than the current U.S. military presence, that is essential for the stabilization of Afghanistan and the region. An open-ended foreign military involvement is as inadvisable as would be a precipitous U.S./coalition military withdrawal, however unlikely. Second, reconciliation is central to achieving peace in Afghanistan. Since the 1978 Saur Revolution, the heart of the problem has been the breakdown of the tenuous national compact of loose tribal allegiances[2] with the monarchy that lasted for two centuries of monarchial rule. A similar compact or national consensus is yet to be restored. The process has to be Afghan-led and promoted indigenously. Afghan history shows that the Afghans have never served as puppets of foreign powers, and outsiders cannot force political conciliation among them.

The U.S. counterinsurgency strategy, described in chapter 3, is based on enhanced military presence to protect population centers; enlist and mobilize local support against insurgent Taliban; rebuild the Afghan army and police to enable them to share responsibility for security; and help promote an environment for reconciliation and economic development. In approving the strategy and the deployment of additional troops, President Obama declared at the same time that U.S. troops would start returning from Afghanistan beginning in July 2011. Subsequent statements suggested that the Afghan army (and police) would be in a position to take over responsibility by 2014, when the U.S. approach could shift to a more circumspect counterterrorism strategy of selectively targeting Al Qaeda and other militant elements. Thereafter, the reduced military presence, largely confined to defensible bases, could be withdrawn gradually. The December 2010 review assessed the strategy to be on course but characterized the "successes" as "fragile and reversible," mainly because of the Karzai government's ineffectiveness and corruption and the existence of Taliban and Al Qaeda sanctuaries in Pakistan's tribal belt, in particular North Waziristan.

The following paragraphs will comment first, on timelines for the drawdown; second, on reconstruction, reconciliation, and rebuilding the Afghan army—the three pillars for stabilizing Afghanistan; and third, on the problem areas identified by the December 2010 review.

---

2. Some Afghans described this loose allegiance of tribes as *Mithaq e Milli* (national compact or concord), holding together under the monarchy since the Loya Jirga that decided to accept Ahmed Shah Durrani as king in 1747. The constitution adopted in 1964 under the rule of King Zahir Shah was also referred to as *Mithaq e Milli*.

Date for the Drawdown

The timeline of July 2011 for the start of the U.S. military drawdown has been criticized, especially by Republican politicians, on the grounds that it would only alert the Taliban, who could bide their time or devise a tactical retreat and fight at a time of their choosing. The question is whether indicating the timeline would help or impede the aim of breaking the momentum the Taliban and other elements of the Afghan militant opposition have gained in the past several years. The critical factor is not the hard-line Taliban leaders, who are likely to continue their guerrilla war tactics. It is how the Taliban sympathizers in the Pushtun-dominated parts of Afghanistan would respond to the start of a U.S. military drawdown and the simultaneous reinvigorated efforts for reconciliation. If Afghan history and circumstances are any guide, adherence to the stated timetable and a clear process for reducing military presence, instead of pointless ambiguity, may turn out to be a helpful factor in promoting stabilization by weakening motivation for the conflict. There are several reasons why this may be so.

First, the U.S. military presence has become part of the problem. The weight of the Afghan tradition and history of resisting outside forces is now pushing against the continued U.S. military presence in the country. As long as the U.S. forces remain in Afghanistan in large numbers actively engaged in military operations, they will paradoxically lend legitimacy to the Taliban resistance in the eyes of their sympathizers. At the same time, the option of maintaining U.S. troops at their present levels will become increasingly untenable for lack of U.S. public support.

Second, an active and indefinite U.S. military presence would detract from the legitimacy and respect that the government in Kabul ought to command among all Afghans. The perceived dependence of the Kabul government on U.S. military forces impairs its ability to promote the process of political consolidation and reconciliation. Quite possibly the indication of the drawdown date and the apparent U.S. unhappiness with Karzai's re-election has enhanced by a notch his credibility as a leader among the Afghans. His government should be able to keep its hold on power after the U.S. forces start moving out. That scenario could improve the ability of Karzai to reach out to the opposition to promote reconciliation, employing traditional Afghan mechanisms, in particular mobilization of local jirgas.

Third, the U.S. exit strategy will not be a precipitous retreat but rather a gradual and coordinated process. The withdrawal of the U.S. military force is unlikely to result in a Taliban surge taking over Kabul and sweeping across Afghanistan. Under the circumstances, they cannot replay the events of the mid-1990s. On the contrary, the anticipation and start of the withdrawal process might help shape natural political alliances, allow chips to fall where they should, and become a catalyst for cohesion among the forces of moderation.

Fourth, a factor of relatively less significance is public opinion in Pakistan. Here an approximate parallel exists with the popular opinion in the Arab world that opposed the U.S. military presence in Iraq. In Pakistan, despite the shift in public sentiment over the Pakistani Taliban and their excesses, there is a widely shared sympathy with the Afghan Taliban, especially among the Pakistani Pushtuns, and a feeling that links the continuing turmoil in the area to the U.S. military presence in Afghanistan. Diminishing this external factor could correct the distorted perception of the challenge Talibanization poses to the region's well-being. It may be apposite to remind U.S. policy analysts of Vorontsov's apt remark in Islamabad in February 1988 when conveying the Soviet decision on withdrawal, that "Moscow no longer wanted to be blamed for all the troubles in Afghanistan."

The criticism of the U.S. administration for indicating July 2011 for the drawdown prompted a clarification from the U.S. military leadership that the reduction of troops would depend on an assessment of the ground situation. The U.S. administration is downplaying the July 2011 deadline and attaching importance to the 2014 transition. This shift in emphasis owes largely to domestic political expediency rather than a change in ground realities in Afghanistan, where U.S. troops are engaged in an uncertain asymmetrical warfare against an elusive adversary. It is clear, however, that the current level of U.S. deployment represents a peak and that this level can be maintained only for a limited period. A new surge is highly unlikely, and the effort to degrade the Taliban will increasingly shift to counterterrorism operations. More than on the military effort, success will depend on a change in the environment that sustains support for the Taliban inside Afghanistan.

To sum up, the discussion is about drawdown, not the end of the U.S. military presence in Afghanistan, which is not yet on the horizon. Drawdown will not undo the political dispensation that has evolved as a result of the Bonn process. Even Najibullah initially survived the exit of the Soviet forces; and unlike the Soviet Union, the sponsors of the Bonn process will neither disengage nor disappear from the scene. The start of the drawdown could, however, break the political impasse that persists in Pushtun regions of Afghanistan. Like the Afghan population, the Taliban fighters may be tired of the conflict, but foreign military presence and operations provide them the motivation and their movement its legitimacy and momentum. Any ambiguity over the start of withdrawal would continue to inject uncertainty in the Afghan situation and prolong the conflict. The drawdown, on the other hand, would signal a change in the dynamic of the conflict that can correspondingly dampen the Taliban motivation and improve the environment for reconciliation and prospects of stability.

Reconciliation and Reconstruction

Reconciliation in Afghanistan will have to be steered by the Afghan leadership, with low-key and necessary input and advice from outside sources. Hamid Karzai's reelection, despite his government's record of corruption, augurs well for the reconciliation process, because among the array of personalities contesting the presidential election, he has the best credentials to reach out to the disaffected south. There is a legitimate expectation of improved governance during his second term of office, but he would be well advised to keep at bay overweening interference by the UN or the Americans in what ought to be an essentially domestic political process. President Karzai should not hold back on political initiatives in deference to the coalition, as he did, according to his own admission, in the early years of the Bonn process.[3]

Even if some top Taliban leaders remain obdurate, efforts must be made to reach out, especially to those seeking to retain local/regional influence. Simultaneously, there is a need to whittle down Taliban support at the lower levels through local initiatives, funds, projects, and employment. The international community can facilitate the process through appropriate and effective financial and economic assistance. Because of the unique ethnic overlap and peculiar cross-border tribal affinities, Pakistan can offer constructive support to the process and play a helpful role with Pushtun tribal elements. Such a role was acknowledged by the Kabul grand jirga held in August 2007. More important, Pakistan would need to restrain the Afghan Taliban residing within its territory and, depending on Kabul's expressed interest, help with efforts to bring them into the fold of reconciliation.

---

3. On the eve of the London Conference on Afghanistan in January 2010, speaking to the media, Karzai remarked that he had all along favored reaching out to the Taliban, but "our allies" did not agree as "they did now." Incidentally, as reported by the *New York Times,* January 25, 2010, in a comment sent to Washington in November 2009 on Karzai's role, U.S. ambassador Eikenberry observed that Karzai "is not an adequate strategic partner . . . and continues to shun responsibility for any sovereign burden."

The February 2010 arrests of Mullah Abdul Ghani Baradar, the second in command to Mullah Omar, and his associates in Karachi pointed to the need for improved coordination between Kabul and Islamabad in contacting or targeting Taliban leaders inside Pakistan. The arrests gave rise to speculation that Baradar was nabbed only because he was in direct touch with the Afghan government, bypassing the Pakistani intelligence. A remark by former UN special envoy Kai Eide that the arrests could damage the reconciliation effort lent strength to this speculation, until U.S. Secretary of State Hilary Clinton stated that the arrests resulted from close collaboration between the ISI and the CIA. It was quite possible that Kabul had reached out to Mullah Baradar, even though there was no evidence of such contacts. But clearly, Pakistani and American intelligence services were not in the loop. The Pakistani reluctance to hand over Mullah Baradar to Kabul was also understandable. Pakistan would not risk provoking the large pro-Taliban Afghan refugee population while it was taking measures to counter domestic militancy and consolidating the army's gains in the tribal areas and in Swat.

Another issue is that of conditions that may circumscribe the reconciliation process. According to well-informed sources,[4] the Afghan Taliban leadership has put forward a number of demands, including release of detainees, removal of its stigma as a terrorist organization and, significantly, withdrawal of foreign forces, but it remains silent on Al Qaeda. At the same time, many in Kabul insist that the Taliban accept the 2004 Afghan constitution, renounce violence, and sever links with Al Qaeda as preconditions for dialogue and reconciliation. There is a strong case that dialogue and reconciliation should be without preconditions, with the exception of prior understanding on abandoning Al Qaeda. The federal character of the Afghan constitution could pose a difficulty, because Taliban leaders amenable to reconciliation would want to have local influence like that of many of the warlords who remain autonomous in their respective areas. However, these are issues that can best be sorted out by the Afghans without outside interference.

The success of the new counterinsurgency strategy of winning hearts and minds in population centers that have been under Taliban influence, such as

---

4. According to Rahimullah Yusufzai, a reporter for the *News International* Peshawar Bureau, the Taliban conditions for dialogue for reconciliation included release of Taliban detainees from Guantánamo Bay, removal of names of the Taliban leaders from the terrorist list, acceptance of the Taliban as a political movement, cessation of all military operations, release of political prisoners, withdrawal of foreign forces, and introduction of Sharia.

Helmand and Qandahar, will depend largely on building the local economy and improving people's lives. On a broader scale, the country needs substantial support to help it revive its economy, particularly agriculture, infrastructure, health, education, and job creation.

For this purpose policymakers must revisit priorities and modalities governing the assistance programs. The experience of the past years should offer lessons as to what works and what does not. The key is what starts making a difference to the people at the local levels. The challenge can by no means be underestimated. Flexibility and innovation are needed to suit local conditions, which vary from region to region within Afghanistan, especially the areas in the conflict zone. Effective use of the assistance will require local partnerships and the involvement of local influentials, elders, and the administrative and military structure. The areas amenable to absorbing assistance could provide the lead by demonstrating a visible peace dividend. The projects must be not only meaningful but also protected and sustained long enough for people to recognize the change and develop a stake in their continuation.

Rebuilding the Afghan National Army

Plans to raise a 240,000-strong Afghan national army are ambitious and need a careful look into their feasibility and impact. The Afghan economy is unlikely to sustain such a large standing military force unless the donor countries continue to underwrite the expenditure. Furthermore, what would be the role of a large standing army in the politically and ethnically fragmented Afghanistan? The use of such a force by the center to integrate the country would be unprecedented, as for most of the last two centuries the country was held together not so much by force of arms as through a web of largely autonomous tribes' allegiance to the monarchy.

Any effort to use non-Pushtun elements in the restive Pushtun areas may aggravate rather than calm the situation. Besides numbers, the ethnic balance in rebuilding the army will be a critical challenge. The deployment of the regular forces in the Pushtun areas could also provoke local tribal resistance. An alternative approach for Pushtun tribes in the southern and eastern parts of Afghanistan could be the example of the Frontier Corps in Pakistan's tribal areas, which is locally raised and mixed with the regular army, especially regarding command. This model has been effective for over a century, has suited the environment in the tribal area, and notably provides employment to local youth, besides winning the allegiance of their families and subtribes.

While the sustainability of a quarter-million-strong military force in Afghanistan is questionable, the prospect of such a buildup is a source of anxiety for the Pakistani military establishment. Any Indian involvement to supplement or supplant NATO efforts to train, maintain, and support this large army would cause a provocation to Pakistan and be fraught with negative consequences for the stability of the region. The task of training the Afghan army should be managed largely by the members of the coalition, if necessary with a lead role for members such as Turkey. Also, a large Afghan army, if it materializes, could create its own dynamic, especially in the disturbed border regions that in the past were the subject of Afghan rhetoric about Pushtunistan and Afghan rejection of the Durand Line. Nonetheless, as discussed in some detail in chapter 4, a conventional threat to Pakistan by a regular Afghan force is quite improbable, given the demography and the intractability of the terrain. This assumption does not imply that Pakistan can afford to be complacent about its tribal areas, which require a careful political approach and economic development to integrate them with the rest of the country.

December 2010 Review

Based on official briefings on the December 2010 review of the counterinsurgency strategy, U.S. media commentaries revealed a certain exasperation with the Karzai government's corruption and weakness and Pakistan's inability to launch full-scale military operations in North Waziristan to eliminate Afghan Taliban and Al Qaeda sanctuaries and put an end to the Afghan Taliban cross-border activity. As compared to the understated tone of the review, media reports suggested serious thinking within the U.S. military establishment about expanding military operations to North Waziristan in case the Pakistani military failed to take action.

The U.S. military intervention in Afghanistan has brought about an irreversible change in the political landscape of Afghanistan, but it cannot engineer a government of its own choosing or steer the country's politics in a direction entirely to its liking. The Karzai government, with all its flaws, is part of the Afghan political reality. It arose from the political process set in motion by the U.S. military intervention. However, this process will not work exactly as its foreign sponsors anticipated. As it settles down, it will assimilate the local dynamics of personal relations, tribal and ethnic affiliations, and corrupt practices.

The threat of military operations inside the Pakistani tribal territory is perhaps part of the pressure on Pakistan to "do more," but it once again dismisses Pakistani limitations and sensitivities and the enormity of its problems. If carried out, coalition incursions into Pakistani tribal areas are unlikely to achieve the desired objective of defeating the Afghan Taliban. However, the consequences would be disastrous. In all likelihood, such incursions would strengthen rather than weaken militancy and spawn even more virulent forms of Taliban radicalism in the area. Pakistan should do whatever it can militarily and diplomatically to stave off such a scenario. Already, of the nearly 150,000 troops deployed in the northwestern border regions, the overstretched Pakistani army has deployed 34,000 in North Waziristan. If necessary, Pakistan should proceed with mining the problematic parts of the border and press the United Nations and the coalition members of the donor community to relocate the notorious Afghan refugee camps in Baluchistan to any suitable regions inside Afghanistan.

In asking Pakistan to seal the border, the United States and the coalition are demanding what they themselves have not been able to achieve after spending hundreds of billions of dollars in military effort and recruiting scores of thousands of Afghan troops. The Afghan Taliban's regaining influence in Afghanistan cannot be attributed simply to alleged Pakistani support and safe havens, as discussed in chapter 3. Regardless of the rhetorical ring in these familiar arguments, the United States must avoid undermining a well-established understanding that could trigger a new cycle of violence, achieve little, and scar its relations with Pakistan beyond healing.

As the current operations progress and when the anticipated phase of drawdown begins, the United States and Pakistan should coordinate closely, especially at the military level, and take into account each other's concerns and sensitivities. Transparency and frankness in these consultations will help avoid mistakes and miscalculations. Both countries are addressing similar challenges, and the problems overlap and impact on both sides of the border. The manner in which the United States decides to withdraw and the conditions it leaves behind are the concern not only of Kabul but of Islamabad as well.

Recommendation for a Pakistan-Afghanistan Modus Vivendi

At this critical stage in the effort to stabilize Afghanistan, the mistrust between Pakistan, Afghanistan, and the United States must be contained so that the three countries do not work at cross-purposes. The world will expect Pakistan to maintain efforts to neutralize Al Qaeda and extremist elements and not to abet the Taliban. Similarly, Kabul ought not to contemplate keeping Pakistan off balance, especially in collusion with India or any other regional power or by virtue of its newly rebuilt large army. That would only prolong the misery of both countries.

If we discount the charge that Pakistan is protecting the Taliban as future assets, it is understandable that for reasons of pre–9/11 amity and cultural mores, Pakistan has not pursued the Afghan Taliban and their leaders. But Pakistan cannot conceivably use these elements to turn the Afghan situation in its favor and must not allow them to operate from its territory. The pre–9/11 period should provide enough lessons about how playing such a game would only keep Afghanistan in turmoil, in turn hurting and debilitating Pakistan in multiple ways.

A stable Afghanistan will serve the best interests of Pakistan. To illustrate this point, it is relevant to recall the words of Sardar Daoud in his address to a Shalimar public reception at Lahore in March 1978: "Your strength is our strength, your welfare is our welfare, and your stability is our stability. . . . Let's walk hand in hand in the warm glow of brotherhood and sincerity. I hope that friendship between Pakistan and Afghanistan will be permanent and everlasting." These words from a man long regarded in Pakistan as the principal protagonist of Pushtunistan had held out a significant promise, not just because of his changed views but also because he presided over a stable Afghanistan. Similar words spoken at the time of the return of Mojaddedi to Kabul in 1992 or by the Taliban leadership in the late 1990s did not carry the same significance because of the conflict and instability then prevalent.

The question arises: how should Afghanistan and Pakistan manage their relations as the presence of outside forces thins out? In that scenario, Kabul may have genuine concerns that Pakistan would return to pushing for an "Islamabad-friendly regime." Pursuit of any such ambitions by Islamabad would be disastrous, complicating further the already difficult situation in Afghanistan and delaying stabilization. The persistence of the conflict as a consequence of any misconceived dreams on the part of religious ideologues or starry-eyed military strategists would continue the bloodshed and inflict a heavy toll on both countries.

Pakistan needs a good deal of introspection regarding its relations with Afghanistan. At present, most urban and educated Afghans who lived in Pakistan and continue to have close personal links in Pakistani cities are critical of Pakistan and accuse its intelligence agencies of interference.

Much of this grievance owes to the support Pakistan gave to hard-line Mujahedin leaders and the Taliban in the 1980s and 1990s, as well as to Pakistan's imprudent opposition to the Northern Alliance, especially during the Taliban period. In the new situation that is emerging, Pakistan has been vindicated to the extent that it was right in suggesting an overture to the Taliban on the eve of the Bonn process. However, it would be wrong for Pakistan to again pitch for one party or the other. The Afghans should sort out their own problems. The Taliban have shown their relevance, but it is for the Afghan leadership in Kabul and the coalition, as the occupying power, to reach out to them in the interest of stabilizing the country. Instead of a gratuitous offer, Pakistan should respond positively if approached to help the process. Pakistan has an indispensable role in helping reconciliation, but it must be played prudently and only in response to expressed interest by Kabul and the coalition, which should welcome Pakistani help in bringing any Afghan Taliban elements into the fold of reconciliation.

Pakistan cannot afford the impression that it regards Afghanistan as a dependency or a hinterland for strategic depth, nor should it allow its policy to fall between the ethnic divide in Afghanistan, as happened in the 1990s. Despite the facts of common demography, geography, and history that join the two countries in a uniquely intertwined complex relationship, Pakistan must reconfigure bilateral relations on the basis of the familiar norms for interstate conduct. Instead of looking for friends and adversaries in Afghanistan, Pakistan ought to pursue state-to-state relations of trust that cut across the ethnic divide.

Afghanistan must similarly avoid playing the Pushtunistan card, which has already lost much of its sting. The reluctance and unwillingness of successive Afghan governments to accept the ground reality of the Durand Line has been another irritant in bilateral relations. Yet, this historical boundary has long been the de facto frontier between the two countries and moreover defines the limits of ISAF operational theater. It would be as futile for Pakistan to push Kabul for formal recognition of the Durand Line as it would be for Kabul to reopen this issue whose parameters it has never been able to define. Kabul should continue to respect the Durand Line as the functional border, which for Pakistan remains the historical and legal border.

This border needs to be better managed rather than leaving it open to unhindered random movement. The Afghan government should respect Pakistan's sound proposals for fencing and for designating crossing points for movement, under easement rights and with issuance of biometric identification cards. The Pakistan government should gradually and nonintrusively introduce these measures, especially as part of its policy to bring normalcy to the tribal areas and integrate them with the rest of the country. Pakistan should also ask the United Nations and the donor community to help in the return and rehabilitation of the over two million Afghan refugees that inhabit sprawling refugee camps inside Pakistan and have become host to Taliban elements, drug trafficking, and other criminal activity. Refugee rehabilitation should be part of the internationally sponsored reconstruction and economic assistance programs.

Afghanistan must not involve itself in Pakistan's troubles in Baluchistan, or worse, become a cat's paw on behalf of another country. Pakistan has concerns, with good justification, about intelligence cooperation between Afghanistan and India in support of dissident and separatist elements in Baluchistan. These games on the part of intelligence operatives have contributed to mistrust and suspicion and vitiated the environment for better relations and cooperation in the region. Intelligence agencies all over the world provide an important input to analysis and policymaking. But their evaluations are often a product of their culture of suspicion and fear and should not be accepted uncritically by policymakers. Judgment at the government level must always be tempered by higher political considerations. As suggested earlier, communication and dialogue at the political, diplomatic, military, and intelligence levels can help assuage fears on all sides. Such dialogue between Pakistan and India can help arrest their using Afghan territory to engage in hostile activities towards each other.

Among the regional countries, Iran, India, and Russia have important influence and interests in Afghanistan that often appear to be at odds with those of Pakistan. Turkey and Saudi Arabia have also been significant players in the area. Turkey, in particular, has actively worked to lessen tension between Islamabad and Kabul, and Turkish leadership enjoys trust in both capitals. Regional rivalries could keep Afghanistan destabilized and hurt its interests and those of Pakistan more than those of any other country in the region. The Afghan government has an unquestionable prerogative to build its relations with other countries in accordance with its best interests. Pakistan cannot resent or interfere if Kabul desires to strengthen its ties with any other country, including India, as long as these relations are not hostile to Pakistan's own interests in the region. However, Pakistan should draw comfort from history and the ground realities that will always impel a stable Afghanistan to seek congenial working relationships, if not close ties, with its southern neighbor.

Since mutual tension and suspicion between Pakistan and India have had an aggravating impact on Islamabad-Kabul relations, improvement of

Pakistan-India relations could have a salutary influence on the situation inside Afghanistan and in the region. India may take the view that the turmoil in Afghanistan is distant and hence affordable. But doing so would be to overlook the potential danger of the turmoil and its impact on Pakistan and the region, thus making a mistake similar to that committed by Pakistani civilian and military leadership in underestimating and remaining complacent about the persistence and growth of militancy and extremism.

In addition to suspected subversive activities, Pakistan worries about the growing Indian economic presence in Afghanistan, especially the Indian infrastructure projects close to the Pakistani border. At the same time, India has a grievance over Pakistan's refusal to allow overland transit for its exports to Afghanistan. The rivalry between the two countries thus not only carries the potential of fueling the conflict in Afghanistan but also constricts opportunities in the region. Pakistani civilian and military leadership need to realize that under the present circumstances, especially after the completion of the Zaranj-Delaram road, it will not be possible to block the growth of Indian-Afghan trade and India's economic presence in Afghanistan. Any attempt by Pakistan to do so will be counterproductive, neither helping the cause of a stable Afghanistan nor promoting trade routes and access to Central Asia.

Pakistani restrictions on overland transit of trade from India to Afghanistan partly stem from the fear that Indian goods would offset Pakistani exports to the Afghan market. This concern is not substantiated by any serious survey and is debatable because of the obvious advantage of contiguity that favors Pakistan. Even more questionable is the argument that overland transit to India should be conditional on progress towards resolution of political disputes. Pakistan's policy is yet to fully reorient itself to the geoeconomics of the region. Its importance lies in being a land-bridge linking South Asia with West and Central Asia, not as a leverage but as a potential to be realized. On the issue of transit, Pakistan's one exception so far relates to possible gas energy pipelines from Iran or Central Asia to Pakistan and India.

Rumblings about the beginning of U.S. disengagement have lent strength to suggestions for a regional and international arrangement to help peace and stability in Afghanistan. The idea is to go beyond the numerous international and donor conferences that routinely commit the international community to help Afghanistan with reconstruction and to respect its territorial integrity, sovereignty, and independence. A formal regional and international arrangement, with suitable guarantees for Afghanistan, that pursues a policy of neutrality echoes similar thinking in the past such as that informally aired on the sidelines of the 1980s Geneva negotiating process. At that time, the problem appeared to be the fears arising from the presence of the Soviet forces in the country. Today, the challenge is qualitatively different and relates to domestic insurgency and ungoverned spaces that have become safe havens for nonstate actors. Today's challenge is rooted in the peculiar conditions and traditions of the bordering regions of Afghanistan and Pakistan. The historical baggage relating to the nature of the border could also become a stumbling block in designing a formal arrangement. Nonetheless, despite the daunting issues of procedure and substance, any proposal for an international/regional arrangement deserves consideration if it could help contain regional rivalries and assuage fears that Afghanistan could become a base for hostile activities against other states.

The Conundrum of U.S.-Pakistan Relations

Pakistan is vital to U.S. interests in the region not simply because of Afghanistan. The United States has a stake in Pakistan's success in countering extremism within the country and the region. Pakistan-U.S. relations must be broad-based and long term and not follow the episodic pattern of relating to single, albeit major, issues such as the Cold War, Soviet intervention in Afghanistan, or the "war on terror." The 2006 communiqué enunciating a framework for a strategic dialogue and wider institutionalized cooperation as well as the 2009 Kerry-Lugar Bill for long-term substantive assistance reflected an increasing realization of this imperative and early efforts in this direction.

Yet the relationship is vitiated by distrust. A strong popular opposition in Pakistan to American policies in Afghanistan and the region, encompassing Iran and the Middle East, has its counterpart in the negative light in which a majority of Americans view Pakistan. The question arises how to better manage bilateral relations and whether it is possible to narrow, if not entirely remove, the disconnect between the officially articulated desire for a strong relationship and the adverse public sentiment in both countries.

Notwithstanding the history of ups and downs in Pakistan-U.S. relations and pronounced anti-Americanism in Pakistani popular perceptions, public opinion in Pakistan would generally regard confrontation with the United States as quixotic. Policymakers are aware that the excessive anti-U.S. and anti-West sentiment, especially since the U.S. intervention in Afghanistan, is inherently damaging to Pakistan. It dissipates opportunities for beneficial

cooperation that Pakistan needs and, more dangerously, builds an environment that can trigger dangerous impulses among individuals to commit acts
of violence against perceived U.S. and Western interests.

Multiple concerns and elements of distrust have weighed down bilateral
relations, as discussed in chapter 4. For their practical relevance, it is useful to examine issues related to bilateral economic cooperation, in particular U.S. economic and military assistance to Pakistan. These issues illustrate the incongruities and troubles besetting mutual interaction, while the
vicissitudes of the overall relationship have conditioned the ebb and flow
of U.S. assistance. The first termination of assistance in 1965, its resump-
tion in 1982, and its termination again in 1990 affected the Pakistani
psyche, engendering mistrust of the assistance and of underlying U.S. motives. When circumstances permitted, successive Pakistani governments actively sought U.S. assistance, often to shore up the country's mismanaged
economy, although the public viewed such aid with suspicion for the perceived strings attached.

The controversy raised by the Kerry-Lugar Bill provides the latest example. The bill's somewhat gratuitous language seeks to link assistance in
the security sector to the monitoring and certification of domestically sensitive subjects and carries a tone of indictment. It has been variously criticized in Pakistan as an affront to the country's sovereignty, a catalogue of
U.S. demands on Pakistan to be part of the "war on terror," or a design to
"defang" the country by targeting its nuclear program. The bill's offensive,
detailed references were avoidable. It is abundantly clear that the assistance
will cease the day Pakistan derails from democracy, is seen to be relenting
on fighting "terrorism," or is found to be faltering in its unilateral commitment to nuclear nonproliferation. In the event, a well-intentioned effort
aimed at helping an ally and building confidence and good will was unnec-
essarily impaired. This unfortunate episode demonstrated the need for U.S.
policymakers to pursue a thoughtful approach that is sensitive to Pakistani
sentiment and concerns.[5] As explained in chapter 3, U.S. demands and con-

---

5. In the *Washington Post,* January 25, 2010, Pamela Constable quoted Pakistani
senator Talha Mehmood of a pro-government religious party: "You are a superpower
and we will help you fight the extremists, but you cannot buy us. . . . You can give us
aid, but you must give us respect and dignity too. Otherwise, you will spill your blood
and spend your money, and people will still hate you." Seemingly minor and avoidable
issues can also become a festering source of bitterness without receiving sufficient attention on the part of the U.S. media and administration. Dr. Afia Siddiqui's incarcera-
tion and trial is a case in point. Dr. Siddiqui had earned a PhD in neuropsychology in the

ditions on Pakistan to "do more," stated publicly or through media leaks, are counterproductive. They distort public debate inside Pakistan, complicate Pakistani efforts to counter extremism and militancy, and do not help bilateral relations.

The use made of U.S. assistance is yet another much-debated issue, especially regarding the benefit it yields as compared to its magnitude. An example is the experience of Afghanistan, where waste and corruption are often cited to explain the failure of assistance to make a material difference on the ground and in the lives of the people. In the case of Pakistan, the $5 billion assistance package[6] approved for 2002–2007 was mostly intended for capacity building, through training programs and consultancies, the strengthening of civil society and advocacy groups, and implementing projects in the health and education sectors. The bulk of the assistance was channeled through nongovernmental organizations, which are largely ineffective in conflict or troubled areas such as the FATA. Even in areas where normal conditions prevail, this modality has led to considerable waste,[7] corruption, and resentment on the part of those NGOs that do not benefit from foreign assistance.

United States. Her strange story came to light through reports of the wails of a woman prisoner at Bagram air base. Reportedly the wife of an Al Qaeda member, she was allegedly kidnapped in Karachi in 2003 under unclear circumstances and moved in 2008 from Bagram to New York for trial on charges of snatching an assault rifle from a U.S. marine during interrogation and firing two shots. The prosecution could not provide evidence of the shooting but in closing remarks appealed to the jury's sense of patriotism, arguing that her acquittal would suggest that the U.S. military had lied and adversely affect the morale of U.S. soldiers. The jury convicted her, notwithstanding the weak evidence, and the judge later sentenced her to 86 years. She also reportedly spoiled her case by attacking the U.S. justice system and the jury. The case set off a storm of emotions in Pakistan, with a stream of articles, especially in the Urdu press, on an almost daily basis during 2009. In the United States, the case garnered barely a mention in the media. Although individuals like Abdullah Mahsud were released from Guantánamo Bay and repeated high-level demarches were made by Islamabad, the U.S. administration was inexplicably reluctant to intercede in a case that so visibly agitated popular sentiment in Pakistan.

6. U.S. officials and media report as assistance $6 billion received by Pakistan during 2002–2007 as coalition support funds. These are in fact reimbursements made to Pakistan for its logistical and other support to Operation Enduring Freedom. These reimbursements were made directly to the national exchequer.

7. An example of waste relates to the procedures for disbursement that require hiring of U.S. contractors. This pushes up the cost several times. For the same quality of construction work, because of overheads U.S. contractors cost three to four times more than if the work were done by local contractors.

A good bit of the 2002–2007 assistance package was spent on capacity building, especially for improvement in governance, and a large part was allocated to support education and health programs. Given the failures in governance and the dismal predicament of education and health in the country, it is widely believed that much of the assistance either reverted to the donor country or was wasted through corruption and bad management. Effective use of assistance is more the responsibility of the recipient than the donor country, and indeed, under the 2009 assistance package, the United States has decided to implement programs through the Pakistani government machinery instead of through U.S.-approved NGOs. It is now for the Pakistani government to select suitable projects, coordinate and monitor them, and ensure their effective implementation.

U.S. assistance has rarely been invested in infrastructure or economic projects that could generate both economic activity and visibility, with symbolic value for the donor. Such projects could positively impact public perceptions of U.S. aid. The U.S.-Pakistan strategic dialogue initiated in 2006 identified a number of projects in education, energy, science and technology, and agriculture that have languished unimplemented for lack of funds. The unprecedented floods in August 2010 that ravaged large parts of Pakistan created a huge demand for construction and restoration of infrastructure and for agricultural projects. Allocating funds available under the current U.S. assistance package for some of these projects, if carefully selected for their impact on the ground and closely monitored for implementation, would be helpful and raise the profile of U.S. economic assistance.

U.S. help would be equally effective and free of controversy, if not more so, if it were limited to U.S. facilitation in trade and investment and U.S. support for assistance to Pakistan by the international financial institutions (IFIs), in particular the World Bank and the International Monetary Fund. IFI support comes with fiscal discipline but is not viewed as imposing political conditions. At the same time, Pakistan's efforts to gain better access to U.S. markets have been unsuccessful. Talks on a possible free trade arrangement stalled because of the requirement that Pakistan first sign a bilateral investment treaty. Pakistan could not accept such a treaty because of onerous legal conditions. Once agreed with the United States, these conditions would have implications under World Trade Organization (WTO) rules for all foreign investment in Pakistan. In 2005 the United States offered Reconstruction Opportunity Zones (ROZs) to help economic activities in the FATA and other economically depressed areas to help Pakistan counter extremist tendencies in these areas. But the proposal was weakened by the exclusion of textile items, the sector in which Pakistan could hope to have an edge. Even in its present form, the proposal has yet to overcome the bureaucratic and legislative hurdles in Washington.

Pakistan needs to deploy its own resources more judiciously and effectively.[8] Perhaps discontinuing grant assistance and bolstering strong IFI support and trade facilitation would impel the Pakistani establishment to improve governance and prevent a certain complacency that comes with the prop provided by grant assistance, a good part of which is wasted. This option may have the added advantage of dampening the criticism of U.S. assistance serving as a carrot for Pakistani governments to do the U.S. bidding.

Trade facilitation is a litmus test for the seriousness that the United States and the European Union have attached to Pakistan's counterterrorism efforts. If these efforts represent a strategic objective, then these countries need to help Pakistan with its economy in an effective manner. The EU had briefly accorded GSP-plus[9] dispensation to Pakistan for its efforts against drug trafficking. Despite Islamabad's repeated requests, neither the EU nor the United States has yet been able to put together any arrangement to boost Pakistan's economy, even though economic development is fundamental to the country's success in addressing the challenge of extremism and terrorism. Regardless of all the rhetoric surrounding this challenge and Pakistan's key role, U.S. and EU policies continue to treat trade and investment matters in the traditional compartmentalized, segregated manner. For concessions or privileges, Pakistan must qualify like any other country. As a consequence, Pakistan has become the most disadvantaged South Asian country in terms of its trade with the United States and the EU.

The officially expressed desire for strong broad-based relations notwithstanding, U.S.-Pakistan relations will remain difficult and tainted by distrust. In the long term Pakistan will have to adjust to a relationship with the United States not conditioned on a well-defined issue of U.S. strategic interest such as terrorism. Pakistan will also have to reconcile to the growing Indo-U.S. strategic cooperation. These factors carry implications for future

8. Once, in a casual conversation on the sidelines of the last Geneva round in March–April 1988, U.S. Deputy Assistant Secretary of State Robert Peck remarked that U.S. officials were at times intrigued that Pakistan launched a huge effort for a U.S. aid package worth $3–$4 billion spread over five years, while it was unable to make proper use of over $32 billion in foreign exchange that Pakistan had received in remittances in the previous eight years. At present, overseas remittances count for over $8 billion annually.

9. GSP stands for Generalized System of Preferences, and GSP Plus is a part of this scheme, as practiced by the EU.

U.S. assistance. Pakistan must view U.S. aid as a short-term effort to help revive Pakistan's weak economy, which suffers largely because of internal insecurity and political instability. The hemorrhage caused by extremist violence more than offsets the assistance that the United States and other donor countries, recently grouped together as "Friends of Democratic Pakistan," can garner for Pakistan.

Once the threat of extremist violence recedes, Pakistan will have to develop a regional and economic orientation for its policy, while maintaining positive and constructive relations with the United States. Pakistan has robust partnerships in the region with China and the GCC countries, but it should not look to alliances for security and economic development.[10] Political stability will determine the pace of economic development, and tension-free external relations will serve as a catalyst. Pakistan also cannot expect the United States or any other power to lean on India for the resolution of Kashmir or other disputes. Sufficient internal impulse exists for both India and Pakistan to be able work out reasonable solutions and ensure a better, more cooperative regional environment.

Expectations of Pakistan

As Operation Enduring Freedom starts winding down, the world community will expect Pakistan to control nonstate actors and not allow its territory to be used against Afghanistan or any other country. The FATA will be no exception. The familiar arguments about the difficult nature of the terrain and porous character of the Pakistan-Afghanistan border will find diminishing appreciation even among friends and those sympathetic to Pakistan. If Pakistan claims sovereignty over these areas, then it cannot retreat from the responsibility that flows from the claim. The fierce independence

---

10. Beyond the early decisions to join the U.S-sponsored alliance systems, Pakistani desire to seek safety in alliances arises from a sense of insecurity and the preoccupation of its policymakers with the country's geopolitical significance, both real and imagined. The long stretches of military rule reinforced this disposition. However, Zulfikar Ali Bhutto, the iconic nonmilitary figure of Pakistan's political history, was no different. In 1974, he suggested to Chinese premier Zhou Enlai a friendship treaty of alliance, a euphemism for a defense pact, disregarding the Foreign Office assessment that the Chinese would not entertain such an idea. The Chinese premier politely declined the suggestion, emphasizing the close friendship that Pakistan and China had already forged. He also said that China had such a treaty only with the Soviet Union and was waiting for its expiration.

of the tribes inhabiting the area or the lawless character of the region would not grant the FATA immunity to the primary requirement that the region not pose a threat to other peoples and states. The proud Pushtun tribesmen of the FATA are not exempt from norms of international conduct, especially in an interconnected globalized world where mischief can be perpetrated from any obscure corner to any other part of the world. If the FATA remains host to the Taliban and Al Qaeda activity, meddling with Afghanistan or threatening other countries, Pakistan will come under international pressure and the FATA will be exposed to military strikes from outside.

The first challenge for the Pakistan government and military is to enforce their control over the FATA through a combination of military action and political, economic, and administrative measures, including political arrangements and understandings with local tribes. The Pakistani Taliban are a motley mix of fanatic ideologues, ambitious soldiers of fortune, and criminals operating under Al Qaeda influence in an area with a tradition of lawlessness. They have intimidated the local population to accept their writ and their harsh version of religion. These elements call for a firm hand that allows no amnesty unless they give up their arms and renounce militancy. They will have to be pacified, and following military action any understandings for peace in the area must be unambiguous on these conditions.

The Pakistani military's ongoing operations provide an opportunity for the government to push for the long-delayed integration of the FATA with the rest of the country. Socioeconomic uplift of the area is the key to the success of the process. The system inherited from British days has outlived its effectiveness. A sustained policy will have to be devised for political integration of the FATA, bringing to an end its reputation as a region with only nominal control by the government.

Pakistan cannot assume the role of spokesman for the Pushtun population of Afghanistan or for that matter the Afghan Taliban. As noted, Pakistan should assist the process of reconciliation only if Kabul so wishes. Unsolicited offers would attract a charge of interference, as observed in Kabul's aversion to any hint from Pakistan on the need for ethic balance or reaching out to the Afghan Taliban. However, at the 2007 grand jirga, the Afghan government did accept Pakistani participation in a small peace jirga to reach out to the "opponent," mainly because the jirga was convened at Karzai's initiative. As the Bonn process has progressed, ethnic balance has improved within the Kabul government. The September 2010 parliamentary elections were an aberration because of alleged fraud and low or nonexistent voter turnout in Pushtun areas under the Taliban influence; but there are voices in Kabul to rectify the reduced Pushtun representation in the new Parliament. The coalition now recognizes that the security forces also need ethnic balance and that a dominant non-Pushtun security apparatus would be a source of rancor as well as dysfunctional in the restive Pushtun areas of Afghanistan.

A deeply emotive issue that would require restraint on the part of the Pakistani civilian and military leadership is the simmering discontent in Indian-controlled Kashmir. Internationally, Pakistan's encouragement of militant activity originating from its territory in support of the Kashmiri cause will be seen as overstepping the norms of international conduct, regardless of Pakistan's perspective on the legitimacy and justice of such support. Sections of the Pakistani public, media, and military establishment blame this attitude of the international community on the failure of Pakistani diplomacy or on double standards in international relations. This stems from a naïve view of international affairs and an inability to factor in the correlation of forces, international trends, and the dynamics of power that quite often prevail over considerations of justice in world affairs. There is sympathy for resolution of the Kashmir issue but no international tolerance for militant activity and random violence to promote the cause.

Pakistan's past patronage of militant groups in support of the Kashmiri insurgency relied on the assumption that low-intensity or limited warfare was possible between two nuclear-capable states that are expected to avoid an all-out Armageddon. Pakistan's objective was to put pressure on India to negotiate a reasonable settlement of Kashmir. Again, such coercive tactics are unlikely to exert enough pressure to bring an equally strong, if not stronger, adversary to the negotiating table. As for limited war, the Kargil episode did not enhance the prospects for diplomatic recourse beyond what had become available following the Lahore summit in February 1999. Kargil also demonstrated that the nuclear capability of the two countries has qualitatively raised the level of international concern about a conflict between the two countries but without a correspondingly high international keenness to intervene for a settlement of the dispute. The much-bruited nuclear capability, when available on both sides, cannot force dispute resolution, nor can it fundamentally alter the parameters for diplomatic efforts.

For progress on the resolution of Kashmir and other issues, Pakistan and India will have to engage seriously on a bilateral basis. The pressure on India for a resolution of Kashmir mainly stems from the Kashmiris' discontent with the status quo and Indian rule, which is being maintained with the coercive presence of over a half-million Indian security forces. Kashmiri disaffection and anger has erupted repeatedly, at times unexpectedly, independent of any instigation from Pakistan. Examples include the 2008 Kashmiri uprisings and, since June 2010, waves of protests with a new generation of Kashmiri youth in the vanguard. A solution is possible. An important and promising effort was developed during the Musharraf period for an interim provisional arrangement based on maximizing Kashmiri self-governance and safeguarding Pakistani and Indian vital interests. The post–Cold War situation lends itself to innovative solutions that do not present a zero-sum dilemma.[11] But such a solution will require strong political leadership in Pakistan and India capable of flexibility and the ability to make difficult decisions.

Experience has shown that jihadi organizations and elements act independently, even if groomed under official patronage in the name of jihad or in the interest of supporting a deeply held moral cause, as in Kashmir. In Pakistan the jihadis turned their guns against the country when they saw that the government policies were adjusting to new circumstances in a direction not to their liking. With a high degree of religious indoctrination, these groups blend their extremism with the legitimacy they derive from a just cause and thus obfuscate the danger they pose to the state. In the process, they have ended up damaging both the state and the cause they ostensibly espouse. Another fundamental flaw in the state patronage of these groups was the failure to think through the policy. There was no blueprint as to where it was heading and what pitfalls it might encounter on the way.

Pakistani society and leadership need a clear vision of the overarching priorities for Pakistan and the region and will have to apply these priorities to the various aspects of its policies, both external and internal. If the priorities are the development and progress of the country and the region, then a peaceful environment is the *sine qua non*. Regarding external affairs, this choice would demand a broadly hands-off policy towards Afghanistan and recourse to diplomacy and peaceful means for the resolution of the Kashmir dispute. A guiding consideration underlying its regional policy, particularly towards Afghanistan, ought to be Pakistan's view of its own potential as a hub of commerce, communications, and energy corridors by virtue

---

11. The diplomatic effort made during 2005–7 developed ideas of autonomous self-governing regions in Kashmir, gradual demilitarization, and a joint mechanism to address issues that involved interests of the three parties—Pakistan, India, and the Kashmiris. In the author's view, this attempted interim arrangement for an eventual settlement rested on a three-way limited sovereignty while maximizing self-rule by the Kashmiris and allowing them free intraregional interaction and movement within Kashmir.

of its geostrategic locale at the crossroads of South Asia, Central Asia, and West Asia.

Domestic peace and security are not a question of choice; they are imperative for survival and necessary for progress. Recent history demonstrates that any state that nurtures or is afflicted with private militias and armed groups, apart from the regular security apparatus of army, state-controlled paramilitary forces, and police, cannot escape trouble. Private militias and armed groups, whether in Somalia or Lebanon, Colombia or Peru, have been a recipe for doom. Pakistan's military action in Swat and Waziristan has been directed primarily at curbing private armed groups that, together with other extremist groups and criminal mafias, posed an existential threat to the state. If Pakistan did not have a strong army capable of meeting the challenge, the numbers and fanaticism of these groups could easily have pushed the country into an abyss of collapse, anarchy, and civil strife similar to the predicament of many failed states.

The Swat and South Waziristan operations, in the wake of manifest excesses by the Pakistani Taliban that changed public opinion, have the potential to rectify the current malignant situation that developed in many of its complex dimensions over thirty years. This difficult military action has created an opportunity to correct past errors and cleanse the society of armed groups, extremism, and violence. Much will depend on the ability of the country's leadership to take advantage of the changed public opinion, move determinedly to eliminate the extremist violence and creed, and evolve and implement a reform agenda. The international community can help, especially through measures that would boost the country's economy.

India can be helpful, too, by responding to or initiating measures to lessen tension with Pakistan. For example, India can revisit its "Cold Start" doctrine (of redeployment close to its border with Pakistan to enable swift strikes), a dangerous concept because of its potential for escalation and miscalculation between two nuclear-armed neighbors. India needs to understand that Pakistan is unlikely to return to its policies of the 1990s or resurrect jihadist groups, given Pakistan's experience of religious militancy and the international environment. Trust can be built in the region on the basis of a forward-looking, constructive approach. Interrupting the dialogue between the two countries adds to risks and uncertainties in the region;[12] the dialogue needs to be resumed and broadened at multiple levels

---

12. The Joint Communiqué issued on April 18, 2005, at the end of President Musharraf's visit to New Delhi, specifically stated that "the peace process was irreversible" and

—political, diplomatic, military, and intelligence—even if initial results of such interaction remain modest. The United States and others can nudge Pakistan and India to move in this direction.

The Dearth of Political and Intellectual Leadership

The region's complex problems have no quick fix. They demand long-term, sustained, and pragmatic policies on multiple fronts, rather than along one linear trajectory. This will first and foremost require responsible and aware leadership in both Afghanistan and Pakistan. The two countries have been wanting in leadership able to measure up to the enormity and complexity of the challenges they face. Absence or weakness of institutional frameworks has compounded difficulties, allowed drift, and aggravated problems that have persisted for three decades. The Soviet Union and then the United States and the regional powers have all made mistakes, mostly of commission and partly of omission. However, the primary responsibility for the sorry state of affairs lies with the leadership of the two countries.

The Afghan leaders are often propelled by their individual ambitions and divided along political and ethnic lines. To suggest that the Mujahedin or Taliban leaders of the 1980s and 1990s were only being manipulated by Pakistan would be an erroneous judgment. Both groups of leaders were driven by narrow, parochial self-interest, with little sensitivity to the continued misery of ordinary Afghans suffering on account of the conflict. The mutual distrust and rivalries, the unwillingness to accommodate or tolerate political opponents, and the deep ethnic divisions continued to fuel the conflict during the twelve-year interregnum between 1989 and 2001, when no foreign forces were in the country. Refusal to share power was not just the hallmark of the obscurantist religious leadership of the Taliban, but was also common in the behavior of their predecessors, who were better attuned to the realities of the world around Afghanistan.

Afghan leaders all too often betray a disposition to exploit the competing interests of outside powers. In pursuing this game they lose sight of larger

---

that "terrorist attacks . . . will not be allowed to impede the peace process." The author, in his capacity as foreign secretary, negotiated this communiqué with his Indian counterpart, Shyam Saran. These sentences were of particular significance because of the underlying anticipation that terrorist acts could take place but must not derail the dialogue. Success in the peace process in resolving disputes and bringing about normalcy would be the best assurance against recurrence of such acts.

national interests. A pronounced trait of personal stubbornness also makes them disdain recourse to accommodation and reasonableness. The problem becomes acute because, in the absence of an institutional framework, politics depends on personalities. The Soviets could not weld the Parcham and Khalq factions together, just as the Pakistanis could not bring the Mujahedin factions onto one platform.[13] A recent, albeit minor, example was the U.S. failure to persuade the main contenders in the 2009 elections to form a government of national unity.

Pakistani leadership, though not facing the challenge of an ongoing domestic conflict like the one raging next door in Afghanistan, nonetheless lacked the vision to grasp the threat of rising militancy and religious extremism in the country. Zia ul Haq was blind to the consequences of his policies and died before they started bearing bitter fruit. The leaders of the 1990s showed a listless disregard for the dangers brewing within the country and remained preoccupied with a spirited, local-level power politics. Meanwhile, the army, as custodian of a narrowly interpreted national interest and confident in the righteousness of its view, maintained its support of the friendly Afghan Taliban and the jihadi militancy in Kashmir. The problems of religious extremism and violence hit the country full blown during the Musharraf period. Musharraf recognized the problem but, while placing ill-judged emphasis on being part of the "global war on terror," displayed diffidence by taking only piecemeal measures and procrastinating on his reform program.

The failure of leadership does not consist only of individual failures. It encompasses the inability of political institutions to mature and develop to the extent they should have in over sixty years of Pakistan's national life. The previous chapter highlighted the absence of political traditions, the hold of feudal and tribal culture, long stretches of military rule, and the diminution of a secular outlook with growing religious and parochial influences, which together stifled the growth of political institutions. The leadership's shortcomings reinforced intellectual confusion in the society. Many in the Pakistani ruling elite, including the elected representatives, the bureaucracy, and the army, show a low grasp of global trends and modernizing influences in other societies and demonstrate an increasingly introverted atti-

13. From the mid-1980s onward, the seven Tanzeemat could not even agree on a spokesman to deliver a speech at the annual Islamic Foreign Ministers Conferences (ICFMs), where despite an invitation no statement could be made on behalf of the Afghan resistance.

tude, reinforced by the society's traditional outlook and the collapse of a more open educational system since the 1970s.

Intellectual equivocation and the absence of a scientific orientation is another weakness of Pakistan's ruling elite. Many advocates of reason and moderation appear to wilt in the face of the religious certitude of extremist scholars and clerics. This was evident in the exchanges on private TV channels that engaged the Taliban representatives and, during the Red Mosque crisis, the Ghazi brothers. The political leaders fare even worse when it comes to defending a modernist perspective in state affairs. One reference to the immutable supremacy of Sharia by clerics demolishes arguments in favor of reason and puts politicians with weak understanding of religion and history on the defensive.

This intellectual tentativeness was one factor leading Pakistan's political leadership to cede ground to religious orthodoxy and obscurantism. At the same time, in many countries that have benefited from globalization, individuals exposed to Western education or with a background in scientific disciplines have provided the political lead. An extreme example is that of China, where more than three-quarters of the Chinese Communist Party Central Committee have backgrounds in engineering and sciences or industrial management. Such leaders and representatives are bound to be more sensitive to the requirements of development and the need to formulate and implement policies along scientific and rational lines. In Pakistan, political leaders are rarely exposed to education in the sciences or associated with endeavors that serve as the backbone of economic and industrial development.

Evidence of the confusion that pervades the ruling elite is manifest in multiple patterns of behavior and outlook. Many Pakistanis would defend the Taliban rule for the security they had ensured in many parts of Afghanistan, while ignoring their harsh and regressive creed and the endemic violence of their military campaigns in the center and north of Afghanistan against non-Pushtun ethnic groups and the Northern Alliance. Similarly, there is empathy among the educated elite for madrassa education, even though they would not send their own children to these institutions. Senior military officers would argue against diversion of resources to education and health on the grounds that a good portion of the funds already allocated to these sectors remained unused or wasted through inefficiency. The feudal elite would question the value of universal education unless the government could ensure employment. The traditional constituencies of prominent "progressive" feudal families remain dismally backward in literacy and development. Political parties defend their youth wings in public universities and colleges, regardless of the havoc their politics has wreaked in these educational institutions. Pakistani leadership and most intellectuals have often shown ignorance if not dangerous misreading of the international environment and the dynamic correlation of forces shaping global trends.

Such conflicted and erroneous thinking finds reflection in arguments justifying the conduct of the Taliban, in particular the Pakistani Taliban, as owing to the U.S. presence in the region, and opposing military action against extremist violence because it is seen as taken in response to the U.S. agenda in the region. Forces of religious extremism and militancy will simply not disappear even if the United States were to withdraw altogether from the region. There was no U.S. or foreign military presence in Afghanistan for the entire 1990s decade, when intra-Afghan conflict continued to ravage the country, fueled by the presence of Al Qaeda and extremist groups from Pakistan.

Such patterns of behavior show how vested interests and political motives underpin resort to religious arguments on matters relating to politics and social development. For Gulbadin Hekmatyar to reject dialogue with Najibullah because Hisb and Mujahedin had engaged in jihad in the name of Islam and then to oppose Ahmed Shah Massoud's control of Kabul because the latter was a Tajik were contrived premises. The stratagems Burhanuddin Rabbani deployed in 1992–93 at Massoud's behest were simply power plays. The arguments by clerics in support of maintaining the integrity of religious education in madrassas and resisting any government interference are motivated by their desire to build and maintain a political constituency for themselves rather than by any religious sanction against scientific or vocational education. A good deal of what transpires in the name of religion and principles in politics is mere conceit.

Yet, in the midst of the deepening uncertainty, Pakistani society has also demonstrated its ability to cut through the confusion and see the danger posed by the Pakistani Taliban, as revealed by their audacity in the wake of the Swat deal. It remains to be seen whether this change of perception will endure. In an environment where religious parties often exploit religious issues in a show of political strength, clarity about the challenge posed by extremism and militancy can easily be lost. Much will depend on both the political and military leadership's clarity of perception and strength of conviction. There will be global pressure on Pakistan to stay the course, but the effectiveness of Pakistan's actions will depend on the determination of its leadership and continued public support. The print and electronic media have a role because of their considerable impact on public opinion. For the present, the media appear mostly to have accentuated the polemical arguments in debates on national issues. In time, however, the freedom and multiplicity of private television channels, a relatively new phenomenon in Pakistan, if sustained, could provide mature scrutiny, understanding, and balance.

Epilogue: Some Observations

The present study has attempted to focus on the evolution of popular thinking in Pakistani society, which for years has struggled with the questions of its identity, role, and destiny in an environment shaped by increasingly intense though amorphous religious influences, Islamization, jihadi policies, and weak institutions of governance. The combination of these factors has induced a resistance to modernization in education, outlook, and behavior, a modernization that is fundamental not just to development and progress but also to the survival of a large and complex society such as Pakistan. The study does not presume to offer any definitive prescription, as societies have to go through their own experience and tribulations to address challenges and adjust to the demands of the times. The purpose is to be part of the debate, in particular on what the study describes as Pakistan's intellectual crisis and the confusion in its public discourse.

Nonetheless, the inescapable question is, what is the way forward? Answers to this elementary question are necessarily subjective, flowing from individual perspectives. The issues that have preoccupied the Pakistani mind have both a local context and a larger frame of reference common to most Muslim societies. The discussion in the foregoing chapters has dwelt in some detail on both aspects and has drawn conclusions. The touchstone for these conclusions has been the author's perception of what counts as progress and strength in societies and states in today's world.

Religious orthodoxy and madrassa education in Pakistan have their own concepts of progress and change. Their aim is to build an Islamic society with the inherent strength and moral rectitude to appeal to much of the Islamic community and replicate the idealized, pristine times of early Islam. However, this dream is pitifully out of sync with present-day realities and oblivious of the transformation of the world in the past few centuries in terms of demographics, technological development, expansion of knowledge, and phenomenal communications. The orthodox or revivalist vision transports a Muslim society to a time warp. Today, no society can ensure its survival, much less progress, without reorienting and readjusting itself to the imperatives of modernity. Every emerging pole of global power—Japan, China, and of late India—and the economic powerhouses of Southeast Asia, the Far East, and Latin America have embraced modernity as part of the blueprint for building strong societies. These societies have given up neither their cultures nor their belief systems. But keeping these aspects of life in their correct perspective, they have endeavored to develop by modernizing their systems of education and governance, their socioeconomic institutions, and the outlook of their populations. Muslims, whether in Pakistan or elsewhere, need a similar orientation.

There is no unique vision or path that would enable the genius of Islamic societies alone to progress, develop, and rebuild their strength. They, too, will have to open themselves to modernizing influences for reform and education. Successful development and modern education have not reduced ascendant societies into replicas of the West; instead they have been rejuvenated culturally and on their progress carry the stamp of their historical experience and social and cultural values even as they become participants in modernity. Muslim societies have much to impart to the changing world, provided they do not remain marginalized in the process of global change.

The Taliban's Afghanistan offered no model for any Islamic society. On the contrary, it proved the reverse—a glaring example of the failure of governance by a radical orthodox Islamist polity identified with the Taliban. Imposing Talibanization or a similarly antiquated creed on a complex country like Pakistan would only be a recipe for civil strife.

Al Qaeda and its extremist ideology pose a qualitatively different challenge. The primary victims of the violent anger that underpins Al Qaeda's ideology are the host Muslim countries and communities that Al Qaeda tends to weaken, disintegrate, or destroy.

The anger that mutates into extremist violence subsists in most Muslim societies for a variety of reasons. These range from the humiliation and sense of impotence in obtaining justice for Muslims seen as subjugated to problems of inequity, poverty, illiteracy, social deprivation, and alienation. A major challenge facing leaders and intellectuals in Muslim societies is to keep this anger contained and to channel the underlying energies into productive venues rather than self-destructive activities. This anger is particularly visible in the middle and lower middle classes in large Muslim populations, which espouse conservative religious values and are becoming increasingly active and empowered with economic development and social and political mobilization. Most unemployed and moderately educated youth also belong to these classes. The situation demands leadership engagement on both economic and social fronts. Economic growth must directly benefit these classes, reducing unemployment and income disparities. Social development must minimize the change-induced stress that conservative and traditional societies have to undergo along with economic development.

In the context of Pakistan, the study has traced the antecedents of religious movements and parties that became active after independence. The colonial experience contributed to both shaping and polarizing political and religious thinking, especially on jihad, a secular outlook, and relations with the West, although the thinking was not dissimilar to debates in other centers of Muslim culture and scholarship. The rise of extremism, however, has a relatively recent origin in the developments of the last several decades. The Afghan Jihad, the policy of Islamization, and the proliferation of madrassas in particular gave birth to religious militancy in Pakistan and the Taliban's rise in Afghanistan.

In the view of most other Muslim countries, the Taliban were synonymous with ignorance rather than standard bearers of Islam. Similar perceptions are common in these countries about madrassas and, much worse, regarding the militant religious groups operating inside Pakistan. The prevalent view of these phenomena within Pakistan is thus out of step with thinking in other Islamic countries, bringing Pakistan's intellectual confusion into sharper relief. Reforms initiated under Musharraf in education, including the madrassas, and those aimed at countering extremism were sound policies with room for improvement. They need to be pushed with increased vigor and conviction.

Because the Saudi Salafi inspiration runs deep in the large majority of madrassas, sustained mainly by largesse from the Saudi Kingdom and other Gulf states, Saudi Arabia has a special responsibility to contribute towards remedial measures. Notwithstanding their great wealth and the development of modern trappings and facilities in the country, built with foreign expertise, the Saudis themselves are not known to have established institutions for scientific learning that would testify to a Saudi endorsement of modern education in countries like Pakistan. At the same time, most Pakistani religious groups and parties that resist modern education and revel in anti-West rhetoric look up to Saudi Arabia as their model, notwithstanding the kingdom's dependence on the West for its defense and for the wealth it earns from exporting its oil to the West. A Saudi contribution towards promotion of scientific education in Pakistan and other Islamic countries might help remove the ambivalence on this count that pervades the minds of Pakistani clergy.

Conservative Pakistani minds need to better understand concepts borrowed from the West that have gained universal currency. Prominent examples include secularism and liberalism, which have been perceived by religious orthodoxy as antithetical to its thinking. Chapter 6 focused on the confusion that swirls around the popular understanding of these concepts, which is at odds with their meanings in many Islamic countries and other societies. Apart from differences in interpretation, the largely visceral prejudice against secular values or systems in Pakistan overlooks the large number of Muslim countries, including those without a colonial experience, that have assimilated and are quite at ease with secular values and systems. Turkey is an example of an inverse paradigm, where the popular ethos is religious but the political system implanted by Mustafa Kemal Atatürk is aggressively secular. In recent decades Turkey has been fortunate in its leadership, achieving a balance, pragmatism, and gradual moderation that have ensured the development and modernization of the country and its emergence as the Islamic world's strongest manufacturing economy and educational base, an honor that once belonged to Pakistan.[14]

Another challenge for Pakistan is to infuse realism and rationality in its politico-religious discourse, in particular on policies and laws introduced as part of Islamization, which, as noted in chapter 6, was formulated in haste and politically motivated. The blasphemy and *Hudud* laws have obvious lacunae in their implementation, apart from legitimate questions about their punitive aspects. The widely reported abuse of the laws and incidents of fanaticism provoked by religious militants, who exploit them to assert their hold on semiliterate sections of society, has done immeasurable wrong, as

14. Since the ascendancy of the Refah Party under Necmettin Erbakan, there has been a growing influence of conservative Islamic sentiment in Turkey's politics. The credit goes to the leadership that kept this trend in balance and focused on bringing the conservative rural classes into the national economic fold and expanding the middle class. The present ruling party, AKP, the Justice and Development Party, has the same conservative disposition, but its agenda focuses on the economy. The leader of the party since 2001 and prime minister of the country, Recep Tayyip Erdogan, is a devout Muslim but does not wear his religion on his sleeve. His conversations are matter-of-fact and devoid of hyperbole and religious caveats, but they reflect seriousness and inspire trust.

well as disservice to the country and the faith internationally. There is need for dispassionate institutional scrutiny that combines scholarship and expertise with reasonableness. Outside Pakistan, a good deal of Islamic scholarship on contemporary legal and social issues exists,[15] combining tolerance and rationalism with compassion and humanity in religious exegeses. Such an appraisal applied to Pakistan ought to begin by recognizing that it is not the only Muslim society and that it needs to be sensitive to the evolution of legal thought and political and human rights in the world.

The building of an economically and politically strong, progressive society that is imbued with eternal Islamic values and at peace with itself and its environment is the idealized vision of Pakistan's founders, as often repeated in textbooks and public rhetoric. To move in that direction, Pakistani society will first have to return to a culture of tolerance and moderation, one that discourages intolerance, polarization, and militancy and nurtures confidence, trust, and harmony. Society would have to become open and receptive to contemporary modernizing influences, without fear that such a course would move it away from its moral and religious moorings. This may sound like a plateful of platitudes, but it underscores the enormity of the intellectual and leadership challenge.

The effort to bring rationalism and tolerance into the society must begin with a focus on education and socioeconomic progress. There is an argument in vogue that tolerance can be instilled by reemphasizing Sufi Islam, as opposed to the Wahabi and Deobandi traditions. This is a false premise. Turning to another regressive and antiquated credo, even one known for its tolerant character, is hardly the prescription for placing the society on a course toward moderation and progress and preparing it to accommodate the challenges of the twenty-first century. Sufi tradition is part of Pakistani culture and should receive support in that context, rather than as a tool for countering extremism or radical political Islam.

Pan-Islamist thinking within Pakistan and among Muslims of South Asia has a long tradition, reflected in strong rhetoric about the unity of the Muslim *Ummah* and an emphasis on support to oppressed Muslim peoples. There are even fringe proponents of the elusive concept of *Khilafat*, who

---

15. The author has conceded his limitation as a student of Islam and contemporary reformist thought in Islam. But scholars and institutions of learning are increasingly focusing on reform and *Ijtehad*. Tariq Ramadan and Javed Ahmed Ghamadi are two examples from, respectively, outside and within Pakistan whose works inject a fresh breath of reason and grasp of contemporary issues in religious discourse.

nurse an outlandish yearning to liberate all lands that were once under Muslim control. A generic sentiment for the unity of the Islamic world and in support of oppressed Muslim communities is understandable and an important ingredient of Pakistan's Islamic persona. But this has to be kept within a realistic perspective. There is little chance of a political merger of Islamic countries beyond the limited platform of the Organization of the Islamic Conference. Contemporary models for meaningful cooperation have been economic and mostly regional, with the European Union an exemplary precedent. These models often have no room for countries with depressed economic conditions. There would be little attraction for oil-rich Muslim countries of the Gulf, for example, to bring a poor Islamic country from Africa or South Asia into their fold to share the fruits of their economies.

Ijtehad, interpreting Islamic law, is the common call among today's Muslim societies confronting new issues and challenges. Despite the ongoing debate, there is little consensus on fundamental issues such as the authority for *Ijtehad* within Islamic countries or within the entirety of the large Sunni Muslim community. (Shiism has a structured religious system with the doctrine of *Vallayat e Faqih,* the guardianship of jurisprudence, which formalizes authority for *Ijtehad.*) Structures of governance and legislation, sanction for Jihad, human rights, especially gender and minority rights, and norms of financial conduct are issues that agitate Muslim minds and need authoritative guidance. A related matter is the authority for issuing fatwas or edicts and the need to eliminate the practice whereby clerics arbitrarily arrogate this privilege to themselves. It appears to be impossible to reach agreement on how this fundamental process can be institutionalized within diverse Muslim societies. But it is vital to delegitimize the practice of whimsical fatwas such as the one issued by a Saudi sheikh justifying slavery in Islam[16] or those by petty clerics declaring jihad.

The Saudis have a program for rehabilitating their radicalized youth. They are treating detained Al Qaeda members as psychologically disturbed and have employed Ulema to use reason and religious arguments to rectify their thinking.[17] It is doubtful that the same program can be replicated else-

16. Khaled Abou El Fadal, *The Great Theft: Wresting Islam from the Extremists* (New York: HarperOne Publishers, 2005), 255, refers to a fatwa by a Saudi jurist, Shaykh Saleh al-Fawzan, declaring slavery as lawful in Islam and calling for its legalization in Saudi Arabia.

17. This was stated to the author by Ali Saeed Awadh Asseri, the Saudi ambassador to Pakistan from 2001 to 2009, and is the subject of his book *Combating Terrorism: Saudi Arabia's Role in the War on Terror* (Karachi: Oxford University Press, 2010).

where, since it relies on heavy funding and specially trained religious scholars. Such an approach would be inconceivable in Pakistan, where people do not speak Arabic and the Ulema are both divided and deeply politicized. In Pakistan, however, public abhorrence of the carnage perpetrated by suicide bombings has gained strength, and government can bank on this reaction to expose and discredit religious extremists.

Saudi Arabia has the distinction of being the birthplace of Islam and custodian of its holiest sites, as well as enormous financial resources. It thus has a critical role to play in bridging the apparent gap between Islamic tradition, orthodox thinking, and contemporary demands. Doing so would require a seminal undertaking and involve Muslim scholars from across the Islamic world for renewal and interpretation of Islamic precepts and norms in light of the transformed circumstances of the Muslim societies. King Abdullah bin Abdulaziz may possibly be the last scion of the House of Saud to command the respect and authority to initiate a process that involves the powerful Saudi Salafi clergy. He has taken steps, as reflected in the reform program and the opinion of religious authorities and senior officials publicly expressed since 2009, that no individual could sanctify or pronounce fatwa on jihad and that each Islamic state could carry out *Ijtehad* in accordance with its specific conditions.[18] The Saudi government needs to persuade its powerful clergy to be more active in containing and countering the extremist and *Takfiri* creeds that were largely inspired by the harsh, austere Wahabi thinking.

The study has touched upon the issues of poor governance and institutional deterioration in Pakistan for their relevance to the rise of extremism and violence and their impact on thinking in Pakistani society. But those issues are not the focus of the study. Similarly, reference has been made to the root causes of extremism and terrorist violence in the existence of long-standing

18. Saudi deputy minister for religious affairs Dr. Abdul Aziz Bin Abdullah Al Ammar, speaking at the Pakistan Council on Islamic Ideology in March 2010, stated that an individual could not decide on any matter that related to community (or society) interests, which must be decided through a collective *Ijtehad* to ensure that the decision is acceptable to the entire community (or society). He further emphasized the need for specialization and expertise on the part of those who deliberate on such issues. Every society has its specific problems and requirements; if one fatwa is given taking into account the concerns of the Saudi society, the same fatwa may not be applicable or appropriate for any other country. In his view, the only way to address the problems faced by the present-day world was for all peoples to rally around common human values (press release issued on March 20, 2010, by the Pakistan Council on Islamic Ideology).

political disputes, in particular Palestine and Kashmir, or in circumstances of illiteracy and economic deprivation. Again, however, the study does not attempt to examine these problems in detail because they are not its focus. A wealth of material is available on the history and state of governance in Pakistan, the political disputes, and other root problems. These subjects will continue to be widely and intensely discussed in the future.

How should one regard the future for Pakistan? A question often asked is whether Pakistan will get out of the quagmire of extremist violence or gradually regress into the condition afflicting Afghanistan. Many Cassandras predict its failure and collapse. A destabilized Pakistan would be a nightmare for the region and the world, given the country's size and its strategic assets that simply must not fall into the wrong hands. There is thus a global stake in the continued stability of this nuclear-weapon state of over 170 million people. Clearly, however, outside assistance or intercession cannot salvage the situation of such a country; its leadership and people alone can address and overcome the problems it faces. On occasion, Pakistan has demonstrated the potential to do so; but as already argued, clarity in thinking and a correct grasp of the challenges are the essential requisites.

While it would be sinful to be complacent, a number of fundamentals appear to work in favor of Pakistan's ability to ride out the current wave of extremism and militancy. The first noteworthy factor is the country's demographics, which constitutes both a challenge and a potential as human resources. Pakistani people are generally high energy, entrepreneurial, and resourceful. Since independence more than six decades ago, their achievements in the development sector have been considerable, even though far short of their potential. Literally starting from scratch, by the late 1960s the country had already developed significant manufacturing capacity in light industries with considerable exports. It has produced in large numbers competent professionals and managerial cadre, who have proved their competitive worth internationally. Despite uneven development and neglect of technological and scientific education, the country has shown significant progress where there have been focused efforts such as the innovative agriculture in the 1960s, and in the defense-production sector. Urbanization is on the increase and involves 35 to 40 percent of the population. The social indicators are low, but in absolute numbers 80 to 90 million literate people constitute a sizable work force. And Pakistan is largely self-sufficient in food and agriculture. All these characteristics are assets the country can deploy to resist collapse and chaos.

With its large urban population and sizable middle class, Pakistan has the ability to survive the bane of extremist violence. Sustained development is the key, and is vital for meeting the needs of its growing population. Fast-paced development in step with the other developing regions of the world would require well-considered policies steered by a leadership, both military and civilian, with a grasp of issues, clarity of vision, and ability to make tough decisions. Alternatively, Pakistan will move forward slowly, drifting along with the powerful global currents for development and progress in the world, as long as it does not start breaking up along ethnic and parochial fault lines.

While extremists and the Taliban can disrupt life in the country, it is inconceivable that they can capture cities or ever rule Pakistan's large urban sprawls. The situation in Pakistan is qualitatively different from the war-ravaged, anarchic, and fragmented Afghanistan of the mid-1990s. Today, the people of Afghanistan and their country's changed circumstances, even without the presence of foreign forces, will not allow the Afghan Taliban to return to power in Kabul. In Pakistan, the extremist and Taliban violence has begun to draw increasingly negative public reaction. Life in the cities has been affected, but the urban centers are also showing resilience.

Another factor in Pakistan's favor, paradoxically, is the country's large army, which is strong enough to be able to hold together a country of its size. This is not to make a case for Pakistan to remain a security-oriented state instead of diverting more resources towards welfare and socioeconomic development; nor is it a justification for the army to resume its erstwhile role in politics. Nevertheless, as already shown during the Swat and South Waziristan operations, the army has an indispensable function as the instrument of last resort against insurgencies and as a strong institution with a stake in the integrity of the country.

Reference must be made to the increasingly mobilized civil society and the powerful media, although their tendency to overreach contributes to an environment of instability. With the passage of time, however, if the democratic transition stabilizes, these informal institutions of democracy will reach equilibrium. The year 2010 was a harbinger of a few good tidings, with an all-party consensus on the Eighteenth Amendment, something not witnessed since the all-party agreement on the 1973 constitution. The parties were able to bridge differences over several prickly issues, such as provincial autonomy and procedures for key appointments of the chief election commissioner and the supreme judiciary. These milestones came in the wake of the 2009 National Financial Award agreement on revenue sharing among the four provinces and the proposal for a Baluchistan package to re-dress the long-standing grievances of that province. Though these develop-ments have an uncertain quality, seen in the context of the tumultuous years since the 2008 elections they augur well for the country's political and dem-ocratic process. Again, much depends on improved governance to sustain political stability, revive the faltering economy, and address the formidable challenges of socioeconomic development.

A final advantage is the society's openness, which imparts to it both the capacity to absorb shocks and the possibility of correcting its direction, as shown in the public reaction to Taliban excesses in Swat. The media has as-serted itself as a strong and, on balance, positive new force that can serve as a check on political leadership. The media has expanded the openness, although in the present circumstances they also contribute to anxiety, agi-tation, and confusion in the public mind.

Pakistan has survived many experiences of deep national trauma and tragedy, sanctions and pressures, which have strengthened its inherent re-silience. Nonetheless, it cannot afford to remain mired in weak governance, ambivalence, and confusion in grasping and overcoming the challenges it faces. The pace of Pakistan's progress will depend on clear thinking in pub-lic discourse about the demands of modernity and on the collective vision of its political and intellectual leaders.

Bibliography

Ahmed, Khaled. *Political Developments in Pakistan: The Musharraf Years Vol 1; Religious Developments in Pakistan: The Musharraf Years Vol 2.* Lahore: Vanguard Publishers, 2010.

Ahsan, Aitzaz. *The Indus Saga and the Making of Pakistan.* Karachi: Oxford University Press, 1996.

Allawi, Ali A. *The Crisis of Islamic Civilization.* New Haven: Yale University Press, 2009.

Antoun, Richard T. *Understanding Fundamentalism: Christian, Islamic, and Jewish Movements.* Oxford: Altamira, 2001.

Asseri, Ali Saeed Awadh. *Combating Terrorism: Saudi Arabia's Role in the War on Terror.* Karachi: Oxford University Press, 2010.

Aziz, Khalid. *Swat: The Main Causes of the Breakdown of Governance and Rise of Militancy,* Regional Institute of Policy Research and Training, Peshawar, June 2010.

Bradsher, Henry S. *Afghanistan and the Soviet Union.* Durham, N.C.: Duke University Press, 1982.

Christia, Fotini, and Michael Semple. "Flipping the Taliban," *Foreign Affairs,* July/August 2009.

Cohen, Stephen P. *The Idea of Pakistan.* Washington, D.C.: Brookings Institution Press, 2004.

Coll, Steve. *Ghost Wars.* New York: Penguin Books, 2004.

Congressional Research Service. *"The Cost of Iraq, Afghanistan, and Other Global War on Terror Operations since 9/11,"* updated October 15, 2008, CRS-6.

Dupree, Louis. *Afghanistan.* Princeton N.J.: Princeton University Press, 1978.

El Fadl, Khaled Abou. *The Great Theft: Wresting Islam from the Extremists.* New York: HarperOne Publishers, 2005.

Ghaus, Abdus Samad. *The Fall of Afghanistan: An Insider's Account.* Washington: Pergamon-Brassey's International Defense Publishers, 1988.

Haqqani, Husain. *Pakistan: Between Mosque and Military.* Lahore: Vanguard Books, 2005.

Hopkirk, Peter. *The Great Game: The Struggle for Empire in Central Asia.* New York: Kodansha International Publishers, 1992.

Huntington, Samuel P. *The Clash of Civilizations: Remaking of World Order.* New York: Simon & Schuster, 1996.

Hussain, Zahid. *The Scorpion's Tail: the Relentless Rise of Islamic Militants in Pakistan and How It Threatens America.* New York: Free Press, 2010.

Iqbal, Dr. Javed. *Zinda Rud.* Lahore: Sang e Mil, Iqbal Academy Pakistan, 2004.

Iqbal, Allama Muhammad. *The Reconstruction of Religious Thought in Islam.* Lahore: Iqbal Academy Pakistan, 1986.

Jalal, Ayesha. *Democracy and Authoritarianism in South Asia: A Comparative and Historical Perspective.* Cambridge, U.K.: Cambridge University Press, 1995.

Khan, Riaz M. *Untying the Afghan Knot: Negotiating Soviet Withdrawal.* Durham, N.C. and London: Duke University Press, 1991.

Kux, Dennis. *The United States and Pakistan, 1947–2000: Disenchanted Allies.* Washington, D.C.: Woodrow Wilson Center Press, 2001.

Masud, Muhammad Khalid. *Rethinking Islamic Fundamentalism in Pakistan,* paper presented at a conference organized by Leicester University's Institute of India-Pakistan Relations, London, November 30, 2002.

Masud, Muhammad Khalid, Armando Salvatore, and Martin van Bruinessen. *Islam and Modernity: Key Issues and Debates.* Edinburgh: Edinburgh University Press, 2009.

Maududi, Syed Abul Ala. *Islam ka Nazriah e Siyasi* (Islamic Political Concept). Ichra, Lahore: Markazi Maktaba e Jamat e Islami Pakistan, 1955.

———. *Islami Riyasat.* Lahore: Islamic Publishers Limited, 1962.

———. *Jihad fil Islam.* Ichra, Lahore: Idara Turjuman ul Quran, 1988.

———. *Khilafat aur Malukiat.* Ichra Lahore: Idara e Tarjuman al Quran, 1966.

Matinuddin, Kamal. *The Taliban Phenomenon: Afghanistan 1994–1997.* Oxford: Oxford University Press, 1999.

Meyssan, Thierry. *9/11: The Big Lie.* Carnot USA Books, 2003.

Milam, William B., *Bangladesh and Pakistan: Fighting with Failure in South Asia.* New York: Columbia University Press, 2009.

Mir, Amir. *The True Face of Jihadis.* Lahore: Mashal Books, 2004.

Mubarak, Ali. *Almiah Tarikh.* Lahore: Fiction House Publishers, 1993.

Muhammad, Sohail Umar. *Khutbat e Iqbal: Naye Tanazur Mein.* Lahore: Iqbal Academy Pakistan, 1996.

Murshed, S. Iftikhar. *Afghanistan: The Taliban Years.* London: Bennet and Bloom, 2006.

Musharraf, Pervez. *In the Line of Fire.* New York: Free Press, 2006.

Nawaz, Shuja. *Cross Swords: Pakistan, Its Army and the War Within.* Karachi: Oxford University Press 2008.

The 9/11 Commission. *The Final Report of the National Commission on Terrorist Attacks on the United States,* July 22, 2004.

Qureshi, Muhammad Ismail. *Namos e Rasool aur Qanoon Toheen e Risalat.* Lahore: Al Faisal Publishers, 1999.

Roy, Olivier. *Islam and Resistance in Afghanistan.* Cambridge U.K.: Cambridge University Press, 1997.

Rashid, Ahmed. *Taliban: Militant Islam, Oil and Fundamentalism in Central Asia.* London: I. B. Tauris, 2000.

———. *Descent into Chaos: How the War against Islamic Extremists Is Being Lost in Pakistan, Afghanistan and Central Asia.* London: Penguin Books, 2008.

Rubin, Barnett R. "Fragmentation of Afghanistan," *Foreign Affairs,* Winter 1989/90; and "A Tribe Apart," *Boston Review,* January/February 2009.

Rubin, Barnett R. *The Fragmentation of Afghanistan: State Formation and Collapse in the International System.* New Haven, Conn.: Yale University Press, 1995.

Syed, Anwar Hussain. *Pakistan: Islam, Politics and National Solidarity.* New York: Praeger Publishers, 1982.

Woodward, Bob. *Bush at War.* New York: Simon and Schuster, 2002.

———. *Obama's Wars.* New York: Simon and Schuster, 2010.

Yunus, S. Fida. *Afghanistan: Political Parties, Groups, Movements and Mujahedeen Alliances and Governments 1879–1997, Vol. II* (collected documents), compiled in collaboration with Area Study Center (Central Asia), Peshawar University, Peshawar, Pakistan, 1997.

Zakaria, Rafiq. *The Struggle within Islam: The Conflict between Religion and Politics.* London: Penguin Books, 1988.

Index